P9-CDC-751

PUBLIC RELATIONS CASES

PUBLIC RELATIONS CASES

Third Edition

Jerry A. Hendrix
The American University

HM
263
.H437
1995

WITHDRAWN
Indiana
Purdue
Library
Fort Wayne

Wadsworth Publishing Company

I(T)P™ An International Thomson Publishing Company

Belmont • Albany • Bonn • Boston • Cincinnati • Detroit • London • Madrid • Melbourne
Mexico City • New York • Paris • San Francisco • Singapore • Tokyo • Toronto • Washington

WP

INDIANA-PURDUE
UNIVERSITY LIBRARY
2101 Coliseum Boulevard East
Fort Wayne, Indiana 46805

Public Relations Editor: Todd R. Armstrong
Editorial Assistant: Joshua King
Production Editor: Robin Lockwood
Interior Designer: Harry Voigt
Cover Designer: Jill Turney
Print Buyer: Randy Hurst
Copy Editor: Betty Berenson
Compositor: Thompson Type
Printer: Vail-Ballou Press

COPYRIGHT © 1995 by Wadsworth Publishing Company
A Division of International Thomson Publishing Inc.

I(T)P The ITP logo is a trademark under license

Printed in the United States of America

1 2 3 4 5 6 7 8 9 10—01 00 99 98 97 96 95

For more information, contact Wadsworth Publishing Company:

Wadsworth Publishing Company
10 Davis Drive
Belmont, California 94002
USA

International Thomson Publishing
Europe
Berkshire House 168-173
High Holborn
London, WC1V7AA
England

Thomas Nelson Australia
102 Dodds Street
South Melbourne 3205
Victoria, Australia

Nelson Canada
1120 Birchmount Road
Scarborough, Ontario
Canada M1K 5G4

International Thomson Publishing GmbH
Königswinterer Strasse 418
53227 Bonn
Germany

International Thomson Publishing Asia
221 Henderson Road
#05-10 Henderson Building
Singapore 0315

International Thomson Publishing-Japan
Hirakawacho Kyowa Building, 3F
2-2-1 Hirakawacho-cho
Chiyoda-ku, Tokyo 102
Japan

International Thomson Editores
Campos Eliseos 385, Piso 7
Col. Polanco
11560 México D.F. México

All rights reserved. No part of this work covered by the copyright hereon may
be reproduced or used in any form or by any means—graphic, electronic, or
mechanical, including photocopying, recording, taping, or information storage
and retrieval systems—without the written permission of the publisher.

Library of Congress Cataloging-in-Publication Data

Hendrix, Jerry A.
  Public relations cases / Jerry A. Hendrix. — 3rd ed.
    p.   cm.

  Includes index.
  ISBN 0-534-24840-3
  1. Public relations—United States—Case studies. 2. Publicity—
Case studies. I. Title.
HM263.H437   1995
659.2—dc20   94-13772

FTW
AFE05269

Contents

Preface

In preparing this third edition, I continue to believe that readers should encounter a clear set of guiding public relations principles accompanied by cases that positively illustrate those principles and thus serve as models of management and practice.

The book is divided into three sections. In Part One, I begin the introductory chapter with a philosophy I have held for a long time — that the best public relations is characterized by interaction, or sometimes interactive participation, between or among sources and receivers of communication. This, in turn, is based on the underlying premise that public relations is mostly persuasion. Some years ago communication researchers discovered that the most effective means of persuasion is *self*-persuasion. Audience involvement thus becomes a crucial ingredient of successful public relations.

In Part One I also formulate a process model involving initial *research*, the *setting of objectives*, *programming*, and *evaluation*. (The elements of this process form a convenient mnemonic device, the acronym ROPE.) This model focuses special attention on the significance of objectives and their arrangement in a hierarchical order of output and impact functions. Another feature of this process model, reflecting my own training and background in speech communication, is special emphasis on the role of interpersonal communication, including speeches, speakers bureaus, small-group and one-on-one formats, and nonverbal aspects of communication. In a word, my process model is interactive.

Part Two consists of audience-centered applications of the process with accompanying illustrative cases. The audience-centered forms of public relations included are media relations, employee and member relations, community relations, public affairs and government relations, investor relations, consumer relations, and relations with special publics. Most of the cases were winners in the Silver Anvil Awards contest, conducted annually by the Public Relations Society of America. They therefore constitute some of the finest examples of public relations practices available. They also follow the prescribed Silver Anvil entry format, which is slightly different from my ROPE model's format. The major difference is that I set objectives apart as a separate category and Silver Anvil does not. My programming phase includes planning and communication (execution), and both Silver Anvil and ROPE begin and end with research and evaluation. Thus, the two models have a simple difference only in format, not substance.

Part Three includes both theory and illustrative cases for emergency, or crisis, public relations. This field of PR is not oriented to a particular audience, and thus I have set it apart in a separate section of the book.

Finally, the appendixes contain exercises or case problems for each of the forms of public relations presented.

Other collections of public relations case studies often present incomplete, open-ended, or negative cases with the presumption that these better serve the needs of students in classroom discussion. I prefer that the reader, whether student or practitioner, see the entire execution of each case, from initial research efforts to finished results or evaluation. I also think that readers profit from exposure to positive models. It is important to learn how corporations and other organizations have *successfully* coped with a variety of public relations problems. I invite those who want to see only the problems, mostly negative, to turn to Appendix II.

More than 75 percent of the cases are new in this third edition, so there are many public relations practitioners who helped me and granted permission to use their cases. I hope they will accept my gratitude and understand that space does not permit a list of their names.

I would like to extend special thanks to Gary D. Strong, vice president and account group manager of The Financial Relations Board, for his help with all three of the investor relations cases. I also want to thank American University graduate fellow Jennifer Evans for writing all the case problems in Appendix II, for preparing answers for those problems in the Instructor's Manual, and for some minor revisions in the text itself.

With this third edition, Wadsworth is providing a new instructional videocassette consisting of short videos produced originally to accompany many of the cases in the book. Along with a revised edition of the Instructor's Manual, the videocassette can be obtained on request from the publisher by instructors who adopt the book. I am grateful to Susanne A. Roschwalb of The American

University Public Communication faculty for coauthoring the Instructor's Manual and coproducing the videocassette.

I am indebted to Sanford Ungar, dean of The American University School of Communication, for his support in approving my sabbatical, for reducing my teaching load, and for financial assistance with this and previous editions of the book.

I also wish to express my appreciation to my editor Todd R. Armstrong and his assistant, Josh King, for their ongoing assistance, support, encouragement, and advice.

I especially want to thank Robin Lockwood of Bookman Productions, who carefully and patiently worked with me on every phase of the production of this book.

Finally, I gratefully acknowledge the following reviewers whose constructive comments helped in the development of this third edition: Ronda Beaman, Northern Arizona University; Joseph Trahan, University of Tennessee, Chattanooga; Kathleen Fearn-Banks, University of Washington; Carolyn Cline, University of Southern California; Kathy Fitzpatrick, Southern Methodist University; and Susan Lucarelli, University of Tennessee, Knoxville.

PART ONE

Solving Public Relations Problems

Chapter **1**   # Public Relations in Action

One of the best ways to learn about public relations is through the study of contemporary examples of its practice. Such case studies can bring public relations to life in a way that theoretical textbooks and classroom lectures cannot. Here we will first examine the nature of public relations through its definition and a process model. Then we will look at various forms of public relations along with several cases to illustrate each form.

One way of defining public relations has been simply to invert the term so it becomes "relations with publics." An improved modification of this definition is "*interrelationships* with publics." This better reflects the nature of contemporary public relations as an *interactive* form of communication in which the targeted audiences yield information to the organization through its research efforts and often *participate* in the public relations programming itself. This interactive or mutual dimension of public relations is seen in the comprehensive description adopted by the Public Relations Society of America in 1982:

Exhibit 1–a   ## PRSA's Official Statement on Public Relations*

Public relations helps our complex, pluralistic society to reach decisions and function more effectively by contributing to mutual understanding among groups and institutions. It serves to bring private and public policies into harmony.

---

*Formally adopted by the PRSA Assembly on November 6, 1982. Reprinted courtesy PRSA.

Exhibit 1-a
(*continued*)

Public relations serves a wide variety of institutions in society such as businesses, trade unions, government agencies, voluntary associations, foundations, hospitals and educational and religious institutions. To achieve their goals, these institutions must develop effective relationships with many different audiences or publics such as employees, members, customers, local communities, shareholders and other institutions, and with society at large.

The managements of institutions need to understand the attitudes and values of their publics in order to achieve institutional goals. The goals themselves are shaped by the external environment. The public relations practitioner acts as a counselor to management, and as a mediator, helping to translate private aims into reasonable, publicly acceptable policy and action.

As a management function, public relations encompasses the following:

- Anticipating, analyzing and interpreting public opinion, attitudes and issues which might impact, for good or ill, the operations and plans of the organization.
- Counseling management at all levels in the organization with regard to policy decisions, courses of action and communication, taking into account their public ramifications and the organization's social or citizenship responsibilities.
- Researching, conducting and evaluating, on a continuing basis, programs of action and communication to achieve informed public understanding necessary to the success of an organization's aims. These may include marketing, financial, fund raising, employee, community or government relations and other programs.
- Planning and implementing the organization's efforts to influence or change public policy.
- Setting objectives, planning, budgeting, recruiting and training staff, developing facilities — in short, *managing* the resources needed to perform all of the above.
- Examples of the knowledge that may be required in the professional practice of public relations include communication arts, psychology, social psychology, sociology, political science, economics and the principles of management and ethics. Technical knowledge and skills are required for opinion research, public issues analysis, media relations, direct mail, institutional advertising, publications, film/video productions, special events, speeches and presentations.

In helping to define and implement policy, the public relations practitioner utilizes a variety of professional communication skills and plays an integrative role both within the organization and between the organization and the external environment.

Process

The public relations process is a method for solving problems. It has four phases: research, objectives, programming, and evaluation. Each element may be modified by the demands of different audiences or publics, including employees, members, customers, local communities, shareholders, and, usually, the news media.

The *research* phase of the process involves identifying and learning about three key elements: (1) a *client* or institution that has (2) a *problem* or potential problem to be solved, which involves (3) one or more of its *audiences*, or publics.

The second phase of the public relations process involves the setting of *objectives* for a program to solve the problem. These objectives may include the kind of influence the client hopes to exert with the audiences, such as informing them or modifying their attitudes or behaviors. The objectives may also include statements about the program itself, such as its composition or how it will operate.

The third phase of the process consists of planning and executing a *program* to accomplish the objectives. The program comprises a central theme, messages, and various forms of communication aimed at reaching the audiences.

Finally, *evaluation*, as defined in this process, consists of two parts. First, it includes an ongoing procedure of program monitoring and adjustment. Second, evaluation refers back specifically to the objectives that were set in the second phase of the process and examines the practitioner's degree of success in achieving them.

Cases

The illustrations of this process in action — the cases — are grouped in this text according to the various audiences that public relations practitioners reach. Each audience calls for some modifications in the overall four-step process, and the cases illustrate the modified process in action.

Cases are presented to illustrate relations with the media, with internal audiences, with the community, with the government, with investors, with consumers, and with special groups.

Effective public relations cases serve as models for students and practitioners alike. They enhance public relations theory, making it come alive with illustrations and examples of the PR process in action. Moreover, audience-centered cases exemplify the constraints involved in conducting research, setting objectives, designing and executing a program, and evaluating what has been done. In sum, cases, especially audience-centered cases, effectively illustrate public relations principles and management and test theoretical applications in real situations and environments.

The Overall Plan of This Book

Part One of this text introduces you to public relations, with special emphasis on the process just outlined. The elements of this process are eclectic, but the arrangement of those elements form the acronym ROPE (research, objectives, programming, evaluation). A major feature is a new emphasis on and new way of classifying public relations objectives. Objectives are viewed as the central and guiding element in the process, and they are arranged in a hierarchical order.

Another feature of this public relations process, consistent with its interactive nature, is a heightened emphasis on interpersonal interaction as a form of controlled communication. The importance of speeches and speakers bureaus as methods of public relations communication is recognized, but this book also advocates the extensive use of small-group and dyadic (one-on-one) interpersonal formats, along with a treatment of nonverbal communication. A recurring theme is that in truly effective communication there can be no substitute for direct interaction.

Part Two explores how public relations reaches major audiences. It looks at media relations; internal communication, including employee and member relations; community relations; public affairs, or government relations; investor and financial relations; consumer relations; and relations with special publics. Following a conceptual treatment of each form of relations are several example cases. Most of these illustrative cases have won Silver Anvil Awards from the PRSA. As such, they represent the very best among models of public relations.

Part Three concentrates on emergency public relations, an important area in contemporary practice. Both students and professionals need to be reminded of the need to study crisis PR procedures. Unlike such audience-centered forms as media relations or community relations, emergency PR is an area in which no one specializes. Yet all practitioners need to be prepared for it.

Finally, the appendixes include the most recent PRSA Code of Professional Standards and its various interpretations, along with exercises for each form of public relations discussed and some problems in applying the code.

General Public Relations Readings

Aronoff, Craig, and Otis W. Baskin. *Public Relations: Profession and Practice*, 3rd ed. Dubuque, IA: Wm. C. Brown, 1992.

Brody, E. W., ed. *New Technology and Public Relations: On to the Future.* Sarasota, FL: Institute for Public Relations Research and Education, 1991.

Cantor, Bill. *Experts in Action: Inside Public Relations*, 2nd ed. Edited by Chester Burger. New York: Longman, 1988.

Center, Allen H., and Patrick Jackson. *Public Relations Practices: Managerial Case Studies and Problems*, 4th ed. Englewood Cliffs, NJ: Prentice-Hall, 1990.

Grunig, James E., ed. *Excellence in Public Relations and Communication Management.* Hillsdale, NJ: Erlbaum, 1992.

Hiebert, Ray Eldon, ed. *Precision Public Relations.* New York: Longman, 1988.

Lesly, Philip, ed. *Lesly's Handbook of Public Relations and Communications*, 4th ed. New York: Amacom, 1991.

Nager, Norman R., and Richard H. Truitt. *Strategic Public Relations Counseling: Models from the Counselors Academy.* New York: Longman, 1987.

Newsom, Doug, Alan Scott, and Judy VanSlyke Turk. *This Is PR: The Realities of Public Relations*, 5th ed. Belmont, CA: Wadsworth, 1993.

Seitel, Fraser P. *The Practice of Public Relations*, 5th ed. New York: Macmillan, 1992.

Wilcox, Dennis L., Phillip H. Ault, and Warren K. Agee. *Public Relations: Strategies and Tactics*, 3rd ed. New York: Harper Collins, 1992.

————, and Lawrence W. Nolte. *Public Relations Writing and Media Techniques*, 2nd ed. New York: Harper Collins, 1994.

Chapter 2 A Public Relations Process

As we saw in Chapter 1, the public relations problem-solving process involves four procedures. First, initial research is performed to establish the basic elements of the communication transaction. Second, objectives for the transaction are established. Third, programming, including all the methods of communication used, is planned and executed to carry out the objectives. Finally, ongoing and follow-up evaluation is conducted both to monitor and to measure how well the program accomplished its objectives.

Now for a detailed look at each of the elements in this process.

Research

Research consists of investigating three aspects of the overall public relations procedure: the client or organization for whom the program is being prepared, the opportunity or problem that accounts for the program at this time, and all audiences to be targeted for communication in the PR program.

Client Research

First, public relations practitioners must be thoroughly familiar with their clients. If the practitioner is working in an in-house PR department, the client will be the organization housing the department. An employee of a PR firm will obviously be independent of the client. In either case, background data about the client or organization — its financial status, reputation, past and present public relations practices, and public relations strengths, weaknesses, and opportunities — are an essential starting point for any program.

If the organization is a business, the practitioner needs to be familiar with its products and services as well as the overall competitive environment. The practitioner should also know about the marketing, legal, and financial functions of the organization in order to coordinate them with the public relations efforts. Interviews with key management personnel and documents such as annual and quarterly reports can provide this information. The location of the organization, whether in a single city or in multiple branches, the delivery system for the products or services (such as the use of a dealer network), the organization's major suppliers, and, of course, the identity and demographics of the customers are all necessary to understand the client.

If the organization is nonprofit, the practitioner must become acquainted with the services provided and the organization's clientele, including major donors.

Other important background information includes the precise mission of the organization, its management's goals, priorities, and problems, and how this proposed public relations program might help accomplish these overall objectives.

Along with this background information the practitioner needs a good working knowledge of the organization's personnel — its total work force, both management and nonmanagement. Special attention must be given to key management people, not just the director of public relations, if there is one. How does top management view the role of public relations? Are PR people regarded as problem solvers and decision makers, or are they simply "hired guns"?

The financial status of a publicly owned corporation is easy to determine. Financial data for such organizations must be reported to the U.S. Securities and Exchange Commission (SEC), and this information is always available in the company's annual report or other financial publications.

Finally, the practitioner needs to raise questions that directly relate to public relations. What is the client's reputation in its field and with its customers or clientele? The answers to these questions constitute the organization's public image, an area of primary concern to PR practitioners. What image liabilities or assets does the organization possess? What are its present and past public relations practices? Does the organization have particular

PR strengths, that is, practices or programs that would enhance its public image? What are its PR weaknesses, the practices or programs that might create an unfavorable image or negative public opinion? What opportunities exist for promoting favorable public opinion or behavior toward the organization?

Thus, the first requisite for effective research in the public relations process is an in-depth understanding of the client for whom the program is being prepared.

Opportunity or Problem Research

The second aspect of research, a logical outgrowth of knowledge of the client, consists of clearly determining why the organization should conduct a particular PR program at a particular time. Is it because of a unique opportunity to favorably influence public opinion or behavior toward the client, or is it in response to the development of unfavorable opinion or behavior toward the client? If it is the latter, extensive research must be done on the source of the problem, whether it be an individual or an organization.

Public relations programs that arise out of opportunities are called *proactive* programs. In the short run, effective proactive programming may seem extravagantly expensive to management, but these programs often head off the need to respond to problems with even more expensive *reactive* programs. The proactive program is like preventive medicine, or the concept of "wellness" now being widely promoted by health maintenance organizations. Preventive medicine is far more desirable than surgery in response to a severe illness. Similarly, an organization should keep close tabs on its ongoing relations with its constituent audiences to avoid PR problems.

This is not to argue that proactive programs are good and reactive programs are bad. In spite of all efforts to avert them, problems may develop. The reactive program then becomes necessary and perhaps beneficial. When a fire breaks out, we must call the fire department. Public relations practitioners must be ready to extinguish "fires," but they should also be skilled in "fire prevention."

Because they are preventive, proactive programs are generally long-range in nature. The organization cannot afford to let its guard down in maintaining good relations with important audiences. Reactive programs, on the other hand, are usually short-range, often ending as soon as the immediate problem is cleared up. But a good, ongoing, proactive program with the same audience may prevent the recurrence of similar problems.

Thus, an investigation of why a public relations program is necessary, whether it should be proactive or reactive, and whether it should be ongoing or short-range is the second aspect of research in the public relations process.

Audience Research

The third aspect of research in the public relations process involves investigating the target audiences, or "publics." This part of the research process includes identifying the particular groups that should be targeted, determining appropriate research data that will be useful in communicating with these publics, and compiling or processing the data using appropriate research procedures.

Audience Identification. All organizations have long-range, and sometimes short-term, "relations," or communications, with certain "standard" publics. The publics of principal concern to most organizations include the media, internal employees or members, the organization's home community, and the national, state, and local governments. A business that provides a product or service for customers is concerned with consumers as an important public. A publicly owned business has the additional, significant audience of its shareowners and the financial community. Finally, all organizations have unique groups of constituent audiences, or special publics. Nonprofit organizations are concerned with donors as a special public. Schools are interested in maintaining communications with parents. Large corporations may need to communicate regularly with their dealers and suppliers.

To address publics most effectively, we should segment each public into its diverse components, so each component may become a separate public to be targeted for special messages. The media, for example, should be segmented into mass and specialized groups. Of the two internal publics, employees should be segmented into management and nonmanagement, and members should be divided into organization employees, officers, members, prospective members, state or local chapters, and related or allied organizations (see Chapter 4). The organization's home community should be segmented into community media, community leaders, and community organizations. Government publics should be subdivided into federal, state, county, and city levels; then each of these levels should be further segmented into legislative and executive branches. Consumer publics can be subdivided into groupings that include company employees, customers, activist consumer groups, consumer publications, community media, and community leaders and organizations (see Chapter 8). Investor publics for financial relations should be segmented into shareowners and potential shareowners, security analysts and investment counselors, the financial press, and the SEC. (See Exhibit 2–a for suggested segmentation of these major publics.)

Targeting. Once the publics have been identified and segmented into their components, the practitioner is ready for the more difficult task of targeting the most important publics on a priority basis. This *prioritizing* calls for a situational assessment of the significance to the client or organization of each potential public. The importance of a potential public is determined by its degree of influence, prestige, power, or perhaps need, and by its level of involvement with the client or organization. Four key questions to consider in targeting and prioritizing publics are:

- Who is this public (demographics, psychographics, and so on)?
- Why is it important to us?
- How active or involved is this public, relative to our interests?
- Which publics are most important to us, in priority rank order?

Desired Data. Once target publics have been segmented into their key components, the practitioner is ready to assess informational needs for each public. Typically, the practitioner will want to know each targeted public's level of information about the organization; the image and other relevant attitudes held about the organization and its product or service; and past and present audience behaviors relevant to the client or organization. Researching the demographics, media habits, and levels of media use of each targeted audience will tell the practitioner how best to reach it. All these data are used to formulate objectives for the public relations program.

Research Methods

With this general framework of informational needs in mind, the practitioner must next decide which research procedures will yield the necessary data. Public relations people use two general methods of research: *nonquantitative* and *quantitative*.

Exhibit 2–a	**Major Publics**

Media Publics

Mass media
    Local
        Print publications
            Newspapers
            Magazines
        TV stations
        Radio stations
    National
        Print publications
        Broadcast networks
        Wire services
Specialized media
    Local
        Trade, industry, and association publications
        Organizational house and membership publications
        Ethnic publications
        Publications of special groups
        Specialized broadcast programs and stations
    National
        General business publications
        National trade, industry, and association publications
        National organizational house and membership
          publications
        National ethnic publications
        Publications of national special groups
        National specialized broadcast programs and
          networks

Employee Publics

Management
    Upper-level administrators
    Midlevel administrators
    Lower-level administrators
Nonmanagement (staff)
    Specialists
    Clerical personnel
    Secretarial personnel

Exhibit 2-a
(*continued*)

Uniformed personnel
    Equipment operators
    Drivers
    Security personnel
    Other uniformed personnel
Union representatives
Other nonmanagement personnel

Member Publics

Organization employees
    Headquarters management
    Headquarters nonmanagement (staff)
    Other headquarters personnel
Organization officers
    Elected officers
    Appointed officers
    Legislative groups
    Boards, committees
Organization members
    Regular members
    Members in special categories — sustaining, emeritus,
      student members
    Honorary members or groups
Prospective organization members
State or local chapters
    Organization employees
    Organization officers
    Organization members
    Prospective organization members
Related or other allied organizations

Community Publics

Community media
    Mass
    Specialized
Community leaders
    Public officials
    Educators
    Religious leaders
    Professionals
    Executives
    Bankers
    Union leaders
    Ethnic leaders
    Neighborhood leaders

Community organizations
Civic
Service
Social
Business
Cultural
Religious
Youth
Political
Special interest groups
Other

Government Publics

Federal
Legislative branch
Representatives, staff, committee personnel
Senators, staff, committee personnel
Executive branch
President
White House staff, advisers, committees
Cabinet officers, departments, agencies, commissions
State
Legislative branch
Representatives, delegates, staff, committee
personnel
Senators, staff, committee personnel
Executive branch
Governor
Governor's staff, advisers, committees
Cabinet officers, departments, agencies, commissions
County
County executive
Other county officials, commissions, departments
City
Mayor or city manager
City council
Other city officials, commissions, departments

Investor Publics

Shareowners and potential shareowners
Security analysts and investment counselors
Financial press
Major wire services: Dow Jones & Co., Reuters Economic
Service, AP, UPI

Exhibit 2-a
(*continued*)

Major business magazines: *Business Week, Fortune,* and
the like — mass circulation and specialized
Major newspapers: *New York Times, Wall Street Journal*
Statistical services: Standard and Poor's Corp., Moody's
Investor Service, and the like
Private wire services: PR News Wire, Business Wire
Securities and Exchange Commission (SEC), for publicly
owned companies

Consumer Publics

Company employees
Customers
    Professionals
    Middle class
    Working class
    Minorities
    Other
Activist consumer groups
Consumer publications
Community media, mass and specialized
Community leaders and organizations

Special Publics

Media consumed by this public
    Mass
    Specialized
Leaders of this public
    Public officials
    Professional leaders
    Ethnic leaders
    Neighborhood leaders
Organizations composing this public
    Civic
    Political
    Service
    Business
    Cultural
    Religious
    Youth
    Other

Nonquantitative Research. One source of nonquantitative data is organization or client *records* (business reports, statistics, financial reports, past public relations records) and communications (speeches by executives, newsletters, news releases, memorandums, pamphlets, brochures).

A second source of nonquantitative data is *published materials*. These include news articles from mass media and trade publications, published surveys or polls, library references, government documents, directories, and published trade association data.

Third, nonquantitative research can be conducted through interviews or conversations with *key members of targeted publics*. Important civic leaders, elected officials, business leaders, religious leaders, educators, influential editors, reporters, and other key individuals in the community can provide invaluable background information for a public relations program.

Fourth, feedback from the client's *customers or clientele* can be helpful as a means of nonquantitative research. Customer responses may come via telephone, mail, or face-to-face interactions.

Fifth, talking with *organized groups* with an interest in the client can be useful. These groups may include the organization's formal advisory boards, committees, commissions, or panels from inside or outside the organization.

Sixth, on-line databases have become an essential source of information for public relations practitioners. The most widely used on-line database service is Nexis, providing access to a vast array of information sources. Other on-line services include DataTimes, Dialog, Dow Jones News/Retrieval, Investext, and NewsNet.

Finally, groups created especially for research purposes can provide valuable insight. The most popular form of this procedure is the *focus group*, usually consisting of 8 to 12 people who are representative of the audience the client wishes to reach. A moderator who is skilled in interviewing and group-process management encourages the participants of the focus group to consider the client's image, products, services, and communication proposals or other issues affecting the client. The focus-group meetings are usually videotaped and carefully studied to identify and analyze participants' reactions and comments.

It should be emphasized that although these seven methods of nonquantitative research may yield useful data regarding all areas of concern in the research process, the data will not be scientifically reliable. For a scientific level of reliability, statistical research methods must be used.

Quantitative Research. Three methods of quantitative research are widely used in public relations: sample surveys, experiments, and content analysis. The key to each is the use of statistical methods.

The *sample survey* is the most frequently used quantitative research method in the public relations process. It is most useful in determining audience information levels, attitudes, behaviors, and media habits. Surveys can be conducted by mail, by telephone, or in person, with cost increasing in that order.

Mail questionnaires are the least expensive survey method because of lower staffing requirements. They can yield more data because length is no problem, and respondents can give thorough answers. The major problem with such questionnaires is the low response rate. Unless the intended respondents have a high level of interest in the subject, mail questionnaires can be a big waste of the researcher's time and money.

Telephone interviews have become the most popular means of conducting surveys. Sampling can be done using the random digit dialing technique and an ordinary telephone directory. Although more expensive than mail questionnaires, telephone interviews provide a more economical use of staff time. The limitations of communicating by voice alone may hamper the rapport between interviewer and respondent since the interviewer cannot make judgments about accuracy and sincerity based on nonverbal cues. Nonetheless, telephone interviewing has become the first choice in the conduct of sample surveys.

Personal interviews remain an important, though expensive and time-consuming, survey method. The interviewer can make judgments based on the respondent's nonverbal as well as verbal cues, so no survey method is more accurate. Getting a good sample, however, is much more difficult than with the random digit dialing technique used for telephone interviews. Many people are reluctant to consent to a personal interview because of the time and inconvenience involved. As with mail questionnaires, personal interviews are most effective with respondents who are truly interested in the subject and willing to sacrifice their time.

With all their limitations, and with the onus of being considered "quick and dirty" by most social and behavioral scientists, surveys remain the most popular of quantitative research methods used in public relations.

Controlled experiments have been gaining in popularity in recent years, however. Conducted either in laboratory settings or in the field, experiments are the most accurate indicator of causality in the behavioral sciences. Experiments are often used in advertising or public relations to determine which forms of communication or messages may be most effective with selected audiences. In the experimental method, two groups of subjects are randomly chosen. One group is exposed to the communication media, and the other is not. Both groups are tested before and after the communication exposure. If the responses of the exposed group change significantly after the communication, then these responses can be attributed causally to the messages.

A third quantitative method of research often used in public relations is *content analysis*. This systematic procedure is used in analyzing themes or trends in the message content of selected media. Content analysis can be used to learn how the media are treating clients — their public image as reflected in the media, negative or positive coverage, and the like. This research procedure is also useful in issues management, in which practitioners identify and analyze the impact of public issues on a client's corporate or organizational interests. Thus, content analysis can be helpful in the evaluation of media treatment in the publicity process and in tracking social, economic, or political trends or issues that may affect clients.

Quantitative research should be conducted only by professional firms with good reputations in their field or by staff members who are trained and experienced researchers. Public relations staff members who have not received formal training in research techniques will waste the client's time and money. Worse, their work will probably be inaccurate and misleading.

With the public relations program's informational needs satisfied through nonquantitative or quantitative research methods, the practitioner is ready to attend to the second phase of the process — that of formulating objectives.

Objectives

Objectives are the single most important element in this public relations process. They represent the practitioner's desired outcomes in communicating with the targeted publics. They are the raison d'être for PR programs. Some writers draw a distinction between "goals" as more general outcomes and "objectives" as specific, immediate results. Here we avoid that confusion by consistently using one term to signify desired program outcomes, and that term is *objectives*. Whether they are to be broad or narrow, long-range or short-range, should be stipulated in the statement of the objective itself. Before we discuss the types of objectives used in public relations, we should examine the method used in formulating such objectives.

Many organizations are now using management by objectives (MBO) to determine both general organizational objectives and those for individual work units, such as the public relations department. MBO is a well-established procedure that involves cooperative goal setting by groups of superiors and subordinates in the employee hierarchy. For example, the director of public relations and the assistant director may represent management, and various writers, graphics specialists, and other staff members may represent the "subordinates" in the MBO process. Together they devise short-term and long-range objectives and evaluation procedures for the work unit and for its particular programs. Then, using these procedures, both groups cooperatively evaluate their work at agreed-on times. They also periodically review and revise their objectives and evaluation procedures.

Our concern here is with objectives for individual PR programs. Regardless of whether such objectives are determined using MBO or more traditional authoritarian means, two criteria apply to all program objectives.

First, objectives should be stated in the form of infinitive phrases, each containing one infinitive and each being a specific and separately measurable desired outcome. An infinitive phrase consists of *to* plus a verb plus the complement, or receiver of the verb's action. For example, a practitioner may hope that, after the PR program is executed, the audience will be informed that a special event is taking place and will attend the event. The phrasing of the objectives in infinitive form could be:

- To publicize special event X
- To stimulate attendance at special event X

These objectives could be combined — to publicize and stimulate attendance at special event X — but this compound phrasing would complicate the measurement or evaluation of both objectives.

Second, public relations objectives should be verifiable. To be verifiable, the desired outcome should be stated in quantified, measurable terms, and a time frame or target date should be set for its accomplishment. Although the objectives just stated meet our infinitive test, they are not stated specifically in quantitative or chronological terms. Thus, they can be reworded:

- To publicize special event X through the community's daily newspaper, its TV station, and its three radio stations during the month of October
- To stimulate an attendance of at least 1,500 persons at special event X on May 15

We can measure the first objective by determining, through the use of a clipping service and a broadcast media monitoring service, how many media outlets actually used the announcement of the special event. We can measure the second objective by checking actual attendance figures or ticket sales at the event itself.

Two basic types of objectives are used in public relations programs: *impact objectives* and *output objectives*. Together, they can be viewed as a hierarchy in ascending order of importance (see Exhibit 2–b). Within each category, however, there is no performance hierarchy or order of importance. For example, informational objectives need not be completed before attitudinal or behavioral objectives, and the importance of each of these subsets of impact objectives is purely situational.

Exhibit 2–b	**A Hierarchy of Public Relations Objectives**

Impact Objectives

Informational objectives
    Message exposure
    Message comprehension
    Message retention
Attitudinal objectives
    Attitude creation
    Attitude reinforcement
    Attitude change
Behavioral objectives
    Behavior creation
    Behavior reinforcement
    Behavior change

Output Objectives

Distribution of uncontrolled media
Distribution or execution of controlled media

Output Objectives

Output objectives, the lower category in the hierarchy, represent the work to be produced, that is, the distribution or execution of program materials. Some writers refer to these activities as "process objectives," "support objectives," or "program effort." Whatever the terminology, these activities should not be confused with desired program impacts. Output objectives, as discussed here, refer to stated intentions regarding program production and effort (or output). They are classified as a form of objective because they describe a type of desired outcome often stated in public relations programs. In fact, the PRSA's Silver Anvil Winners use a much higher percentage of output objectives than impact objectives. In the best of all possible worlds, PR directors would use only impact objectives. But here it seems appropriate to deal with PR objectives as they actually exist in the *real* world. Such objectives can easily be made specific and quantitative. For example:

- To send one news release to each of the community's major media outlets: its daily newspaper, its TV station, and its three radio stations by May 10
- To make an oral presentation to an important conference of security analysts in each of the following five cities: New York, Los Angeles, Chicago, Houston, and Denver, before December 15

These objectives can then be measured easily by counting the number of news releases actually sent to the media outlets and the number of oral presentations actually made to security analysts. Time frames can be added if desired.

Some practitioners use only output objectives in their public relations programs. The advantage of such usage is that output objectives set definite, specific, and attainable goals, which can be measured quantitatively. Once these goals have been met, the practitioner can claim success. Unfortunately, output objectives are unrelated to the actual impact the program may have on its intended audiences, and for this we must move to the top, and more significant, category in our hierarchy of public relations objectives.

Impact Objectives

There are three kinds of impact objectives: informational, attitudinal, and behavioral. These are called impact objectives because they represent specific intended effects of public relations programs on their audiences.

Informational Objectives. Informational objectives include message exposure to, message comprehension by, and/or message retention by the target public. Such objectives are appropriate when the practitioner wishes to publicize an action or event; seeks to communicate instructions, operating procedures, or other forms of information; or wants to educate an audience about a noncontroversial subject. Two examples of informational objectives are:

- To increase awareness of the company's open house (by 10 percent) among all segments of the community (during the month of May)
- To increase employee awareness of new plant safety procedures (by 50 percent during our three-month safety campaign)

Attitudinal Objectives. Attitudinal objectives aim at modifying the way an audience feels about the client or organization and its work, products, or services. Attitude modification may consist of forming new attitudes where none exist, reinforcing existing attitudes, or changing existing attitudes.

There will probably be no public attitudes toward a completely new organization. The task of public relations, then, will be the creation of favorable attitudes toward the organization. Two examples of such objectives are:

- To create favorable public attitudes toward a new department store (among 25 percent of mall shoppers during the grand opening celebration)
- To promote favorable attitudes toward a company's new retirement policy (among 80 percent of current employees during the current fiscal year)

It should be stressed that this type of attitudinal objective (forming new attitudes) applies only to organizations and actions that are not controversial and therefore have not generated prior audience attitudes. Some new organizations or actions immediately create reactions among affected groups. In these cases, objectives that seek to reinforce or change existing attitudes are more appropriate.

The second form of attitudinal objective has as its goal the reinforcement, enhancement, or intensification of existing attitudes. A given audience may have moderately favorable, but weak, attitudes toward an organization. In this case, public relations may seek to strengthen these attitudes through a variety of actions, events, or communications. An example of this might be

- To reinforce favorable public opinion toward a nonprofit organization (among 80 percent of its past donors during March and April)

The final form of attitudinal objective is the changing, or reversing, of (usually negative) existing attitudes. In this case, the practitioner must be careful not to take on a "Mission Impossible." The reversal of attitudes is, of course, the most difficult of all tasks in public relations, so the old military adage "Don't fight a losing battle" may serve as a useful guideline here. Attitude or behavior reversal takes time and, as a rule, it cannot be accomplished with one short-range PR campaign. When Ivy Lee attempted to reverse the public image of John D. Rockefeller, Sr., the task took years. Little by little, Lee was successful in converting Rockefeller's image from that of the ogre responsible for the deaths of Colorado miners and their families to the image of a beloved philanthropist. Many practitioners would rightly have regarded such an enormous task as a "losing battle," given the resources of most individuals or organizations. But with unlimited Rockefeller money, the task was finally accomplished.

Sometimes the practitioner will seek to reverse existing positive attitudes. For example, some Republicans in Congress (and in the White House) have attempted to portray many of the government's social programs in a negative light, although most of these programs have enjoyed great popularity since their inception during President Franklin D. Roosevelt's New Deal era.

Two examples of objectives that seek attitude change are

- To reverse (within a period of one year) the negative attitudes and ill will now being expressed toward the manufacturer of a defective product (among 20 percent of the manufacturer's former and current customers)
- To change the favorable attitudes that exist regarding the proposed program (among 10 percent of the members of the U.S. Congress before the vote on the bill)

Attitudinal objectives, then, may involve any of three goals: formation of new attitudes where none exist, reinforcement of existing attitudes, or change in existing attitudes.

Behavioral Objectives. Behavioral objectives involve the modification of behavior toward the client or organization. Like attitude modification, behavior modification may consist of the creation or stimulation of new behavior, the enhancement or intensification of existing favorable behavior, or the reversal of negative behavior on the part of an audience toward the practitioner's client or organization.

Examples of the creation of new behavior might include:

- To accomplish adoption of new safety procedures (among 75 percent of the organization's employees by September 15)
- To persuade (60 percent of) persons over the age of 50 to regularly take a colon cancer test (during the next two years)
- To stimulate new diet procedures (among 70 percent) of children in the city school system (during the current school year)

Enhancement or intensification of existing positive behaviors might involve such objectives as:

- To encourage (30 percent) greater usage of seat belts in automobiles (this year)
- To stimulate (50 percent) higher attendance at meetings by association members (during the next national convention)

The reversal of negative behaviors could include:

- To discourage defacement of public monuments (by 20 percent) in a city park (over a period of eight months)
- To discourage smoking (by 80 percent) in the east wing of the restaurant (during the next three months)

Objectives, as presented here, result from and are shaped by the findings revealed in the research phase. As mentioned earlier, research data should be sought in the area of audience information levels, attitudes, behaviors, and media habits. If information levels about the client or related matters are low, then informational objectives are called for in the public relations program. If audience attitudes toward the client are nonexistent, weak, or negative, then the practitioner will know the kinds of attitudinal objectives to formulate. Finally, if desired audience behaviors are nonexistent, weak, or negative, the practitioner will have a framework for developing appropriate behavioral objectives. Data regarding audience media habits may not contribute directly to the formulation of program objectives, but these findings are useful in determining appropriate media usage in the programming phase of the process.

In addition to impact objectives, the practitioner may devise output objectives for each PR program. These objectives are of less significance because they represent outcomes that have nothing to do with program effects on target audiences.

In the public relations process, objectives precede and govern programming decisions. The degree of influence these objectives exert can best be seen in the programming phase itself.

Programming

Public relations programming, as presented in this process, includes the following elements of planning and execution:

1. Stating a theme, if applicable, and the messages to be communicated to the audiences
2. Planning the action or special event(s) sponsored by the client
3. Planning the use of the media, either uncontrolled or controlled
4. Effectively communicating the program

Theme and Messages

The first element of a program, its theme and messages, should encompass the program's entire scope and must be carefully planned in conjunction with the action or special event central to the program.

The program theme should be catchy and memorable. The best themes are in the form of short slogans consisting of no more than five words. Not all programs require themes or slogans, but a brief, creative theme can become the most memorable part of the entire public relations effort.

Most PR programs will have one central message epitomized in such a slogan or theme. In some cases, programs may have several messages, possibly one for each separate audience. The practitioner should work out as concisely as possible just what is to be communicated to each audience during the entire program.

Action or Special Event(s)

A central action or a special event to be sponsored by the client should be considered along with the program's theme and message. The client's actions or events will usually be the focal point of the theme and messages, although some PR programs omit this element and concentrate on theme and messages alone. However, it is highly recommended that programs be action oriented. A central action or event can make most programs more newsworthy, interesting, and effective. To best advance the public image of the client, this action or event should be substantive, usually serious, and in the public interest. It will be most effective if the event involves large numbers of people and includes the presence of at least one celebrity. Shallow "pseudoevents" should be avoided; they sometimes do more harm than good by damaging the client's credibility. For the most part, gimmicks and stunts are best left to carnivals and circuses. There are exceptions, of course. Sometimes carnivals, circuses, beauty pageants, and similar activities can be presented as a means of raising funds for worthy causes. If these events can be seen as serving the public interest, they may enhance the client's credibility. Typical public relations actions and special events are included in Exhibit 2–c.

Uncontrolled and Controlled Media

The two forms of communication used in public relations are usually classified as *uncontrolled* and *controlled media*.

The use of uncontrolled media involves the communication of news about the client or organization to the mass media and to specialized media outlets. Specifically, the decision-making editors of these outlets become the target audiences for uncontrolled media. The objective of this form of communication is favorable news coverage of the client's actions and events. The standard formats used to communicate client news to the media include news releases, feature stories, captioned photographs or photo opportunities, and news conferences. A more complete listing of these formats can be found in Exhibit 2–d. They are called uncontrolled media because the practitioner loses control of these materials at the media outlet itself. An editor may choose to use the practitioner's release or feature story in its entirety, partially, or not at all; or editors may send reporters who will write or videotape their own stories about the client, ignoring the practitioner's efforts. Since the client or practitioner does not pay the media outlet to use the story as advertising, the use of the material is at the complete discretion of the media outlet.

Exhibit 2-c   **Actions and Special Events**

Special days, nights, weeks, months
Displays and exhibits
Trade shows and exhibitions
Fairs, festivals, expositions
Meetings, conferences, conventions, congresses, rallies
Anniversaries, memorial events
Special awards, retirements, salutes
Open houses, plant tours
Town meetings, public debates, parties
Coffee hours, teas
Contests
Parades, pageants, beauty contests
Sponsoring community events
Sponsoring organizations (community youth organizations,
   Little League, Junior Achievement Organization)
Sponsoring scholarships, contributions
Creating charitable and educational foundations
Receptions
Concert tours, theatrical tours
Performing and graphic arts tours
Visits, pleasure tours for selected publics and groups
Picnics, outings, cookouts, barbecues
Nature trails, flower shows
Ground-breaking ceremonies, cornerstone layings, safety
   programs
Product demonstrations
Traveling demonstrations, home demonstrations
Visits by dignitaries, celebrities
Guest lectures, kickoffs, farewells, going-aways, welcome-
   backs, welcoming ceremonies
Elections of officers
Issuing reports or statistics
Announcing results of polls or surveys
Grand openings
Announcing an appointment
Announcing a new policy or policy change
Announcing a new program, product, or service
Announcing important news about the client or organization
Public relations personalities (Miss America, Miss Universe,
   Maid of Cotton)
Dedications
School commencements, assemblies, events, convocations

Fetes, galas, proms, dances, balls, disco parties
Banquets, luncheons, breakfasts, dinners, buffets
Art shows, openings, exhibits
Concerts, plays, ballets
Film festivals, fashion shows
Animal shows (dogs, cats, birds)
Sporting events, ski trips, ocean cruises, pack trips, hikes, marathons, bike-a-thons, swim-a-thons, miscellaneous-a-thons, races
Celebrity sporting events, cruises
Museum tours, home tours
Embassy tours
Celebrity appearances, autograph-signing ceremonies
Car washes, neighborhood cleanups, services for the elderly
Health screening tests
Committee hearings
Training programs
Opinion-leader meetings and conferences
Special education programs: thrift education, health education, conservation education
Leadership programs
Participation in community events
Celebrations of national holidays
Theme events and celebrations: "Roaring Twenties," "Old New Orleans," "Colonial New England," "Ancient Greece"
Events honoring other nations or cultures
Events honoring the client or organization

The use of controlled media, on the other hand, involves communication about the client that is paid for by the client. The wording of the material, its format, and its placement in the media are all at the discretion of the client. The formats for controlled media include print materials, such as brochures, newsletters, and reports; audiovisual materials, such as films, slide shows, and the like; and interpersonal communication, including speeches, meetings, and interviews. Also included in controlled media are institutional advertising, aimed at enhancing the client's image; advocacy advertising, communicating the client's stand on a controversial issue; and other forms of nonproduct advertising. Exhibit 2–d includes a more detailed listing of the forms of controlled media.

Exhibit 2–d	**Uncontrolled and Controlled Media**

Uncontrolled Media

News releases — print and video news releases (VNRs)
Feature stories
Photographs with cutlines (captions) or photo opportunities
News conferences
Media kits
Radio/TV public service announcements (PSA's) (nonprofit
   organizations only)
Interviews
   Print media
   Broadcast media
Personal appearances on broadcast media
News tapes for radio
News slides and films for TV
Special programs for radio and TV
Recorded telephone news capsules and updates from an
   institution
Informing and influencing editors, broadcast news and public
   service directors, columnists, and reporters (phone calls, tip
   sheets, newsletters with story leads, media advisories)
Business feature articles
Financial publicity
Product publicity
Pictorial publicity
Background editorial material (backgrounders and fact
   sheets)
Letters to the editor
Op-ed pieces

Controlled Media

Print communication methods
   House publications
   Brochures, information pieces
   Handbooks, manuals, books
   Letters, bulletins, memos
   Bulletin boards, posters, flyers
   Information racks
   External periodicals: opinion-leader periodicals, corpo-
      rate general public periodicals, distributor-dealer peri-
      odicals, stockholder periodicals, supplier periodicals,
      periodicals for special publics
   Annual reports

Commemorative stamps
Exhibits and displays
Mobile libraries, bookmobiles
Mobile displays
Attitude or information surveys
Suggestion boxes, systems
Instructions and orders
Pay inserts
Written reports
Billing inserts
Financial statement inserts
Training kits, aids, manuals
Consumer information kits
Legislative information kits
Teacher kits, student games
Teacher aids
Print window displays

Audiovisual communication methods
Institutional films
Slide shows
Filmstrips
Opaque projectors, flannel boards, easel pad presentations
Transparencies for overhead projectors
Telephone calls, phone banks, dial-a-something, recorded messages
Multimedia exhibits and displays
Audio tapes and cassettes
Videotapes and cassettes
Visual and multimedia window displays
Oral presentations with visuals
Multimedia training aids
Teacher aids, student games
Specially equipped vans, trains, buses, boats, airplanes, blimps

Interpersonal communication methods
Formal speeches, lectures, seminars
Roundtable conferences
Panel discussions
Question-and-answer discussions
Oral testimony
Employee counseling

Exhibit 2-d
(*continued*)

Legal, medical, birth-control, miscellaneous counseling
Committee meetings
Staff meetings
Informal conversations
Demonstrations
Speakers bureaus: recruiting and training speakers, speech preparation, clearance of materials with management, list of subjects, speakers' guide, engagements and bookings, visual aids, follow-up correspondence
Training programs
Interviews
Personal instructions
Social affairs
Face-to-face reports
Public relations advertising (not designed to stimulate product sales)
  Print and broadcast advertising
    Institutional advertising — image building
    Public affairs (advocacy) advertising: institutional or organizational statements on controversial issues
  Direct mail institutional advertising
  Outdoor advertising: billboards, signs
  Yellow Pages institutional advertising
  Transit advertising, skywriting, fly-by advertising
  Specialty items: calendars, ash trays, pens, matchbooks, emery boards, memo pads

Effective Communication

The final aspect of programming is the effective communication of the program. Thus, the factors of source, message, channel, receivers, and feedback will be useful in our examination of communication principles. That is, effective communication depends on:

1. source credibility
2. salient information (message)
3. effective nonverbal cues (message)
4. effective verbal cues (message)
5. two-way communication (channel and feedback)
6. opinion leaders (receivers)

7. group influence (receivers)
8. selective exposure (receivers)
9. audience participation (feedback)

Source Credibility. The success or failure of the entire public relations transaction can hinge on how the *source* of communication, the spokesperson for the client or organization, is perceived by the intended audience. Credibility involves a set of perceptions about sources held by receivers or audiences. The personal characteristics of believable sources that continually appear in communication research are trustworthiness, expertise, dynamism, physical attractiveness, and perceived similarities between the source and receivers.[1] These characteristics should serve the PR practitioner as guidelines for selecting individuals to represent the client or organization. Communication coming from high-credibility sources will clearly be in the best interests of the PR program.

Salient Information. A second principle of effective communication involves the use of salient information in the client's messages addressed to target audiences. Members of audiences can be viewed as information processors whose attitudes and behaviors are influenced by their integration of significant new information into their preexisting beliefs.[2] This is another way of saying that the message content must be motivational for the intended audiences — it must strike responsive chords in their minds. Information that is not salient to a given audience in a given context should be discarded.

Nonverbal Cues. A third principle of effective communication involves the use of appropriate nonverbal cues in the PR program's messages. Countless volumes have been published on a variety of aspects of nonverbal communication. But for purposes of effective programming, the PR practitioner should closely examine the nature of the client's actions or special events that are to serve as a basis for the overall effort. Choosing appropriate symbols to represent the client or the cause can be the most important aspect of nonverbal communication. Questions involving the mood, or atmosphere, desired at the event, the personnel to be used, the guests to be invited, the setting, the forms of interpersonal interaction, and the scheduling should be raised. These are essential details that can make the difference between success and failure for the client. Exhibit 2–e provides more details useful in planning effective nonverbal communication for the client.

Verbal Cues. The use of effective verbal message cues, or the actual wording of the client's messages, is the fourth principle of communication considered here. The two most important characteristics of effective language usage are *clarity* and *appropriateness*.

To be clear, language must be accurate. The forms of communication used in a PR program should use words precisely, so the practitioner may need to consult a dictionary or thesaurus. Messages should be tested with a small audience to eliminate ambiguity before their actual use in a PR program. In addition to accuracy, simplicity of word choice contributes to language clarity. Why use big words when simple ones will do? Audiences will relate to such words as *try* better than *endeavor, help* better than *facilitate, explain* better than *explicate, tell* better than *indicate,* and *learn* better than *ascertain.* Finally, coherence is an important factor in clear language. The words in a message should be logically connected — they should hang together well. The use of simple sentences rather than compound or complex ones contributes to coherence. Clear transitions and summaries in messages also aid coherence. Accuracy, simplicity, and coherence, then, are the major factors in constructing clear messages.

Messages should also be appropriate to the client, the audience, and the occasion. If the client is the city's leading bank, some levels of language may be inappropriate. Language used by a fast-food chain is different from that used in the messages of a funeral home. Similarly, language must be appropriate to the demographic level of the audience. Teenagers will obviously respond to a different use of language than senior citizens. The occasion for the use of the message also influences the level and type of language to be used. A diplomatic function held in a Washington embassy requires a different level of language from that used at a locker room gathering of an athletic team. Thus, appropriateness and clarity are the two major requisites for effectiveness in the use of verbal message cues.

Exhibit 2–e   **Nonverbal Communication**

Appropriate symbols
Mood or atmosphere desired: excitement, quiet dignity
Organizational personnel involved, including spokesperson(s)
    to be used
      Demographics of the audience: white/anglo, African American, Hispanic, Jewish, Asian, Arab (if applicable)
      Appearance, dress, actions/interactions expected

Guests: appearance and dress expected

Setting

    Buildings, rooms, or exterior environment desired

    Colors

    Background: banner, logo

    Lighting

    Sound system

    Nature and use of space

    Types and arrangement of furniture, seating arrangements

    Other artifacts to be used: paintings, wall tapestries, sports banners, colored balloons

    Nature of central presentation appropriate for setting (vice versa)

    Music: type, volume

    Entertainment (if any)

    Food, beverages, refreshments (if any)

Forms of interpersonal interaction: sit-down dinner, stand-up cocktail party, reception

Use of time: where will emphasis be placed; will activity build to climax?

Two-Way Communication. The fifth principle of effective communication involves two-way interaction. Communication was once considered a linear process involving the transmission of a message from a source through a channel to a receiver. On receipt of the message at its destination, the communication transaction was considered complete. Today, however, the PR practitioner must program two-way communication activities that permit audience response — or feedback — in brief, the interactive aspects discussed earlier.

A variety of print-oriented response mechanisms are available, such as the suggestion box for employee communication, response cards to be returned to the source of communication, and letters to the editors of publications. The most effective means of two-way interaction, however, is interpersonal communication activities: speeches with question-and-answer sessions, small-group meetings, and one-on-one communication. It is usually possible to divide target audiences into small groups that provide excellent opportunities for interpersonal communication. This is the most effective form of persuasion because of the high level of source-receiver engagement.

Opinion Leaders. The sixth principle of effective communication involves the identification and targeting of opinion leaders as receivers of communication. Sometimes communication operates efficiently in a direct, one-step flow from source to receiver. On many occasions, however, communication is more effective when staged in a two-step or multiple-step flow. In these cases, the practitioner should seek opinion leaders, or "influentials," who in turn will communicate with their followers or cohorts. One simple way to identify opinion leaders is to catalog the leadership of all important groups in a given community or institution. These may include elected political leaders and others who hold formal positions in the community. In some cases, opinion leaders may hold no formal positions, but their advice is nonetheless sought and respected within given groups, institutions, or communities. Practitioners should create a list of opinion-leader contacts, much like their media contacts list, including all relevant data about the leaders, their positions, their availability, and their influence on other audiences.

Group Influence. A seventh effective communication principle involves the use of group influence. People belong to a variety of formal and informal groups. The most valued groups, which exert the greatest influence on their members, are known as *reference groups*. Members feel a sense of cohesiveness, of belonging together; have mutual, face-to-face interactions and influence each other; and share a set of norms and roles that structure and enforce a degree of conformity by each member.

The practitioner's task is to identify and target for communication key groups that can be most useful to the client or organization. Special effort should go into the preparation of a group contacts list, similar to the media and opinion-leader lists. Groups should be reached through interpersonal communication (speeches or presentations) as well as other appropriate methods. It is especially important to contact a formal group's program chairperson to schedule a speech or other presentation on behalf of the client. Acceptance of the client's message or position by key group leaders will then effectively engage the essential nature of group influence: acceptance by all members because of the group's operative cohesiveness and conformity.

Selective Exposure. An eighth principle of effective communication that should be observed by the public relations practitioner is selective exposure. Since the objectives of public relations include attitude and behavior modification, the temptation is always present to take on the most difficult of all tasks: changing existing attitudes or behaviors. Why is this the toughest task? The principle of selective exposure holds that people will accept and even seek out communication supporting their beliefs. However, communication researchers have also found that people will not necessarily avoid information incompatible with their views, as was once thought to be the case.[3] Moreover, other communication research indicates that when a persuasive message falls within the region (latitude) of personal acceptance, opinion or attitude will change in the direction of the advocated position. But when it falls within the region of rejection, attitudes will not change.[4] These communication research findings send a clear message to the PR practitioner—the easiest task in persuasion is reinforcement of existing attitudes or behaviors.

Clearly, trying to change attitudes or behavior is difficult and counterproductive, particularly in the face of strong resistance. Always avoid fighting a losing battle.

When controversial messages are necessary, audiences or individual receivers should always be categorized on the basis of their agreement or disagreement with the message in question. Using terms that coincide with the Likert scale often used in attitude surveys, audiences can be categorized as "positive" (those who strongly agree with the message); "somewhat positive" (those who agree with the message); "undecided"; "somewhat negative" (those who disagree with the message); and "negative" (those who strongly disagree with the message).

The principle of selective exposure dictates that the practitioner first target the "positives," then the "somewhat positives," next the "undecideds," and last, if at all, the "somewhat negatives." The pure "negatives," those strongly opposed or in disagreement with the program's message, should usually be written off. If their attitudes are hardened, and especially if they have publicly expressed their disagreement, they are highly unlikely to change their minds. Given a long period of time, along with perhaps unlimited funds, the hard-core negatives may be slowly changed; but for most practical and immediate situations requiring persuasion, conversion of the negatives is not worth the time, effort, or money.

Audience Participation. A final principle of effective communication, observed whenever possible, is the use of audience participation. This is the only means of communication that encourages audience self-persuasion through direct experience or involvement with the client's services or products. Communication researchers have found that self-persuasion is more effective, by far, than any other means of influence.[5] Therefore, the practitioner should constantly seek opportunities to include audience participation in PR programs.

In summary, public relations programming consists of planning, including attention to theme and message, the use of an action or special event, the use of uncontrolled and controlled media, and program execution following the principles of effective communication.

Evaluation

Evaluation as discussed here is an ongoing process of monitoring and, when appropriate, final assessment of the stated objectives of the PR program. It is usually inadvisable to wait until the execution of the program has been completed to begin the evaluation process. Instead, the practices described here should be engaged in at stipulated intervals during the execution, with program adjustments made as deemed appropriate.

Evaluating Informational Objectives

The measurement of informational objectives includes three dimensions: message exposure, message comprehension, and message retention.

Message exposure is most commonly determined by publicity placement through national or local clipping and media monitoring services. It can also be measured through the circulation figures and audience-size data readily available for publications and broadcast media. Attendance figures for events or meetings also provide an index of message exposure. Finally, exposure is measured by computerized tracking systems that have been developed by some public relations firms for monitoring their effectiveness in delivering messages to audiences.

Message comprehension, or at least the potential for comprehension, is most frequently determined by the application of readability formulas to the messages used in PR programs. The most often used are the Flesch Reading Ease Formula, the Gunning Fog Index, the Dale-Chall Formula, the Fry Formula, and the Farr-Jenkins-Patterson Formula.[6] These predict ease of comprehension based on measuring the difficulty of the words and the length of the sentences used in messages, but surveys must be used to measure actual message comprehension.

Message retention is usually tested by asking appropriate questions designed to check target audiences' knowledge of the client's message. Although message retention can be measured by the nonquantitative research methods discussed earlier, retention questions are usually administered in the form of sample surveys.

Thus, the key to determining the effectiveness of informational objectives lies in the assessment of message exposure, comprehension, and retention. The more of these measurements used, the more accurate the evaluation of effectiveness is likely to be.

Evaluating Attitudinal Objectives

Attitudinal objectives can be measured by several well-established survey research instruments, the most frequently used being Likert scales and the Semantic Differential.[7] Both of these instruments measure attitude intensity and direction; thus, they are useful in assessing whether new attitudes have been formed or whether existing attitudes have been reinforced or changed. These measurements require both pretesting and posttesting of target audiences to determine the degree of influence on attitudes attributable to the PR program. To be of any value at all, attitude measurement must be done by competent professionals well-schooled and experienced in quantitative research methods.

Evaluating Behavioral Objectives

Finally, behavioral objectives can be measured in two ways. First, target audiences can be asked what their behaviors have been since exposure to the PR program. Like attitude measurement, assessment of audience behaviors requires testing before and after program exposure. However, the questions used will be different from those used in attitude research. Closed-end multiple-choice questions or checklists designed to determine audience behaviors are commonly used for this measurement.

A second means of assessing audience behavior is simply observing the behaviors of target audiences. In some cases, these can be counted, as in attendance at special events or numbers of telephone calls received. And in many situations, audiences may be small enough to observe before, during, and after exposure to the PR program.

Nonquantitative research methods can provide useful information both in asking audiences about their behaviors and in observing these behaviors. To obtain the most reliable evaluations of all three types of impact, however, competent professionals with established reputations in research should be retained.

Evaluating Output Objectives

In addition to measuring impact objectives, the PR practitioner must be concerned with assessing the effectiveness of output objectives, which involve the distribution of uncontrolled and controlled media. This effectiveness can be evaluated by keeping records of the number of news releases sent to publications and broadcast stations, the number of contacts made with journalists, the number of speeches given to targeted audiences, the number of publications distributed to each public, and the number of meetings held with key audiences. In the realm of output objectives, practitioners accomplish their goals by distributing appropriate quantities of media according to their original plans. Although these are easily achievable objectives, it should be reiterated that they have no bearing whatever on the PR program's priority goal — audience impact.

Evaluation of the two general forms of program objectives — impact and output — constitutes an ongoing dimension of this public relations process model. The process will not be completed, however, when the program objectives are evaluated. These evaluative data are recycled as part of a continuing procedure. They are useful in adjusting ongoing relations with various audiences, and they can be helpful when planning the client's next short-term PR program with similar audiences.

Summary

The public relations problem-solving process includes four parts: research, determination of objectives, programming, and evaluation. The following outline provides a useful summary and review of the whole process.

Outline of the Public Relations Process

 I. Research
   A. Client/organization: background data about your client or organization — its personnel, financial status, reputation, past and present PR practices, PR strengths and weaknesses, opportunities
   B. Opportunity/problem: proactive or reactive PR program; long-range or short-range campaign
   C. Audiences (publics): identification of key groups to be targeted for communication
     1. Desired research data: each targeted audience's level of information about your client/organization;

image and other relevant attitudes held about your
client/organization and its products or services; audience behaviors relevant to your client/organiza-
tion; demographics, media habits, and media-use
levels of each targeted audience
2. Research procedures: nonquantitative and
quantitative
II. Objectives
A. Impact objectives
1. Informational objectives: message exposure, comprehension, retention
2. Attitudinal objectives: formation of new attitudes,
reinforcement of existing attitudes, change in existing attitudes
3. Behavioral objectives: creation of new behavior; reinforcement of existing behavior; change in existing
behavior
B. Output objectives: distribution or execution of uncontrolled and controlled media
III. Programming — planning and execution of:
A. Theme (if applicable) and message(s)
B. Action or special event(s)
C. Uncontrolled media: news releases, feature stories,
photos; controlled media: print, audiovisual, interpersonal communication, PR advertising
D. Effective communication using principles of: source
credibility, salient information, effective nonverbal and
verbal cues, two-way communication, opinion leaders,
group influence, selective exposure, and audience
participation
IV. Evaluation — ongoing monitoring and final assessment of:
A. Impact objectives
1. Informational objectives: measured by publicity
placement, surveys
2. Attitudinal objectives: measured by attitude surveys
3. Behavioral objectives: measured by surveys and observation of behaviors
B. Output objectives: measured quantitatively by simply
counting the actual output

Notes

1. For a summary of this research, see Erwin P. Bettinghaus and Michael
Cody, *Persuasive Communication*, 4th ed. (New York: Holt, Rinehart &
Winston, 1987), and Mary John Smith, *Persuasion and Human Action*
(Belmont, CA: Wadsworth, 1982), pp. 219ff.

2. For a detailed discussion of the information integration approach to persuasion, see Smith, *Persuasion and Human Action*, pp. 243–61.

3. The best discussion of selective exposure is David O. Sears and Jonathan L. Freedman, "Selective Exposure to Information: A Critical Review," *Public Opinion Quarterly* 31 (1967): 194–213.

4. For a good explanation of this research, called *social judgment theory*, see Nan Lin, *The Study of Human Communication* (Indianapolis: Bobbs-Merrill, 1977), pp. 118–22. Also see Smith, *Persuasion and Human Action*, pp. 264–74.

5. For a review of this research, see Smith, *Persuasion and Human Action*, pp. 191–207.

6. For the Flesch Formula, see Rudolf Flesch, *How to Test Readability* (New York: Harper & Row, 1951); Gunning's Fog Index is found in Robert Gunning, *The Technique of Clear Writing*, rev. ed. (New York: McGraw-Hill, 1968); for the Dale-Chall Formula, see Edgar Dale and Jeanne Chall, "A Formula for Predicting Readability," *Educational Research Bulletin* 27 (January and February 1948); the Fry Formula is found in Edward Fry, "A Readability Formula that Saves Time," *Journal of Reading* 11 (1968): 513–16, 575–78; for a review of readability research, see Werner J. Severin and James W. Tankard, Jr., *Communication Theories: Origins, Methods, Uses* (New York: Hastings House, 1979), chap. 6.

7. For a discussion of these and other research instruments used in attitude measurement, see Kathleen Kelley Reardon, *Persuasion: Theory and Context* (Beverly Hills, CA: Russell Sage Foundation, 1981), pp. 220–32.

Readings on the Public Relations Process

Research

Brody, E. W., ed. *New Technology and Public Relations: On to the Future.* Sarasota, FL: Institute for Public Relations Research and Education, 1991.

———, and Gerald C. Stone. *Public Relations Research.* New York: Praeger, 1989.

Broom, Glen M., and David M. Dozier. *Using Research in Public Relations: Applications to Program Management.* Englewood Cliffs, NJ: Prentice-Hall, 1990.

Grunig, James E., and Larissa A. Grunig, eds. *Public Relations Research Annual.* Hillsdale, NJ: Erlbaum (annual volumes since 1989).

Hamilton, Seymour. *A Communication Audit Handbook: Helping Organizations Communicate.* New York: Longman, 1987.

Masterton, John. "Discovering Databases." *Public Relations Journal* 48 (November, 1992): 12ff.

Nasser, David L. "How to Run a Focus Group." *Public Relations Journal* 44 (March 1988): 33–34.

Pavlik, John V. *Public Relations: What Research Tells Us*, Vol. 16. Newbury Park, CA: Sage CommText Series, 1987.

Simpson, Andrea L. "Ten Rules of Research." *Public Relations Quarterly* 37 (Summer 1992): 27ff.

"Using Research to Plan and Evaluate Public Relations" (special issue). *Public Relations Review* 16 (Summer 1990).

Objectives

Broom, Glen M., and David M. Dozier. "Writing Program Goals and Objectives." In *Using Research in Public Relations: Applications to Program Management*. Englewood Cliffs, NJ: Prentice-Hall, 1990, pp. 39–44.

Grunig, James E., and Todd Hunt. "Defining and Choosing Goals and Objectives." In *Managing Public Relations*. New York: Holt, Rinehart & Winston, 1984, pp. 114–37.

Koestler, Frances A. *Planning and Setting Objectives*. New York: Foundation for Public Relations Research and Education, 1977.

Nager, Norman R., and T. Harrell Allen. *Public Relations Management by Objectives*. New York: Longman, 1984.

Programming

Aronoff, Craig, and Otis W. Baskin. *Public Relations: Profession and Practice*, 3rd ed. Dubuque, IA: Wm. C. Brown, 1992.

Grunig, James E., ed. *Excellence in Public Relations and Communication Management*. Hillsdale, NJ: Erlbaum, 1992.

Hunt, Todd, and James E. Grunig. *Public Relations Techniques*. Fort Worth, TX: Harcourt Brace, 1994.

Lesly, Philip, ed. *Lesly's Handbook of Public Relations and Communications*, 4th ed. New York: Amacom, 1991.

Newsom, Doug, Alan Scott, and Judy VanSlyke Turk. *This Is PR: The Realities of Public Relations*, 5th ed. Belmont, CA: Wadsworth, 1993.

Seitel, Fraser P. *The Practice of Public Relations*, 5th ed. New York: Macmillan, 1992.

Wilcox, Dennis L., Phillip H. Ault, and Warren K. Agee. *Public Relations: Strategies and Tactics*, 3rd ed. New York: Harper Collins, 1992.

Evaluation

Broom, Glen M., and David M. Dozier. "Using Research to Evaluate Programs." In *Using Research in Public Relations: Applications to Program Management*. Englewood Cliffs, NJ: Prentice-Hall, 1990, pp. 71–88.

Grunig, J. E. "Basic Research Provides Knowledge that Makes Evaluation Possible." *Public Relations Quarterly* (Fall 1983): 28ff.

Hauss, Deborah. "Measuring the Impact of Public Relations." *Public Relations Journal* 49 (February 1993): 14–21.

Holloway, Deborah. "How to Select a Measurement System That's Right for You." *Public Relations Quarterly* 37 (Fall 1992): 15ff.

Lindenmann, Walter K. "An 'Effectiveness Yardstick' to Measure Public Relations Success." *Public Relations Quarterly* 38 (Spring 1993): 7–9.

"Measuring Public Relations Impact" (special issue). *Public Relations Review* (Summer 1984).

Richter, Lisa, and Steve Drake. "Apply Measurement Mindset to Programs." *Public Relations Journal* 49 (January 1993): 32ff.

Rossi, Peter H., and Howard E. Freeman. *Evaluation: A Systematic Approach*, 3rd ed. Beverly Hills, CA: Russell Sage Foundation, 1985.

"Using Research to Plan and Evaluate Public Relations" (special issue). *Public Relations Review* 16 (Summer 1990).

Wiesendanger, Betsy. "Electronic Delivery and Feedback Systems Come of Age." *Public Relations Journal* 49 (January 1993): 10–14.

PART TWO

Reaching Major Audiences

Chapter 3   Media Relations

Journalists representing the mass and specialized media usually make up the external audience of highest priority for public relations practitioners. Media relations consists essentially of obtaining appropriate publicity, or news coverage, for the activities of the practitioner's client or organization. The field of public relations began as publicity and for many years was called that. Indeed, this process remains the basis for the burgeoning disciplines of public relations, public affairs, and corporate communications.

Media relations involves targeting the "gatekeepers" of the mass and specialized media for communication about the client or organization. However, the media are actually intermediate audiences. The ultimate targeted audiences in media relations are the *consumers* of the media.

Research

The research process for media relations includes investigation of the practitioner's client or organization, of the opportunity or problem that accounts for communication with the media, and of the various audiences themselves to be targeted for the PR effort.

Client Research

First, the practitioner should be familiar with background data about the client or organization, including its personnel, financial status, and reputation. Special attention must be given to past and present relations with media representatives. Has the client had negative or positive news coverage in the past? Has there been little or no coverage? Does the client have any particular media coverage strengths, such as unusual or glamorous products or a newsworthy chief executive officer? On the other hand, what are the client's publicity "negatives"? In what areas is the client vulnerable? Finally, the practitioner should assess the client's publicity opportunities. What special events can be most profitably staged for the client? What can be done to tie the client in with ongoing community or national special events? With information of this kind the practitioner will be better prepared to serve the client's publicity or media relations needs.

Opportunity or Problem Research

The second aspect of research in preparation for media relations involves determining the reason for the program. Is it because an opportunity has presented itself for good news coverage, or has some problem arisen that will bring media representatives to the client's doorstep? This chapter is concerned more with the former situation, the publicity *opportunity*. For information on managing the media when a problem or crisis develops, see Chapter 10, "Emergency Public Relations."

Audience Research

The final aspect of research for media relations is thought by most practitioners to be the most important — identifying the appropriate media and *their* audiences to target for communication. These media fall into two broad categories, mass and specialized, each of which can be further subdivided (see Exhibit 3–a).

With these media categories, the practitioner's task is to prepare a comprehensive list of media contacts. Appropriate *media directories*, such as those listed in the suggested readings in this chapter, should be consulted in preparing such a list. Practitioners may find that much of their work has already been done for them by these directories. The national, regional, state, and city directories are thorough, but in some cases more information must be gathered. To be of optimal use, the media contacts list should include:

1. The type and size of the audience reached by each media outlet

2. The type of material used by the media outlet — spot news, feature material, interviews, photos

3. The name and title of the appropriate editor, director, re-porter, or staff writer who handles news of organizations such as the client's

4. The deadlines for that media contact—monthly, weekly, daily, morning, afternoon, evening, date, day, or hour

The best advice for the practitioner in media relations is simply to *know the media outlet.* Each outlet has its own unique set of departments and editorial staffing, with particular requirements for submitting material. If in doubt, call the media outlet to obtain the necessary guidelines, along with the name and address of the person who holds the editorial position. It is usually best not to ask to speak with journalists themselves. They may be very busy and resent intrusions for routine information. As a rule, news releases for newspapers should be addressed to the city editor if general in nature or to the appropriate section editor if they are of special interest. For broadcast stations, news releases should usually be addressed to the news director or, in some cases, to the public service director.

Practitioners should never feel that their media contacts lists are complete when they have compiled necessary information about the mass media alone. Each client or organization will be operating in a special field. Automobile manufacturers, fashion designers, dentists, rock music groups—all have their own organizations or associations. And all are served by their own specialized publications. Public relations practitioners must be aware of all such publications that serve their client's field. The process of compiling a list of specialized media contacts begins with consulting a media directory. Among the best of such publications for comprehensive listings in a great variety of fields are *Bacon's Publicity Checker* and *Working Press of the Nation*, both listed later in this chapter. Also listed are directories for medical, scientific, military, and minority media contacts.

Among the finished products of the practitioner's audience research, then, will be *two* media contacts lists: one for mass media and the other for specialized media. News releases, photos, and feature stories directed to and published in specialized publications can often be of greater value to the client than similar exposure in the mass media. It should be emphasized that the purpose of compiling these two media contacts lists is communication with the consumers of both the mass and specialized media—the client's ultimate intended audiences.

In the cases included later in this chapter, these audiences are sometimes specialized and sometimes mass in character.

Exhibit 3–a	Media Publics

Mass media
  Local
    Print publications
      Newspapers
      Magazines
    TV stations
    Radio stations
  National
    Print publications
    Broadcast networks
    Wire services

Specialized media
  Local
    Trade, industry, and association publications
    Organizational house and membership publications
    Ethnic publications
    Publications of special groups
    Specialized broadcast programs and stations
  National
    General business publications
    National trade, industry, and association publications
    National organizational house and membership
      publications
    National ethnic publications
    Publications of national special groups
    National specialized broadcast programs and
      networks

Thus, the research process in media relations involves a thorough understanding of the practitioner's client or organization; the reason—opportunity or problem—for communicating with the media; and, most important, knowledge of the targeted media themselves—the nature of the media outlets, audiences reached, types of material used, specific names and titles of staff contacts, and their deadlines.

Objectives

Media relations uses both impact and output objectives. Some typical examples of both types are examined here, along with a sampling of the objectives used in the media relations cases included in this chapter.

Impact Objectives

Impact objectives represent the desired outcomes of modifying the attitudes and behaviors of target audiences. In media relations they usually include such statements as:

1. To increase knowledge of news about the client among community media representatives
2. To enhance the client's credibility among media people
3. To reinforce favorable attitudes toward the client on the part of media representatives
4. To increase favorable client news coverage

Note that in each of these statements, percentages and time frames can be added as desired. The first statement could be rephrased to read: to increase knowledge of news about the client by 30 percent among community media representatives during the period June 1–December 1. However, a majority of the award-winning cases in this book do *not* quantify their objectives or set time frames.

Almost invariably the objectives used in our sample cases targeted the client's ultimate audiences, rather than the media audiences, for desired impact. It is understood in each case, however, that the media must be the intermediate target audience. Perhaps the objectives would have been clearer and easier to measure if they had targeted *both* the desired media and the ultimate audiences.

Output Objectives

Output objectives in media relations refer to the efforts made by the practitioner on behalf of the client. These statements have nothing to do with the client's desired influence on audiences. Output objectives may include:

1. To be of service to the media — both proactively and reactively
   a. proactively, to provide *newsworthy* stories about the client or organization
   b. reactively, to be available for responses to media inquiries
2. To coordinate media interviews with client or organizational officers and personnel

Programming

Programming for media relations includes the same planning and execution elements used in other forms of public relations: (1) theme and messages, (2) action or special event(s), (3) uncontrolled or controlled media, and (4) principles of effective communication.

Theme and Messages

Program themes, especially in connection with special events, should be included in the messages sent to media outlets. In media relations, the messages themselves should always be governed by the requirements for newsworthiness applicable to the targeted media outlets. Since media relations essentially involves the communication of client news to media outlets or the stimulation of news coverage of the client, the practitioner must understand the nature of news and the criteria for newsworthiness.

Some practitioners believe there are two kinds of news: "hard" and "soft." It is more accurate, however, to think of *spot news* and *feature material* as the two kinds of news.

Spot news is temporal, or time-bound, in nature. Within the rubric of spot news are two subcategories: hard and soft. *Hard spot news* is normally found on prominent pages of major metropolitan dailies. It affects large numbers of people and is of great and immediate interest to the audiences of most mass media outlets. Unfortunately, most hard spot news handled by PR practitioners is *bad* news about the client, such as disasters, plant closings, or layoffs. *Good* news about clients can usually be classified as *soft spot news*. It may not be of much interest outside the organization itself, in which case it should be printed in a house publication and not sent to a mass media outlet. A major challenge to the practitioner is to create special events or *make* good news about the client that will receive favorable coverage in the media.

Feature material, on the other hand, is not time-bound but may be used as "filler" for print and broadcast media. Feature stories for both kinds of media usually focus on human interest topics. Types of feature stories include "a day in the life of. . ."; profiles of personalities; interviews; descriptions of events that emphasize human interest factors and the personalities involved; and sidebars, or feature stories designed to accompany spot news stories in newspapers.

Keeping in mind the differences between spot news and feature material, the practitioner should also be sensitive to the general criteria used by journalists to determine what is newsworthy. The usual characteristics of news include what is new or novel, involves famous persons, is important to large numbers of people, involves conflict or mystery, may be considered confidential, will have significant consequences, is funny, is romantic, or involves sex.

News has also been defined as anything a media outlet chooses to print, broadcast, or film as "news." Since the selection is always the outlet's choice, the public relations practitioner must become familiar with the criteria used by that particular group of editors. This is simply another way of saying, *Know the media outlet.*

Like other aspects of programming, theme and messages should be governed by the practitioner's understanding of what is news and both the general and particular newsworthiness criteria in use at individual media outlets.

Action or Special Event(s)

The use of actions on the part of the client and the staging of special events assumes special importance in media relations. They provide the basis for news coverage. They *are* the news about the client. Thus, the PR practitioner should review the list of actions and special events included in Exhibit 2–c. These can serve as methods of *making* news for the client. Each action or special event should be carefully planned and orchestrated for its maximum news value. If possible, celebrities should be present, and as many other news criteria should be incorporated as is feasible.

The cases in this chapter illustrate a broad range of special events, including a grand opening, an anniversary, and the introduction of a new product line.

Uncontrolled Media

Uncontrolled media are the major vehicles for reporting client news to media representatives. The most commonly used forms are:

1. News releases — print and video
2. Photographs and photo opportunities
3. News conferences
4. Media interviews

News Releases. Of these four frequently used formats, news releases are the most popular with public relations practitioners.

News releases provide a quick, economical means of communicating client spot news or feature material to appropriate media outlets.

Unfortunately, news releases have become overused in major markets throughout the United States. Each morning, editors may be confronted with a stack of 70 to 100 or more releases from practitioners seeking news coverage for their clients or organizations. A prominent Washington bureau chief confided to one of my classes that, faced with his daily pile of news releases, he simply pulls a large, desk-top-high wastebasket over to the edge of the desk and "files" most of the morning mail.

How, then, can practitioners expect to break through the blizzard of news releases to call attention to their own client's news? The "secret" of successful news releases lies in the first word of the term itself—*news*. A really newsworthy story about a client can easily be telephoned to a city editor. The editor, if interested in the story, will assign a reporter to cover it. Major metropolitan editors or broadcast news directors rarely use news releases verbatim or even partially. If a story is there, the news release may alert them to it; but they invariably prefer to assign their own staff people to do the actual news gathering and writing.

Practitioners' news releases may be used verbatim in smaller markets, served by low-circulation dailies or weekly newspapers. Faced with staff and time limitations, these small-market media outlets rely heavily on the work of public relations people.

All media outlets, in markets large or small, depend on PR practitioners for *information* about news events in their market areas. News releases, despite their overuse, remain the major method of transmitting information from the client to the journalist.

An increasingly popular form of client news is the *video news release (VNR)*. Like their print counterparts, successful VNRs must focus on *news* rather than on promotional pap about the client. These news releases are used most frequently in medium or small, rather than major metropolitan, markets. They should be produced by a reputable firm specializing in VNRs and, ideally, the firm should be equipped to handle the entire task, including scripting, production, and distribution.

Photographs and Photo Opportunities. Photographs are a second widely used form of uncontrolled media. As with news releases, public relations photographs are seldom used by major metropolitan daily newspapers. But, like news releases, they may serve to attract the attention of major editors to client news that might otherwise be overlooked. Public relations photographs have a better chance of being used by smaller publications in smaller markets. They are important enough to warrant attention to the details of their proper composition and preparation for PR purposes.

Good public relations photographs should be creative and imaginative in composition, avoiding the clichés a client may request, such as a speaker standing at a podium, one person handing something to another, a group shot of ten or more people, or one person sitting at a desk. Photographs of this kind usually find their way into house publications. A good public relations photograph depicts something a newspaper photographer cannot duplicate or restage. Unique and interesting photographs may be used because of their creativity and news value.

A frequently used contemporary technique is the staging of a "photo opportunity," especially in markets where the major dailies or magazines are likely to assign their own photographers to a story. The photo opportunity should be carefully planned in advance and staged in a natural — not theatrical — way, so that it becomes an integral or necessary part of the news story and not something that can be missed by the assigned journalists and photographers.

News Conferences. A third frequently used form of uncontrolled media is the news conference. News conferences should be used sparingly since they are usually inconvenient for journalists. A good one-word rule for holding news conferences is *don't*. Of course, all rules have exceptions, and news conferences should be staged under exceptional circumstances. If staged, the conference must live up to its descriptive adjective, *news*. Even on their very best days, metropolitan journalists are easily annoyed. They can resent being summoned to a news conference to hear a routine announcement that could have been faxed to the city desk or reported in a written release.

Many organizations use news conferences for significant announcements, such as major corporate changes, takeovers, mergers, introductions of new product lines, or responses to false accusations of wrongdoing. Other than for major government agencies, news conferences should never be routine. They should be reserved for truly newsworthy occasions that call for a personal presentation by the organization's chief executive officer or by a visiting celebrity or dignitary.

News conferences can be conducted profitably, but the practitioner should always keep the preceding reservations in mind and usually resist the urge to hold one.

Media Interviews. Media interviews are a fourth frequently used form of uncontrolled media. Whether given to print or broadcast journalists, interviews provide the most direct contact between the client and the media. The practitioner's role in this situation is that of a link, or coordinator, and sometimes also that of a trainer or coach for the client.

In the case of print interviews, clients may have the options of declaring beforehand that their comments will be for background, not for attribution, or completely off the record. In these cases the client's name cannot be used; and in off-the-record interviews the content of the interview cannot be used in the media. Aside from interviews with high government officials in sensitive positions, however, most clients want to be both quoted and identified in the media as a means of promoting their organizations' interests.

Broadcast interviews do not permit the luxury of being off the record. If clients consent to broadcast interviews, they do so with the knowledge that while on camera (or microphone), they may be put through a "third degree" by an enterprising journalist. Moreover, the client loses control of the editing function. For this reason many organizations insist on bringing their own videotaping equipment and crew in order to have an independent record of the interview. Increasingly, organizations are paying specialized consultants for "media training" for their executives, who can then significantly influence favorable public opinion about their organizations.

Print and broadcast interviews, then, are one of the four most frequently used forms of uncontrolled media in the client's communication with journalists. In addition to news releases, photographs, news conferences, and interviews, the practitioner should consider the other communication vehicles listed in Exhibit 2–d.

Controlled Media

A variety of forms of controlled media can be used to provide journalists with background information. For example, the typical *media kit* includes such printed materials as brochures, folders, annual reports, speeches, and backgrounders. In the true sense of the term, however, controlled media are not used in media relations. When journalists are given controlled communications, they make their own uses (or nonuses) of them. Thus, the client or practitioner has no control over how such materials will be used by journalists.

A case can be made that public relations advertising constitutes the use of controlled communications in media relations. The practitioner *does* deal with media outlets in such cases, but not with journalists. Advertising is purchased directly from the media outlet's advertising department.

The exhibits included with the cases in this chapter demonstrate the scope of both uncontrolled and controlled communications used in media relations.

Effective Communication

In media relations, the communication process can be aptly described as a two-step flow. The traditional two-stage model depicts a stream of messages from a mass media source to opinion leaders and then to the colleagues of the opinion leaders. In media relations, this process is partially reversed. Communication flows from the practitioner's client to the media and then in turn to the media audience.

Because of the special nature of media relations, not all of the nine principles of effective communication discussed in Chapter 2 apply.

Source credibility clearly *is* applicable in the case of media relations. Media representatives must perceive the client or organization and its spokesperson as trustworthy and reliable. Salient information, on the other hand, must be redefined for media relations. Information that meets the criteria of newsworthiness constitutes the salience for journalists. Both nonverbal and verbal cues contribute to communication effectiveness in media relations, just as they do in other forms of public relations. The use of two-way communication, however, plays a less important role in media relations than in other forms. Journalists generally resent inquiries from practitioners to see if a client's news releases are going to be used. The feedback that practitioners really want in media relations is the use of their materials in the media.

The use of opinion leaders in the usual sense is not a part of media relations. In media relations, practitioners communicate directly with journalists. In some instances, journalists *are* regarded as community opinion leaders, but this principle applies more directly to community relations. The selective exposure principle may apply in some cases to media relations but, in general, journalists are more open-minded and often seek information that they may personally disagree with. Finally, the audience participation principle is valid and useful in media relations. When introducing new product lines, for example, many companies invite journalists to use the product on an introductory basis. Journalist participation at news conferences and other meetings arranged by PR practitioners provides other instances of effective audience participation in media relations.

Thus, most of the principles of effective communication apply to media relations to some degree. However, the group-influence principle is rarely used in media relations since journalists pride themselves on their independence of thought and action. But on the whole, principles of effective communication should be a priority concern of the public relations practitioner in media relations.

Evaluation

The evaluation process in all forms of public relations always refers to the program's stated objectives. In media relations, as in all of public relations, impact objectives are of the highest priority.

Evaluating Impact Objectives

The impact objective of informing the media about the client is generally measured by assessing the exposure of the message in the media, or publicity placement. National or local clipping and media monitoring services are usually retained to take this measure of effectiveness. Message exposure can also be measured by the circulation figures and audience-size data available from the publications and broadcast media themselves. Additionally, some public firms use sophisticated computerized tracking systems to evaluate effectiveness in delivering messages to audiences. Publicity placement, however, remains the predominant method for evaluating the success of message exposure.

Attitude objectives in most forms of public relations are measured by conducting sample surveys of the target audiences, but this may not be feasible with journalists targeted for communication. Some might react negatively to such an intrusion from a PR practitioner. Content analyses of media placement, however, can yield the desired measurements. A scientific assessment of attitudes is therefore possible and relatively easily obtained.

This same procedure is also useful in measuring favorable client news coverage. This objective is the ultimate goal of *all* media relations.

Evaluating Output Objectives

Along with the measurement of impact objectives, practitioners want to determine the effectiveness of their media relations output objectives. These consist essentially of distributing uncontrolled media to outlets, being responsive to media inquiries, and coordinating media interviews. They can be evaluated by keeping records of all such transactions. Although these objectives are easily accomplished, the practitioner should be reminded that these goals have no bearing on media relations impact.

Evaluation of media relations, then, is heavily concentrated on successful and favorable placement of the practitioner's uncontrolled media. Other objectives are useful, but successful media relations ultimately boils down to the matter of placement. This is clearly visible in the priority given to placement in the evaluations of the cases in this chapter.

Summary

With some modifications, the four-stage process is as useful in media relations as it is in other forms of public relations. Essentially, media relations involves establishing a favorable working relationship between PR practitioners and journalists representing appropriate mass and specialized media.

The most important aspect of research for media relations is the preparation of up-to-date lists of media contacts for both mass and specialized outlets. Objectives in media relations usually emphasize the desired behavioral impact of obtaining favorable news coverage for the client. An absolute essential for media relations programming is an understanding of the particular media outlets' audiences and the media's definitions of news for those audiences. This information should provide criteria for the development of newsworthy, client-centered special events, news releases, photographs, news conferences, interviews, and/or other forms of uncontrolled media used in reaching journalists.

Evaluation of media relations always refers back to the program's stated objectives. Impact objectives are generally measured through publicity placement, circulation and audience data, computer tracking of messages, or content analysis. The accomplishment of output objectives can be simply determined by counting or otherwise observing the desired outputs as they are set in motion. In essence, however, the effectiveness of media relations always comes down to media placement, that is, obtaining the desired publicity for the client.

Readings on Media Relations

Bernstein, Gail. "Meet the Press." *Public Relations Journal*, 44 (March 1989): 28–32.

Detweiler, John S. "Source Power: New Leverage in Media Relations." *Public Relations Quarterly* 37 (Summer 1992): 19ff.

Dilenschneider, Robert L. "Use Ingenuity in Media Relations." *Public Relations Quarterly* 37 (Summer 1992): 13ff.

Goff, Christine F. *The Publicity Process*, 3rd ed. Ames, IA: Iowa State University Press, 1989.

Grabowski, Gene. "Seven Deadly Sins of Media Relations." *Public Relations Quarterly* 37 (Spring 1992): 37ff.

Graham, Barbara Florio. "Two Dozen Ways to Guarantee Failure in Media Relations." *Public Relations Quarterly* 37 (Summer 1992):

Howard, Carole, and Wilma Mathews. *On Deadline: Managing Media Relations.* New York: Longman, 1985.

Klein, T., and F. Danzig. *Publicity: How to Make the Media Work For You.* New York: Scribner's, 1985.

Martin, Dick. *Executive's Guide to Handling a Press Interview.* Babylon, NY: Pilot Books, 1990.

"Media Relations: What's News?" (special section). *Public Relations Journal* 45 (November 1989): 14–22.

Morton, Linda P. "Producing Publishable Press Releases: A Research Perspective." *Public Relations Quarterly* 37 (Winter 1992): 9ff.

_____, and John Warren. "News Elements and Editors' Choices." *Public Relations Review* 18 (Spring 1992): 47–53.

Wester, Natalie. "Build Confidence with Media Training." *Public Relations Journal* 48 (February 1992): 26ff.

Winter, Grant. "Improving Broadcast News Conferences." *Public Relations Journal* 46 (July 1990): 25–26.

Media Directories

Bacon's Media Alerts. Chicago: Bacon's Publishing Co., published annually with bimonthly updates. Publicity opportunities.

Bacon's Publicity Checker. Chicago: Bacon's Publishing Co., published annually with quarterly supplements.

Bacon's Radio/TV Directory. Chicago: Bacon's Publishing Co., published annually with quarterly supplements.

Broadcasting/Cablecasting Yearbook. Washington, DC: Broadcasting Publications, published annually.

Burrelle's Media Directories. Livingston, NJ: Burrelle's, published annually.

Burrelle's Special Directories: Black Media: Hispanic Media: Women's Media. Livingston, NJ: Burrelle's, published annually.

Editor and Publisher International Yearbook. New York: Editor and Publisher Co., published annually.

Gale Directory of Publications (formerly *Ayer Directory of Publications*). Detroit: Gale Research, published annually.

Guide to U.S. Business, Financial and Economic News Correspondents and Contacts. New York: Larriston Communications, published annually.

Guide to U.S. Medical and Science News Correspondents and Contacts. New York: Larriston Communications, published annually.

Hudson's Washington News Media Contacts Directory. Rhinebeck, NY: Hudson's, published annually with quarterly updates.

Military Publications. New York: Richard Weiner, published annually.

TV Publicity Outlets Nationwide. Washington Depot, CT: Public Relations Plus, published three times a year.

Working Press of the Nation. Chicago: National Research Bureau, published annually.

Media Relations Cases

The opening of the Ordway Music Theatre is an outstanding case because of the extent of its opening activities, all coordinated with a 10-day celebration of New Year's Day. Another strength of the case was the extension of media relations well beyond Minnesota's Twin Cities. The exhibits included here clearly indicate the thoroughness and the marketing orientation used in the campaign. Exhibit 3–1b illustrates the use of the VALS typologies (achievers, the societally conscious, experientials, and integrateds) as a means of determining the theater's programming and marketing its various shows. Exhibit 3–1c, the communications plan for the theater opening, is an outstanding example of thorough public relations planning. Every staff activity connected with the campaign is listed under the categories of Events, Printing, Media Relations, Community Relations, Advertising, Marketing, Objectives, Audiences, and Current Audience Knowledge. Finally, Exhibit 3–1d, "Positioning the Ordway Music Theatre," is an instrument used in sophisticated marketing. Its purpose is to differentiate Ordway from all its competitors in the Twin Cities area. The emphasis in positioning is on such marketing aspects as need, uniqueness, the competition, and the development of messages about the theater based on this information. The Ordway Theatre campaign truly exemplifies a "grand opening" as it should be planned and executed.

Case 3–1   Opening of the Ordway Music Theatre

Ordway Music Theatre, St. Paul, MN, with Padilla and Speer, Inc., Minneapolis, MN

The Ordway Music Theatre is a multiuse performing-arts hall that opened in St. Paul on January 1, 1985. The Ordway houses two separate theater facilities: a 1,815-seat Main Hall and a 315-seat Studio Theatre.

Preface

January is a difficult time to open a theater in Minnesota. Although Minnesotans are accustomed to winter, January nights are cold and people are content to remain at home after the holidays. Because of this, we knew we had to find a way to create excitement

Courtesy Ordway Music Theatre

that would persuade people to attend a theater performance. Although the Twin Cities of Minneapolis and St. Paul adjoin, many Minneapolitans have never been to St. Paul. This, along with the fact that Minneapolis is the home of the 2,500-seat Orchestra Hall, meant obstacles would have to be overcome. Without support of both Minneapolis and St. Paul patrons, arts facilities in the Twin Cities cannot hope to succeed.

Research

The problems were turned into opportunities, partly by using a research framework developed by SRI International (formerly Stanford Research Institute). Using SRI's VALS (Values and Life Styles) framework, we identified (1) types of people who would be most apt to attend the theater, and (2) messages we should attempt to convey. The primary target group we identified is described by VALS as "achievers." The message to this group emphasized "the experience of going to the theater" rather than specific performances.

Planning

The objectives of the program were to:

1. Interest New York–based music critics in coming to St. Paul to see the Ordway so that national attention would be focused on the theater and top-quality artists would want to perform here.
2. Demonstrate the versatility of the Main Hall and Studio Theatre so that many types of audiences would be attracted to the Ordway.
3. Build a solid base for future ticket sales.
4. Get large numbers of people to see the building so they would be familiar with its location and offerings.
5. Generate favorable local publicity about the theater and its mission.

Strategies

- "Model Road Show" — The architect's scale model of the theater was taken to meetings all over the Twin Cities, providing a preview.

- New Year's Day Open House — The public was invited to see the theater before its inaugural performances. The all-day open house featured backstage tours of the Main Hall and entertainment.
- 10-Day Gala Opening Festival — A 10-day opening series was planned to illustrate the broad range of music, dance and theater forms that can be presented at the Ordway.
- Consistent Message — News information, advertising and promotional materials emphasized the elegance and ambiance of the theater, care taken in planning the acoustics and sight lines, and opportunities for socializing.
- Variety — To appeal to a wide range of audience tastes and to build rapport with the Twin Cities arts community, we invited all types of local music, dance, and theater groups to perform at the Opening Festival.
- Early Contact with Critics — Five months before the opening, we sent background material to national music critics and architecture critics. They also received invitations to take part in the Opening Festival.
- Early Contacts with the Media — We developed unique angles for each major local media outlet, beginning 8 months prior to opening.

Budget

The opening events, public relations, and advertising budget combined was $240,000. The amount spent on advertising was less than one-sixth of the budget. The program was executed by the Ordway's marketing and communications director, two part-time assistants, and two representatives of the public relations firm until 3 weeks before the opening. At that time, one person was added to the theater's communications staff. The project was completed within budget.

In-Progress Adjustments

- We came up with the idea of positioning every performance of the 10-Day Opening Festival as "an opening night." This would give every festival goer the opportunity to experience the magic traditionally connected with any opening night. Second, it avoided problems connected with having three major tenants — the Schubert Club, the St. Paul Chamber Orchestra, and the Minnesota Opera — and only one opening night.

- We heard concerns that the theater didn't have a connecting parking ramp. We made a special effort to identify the on-street, surface lot and ramp parking spaces in close walking distance to the theater (there were more than 5,000, we learned). We communicated this and also the message that many local restaurants had shuttle buses to the theater.

Evaluation

We measured the program's effectiveness by attendance figures at opening events and the scope of news-media coverage.

- More than 550 articles, photos, or editorials about the theater have appeared in approximately 85 publications across the country. In addition to massive local news coverage in both Minneapolis and St. Paul, the theater was the subject of articles in *Time* and *Newsweek*, the *New York Times*, the *Boston Globe, San Francisco Chronicle, Chicago Tribune*, and 3 airline in-flight magazines. Broadcast coverage was also extensive. CBS "Sunday Morning" featured a tour of the theater with architect Ben Thompson, and American Public Radio aired three nationwide broadcasts. Both the "Today Show" and "Good Morning America" sent crews for live coverage. All five Twin Cities television stations did live broadcasts from the Opening Festival and/or the New Year's Day Open House. (OBJECTIVES 2 AND 5)
- The theater was well received by music and architecture critics. Their reviews applauded the theater's acoustical and staging versatility and its spaciousness and warmth. (OBJECTIVES 1 AND 2)
- A total of 19,655 tickets were purchased for performances of the Opening Festival. (OBJECTIVES 3 AND 4)
- To date, 35,383 tickets have been purchased for the Ordway's own inaugural season of visiting artists. (OBJECTIVE 2)
- Attendance at the New Year's Day open house included 23,000 children and adults, four times greater than expectations. (OBJECTIVE 4)

Exhibit 3–1a   Ordway Music Theatre, St. Paul, Minnesota

Courtesy Ordway Music Theatre

Exhibit 3–1b   **Marketing Ordway Music Theatre Using SRI International's VALS Typologies**

Memorandum

TO: OMT Operations Staff
FROM: Jane Cooper
RE: Sneaking up on marketing acts booked for opening season
DATE: August 26, 1984

The Initial Question: how best to spread acts across four columns?

#1   Subquestion: What types of acts do four VALS typologies prefer?

#2   Subquestion: In what proportion do VALS types attend any acts?

#3   Subquestion: What OMT-booked acts are preferred by each VALS type?

#4   Subquestion: Can we spread achiever-preferred acts (etc.) across the four columns evenly so each VALS type has plenty to select from?

#5   Subquestion: What media placements are implied by the categorizing of booked acts according to VALS type?

#6   Subquestion: What advertising costs must be incurred for each act and for the overall season promotion?

#1   What types of acts do four VALS typologies prefer?

Achievers	Societally Conscious	Experientials	Integrateds
Generally popular modern contemporary classics	classics modern contemporary popular	popular modern contemporary classics	popular classics modern contemporary

Courtesy Ordway Music Theatre

Music			
rock, c&w, blues	symphonies	rock, c&w, blues	rock, etc.
mid-road pop	rock, c&w, blues	jazz	mid-road pop
symphonies	jazz	mid-road pop	symphonies
jazz	mid-road pop	symphonies	jazz
Theater			
musical comedy	musical comedy	modern comedy	modern comedy
modern comedy	modern comedy	musical comedy	musical comedy
Vegas spectacular	modern drama	modern drama	Vegas spectacular
modern drama	classics	Vegas spectacular	modern drama
Dance			
modern	ballet	tap, show, jazz	ballet
tap, show, jazz	modern	modern	tap, show, jazz
ballet	tap, show, jazz	ballet	modern
folk	folk	folk	folk
Reasons for Attending			
entertainment	entertainment	entertainment	entertainment
show	show	group, star	show
group, star	performer, conductor	show	performer, conductor
performer, conductor	group, star	performer, conductor	group, star
old favorite	old favorite	new, different	old favorite
to be sociable	be emotionally moved	given tickets	improve self
part of business	season tickets	dressing up	see facilities
to be seen	personally involved	escape routine	= users, not enjoyers
discuss it later	see performer first time	celebrate event	
to feel special	sake of children	judge the show	
vacation event	fulfill self	experience new	
= hard sells	meet interesting people	asked to go	
	performers from other countries	= desire to be au courant, celebrate	
	support college, university		
	= deeply personal		

Exhibit 3-1b
(*continued*)

"Aha's"* from reasons for attending:
* Entertainment is key element.
* Seeing a known show is more important than seeing an un-known piece.
* Seeing a star or specific individual — group, performer, con-ductor, is important; not just anyone will do.
* Old favorites are appealing, but only after all other reasons.
* Something new and different is appealing ONLY to Experientials.
* Seeing performers never seen or heard of before is NOT appealing.
* Achievers need to attend for business, to-be-seen reasons, but there's a hint of "ought to go but really don't want to."
* Supporting the college is important to Societally Conscious, but much less to others.
* Experientials, with less disposable income, are stimulated by free (or low-priced) tickets.

*Insights (author's note).

Concerns about Attending:
Generally, top five reasons for not attending are preferences for other ways to spend leisure time, expense, prefer not to commit time, lack of time, inability to follow performance in a foreign language. Plus:

parking	best informed	impulsive	show quality
good seat	(read ads, etc.)	last-minute	best informed
show quality	expense	waits in line	expense
safety	best educated	procrastinate	safety
	(less concern	in buying	best educated
	re language)		(less concern
			re language)

#2   In what proportion (by millions) do VALS types attend any acts?

Achievers	Societally Conscious	Experientials	Integrateds
Music			
68	59	23	6
Theater			
37	36	9.5	3.5
Dance			
14	14	5.4	1.5
119	109	38	11
(43% audience)	(39% audience)	(14% audience)	(4% audience)

Note: Census figures indicate the following representation in the northcentral region of the United States:

(50% audience) (29% audience) (16% audience) (5% audience)

* This indicates there are more achievers in our region than show up at performances, something we should be aware of in booking.
* On the other hand, societally conscious people here are attending in greater proportion than their numbers would suggest.

"Aha's" from attendance figures:
* Achievers are the largest single market segment, but the Societally Conscious are gaining — fast!
* Only Experientials as a group report more increases than declines — probably due to age factor and baby boom stuff.
* For musical events, concentrate on those who attend three plus times a year.
* For theater, focus on all groups equally.
* For dance, focus on those who attend fewer than six times a year. . . .

Exhibit 3-1b
(*continued*)

#5   What media placements are implied for 1984–85 by the categorizing of booked acts according to VALS types?

* Achievers usually hear about performances by the following:
(Note: booked acts appeal 35% to Achievers)

Newspaper/magazine
ads 80%
TV....................................74%
Radio 69%
Newspaper/magazine
review 66%
Newspaper/magazine
story 65%
From a friend 62%
Word of mouth 56%
Billboards......................34%
Mailed notice 25%

* Societally Conscious, by the following:
(Note: booked acts appeal 85% to Societally Conscious)

Newspaper/magazine
review.............................78%
Newspaper/magazine
story 71%
From a friend 67%
Word of mouth 63%
Calendars of events........62%
Radio 60%
TV....................................55%
Mailed notice 42%

* Experientials, by the following:
(Note: booked acts appeal 61% to Experientials)

Radio 90%
Newspaper/magazine
advertisements...............82%
From a friend 71%
Word of mouth 69%
TV....................................68%
Calendars of events........58%
Newspaper/magazine
story 54%
Billboards......................54%
Newspaper/magazine
review.............................51%
Mailed notice 19%

* Integrateds, by the following:
(Note: booked acts appeal 65% to Integrateds)

Newspaper/magazine
advertisements...............82%
Word of mouth 75%
TV....................................67%
From a friend 65%
Newspaper/magazine
review.............................55%
Radio 52%
Newspaper/magazine
story 49%
Calendars of events........50%
Billboards......................34%
Mailed notice 39%

Exhibit 3–1c   **Communications Plan for Opening of Ordway Music Theatre**

Events

1. Research openings of "great halls"
2. Construction workers dinner
3. Media preview night
4. New Year's Day public open house
5. Funders recognition dinner
6. Determine gifts for any/all events
7. Develop 6–9-minute slide/video program on construction to show at events (not performances)
8. Consider commemorative medal for special gifting
9. Determine and invite special guests for opening events
10. Consider appropriate persons for M.C. of opening events
11. Consider drawing/contest for open house
12. Series of events/performances by arts groups
13. Conduct hall-tuning events with: senior citizen groups, downtown employees, Landmark and other location staffs, etc.

Printing Needed for Opening Events

1. Invitations for construction dinner
2. Invitations for media preview night
3. Invitations (publicity and advertising) for public open house
4. Invitations for funders recognition dinner
5. Programs for construction dinner and funders dinner
6. Special brochure for public open house, with floor plans, events of the day
7. Commemorative program for opening performances
8. Poster for opening, perhaps as gift, perhaps through contest
9. Determine overall design theme for opening, as differentiated from "regular" Ordway look

Media Relations

1. Staff announcement release
2. TV release as a "walk" through the model
3. Acoustics as a financial risk release to business writers or special placement
4. Milestone of construction releases as they occur
5. Great halls of the world and how Ordway fits in release or placement

Exhibit 3-1c
(*continued*)

6. Sound engineering release to science writers
7. How to listen to music at the Ordway (from the perspective of top artists) placement
8. Contact with KTCA-TV re half-hour documentary
9. Contact with KSTP-TV re feed to local and network TV pool (performances)
10. Contact with St. Paul papers re feed still shots to newspaper pool (performances)
11. Advance work with all media re house configuration, photo rules, etc.
12. Contact with MPR re broadcast of opening performances
13. Architecture story to architecture writers/critics local and national
14. Contact with all critics, local and national
15. Regular newsletter to all key media, with update
16. Quarterly media tours, lunches
17. Opening events news kit (coordinated with tenants)
18. Public open house news kit
19. Media preview night
20. Determine policy for comp tickets to media, in conjunction with tenant organizations
21. Release or placement on the orchestra shell as a key component of the acoustics, and how it will be stored and moved up and down stage
22. Work with MPR on "how to be your own critic"

Community Relations

1. Pursue linkages with Rice Park community: Amhoist Tower, St. Paul Hotel, Library, Minnesota Club, St. Paul Companies, Landmark Center, Civic Center, etc.
2. Buttons celebrating opening
3. Pursue linkages with retail community: Dayton's, etc.
4. Display theater model at a variety of locations available to the public: hotels, skyway concourses, corporate headquarters, libraries, city hall, capitol, governor's office, etc. Include flyer on the theater
5. Work with state and city offices re highway and street signs directing public to the theater.
6. Seek Winter Carnival connection, particularly for 1985 and 1986
7. Work with nearby garages to use signs indicating space available for Ordway patrons
8. Produce wallet-sized maps to the theater
9. Mail releases to internal communications departments of St. Paul area firms

10. Monthly newsletter to go to key audiences: funders, board, funding prospects, key media, arts organizations, Ordway family, corporate funders, volunteers
11. Pursue use of bill stuffers highlighting OMT opening with Northwestern Bell, banks, retailers, etc.

Advertising

1. Develop format for Ordway opening ads
2. Consider co-op advertising with tenant arts organizations
3. Develop and produce PSAs
4. Make linkage with Paragon Advertising for free creative help
5. Produce ads for public open house
6. Produce ads for all opening events
7. Set schedule for media buys
8. Determine media mix appropriate for the public open house and opening events

Marketing

1. Determine key markets and how to reach them
2. Research tourism marketing techniques
3. Produce brochure for marketing OMT to local, national performing arts groups
4. Produce brochure for marketing OMT as a convention, meeting site
5. Determine mailing lists, procedures for above brochures
6. Investigate tour packages with area hotels for out-of-state patrons
7. Work on bus trips to St. Paul for opening
8. Work with Forepaughs and other restaurants on dinner-and-OMT events
9. Contact Forepaughs re their interest in producing OMT schedules for their guests

Objectives

1. Make OMT known to key audiences, so that they can come and tell their friends about OMT
2. Fill the house, so that we make money
3. Develop long-term relationships with arts lovers, so that we have a steady base of patrons
4. Enhance reputation of OMT as a high-quality hall, so that top-quality artists will want to perform here, and will therefore call us

Exhibit 3-1c
(*continued*)

5. Enhance the reputation of the OMT so that our international patronage may be increased
6. Encourage local arts groups to perform at the OMT, so that we can represent the best in Minnesota and upper Midwest artists
7. Generate name familiarity and good attendance so that our funders are happy

Audiences tc Be Reached

1. Current patrons of the performing arts in the Twin Cities
2. Current patrons of the performing arts in the upper Midwest
3. Current patrons of the performing arts in key cities of the U.S. and abroad
4. Performing arts critics in the local area, nationally and internationally
5. Potential patrons locally, regionally, nationally
6. Funders and potential funders: corporate, foundation, individual
7. Architecture and engineering/sound writers
8. Acousticians
9. Performing arts groups and individual artists: local, regional, national, international
10. Twin Cities business community
11. Arts students
12. Children
13. General media

Current Audience Knowledge/Attitudes toward Ordway

1. Top echelon of business community is getting the word to give money to a winner
2. Local arts organizations know a little about the OMT, and are interested in their own affiliation possibilities
3. Current patrons of the performing arts everywhere know virtually nothing
4. Performing arts critics locally are aware of OMT and generally supportive (for now)
5. Performing arts critics regionally and nationally are far less aware, will be supportive only so long as the OMT "works"

6. Architecture, engineering/sound writers, and acousticians know virtually nothing
7. Arts students probably know virtually nothing
8. Children certainly know nothing re OMT
9. Potential patrons of the performing arts will have to be "sold" on OMT as a nonstuffy, people's place

---

Exhibit 3–1d   **Positioning the Ordway Music Theatre**

1. Need for the OMT

   - With the close of the Civic Center Theater in 1980, struggling local arts organizations were thrown out on the street, making their lives still more nomadic than usual.
   - No performing arts organization can long survive in the Twin Cities without support from the entire metro area. Audience breakout between St. Paul and Minneapolis for major organizations is as follows: SPCO 50/50, MOC 50/50, Schubert Club 30/37 and the Minnesota Orchestra's St. Paul series 67/33 and its overall breakout 15/85.
   - The OMT is located very centrally in the Twin Cities metro area.
   - Downtown St. Paul needs additional activity in the evening to encourage people to stay after work, or to return downtown later in the evening. The Ordway can be such a catalyst, offering lighted, active, people-oriented events 18 hours a day, between meeting use and performances.

2. Uniqueness of the OMT

   - The Ordway is the only facility in the Twin Cities that is truly multipurpose. Virtually all other facilities are committed to a particular artistic form: the Guthrie to theater, Orchestra Hall to orchestral music, Northrop Auditorium to dance (although it purports to work for other forms but lacks an orchestra shell), O'Shaughnessy to smaller instrumental works.
   - OMT can provide the optimum performing space for all its major tenants: solo voice or instrument presentations of the Schubert Club, full opera by the Minnesota Opera, and full orchestra by the SPCO. Acoustics and staging opportunities and flexibility have been maximized in the OMT design.

Courtesy Ordway Music Theatre

Exhibit 3-1d
(*continued*)

- The OMT has been built along the lines of the great, classical European music halls. This creates an aura of informal elegance and intimacy in the large hall. The side boxes don't add many additional seats and could even be termed an extravagance, but they permit the maximum experience for patrons, who find that watching each other can enhance what's happening on stage. This second layer of activity and interest is a characteristic of many of the great halls of the world. Third, the lobby, which is large enough to serve two theaters, also permits patrons to "promenade" at intermission and before performances, thereby completing the evening.
- Design of the hall was based on gleanings from an extensive tour of many of the great halls of Europe. More than a dozen halls were visited by Sally Irvine, Ben Thompson, and Henry Blodgett, in the following cities: London, Venice, Vicenza, Milan, Vienna, Salzburg, Munich, and Paris. Purpose of the tour was to inculcate into the architecture of the OMT the "feeling" of elegance, warmth, and intimacy that makes those halls so great.

3. OMT Service to Arts Organizations

- The OMT will provide a permanent base for the three principal tenants. Identifying with the facility will help these groups build their audience base on a continuing basis. By centering their activities in the OMT, the groups can achieve greater consistency in costs and performance quality, thereby helping their revenues. It's hard to stay alive as a gypsy.
- OMT will also help organizations build their outstate audiences by providing a place where visitors can contact to see what's going on around town. Visitors are more inclined to call a hall than a particular organization when they are seeking information on entertainment options.
- A centrally located permanent base helps groups with their operating costs by reducing travel and transportation of people and staging and potentially by sharing certain central administrative services.

4. OMT and Its Competitors

- OMT offers high-quality rehearsal space close to the actual performance space.
- OMT offers a quality facility of the type that "they just don't build any more," with fine metal work and wood finishes.

- The acoustical quality of OMT has been scrupulously designed to accommodate a variety of musical performances and to show off each one to its most magnificent.
- The OMT will offer space for corporate meetings, large-group seminars, and other convention-oriented programs to a wide variety of organizations.

5. Messages about OMT

- The Ordway Music Theatre is a public assembly facility that offers the opportunity to come together and share a variety of experiences — in the performing arts, special events, meetings, and conventions.
- Built in the likeness of the great halls of Europe, the Ordway offers guests an atmosphere of warmth, informal elegance, and intimacy.
- The Ordway performing space is technically the finest in Middle America. Patrons may enjoy a great variety of musical, dance, and theatrical events in either of the OMT's performing spaces.
- Local, national, and international artists will perform at the Ordway. The Theatre will serve as the performing home of The Saint Paul Chamber Orchestra, the Minnesota Opera, and the Schubert Club and will host the St. Paul Series of the Minnesota Orchestra and occasional performances of the Children's Theatre Company and School. Ordway will also present other national and international artists and will offer performing space to small local performing arts organizations.
- Facilities of the Ordway are also available for a variety of special events — conferences, dinners, receptions, annual meetings, and conventions.

*Faced with declining consumption of beef by the general pub-
lic and, in turn, by food-service operations, the Beef Industry
Council targeted food-service operators in a campaign to re-
establish and maintain beef's dominance in the food-service
marketplace. Exhibit 3–2a is a news release about the Beef
Industry Council's* BE A STAR *kids' promotion to be used in restaurants. Exhibit 3–2b is a page from the* Kids' Star Tribune.
Exhibit 3–2c is a photograph of the BE A STAR *program in action, and Exhibit 3–2d is a beef recipe.*

Case 3–2   ## Beef Industry Council Marketing Communications Program

Beef Industry Council, Chicago, IL, with Ketchum Public
Relations, San Francisco, CA

Research

The beef industry estimates that 40 to 45% of its sales are to food-
service operations — up from 35% in 1982. *Restaurants & Institutions Menu Census* has tracked beef as the number 1 food-
service entree for more than 20 years. The Beef Industry Council
asked Ketchum to help it maintain that dominance. Analyses of
secondary and primary research defined (a) vulnerability in key
segments; (b) tactics likely to be most effective; (c) operator "hot
buttons."

- Simmons data showed that the most important base is
  restaurant/hotel dining establishments, accounting for 51%
  of food-service beef buyers. Agency-commissioned Purchase
  Dynamics study (projectable random telephone survey of
  204 homes) showed erosion within that vital base: only 23%
  of these key customers said that new menu items featured
  beef — versus 38% chicken or seafood; even worse, only
  15% said that they expected their next entree additions to
  be beef, versus 33% chicken/seafood (and 33% unknown).
  The main problem was operators feeling that their customers were concerned about health: 60% of all survey re-

Courtesy Beef Industry Council of the Meat Board

spondents (70% of key beef customers) agreed that patrons order chicken because they feel it's healthier than beef; 68% said the same about fish.

- Purchase Dynamics survey also guided prioritization of tactics: (1) Two-thirds of restaurateurs who serve beef menued new entrees in the preceding year; (2) 57% get ideas for new menu items from food-service magazines, 50% from other restaurants; (3) 50% were interested in innovative menu ideas; (4) 40% requested recipes (including 4-color photos); (5) 20% requested preparation/selection tips.

- Agency conducted focus groups exploring "hot buttons" to incorporate in messages, confirming that restaurateurs are motivated by changing patron demographics (increasing number of ethnics in the United States) and psychographics (health-conscious consumers) when developing menu items.

Planning

- Objective — To maintain beef's dominance in the food-service marketplace, we needed to increase operator awareness that beef is suited to new, contemporary menu items.

- Strategy — A zero-base look at beef, at its competition, and the food-service market, led us to focus on the single key message: "Beef is the lead ingredient for healthful menu creativity because it adapts to contemporary eating styles."

- Target Audience and Budget — We determined that the greatest opportunity lay in influencing decisions at the 476,300 U.S. restaurants and hotels allocating 72% of the $857,000 budget to them; 20% to noncommercial operations (schools, employee cafeterias, colleges); 8% to the 2,500 + distributors and purveyors selling beef in food services. We decided to deliver our key message to our targets by: (1) providing recipes/menu ideas with emphasis on the leading-edge chefs who influence other restaurateurs; (2) increasing positive perceptions of the beef industry in the food-service industry; (3) motivating our traditional food-service supporters to actively promote beef to their patrons; (4) educate sellers and operators regarding usage, handling, and profitability of beef.

Execution

1. To increase awareness of beef's adaptability to contemporary menu items:

- The *In Search of Real Food* recipe brochure showcases beef as an ingredient in trend-oriented dishes. Ten ethnic and "new traditional" beef recipes, solicited from trend-setting restaurants across the United States and tested/refined by the Ketchum Food Center, were dramatically photographed. Dissemination tactics included product releases, trade shows, and write/phone-in requests to the BIC and offered via trade ads (a *separate* $900,000 effort).

- Ketchum developed the *Lite Styles with Beef* portfolio filled with creative beef recipes, each under 300 calories, on the "cutting edge" of contemporary cuisine. The portfolio will be mailed to a hand-selected list of 1,500 "leading-edge chefs" (for example, Wolfgang Puck) in March of 1991.

2. To further increase operator perceptions that beef is contemporary, healthy, and nutritious:

- Ketchum secured a wide variety of feature articles and placements in food-service publications by providing a press kit, exclusive recipes, full-color photographs, and case histories (emphasizing leading-edge chefs who influence other restaurateurs).

3. To encourage traditional food-service beef supporters to actively promote beef to customers:

- The *Around the World with Beef* and *Beef Barbecue Americana* point-of-sale kits were direct-mailed to noncommercial operators responding to publicity placements. Each promotion included 4-color posters, recipes, counter cards, crew badges, bunting, an activity sheet, and a waitstaff poster. A sales incentive contest was also conducted.

- Additionally, new materials were developed to help restaurants serve families by keeping kids happy while providing nutrition education to these "customers of tomorrow." The BE A STAR kids' promotion contains an activity sheet, waitstaff poster, counter card, "star packs" filled with activities to keep kids busy while dining, stickers, and an evaluation card. A calculator was offered to operators as an incentive to return the evaluation card. In January 1991, a sample mailer describing the program was sent to 17,500 family-oriented, independent restaurant operators. A total of 2,500 of these mailers will also be offered to state beef councils to target local restaurants.

4. To educate the food-service industry regarding usage, handling, and profitability of beef:

- Ketchum developed the *Everything You've Always Wanted to Know about Beef* training kit. The kit consists of two videos and a self-study notebook. Kits were disseminated through direct mail to a list of meat buyers at the nation's 2,500 major distribution locations.

Evaluation

Every program element Ketchum develops for the Beef Industry includes a bounceback mechanism.

1. A phone survey of *Search* brochure recipients showed that: (a) 90% used one or more of the recipes featured; (b) 60% said the brochure inspired them to create new beef dishes based on the information included; (c) 30% added at least one recipe to their menu permanently. Four magazines featured one or more recipes in publicity features, and five magazines placed the brochure as a product offer. Product releases secured in *Restaurant Business, Restaurant Hospitality,* and *Nation's Restaurant News* generated 562 requests for the brochure. State beef councils distributed 50,000 brochures through national and local food-service trade shows, and direct mail. The Beef Industry Council has fulfilled over 10,000 write/phone-in requests.

2. A follow-up survey will be conducted in May 1991 to determine operator usage of the recipes and overall impressions of the Lite Styles portfolio.

3. A total of 2,292,211 trade publication impressions were secured via feature placements/publicity in 14 magazines in 1990. (There are 650,000 total food-service outlets.) Many magazines pick up Ketchum copy verbatim and rely on the agency for quality photos, copy, and recipes.

4. Encouraging operators to actively promote beef, 1,462 kits of *Beef Barbecue Americana* and *Around the World with Beef* were distributed in 1990. A phone survey revealed that 53% planned to use the recipes; 70% had or planned to run the promotion — operators who ran the promotion reported increased sales; 100% indicated good patron response. Harris Trust and Savings Bank cafeteria of Chicago won the operator incentive contest with representative results: 53% increase in beef sales, 10% increase in lunch sales, and 5% increase in patron traffic resulting from the promotion. A feature of the promotion was secured in The Society for Foodservice Management's spring newsletter and a product placement was secured in *Restaurants & Institutions* and *Food Management* magazines. Since its dissemination in January 1991, The BE A STAR kids' promotion mailer has generated 1,008 requests for materials — a response rate of 6.7% — more than three times the industry norm.

5. In the sales education effort, regional sales managers and district sales managers have responded to the initial mailing of the video kit with seminars reaching 7,500 salespersons.

Exhibit 3–2a   BE A STAR News release

BEEF INDUSTRY COUNCIL
of the MEAT BOARD 444 NORTH MICHIGAN AVENUE / CHICAGO, ILLINOIS 60611 / 312/467-5520

FOR: BEEF INDUSTRY COUNCIL
        444 North Michigan Avenue
        Chicago, IL 60611
        Maureen Lambe (312) 670-9261
        Jane Lindeman (312) 670-9297

FROM: KETCHUM FOODSERVICE
        55 Union Street
        San Francisco, CA 94111
        Steve Siegelman (415) 984-6347

                                        FOR IMMEDIATE RELEASE

            BEEF INDUSTRY COUNCIL KIDS' PROMOTION
            GIVES FAMILY-STYLE OPERATIONS A BOOST

        Less than a year ago, City Lights restaurant in Baltimore's
upscale Harbor Place was a quiet waterfront dinnerhouse and bar
catering to couples and singles. And business was just that:
quiet. Today, an aggressive new family marketing focus --
including a "kids eat free" program and promotional materials
furnished by the Beef Industry Council -- has turned the business
around, and sales are brisker than ever.

        "It took us a long time to accept that the kids' market is
our market," says manager Landie Logston. "We're in the heart of
a major tourist area. Instead of being resistent to kids and
families, we finally decided to 'go with the flow' and make them
our most valued customers. Once we made that decision, our
business took off."

                        (more)

Courtesy Beef Industry Council of the Meat Board

Ready Or Not, Here They Come

It's a story that has become commonplace in foodservice operations around the country. The baby boomers -- now parents themselves -- are still dining out. But as their families grow, they're becoming more budget-conscious. And they're as likely to choose a restaurant for its kids' menu as for its winelist.

Statistics point to a major demographic shift that operators can no longer ignore. Since 1982, the number of children eating in restaurants increased 36% -- more than twice the rate of adult diners. Kids ages 6 to 17 now account for 8% of traffic in full-service family-style restaurants, and in the next five years, their numbers will increase by 6.6%.

As the demand for casual, mid-priced, "kid-friendly" dining increases, restaurants of all kinds -- from independent dinner-houses to midscale chains -- are hastening to develop merchandising and promotion strategies to tap into the kids' market.

But this retooling can be expensive and time-intensive. Many operations lack the time and resources to develop promotion programs of their own. The need for more and better family marketing materials has given rise to profit-building promotion partnerships between restaurants and other industry players, from manufacturers to distributors and commodity boards.

(more)

BE A STAR Kids' Promotion Gives Families Star Billing

Earlier this year, the Beef Industry Council debuted its "BE A STAR" kids' promotion -- a free merchandising kit including activity packs for kids, point-of-sale materials, and merchandising, recipe and training ideas -- in midscale independent restaurants and chains nationwide.

"We recognized a tremendous need for family marketing materials that could give any restaurant a foundation for developing their own customized kids' promotion," says Maureen Lambe, director of foodservice programs for the Beef Industry Council. "And because beef is the number one selling kids' entree in America, we felt that this program was a natural for the Beef Industry Council. The response has been phenomenal. More than a thousand restaurants have used our BE A STAR kits to stage promotions, train their staff or revamp their kids' menus."

Preliminary sales figures indicate success with patrons as well. The Beef Industry Council reports an average 12 percent increase in beef sales among participating operations during the promotion period.

At the heart of the program are star-shaped folding activity packs designed to keep waiting kids busy at the table. Through colorful games and projects, the "star packs" teach children about nutrition and the four food groups, encouraging them to "Be A Star...Eat Smart!"

(more)

City Lights restaurant used the "star packs" to kick off its "kids eat free" program. "We were attracted to the materials because of their educational and nutritional focus. It's not just another kiddie coloring book," says manager Logston. "Parents appreciate that. And when you please one parent, they'll spread the word to five or six others."

Boring Restaurant is Kid Heaven

Across the country in the unlikely-sounding tourist destination of Boring, Oregon, brothers Frank and Bill Hartner are facing a similar challenge. In the fall of 1990, they purchased an abandoned roadside family amusement complex, including two full-service restuarants, a bakery and a variety of shops and amusement concessions. Banking on attracting families on their way to the nearby Mount Hood ski resort, the Hartners restored the complex, renaming it "Ashley's Swiss Village."

"It's been an education," says Bill Hartner of this first venture into the children's market. "This place is kid heaven with all the rides and attractions. But now that we've got the place running, we still need to learn how to make the _restaurant_ kid-friendly. We've got a great kids menu worked out, but the real challenge has been working with our staff to brush up on our 'kid behavior.' _That's_ what keeps the kids and parents coming back."

(more)

During their first few months of operation, the Hartners sent for the BE A STAR promotion kit. "We need a tool like this" says Bill Hartner. "It's more than just a box full of materials to hand out and hang on the walls. It's given us ideas we can put into effect right away. We're using it, and it's working." The brothers found the training materials -- an operator activity guide and poster with tips for the waitstaff on "serving kids right" -- particularly useful.

"We're glad to see that the Beef Industry Council is sponsoring a program like this," adds Hartner. "At Ashley's, we sell more beef to kids than anything else, and this kit has helped us merchandise beef and build up our kids' menu."

Midscale Chain Reaction

For the Bonanza family-style steakhouse chain, kids and beef have always been central to the operation's marketing focus. So when Trudy Moore, who handles advertising and marketing for 55 Bonanza units, heard about the BE A STAR promotion, she immediately ordered kits for the 25 Arkansas and Kansas units.

How can a "generic" promotion kit meet the needs of a major chain? "We have no problem using the materials even though they aren't customized with the Bonanza name and logo," says Moore, "because the Beef Industry Council logo gives the program a 'seal of approval.' The bottom line is, this program can help us sell more beef."

(more)

Peter Poblete, general manager of a Manahawkin, NJ franchise of the Ponderosa chain, agrees. "Of course beef is a product we want to promote. But the real question is 'who are we promoting to?' We're undergoing a transition from being a steakhouse to being recognized as an affordable, family-style restaurant. The BE A STAR promotion is helping us to compete with fast food by showing parents that we welcome kids and have more to offer them than the competition. It gives the kids something fun to play with and teaches them about the food they're eating. And that's helping us make friends with a lot of parents."

BE A STAR promotion kits are available free of charge on a first come, first served basis. To order promotion materials, contact the Beef Industry Council at (800) 922-2373 or write:

BEEF INDUSTRY COUNCIL
BE A STAR PROMOTION
P.O. BOX 1003
AUSTIN, MN 55912-9912

# # #

0061B/58-63

FINAL

KIDS' STAR TRIBUNE

BE A STAR · BEEF · EAT SMART

★★★★★

© 1990 BEEF BOARD AND BEEF INDUSTRY COUNCIL

The "BE A STAR" Kids' Promotion

There's never been a better time to expand your business by attracting families with children. And the Beef Board and Beef Industry Council are here to help. Your "BE A STAR" promotion kit contains everything you need to be a star with kids and families.

Start generating excitement and increased sales today with these high-powered promotional materials:

Kids' STAR PACKS—Keep kids busy at the table with these star-shaped activity packs. They're loaded with games and projects kids will love. And parents will appreciate their nutritional message, too.

- *Keep plenty of crayons and pencils on hand.*
- *Assemble a few star packs to use as colorful ceiling danglers during the promotion.*
- *Children as young as 2 years old can color the black and white side of the star. Kids ages 4-10 will enjoy the games and puzzles.*

BE A STAR SWEEPSTAKES Entry Blanks (one in each Kids' Star Pack)—Your young patron will have a chance to win a Macintosh SE computer by mailing entry blanks to the Beef Industry Council.

- *Create excitement by displaying sample entry blanks and signs announcing the sweepstakes.*

I'M A STAR. I EAT SMART! Stickers (one in each Kids' Star Pack)—Kids love stickers. These fun stick-on badges encourage them to think about healthy eating.

KIDS ARE STARS WITH US Counter Card—Display prominently at register or hostess station to let families know they're valued customers the minute they walk in the door.

EIGHT WAYS TO SERVE KIDS RIGHT—A waitstaff training poster to hang in the kitchen (see over).

★★★

The ABCs of Kids' Promotions

The materials in your "BE A STAR" promotion kit are ready to go to work for you right now, with minimal planning and waitstaff training.

But because every restaurant has different promotional needs, you may want to expand on these materials and plan a customized promotion tailored to the style of your operation.

Setting Your Objectives

Once you've established a time frame for your promotion, it's important to think through your objectives. These should include clearly measurable results, such as "increase kids patronage by 25 percent during the promotion period."

Next you'll want to determine what strategies and specific tactics—like the ones listed below—will help you reach your promotion goals.

The Waitstaff—Your Key to Promotion Success

Because they provide the point of contact between families and your operation, your waiters and waitresses can make or break a promotion. Build team spirit by involving them in promotion planning right from the start. Their perspective can be invaluable in determining what strategies will work with your patrons. Fire up their enthusiasm to bring your promotion to life.

Meet with your waitstaff to familiarize them with the "BE A STAR" promotional materials. Conduct a staff contest with a cash prize for best promotion idea. Hold a tasting party, where employees can sample special kids' menu items. And invite them to bring *their* kids for some first-hand opinions.

Emphasize to your staff the importance of treating children like valued customers, and give them the leeway to fill special requests. Explain how suggestive selling can build check averages.

The Kids Are Coming!

*More kids are eating out today than ever before. And kids' patronage is still rising—at more than twice the rate of adults. Kids ages 6 to 17 now account for 8% of traffic in full-service family-style restaurants. In the next five years, their numbers will increase by 6.6%.**

Now that the baby boomers are having kids of their own, they're looking for restaurants where the whole family can feel comfortable—restaurants like yours.

*Source: Restaurants USA, April May, 1990.

Begin With the Basics

Even if you're not ready to plan an ambitious family promotion, you can begin increasing family traffic right away with a few simple promotion ideas:

Crayons: Keep them at the waitstation in plastic cups so kids can color their star packs or paper placemats. Or hand out "4-packs" of crayons for kids to keep.

Cameras: Many family-oriented restaurants keep instant-film cameras on hand. A photo makes an ideal souvenir—a lasting memory of a fun meal that will keep kids and parents coming back for more.

Giveaways: A wide variety of inexpensive toys and prizes are available through mail-order merchandising companies. Set up a "treasure chest" or "grab bag" at the register to reward kids for good behavior after the meal.

Balloons: Whether plain or custom-printed with your logo, balloons are a proven favorite with kids—an inexpensive way to create a fun and colorful atmosphere in your operation. And when kids take printed balloons home, they spread your name all over town.

Contests Build Sales

Patron contests—from simple drawings to more elaborate competitions—are a sure-fire way to generate excitement. And by tabulating contest entries, you can build a powerful mailing list of regular customers.

Even a simple guessing game—like guessing the number of jelly beans in a jar—can become a fun contest for kids. And you can start building your mailing list by having kids fill out their name and address on a contest entry blank. More elaborate contest ideas include:

- *"Color the Star" contest—As part of your "Be a Star" promotion, have kids color the outside of their star packs. Fold winning entries into mobile shape to display.*
- *Other drawing contests—kids color on paper or on paper placemats. Judge drawings by age groups and display winning entries each month so kids—and proud parents—come back to see results.*
- *"Make a Menu" contest—Have kids design their dream menu. Incorporate winning designs and suggested dishes into your regular kids' menu.*

Contest prizes need not be expensive. Kids love the idea of "taking their family to dinner." What could be simpler—and more cost effective—than a free meal or gift certificate?

Your promotional materials, such as logo tee-shirts, also make perfect prizes. Or consider offering educational prizes (e.g., a scholarship to a local summer camp) that appeal to parents, too.

Return Business Progams

Return business programs may require some follow-up and tracking. But they can also bring families back to your operation time and again.

- ***Couponing***—hand out coupons for kids' menu items, such as a beef entrée or beverage, redeemable on the next visit.
- ***"Frequent Diner" Club***—Give kids membership cards that can be punched or stamped each time they visit the restaurant. Completed card qualifies family for discount or free meal.
- ***Birthday Club***—Kids get a free meal or dessert on their birthday.

Activities and Special Events

As competition for family business increases, many operators are planning special events for kids and families. These events help build a loyal patron base and—if aggressively publicized—provide excellent opportunities for free media exposure.

Examples range from weekend classes for kids (including hands-on cooking classes; demonstrations and tastings; and restaurant etiquette workshops) to more "splashy" special events (such as themed parties, holiday tie-ins, games and competitions).

Sponsoring or hosting a fund-raising event for a local non-profit children's organization is another effective way to generate publicity and build goodwill in your community.

Building a Mailing List

The mailing list you assemble from contest entries, drawings, "clubs" and event sign-ups can help you identify and reach proven customers.

One way to build your existing list is to offer a kids' newsletter. Kids love the idea of receiving their own mail, and will gladly supply their addresses. Your newsletter will increase visibility for your operation and strengthen your relationship with patrons. And, of course, you can use it for a variety of promotional purposes—to announce events, offers, menu specials and contests. Be sure to include a "mail-back" portion or coupon to get patrons involved and help you measure response.

Real Food for Today's Kids

Good news! The taste kids love is good for them, too.

Children need a balanced diet that draws from the four food groups. And beef is an important part of that diet.

- Beef is packed with nutrients, supplying much of the protein, iron and zinc kids need.
- Amazing, but true: a lean, trimmed portion of beef has no more cholesterol than chicken—without the skin. And only 1.5 grams more saturated fat (or about 14 calories).
- A three-ounce portion of lean, trimmed beef averages about 200 calories.

Kids' Menus Beef Up Profit

Planning a kids' menu can be tricky. To please the entire family, offer dishes that appeal to kids, but don't underestimate the nutritional concerns of parents.

Instead of creating a full-blown kids' menu, you may wish to introduce one or two daily kids' specials to your regular menu. By experimenting with specials, you can build a repertoire of tried-and-true kids' dishes that work well in your operation.

Offer half-orders of regular menu items at reduced prices. Or try a "family hour" promotion, with reduced rates for kids during early dinner hours.

To develop a full kids' menu, begin by taking a look at which items can be adapted from your regular menu. Then add specials designed especially for kids. Some helpful guidelines:

- *Kids' food should be ready to serve or quick to prepare to avoid prolonging the wait at the table.*
- *Keep portions kid-sized and pieces bite-sized.*
- *When possible, serve kids finger foods that don't require utensils.*
- *Keep it simple. Avoid mixing a lot of textures and flavors.*
- *Consider serving kids meals in colorful meal boxes (available from promotion companies).*

Beef—A Family Favorite and a Great Value

Today's parents want it all: flavor, nutrition, convenience and economy. By making kids' food fun *and* nutritious and keeping prices low, you'll win over the whole family.

How can you offer all that? It's easy—with the great taste and high nutritional value of beef.

Kids love beef. That's why hamburgers are their number one menu choice. But beef is more than burgers. It's a versatile ingredient that can turn up in all kinds of kid-pleasing dishes. And it's real food that satisfies parents, too, because they know they're getting their money's worth.

Try these kid-sized adaptations of time-honored beef favorites:

- **Hand Burgers** Serve miniature burgers garnished with pickle chips; use small dinner rolls for buns.
- **Beef Nuggets** Bite-sized nuggets of ground beef, breaded and fried or baked in a hot oven. Serve with ketchup or barbecue sauce for dipping.
- **Pocket Philly Cheese Steak** Paper-thin slices of grilled beef and melted cheese in a halved pita bread.
- **BBQ Beef Kabobs** Tender beef cubes and vegetables skewered and grilled or broiled. Brush with barbecue sauce; remove skewers at table before serving.
- **Pizza Burger** Top an open-faced burger with tomato sauce and mozzarella; melt cheese under broiler.
- **Spaghetti with Mini-Meatballs** Break spaghetti in half before cooking for easier eating. Top with tiny meatballs in red sauce.
- **Starburst Soft Tacos** Layer shredded cheese and cooked ground beef flavored with taco seasoning on a soft tortilla. Top with another tortilla. Heat and cut into wedges.
- **Small Fry's Stir Fry** Marinate strips of tender beef in soy sauce. Stir fry with mixed vegetables. Add beef broth and thicken with cornstarch. Serve over rice and garnish with chow mein noodles.
- **Stroganoff Spirals** Top corkscrew noodles with made-ahead ground beef stroganoff.

★★★

Courtesy Beef Industry Council of the Meat Board

Exhibit 3–2c   Photograph of the BE A STAR Program in Action

The Beef Industry Council's BE A STAR kids' promotion keeps children busy at the table while teaching them about healthy eating.

Photo Credit: Beef Industry Council

Courtesy Beef Industry Council of the Meat Board

Exhibit 3–2d   **Beef Recipe**

San Francisco, California
The Four Seasons Clift Hotel
Kelly Mills, Executive Chef
Spiedini of Beef Sirloin Mediterranean-
Style with Minted Tabouleh

Courtesy Beef Industry Council of the Meat Board

Tuesday 3:00 p.m.

From the Golden Gate to the Bay Bridge, worldly feasts tempt the eye and tastebuds. Cosmopolitan capital of fresh market cuisine, sourdough bread and Napa Valley wines.

"Lighter" and California cuisine are one—no need to sacrifice taste or the dining adventure— just calories.

SPIEDINI OF BEEF SIRLOIN MEDITERRANEAN-STYLE WITH MINTED TABOULEH
from The Four Seasons Clift Hotel, San Francisco, California

INGREDIENTS:	WEIGHTS:	MEASURES:	DIRECTIONS:
Dry red wine		1¾ cups	1. To make marinade, mix ingredients
Chopped herbs (mixture of		1½ cups	except beef in large shallow pan. Add
rosemary, thyme and parsley)			beef; cover, refrigerate and marinate 2
Balsamic vinegar		1¼ cups	hours or overnight, turning occasionally.
Olive oil		¼ cup	2. Remove beef from pan; reserve
Garlic, minced	2½ ounces		marinade.
Beef Top Sirloin Butt, closely	6 pounds		
trimmed, cubed 1½ inches			
(NAMP/IMPS 184)			
Minted Tabouleh			
Cracked wheat bulgur,	2 pounds, 4 ounces		3. Thoroughly toss ingredients in large
cooked, cooled	(raw weight)		bowl. Cover and refrigerate 1 to 24
Tomatoes, diced ¼ inch	2 pounds, 4 ounces		hours; bring to room temperature before
Chopped mint		¾ cup	serving.
Fresh lemon juice		½ cup	
Chopped basil		6 tablespoons	
Chopped parsley		6 tablespoons	
Olive oil		6 tablespoons	
Grated lemon peel		¼ cup	
Garlic, minced	½ ounce		
Salt		2½ teaspoons	
Pepper		2 teaspoons	
Zucchini, sliced ½ inch	1 pound, 8 ounces		4. On *each* of 48, 10-inch skewers,
Yellow bell peppers, chunked 1 inch	1 pound, 8 ounces		alternate 2 ounces beef, and ½ ounce
Red onions, chunked 1 inch	1 pound, 8 ounces		*each* zucchini, bell pepper and onion.
			For each serving: brush 2 skewers with
			reserved marinade. Grill to desired
			doneness. Plate approximately 1 cup
			Minted Tabouleh; top with beef
			skewers.

Yield: 24 servings

*As worldwide leader of the power tool industry, Black &
Decker took advantage of its 75th anniversary to "recycle" a
stagnant market by introducing its new drills featuring a keyless chuck. Several special events, including a ceremony at the
Smithsonian Institution, made this outstanding media campaign a model of marketing communications as well. Exhibit
3–3a is a news release announcing the seventy-fifth anniversary. Exhibit 3–3b is a photograph of the Limited Edition
Seventy-Fifth Anniversary drill. Exhibit 3–3c is a photograph
of the ceremony at the Smithsonian Institution. Exhibit 3–3d
is the U.S. Patent Office drawing of the first Black & Decker
drill.*

Case 3–3	**Black & Decker Seventy-Fifth Anniversary**

Black & Decker U.S. Power Tools Group, Towson, MD, with
Image Dynamics, Inc., Baltimore, MD

Overview and Objectives

Black & Decker, the worldwide leader in the power tools industry,
has built its multibillion dollar success on the drill, a market the
company still dominates. After a five-year stagnation in sales of
electric drills, Black & Decker decided to "recycle" the market by
motivating consumers to buy replacement or additional drills.

Coinciding with the introduction of the keyless chuck was the
75th anniversary of the pistol-grip, trigger-switch drill—the tool
that launched the company. The anniversary presented an unprec-
edented opportunity to capitalize on the company's heritage,
product innovation, and world-renowned brand recognition. It
also provided a meaningful, historical story in which to position a
new product feature and ultimately revitalize the market.

Our communications objectives included:

- Create awareness among consumer and industry audiences
  of Black & Decker's 75th anniversary and the company's
  heritage of product innovation

Courtesy Black & Decker

- Create awareness among consumers and industry audiences of the commemorative, limited-edition drills featuring the keyless chuck
- Position Black & Decker as an industry leader and a legend in U.S. manufacturing

Research

Company research figures revealed that sales of electric power drills had leveled off during the last five years. Household penetration of the products had reached 75 percent, indicating a saturated market condition. Research also noted that the addition of the keyless chuck feature would spark sales. We also learned that 1992 marked the 75th anniversary of the patenting of the first pistol-grip, trigger-switch drill. Research on the company's heritage was undertaken via corporate archives.

Extensive studies were conducted to determine the feasibility of organizing critical events and related activities.

Planning

Planning first identified two opportunities — new product innovation and the seventy-fifth anniversary. "75 Years of Leadership and Innovation" was developed as the theme.

Clear objectives and strategies supported a comprehensive public relations plan. Media relations was the plan's core, with strategic events propelling the story throughout the year. Several considerations needed to be addressed:

- How and when to reach a range of key hardware industry trade and DIY-consumer publications, which face extended production lead times, to achieve anticipated coverage before the year's end? How will product availability affect media relations planning and sales force efforts?
- How to achieve national media coverage that will enhance awareness and stimulate increased sales?
- Given the historical nature of the anniversary, what opportunities existed relating to the Smithsonian Institution?

Execution

- <u>May Media Tour</u> — As a prelude to the 1992 Hardware Show and as an opportunity to sell a softer story to long leadtime trade and end-user media, our May press tour piqued editors' interest in both the 1917 drill and the new, more innovative consumer drill. Coverage that was generated coincided with product availability in stores.

- <u>Matte Article</u> — Distributed to over 11,000 newspapers, the matte article offered a grassroots approach to a primary target audience — the end user.

- <u>Hardware Show</u> — This top annual gathering of industry media and manufacturers provided a perfect opportunity to showcase the campaign. A press reception attracted a wide variety of national end-user and trade media as well as general consumer and local and national print and electronic press.

- <u>Newspaper Campaign</u> — Blanket mailing targeted Home/ DIY editors at 100 largest outlets. Also targeted were prominent do-it-yourself syndicated columnists. Both efforts were geared at reaching the general consumer audience.

- <u>Assembly Line Event</u> — At Black & Decker's Easton, Maryland, manufacturing plant, production of the 50-millionth drill was commemorated. Al Decker, Jr., son of a company founder, participated along with other VIPs such as Maryland's governor. Media coverage included national, regional, and local print and electronic outlets.

- <u>Smithsonian Institution</u> — Donated the first pistol-grip, trigger-switch drill and Limited Edition drill at a ceremony at the Smithsonian's Museum of American History to complement exhibit of Black & Decker's moon drill developed for NASA. The Smithsonian's implied endorsement of Black & Decker as a quality- and tradition-oriented manufacturer provided the campaign with added news value.

- <u>Video News Release</u> — Through a dynamic VNR, we packaged all campaign elements, including manufacturing success story, heritage, Smithsonian Institution, and new product innovation. Provided to 800 television stations.

Evaluation

The 75th anniversary campaign was successful in achieving its marketing goals — increasing sales of electric drills and revitalizing a stagnant market for do-it-yourself electric power drills. Black & Decker directly credits the 75th anniversary public relations campaign with boosting sales of power drills by a remarkable 22 percent, which roughly translates into a $10 million sales increase.

Media coverage throughout the six month campaign period was remarkable. A strategic media effort resulted in 22,378,326 print impressions and 7,361,000 households viewing.

Follow-up telephone contact with media revealed that the successful campaign served to not only promote the 75th anniversary product but also reminded media about the company's longstanding reputation for quality as well as its unique, all-American heritage. As a result, the 75th anniversary drills were featured by *Workbench* and other media as one of 1992's top ten "Gifts to Give."

Exhibit 3–3a   News Release Announcing the 75th Anniversary

BLACK&DECKER

U.S. Power Tools Group
10 North Park Drive
P.O. Box 798
Hunt Valley, Maryland 21030-0748

BLACK & DECKER
75 YEARS

CONTACT ▷   Diane Sullivan
Black & Decker
(410) 527-7106
or
Anita Galloway
Image Dynamics, Inc.
(410) 539-7730

news

BLACK & DECKER CELEBRATING 75TH ANNIVERSARY
WITH LIMITED EDITION KEYLESS-CHUCK DRILLS AND ACCESSORY SETS

HUNT VALLEY, MD -- Black & Decker is celebrating its invention and patenting of the

world's first pistol-grip, trigger-switch electric drill with the introduction of three Limited

Edition keyless-chuck drills and three Limited Edition Bullet® Pilot-Point® drill bit sets.

"For 75 years, Black & Decker has been providing innovative solutions to make the

do-it-yourselfer's life easier, explained Joe Galli, Vice President of Sales & Marketing, Black

& Decker U.S. Power Tools. "With these new Limited Edition drills and drill bit sets,

we're embarking on our next 75 years of innovation."

Black & Decker's Limited Edition drills include the 3.0-amp VSR Model 7191A and

the 4.0-amp VSR Model 7196A corded drills, and the Ranger™ 6-volt cordless drill, Model

9049A. All three Limited Edition drills feature a keyless chuck. The Black & Decker

keyless chuck has the gripping power of a keyed chuck, simplifies bit changing and solves

the mystery of the missing chuck key.

- more -

Courtesy Black & Decker

B&D LIMITED EDITION DRILLS & ACCESSORIES -- PAGE TWO

"The keyless-chuck design offers exceptional gripping power -- up to 25 percent more gripping power than comparable keyed chucks," explained Mr. Galli. "It has a durable coating that resists rust and keeps dirt and moisture out of the jaws and gears. The reinforced jaws reduce bit wobble, so holes start more easily and run more smoothly. Furthermore, the jaws ensure that the grip will not come loose or overtighten during use."

Black & Decker also has designed three Limited Edition Bullet® Pilot-Point® accessory sets, which are a perfect complement to the Limited Edition drills. The unique Bullet® Pilot-Point® drill bit has a patented design which allows it to drill up to four times faster than conventional bits, requires no center punch, eliminates walking when drilling in metal, and avoids lock-up at breakthrough in wood or metal.

LIMITED EDITION DRILLS: POWER AND FEATURES

The Limited Edition Model 7191A 3/8" drill features a keyless chuck, 3.0-amp motor, double gear reduction for added torque, variable speed reversible (0-1200 RPM) and infinite speed lock for drilling and screwdriving into a variety of materials.

The Limited Edition Model 7196A 3/8" drill features a keyless chuck, a powerful 4.0-amp motor, variable speed reversible (0-2500 RPM) and infinite speed lock for preselected speed. The 7196A also features comfortable gripping surfaces and the Accu-Bore™ two-way level for accurate horizontal and vertical drilling.

The Limited Edition Ranger™ 3/8" cordless drill, model 9049A, features a keyless chuck, a high-performance 6.0-volt motor, two speeds (225 and 550 RPMs) for screwdriving and drilling, and it is reversible for backing out stuck bits and removing screws.

- more -

B&D LIMITED EDITION DRILLS & ACCESSORIES -- PAGE THREE

All of Black & Decker's Limited Edition keyless-chuck drills are U.L.-listed and come with a full two year home use warranty.   For more information on Black & Decker's 75th Anniversary Celebration, write Black & Decker, Communications Dept., 10 North Park Drive, P.O. Box 798, Hunt Valley, MD 21030.

# # #

Exhibit 3–3b   **Photograph of the Limited Edition 75th Anniversary Drill**

BLACK & DECKER LIMITED EDITION 75TH ANNIVERSARY DRILL

(Spring 1992) — The Limited Edition Model 7196A ⅜-inch keyless-chuck drill is being introduced as part of Black & Decker's celebration of the invention and patenting of the world's first pistol-grip, trigger-switch electric drill 75 years ago. This Limited Edition model features a 4.0-amp motor, variable speed reversible (0–2,500 rpm), and infinite speed lock for preselected speed. The 7196A also features comfortable gripping surfaces and the Accu-Bore™ two-way level for accurate horizontal and vertical drilling.

Courtesy Black & Decker

Exhibit 3–3c   **Photograph of Ceremony at Smithsonian Institution**

(Pictured left to right: Dr. Spencer Crew, acting deputy director of the Smithsonian Institution's National Museum of American History, and Gary DiCamillo, president, Black & Decker, U.S. Power Tools Group)

Smithsonian Institution's Museum of American History Accepts First Pistol-Grip, Trigger-Switch Drill into its Collection

Washington, DC — (October 22, 1992) — Gary DiCamillo, president Black & Decker U.S. Power Tools Group, presents the world's first pistol-grip, trigger-switch electric drill to Dr. Spencer Crew, acting deputy director of the Smithsonian's National Museum of American History. The drill was patented 75 years ago by S. Duncan Black and Alonzo G. Decker.

Courtesy Black & Decker

Exhibit 3–3d   U.S. Patent Office Drawing of First Black & Decker Drill

UNITED STATES PATENT OFFICE.

SAMUEL DUNCAN BLACK AND ALONZO GALLOWAY DECKER, OF BALTIMORE, MARYLAND, ASSIGNORS TO THE BLACK & DECKER MANUFACTURING COMPANY, OF BALTIMORE, MARYLAND, A CORPORATION OF MARYLAND.

ELECTRICALLY-DRIVEN TOOL.

1,245,860.   Specification of Letters Patent.   **Patented Nov. 6, 1917.**

Application filed December 4, 1914.   Serial No. 875,439.

S. D. BLACK & A. G. DECKER.
ELECTRICALLY DRIVEN TOOL.
APPLICATION FILED DEC. 4, 1914.

1,245,860.   Patented Nov. 6, 1917.

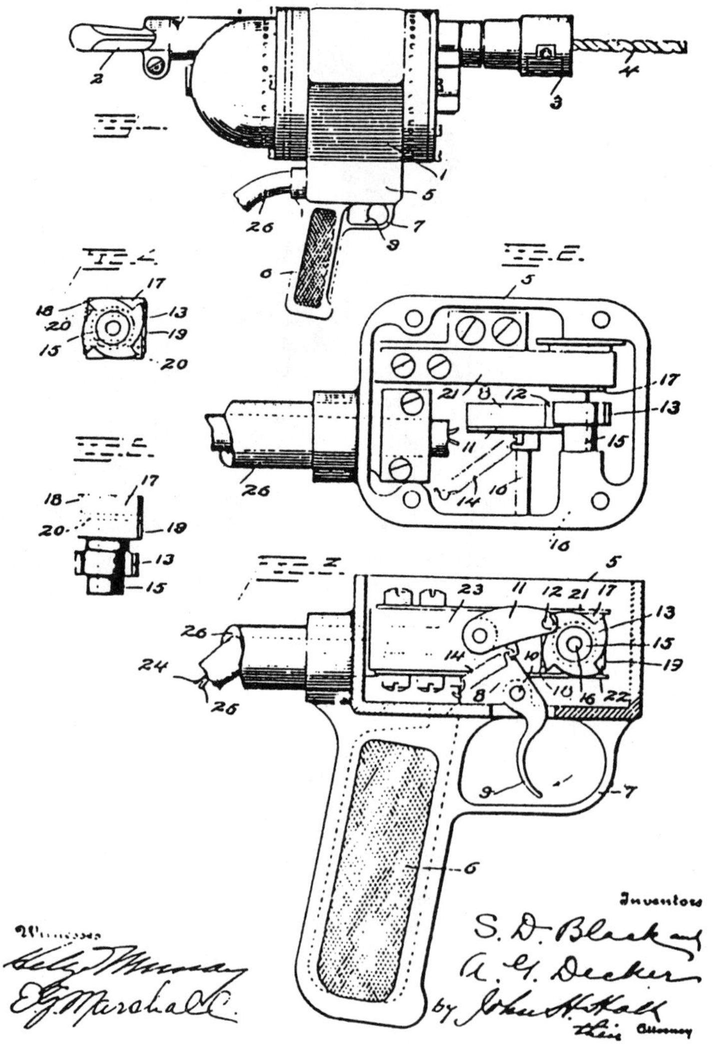

Courtesy Black & Decker

To publicize its grand opening, the Liberty Science Center developed dozens of different story angles and background materials for a variety of targeted media. Exhibit 3–4a is a news release announcing the exhibit areas in the center. Exhibit 3–4b is a news release featuring the center's laser light show. Exhibit 3–4c is a photograph illustrating the center's slogan, "Where Science = Fun."

Case 3–4   **Liberty Science Center Public Relations Program**

Liberty Science Center, Jersey City, NJ, with GCI Group,
New York, NY

Background

Liberty Science Center (LSC), the New York area's first world class, interactive science and technology center, mounted a public relations campaign in January 1992 in support of its opening, scheduled for late 1992. The $67 million facility located in Liberty State Park, New Jersey, would offer exceptional activities designed to help improve science education.

The business plan called for a PR program to create awareness and ongoing support for this new attraction and to help generate the 1.5 million visitors needed annually to keep LSC operational. This goal presented three significant challenges: (a) LSC had to be perceived as fun since science was seen as dull; (b) LSC had to be perceived as accessible to residents of New York City—a large and important base of LSC visitors; and (c) LSC had to receive national attention to achieve its goal, but it was really a regional attraction.

Research

Marketing studies, surveys, and focus groups conducted by outside marketing firms were used with secondary research to develop an effective communications plan. Key findings were that:

- Science and science centers were perceived as serious and boring
- LSC would compete with established family attractions in the area. Potential visitors would be unfamiliar with a hands-on museum experience

Courtesy Liberty Science Center

- LSC's location in Liberty State Park appeared inaccessible to many
- LSC was one of four science centers opening in 1992, making the regional story even less significant on a national basis.

Planning

Based on these research findings, LSC, together with GCI Group, developed a strategic public relations approach to generate widespread, positive coverage that would help generate the traffic goal as follows:

1. Positioning

- LSC is fun. With more than 250 hands-on exhibits covering contemporary issues, LSC provides a unique day of experimentation and discovery.
- LSC benefits the entire country. Since New York City is a major tourist attraction, LSC is accessible to a much larger audience than other regional science centers.
- LSC's mission is to get visitors interested in science and excited about further study and to help address the science illiteracy problem in the United States. This is critical for the country's competitiveness in the future.
- LSC is accessible. Convenient public transportation services make it "worth the trip."

2. Strategies

- Generate national publicity to reach out-of-town visitors and stimulate corporate funding by pitching a story about the nation's science illiteracy problem, positioning LSC as a key contributor to the improvement of this situation.
- Make LSC stand out among the other science center openings nationally by accentuating what's new and innovative about LSC and its leading role in the science center "industry."
- Attract a broadbased audience by developing a wide variety of media pitches tailored to different interests, concentrating on key target audiences — parents, children, teachers, corporations, etc. — for maximum impact.

- Conduct outreach programs with schools and students to engage them in LSC for the long-term.
- Arrange for the media to include LSC's information number and/or direction to LSC to help make LSC accessible.
- Prepare the marketplace for coverage to break near the opening for maximum traffic impact, with select placements before the opening.
- Show the "fun" side of LSC by: (a) inspiring journalists to "play" with the exhibits and (b) by arranging for third-party testimonials with children while they interact with the exhibits.

3. Tactics

- Pitch all long-lead media one year before the opening and conduct regular phone follow-ups to build relationships for LSC and inspire coverage.
- Do the media's "homework" by providing up-to-date statistics about science illiteracy in the United States.
- Provide frequent updates to regional and local media to bring them completely on board. This included construction tours and distribution of press releases about the work-in-progress.
- Arrange interviews for LSC's spokespeople — including LSC's president, major corporate supporters, staff scientists, and LSC's "bug lady" — with all target media, with an emphasis on national, consumer broadcast and print outlets.
- Provide tours for all interested media when LSC is near completion.
- Distribute mailings and arrange meetings with the academic community.

Execution

Liberty Science Center and GCI developed dozens of different suggested story angles and background materials for the various target media; contacted more than 300 long-lead publications, and maintained relationships with local and national editors for preview and opening coverage.

National and regional media with short leads — "Good Morning America," *The New York Times*, CNN — were aggressively pitched beginning three months before the opening. All local media were continually updated on LSC's progress. Contact extended beyond science reporters, targeting travel, business, education, and life-style reporters.

Six executives from LSC were professionally media trained and drilled in preparation for the influx of media interviews. Opening plans were developed and large numbers of media tours were coordinated. Every school in the tri-state area was contacted.

When LSC's opening was postponed from October 1992 to January 1993, a crisis communications plan was initiated to maintain positive momentum. The delay was positioned as a common occurrence that would lead to a better museum, resulting in no criticism.

Results

Liberty Science Center opened on January 24, 1993, receiving extensive publicity in national and regional media. All coverage included one or more of LSC's key messages: LSC is a place where science equals fun; LSC is accessible; LSC is addressing science illiteracy; and LSC is a national attraction.

Print coverage included more than 1,300 placements 4 months before the opening, including *The New York Times, New York Magazine, Associated Press, Ladies Home Journal, Time, Weekly Reader, Continental Profiles, Travel & Leisure, Business Week*, and more.

Television coverage totaled 225 minutes. "Good Morning America" produced a 4-minute feature 2 weeks before the opening. Science correspondent Michael Guillen said, "I cannot cover most of the science center pitches I receive, but LSC stood out and appeared special."

The other 37 television placements included repeated features on CNN, WABC-TV, WCBS-TV, and NJ Network. WNYW-TV's "Good Day New York," and WNBC-TV's "Sunday Today in New York" produced live remote broadcasts. The television coverage communicated LSC's accessibility and stature as a national attraction.

The excitement generated by LSC's opening has given a boost to LSC's corporate fund-raising effort and new negotiations are underway as a result. Liberty Science Center greeted 8,000 visitors its first day—almost double the expected daily capacity. Liberty Science Center's school group program sold out 1 week after opening for the 1992–1993 school year.

LIBERTY SCIENCE CENTER EXHIBIT AREAS
From Touch Tunnels to Tarantulas
WHERE SCIENCE = FUN

Liberty Science Center's (LSC) interactive exhibits encompass three themes -- Environment, Health, and Invention -- enabling guests to discover a place WHERE SCIENCE = FUN.

The exhibits, activities and demonstrations in the 170,000-square-foot Center give guests a special opportunity to see, feel, explore and understand the world. Planned scientific demonstrations throughout the building further enliven the daily program of films and talks. For example, LSC's "Bug Lady," Dr. Betty Faber, might casually walk by with a giant live millipede or tarantula for guests to see and feel. And each floor has a "Discovery Room" where hands-on activities are guided by museum staff.

LSC contains more than 250 exhibits with plans to continually change and enhance the experience for guests. Following is a small sampling of key LSC exhibits:

ENVIRONMENT EXHIBITS HIGHLIGHTS

"We want to provide activities that enable the guest to observe, investigate, question, share with others and wonder about the world around them," says Arlene Jangaard, Manager of Exhibit Floor Programs.

The Estuary -- Guests come nose-to-nose with fish, hold a horseshoe crab or a starfish, and gaze through microscopes at tiny algae and single-cell organisms from three 20-foot tanks filled with living plant and animal species native to the Hudson River ecosystem.

MicroZoo -- Features an insect "zoo" displaying local and exotic species of live insects including tarantulas, gigantic Madagascar cockroaches, rare red-kneed Mexican spiders and African scorpions, with many available to touch at special demonstrations.

Interactive Theater -- a unique theater in which audiences make decisions effecting the fate of the environment. Audience groups, divided by seating areas, punch in answers to questions, causing the film to evolve in different ways each time it is seen.

- more -

Courtesy Liberty Science Center

Atmosphere -- An introduction to the physical properties of the earth's atmosphere and oceans. Sunspots and solar flares can be seen by guests via a solar telescope mounted in a 20-foot, floor-to-ceiling "lighthouse". On the outdoor deck, guests use a weather station's rain gauge, wind vane and barometer to forecast the weather.

The Green House (Discovery Room) -- Guests study rare insects, experiment with water, and identify unknown objects with the help of staff and local scientists.

HEALTH EXHIBITS HIGHLIGHTS

"Our overall goal is to create a sense of celebration and wonder about what makes us human," says Janice Walker, Manager of Training and Development.

Perception -- The Touch Tunnel tests guests' vital sensory skills in an eerie crawl through a pitch-black, 100-foot world with only the sense of touch as a guide. The Illusion Labyrinth, a 1,000-square-foot maze of mirrors, challenges guests' visual acumen.

The Heart -- The guest's pulse creates a striking particle suspension within a cone of light. Guests also receive a full introduction to the most vital of organs through displays such as EKG monitors and a capillary racer computer game. A thermography display uses infrared heat to graphically show the body's "hot spots."

Bodies in Motion -- LSC's "fitness center" includes testing stations for balance, center-of-gravity, endurance and flexibility. By "pedaling" a bike illustrating aspects of the muscle system, or by manipulating a skeleton, guests learn the "inside story" of movement.

Choices -- Focuses visitor's attention on many of today's most critical health issues -- AIDS, cancer, nutrition and substance abuse -- through provocative displays and videos, including a drunk driving simulator.

The Living Room (Discovery Room) -- This 2,000-square-foot area encompasses hands-on sensory activities and includes a laboratory room, a fully-equipped ambulance, and an "Empathy Belly", or pregnancy simulator.

-more-

INVENTION EXHIBITS HIGHLIGHTS

"The goal of these exhibits is to explore the process of invention -- not just as an end-product, but as a vital form of problem-solving and creativity," says Max Cameron, Manager of Design & Production.

Buildings & Bridges -- A dazzling display of architectural and engineering systems, with the expanding and contracting Hoberman Sphere as a focal point. This first-ever museum installation was created by artist/engineer Chuck Hoberman, whom DISCOVER Magazine dubbed the "Buckminster Fuller of the 1990s" in a recent article. The globe is a 700-pound suspended aluminum structure that unfolds from 4.5 to 18 feet in diameter with a motor control. Also in this area, guests use their bodies as "supports," to experience first-hand how arches and bridges work. And an almost 10-foot-high boom crane with an electromagnetic pick-up allows guests to build block structures.

Machines and Motion -- An Indy racecar donated by industrialist Roger Penske encircled by a remote-controlled racetrack exploring aerodynamics, speed and fuel economy. Accompanying tabletop exhibits further pursue the topic, focusing on speedometers, gears, brakes, pumps and cooling systems.

Light and Optics -- A laser light and sound display designed by MIT consultant and composer Paul Earls "plays" throughout the LSC atrium. Computer-controlled laser images accompanied by electronic music "dance" on hanging screens crafted by a Finnish weaver from copper wire and nylon filament threads.

Sound and Music -- In the sound booth, guests use a mix of everyday and high-tech electronics to compose music. A strobe light is used to see sympathetic vibrations in piano wires; and guests hear how sound travels through different materials with gigantic "whisper balloons".

Media -- Exhibits enable guests to create their own special effects and animation. The Chromakey exhibit uses video technology to place guests in unexpected locales. In Digital Darkroom, guests transform their facial features with a computer.

The Workshop (Discovery Room) -- Self-directed and staff-assisted activities such as invention kits and build-your-own structures. Guests of all ages bring ingenuity to life by mixing ordinary objects such as hammers, scissors and popsicle sticks with more technical items including computers, lasers and transistors. In the Swap Shop, guests can exchange high-tech and everyday artifacts they bring to LSC.

##

CONTACT: Elizabeth Graham, LSC (201) 451-0006, ext. 295

Exhibit 3–4b 　　　**News Release Featuring the Center's Laser Light Show**

Liberty Science Center

LASER IMAGERY LIGHTS UP LIBERTY SCIENCE CENTER

Spectacular multi-colored laser imagery modulated by original synthesized music dazzles guests when they enter Liberty Science Center (LSC).

The installation is the first of its kind to be on permanent display, unlike most "laser shows." Created by Paul Earls, a Fellow at the Center for Advanced Visual Studies at Massachusetts Institute of Technology (M.I.T.), the exhibit fills LSC's atrium with polychromatic laser activity modulated by customized electronic music. The laser imagery is projected onto and through 20 layers of large handwoven wirecloth screens, created by Finnish artist Maarit Salolainen specifically for this installation. The result is varying animated images, including fish, faces, bugs, birds, and abstract geometric designs.

Mr. Earls describes his exhibit as "kinetic art that undergoes constant evolution. The projected images transform synergistically with the changing electronic sounds." As guests make their way around LSC's four floor levels, they can view the ever-changing exhibit from many different angles.

Trained as a composer, Mr. Earls began working at M.I.T. 22 years ago and currently is creating interdisciplinary environmental art for public use and display.

Ms. Salolainen produced 20 screens for the LSC atrium with the assistance of two weavers provided by the University of Industrial Arts - Helsinki. Ranging in size from three to 10 square feet, production took six months.

"Liberty Science Center is the place 'Where Science=Fun' and is designed to both entertain and educate our guests," says LSC's President Chuck Howarth. "Paul Earl's laser exhibit truly captures this spirit."

CONTACT: Elizabeth Graham, LSC 　　　(201) 451-0006, ext 295

Exhibit 3–4c   A Photograph Illustrating the LSC's Slogan,
                  "Where Science = Fun."

Liberty Science Center. Where Science = Fun.
Encounter a surprising new world of invention and wonder at Liberty Science Center.
☞ With over 250 hands-on science and technology exhibits, and the world's largest
OMNIMAX® theater, it's all just a stone's throw from the Statue of Liberty. ☞ Liberty Science
Center is easy to reach by ferry from New York and New Jersey, PATH/bus or car (Liberty
State Park, Exit 14B, NJ Turnpike). Call (201) 200-1000 for advance tickets.

Chapter 4   Internal Communications

Public relations conducted inside organizations falls into two general categories: employee relations and member relations. Employee relations includes all communications between the management of an organization and its personnel. Member relations refers to communications inside a membership organization between the officers and members.

Employee Relations

Research, objectives, programming, and evaluation are useful problem-solving tools in employee relations.

Research

Research for employee relations concentrates on client research, studying the reason for communication, and identifying the employee audiences to be targeted for communication.

Client Research

Client research for employee relations focuses on *information* about the organization's personnel. What is the size and nature of the work force? What reputation does the organization have with its work force? How satisfied are the employees? What employee communications does the organization regularly use? Are any special forms of communication used? How effective are the organization's internal communications? Has the organization conducted special employee relations programs in the past? If so, what were the results of such programs? What are the organization's strengths, weaknesses, and opportunities regarding its work force? These questions might guide the initial research in preparation for an employee relations program.

Opportunity or Problem Research

A second focal point for research is the *reason* for conducting an employee relations program. Is a new program really necessary? This question should be answered with care because it justifies the necessary expenditure for a program. Would the program be reactive — in response to a problem that has arisen in employee relations — or would it be proactive — taking advantage of an opportunity to improve existing employee relations?

A survey of employee attitudes may reveal a variety of issues, including: low levels of satisfaction and morale, dislike of the physical surroundings, and/or frustration with internal policies. The survey results may thus demonstrate a strong need for a reactive employee relations program.

Audience Research

The final area of research involves precisely defining the *employee audiences* to be targeted for communication. These audiences can be identified using the following terms:

Management
    Upper-level administrators
    Mid-level administrators
    Lower-level administrators
Nonmanagement (staff)
    Specialists
    Clerical personnel
    Secretarial personnel
    Uniformed personnel
        Equipment operators
        Drivers
        Security personnel
        Other uniformed personnel
    Union representatives
    Other nonmanagement personnel

Effective research on employee relations is built on an understanding of the client's personnel, the opportunity or problem that serves as a reason for communication with the work force, and the specific identification of the employee audiences to be targeted for communication.

Objectives

Objectives for employee relations include the two major categories of impact and output. Employee relations objectives may be specific and quantitative to facilitate accurate measurement. Optional percentages and time frames are included here in parentheses.

Impact Objectives

Impact objectives for employee relations include informing employees or modifying their attitudes or behaviors. Some typical impact objectives are:

1. to increase employee knowledge of significant organizational policies, activities, and developments (by 60 percent during March and April)
2. to enhance favorable employee attitudes toward the organization (by 40 percent during the current fiscal year)
3. to accomplish (50 percent) greater employee adoption of behaviors desired by management (in a three-month period)
4. to make (60 percent of) the employee force organizational spokespersons in the community (during the next two years)
5. to receive (50 percent) more employee feedback from organizational communications (during the coming year)

Behavioral, informational, and attitudinal impact objectives may be used in any combination in a public relations plan. The chosen objectives should be carefully determined so they demonstrate the program's goals.

Output Objectives

Output objectives in employee relations constitute the efforts made by the practitioner to accomplish such desired outcomes as employee recognition and regular employee communication. Some examples include:

1. to recognize employee accomplishments and contributions in (80 percent of) employee communications (during the current year)
2. to prepare and distribute employee communications on a weekly basis
3. to schedule interpersonal communication between management and a specific employee group each month (specify groups and months)

Programming

Programming for employee relations should include the careful planning of theme and messages, action or special event(s), uncontrolled and controlled media, and execution using the principles of effective communication.

Theme and Messages

The theme and messages for employee relations depend on the reason for conducting the campaign or program. Both of these elements should grow out of the opportunity or problem that accounts for the particular program. That is, themes and messages usually grow out of the problems faced by companies and the methods chosen to solve them. For example, a practitioner working for a company that is moving its facilities and offices to a new building could produce a brochure entitled "A Company on the Move."

Action or Special Event(s)

Action and special events used in employee relations programs include:

1. training seminars
2. special programs on safety or new technology
3. an open house for employees and their families
4. parties, receptions, and other social affairs
5. other employee special events related to organizational developments

A bank, for example, could sponsor a surprise Dividend Day for participants in the employee stock program, and a company moving into a new facility could arrange an employee open house and party.

Uncontrolled and Controlled Media

The use of uncontrolled media in employee relations is usually limited to sending news releases or announcements about employees' accomplishments to outside mass and specialized media as warranted. Actually, this is media relations, not employee relations, but it is often considered part of the employee relations program.

Controlled media, on the other hand, are used extensively in employee relations programs. The most frequently used controlled media are employee publications such as magazines, newspapers, and newsletters addressed to particular groups or levels of employees in larger organizations. These publications are often highly professional and creative, both in writing and design.

In addition to house publications, employee relations programs use a variety of other forms of controlled media, such as:

1. bulletin boards
2. displays and exhibits
3. telephone hot lines or news lines
4. inserts accompanying paychecks
5. internal television
6. films
7. video cassettes
8. meetings
9. teleconferences
10. audiovisual presentations
11. booklets, pamphlets, brochures
12. speakers bureaus (employees address community groups)

The use of media in employee relations differs from that in other forms of public relations because of the heavy emphasis on controlled media.

Effective Communication

Principles of effective communication are virtually the same for employee relations as for most other forms of public relations, although two-way communication and audience participation should be stressed. Special events are an excellent way to employ these elements in employee relations.

Evaluation

Impact and output objectives in employee relations can be evaluated using the same tools of measurement as in other forms of public relations (see Chapter 2). In addition, a variety of research techniques have been developed to deal exclusively with internal organizational communication. These techniques include network analysis, which measures the effectiveness of internal communication channels using such methods as the ECCO (*episodic communication channels in organizations*) analysis. This method traces one message unit as it flows through an organization. A duty study involves employees recording their daily communication activities in a detailed diary. Observational studies use trained observers to record employees' communications during their work schedules, and cross-sectional interviews ask employees about their communication interactions.

The most extensive of these research activities designed to assess internal organizational communication is the communication audit developed by the International Communication Association (ICA). The ICA audit includes some of the network analysis techniques just mentioned and also queries employees about the nature of their communication experiences and their overall job satisfaction.

Follow-up surveys were used in most of the case studies in this chapter. These yield quantitative measures of the stated objectives. Objectives were also assessed through publicity placement and employee participation in the programs.

Again, remember that to be effective and useful to the organization, research—both initial and evaluative—should be conducted by trained, experienced professionals who work for reputable research firms.

Summary

The ROPE process provides a useful approach to the planning and execution of employee relations programs.

Research for employee relations concentrates on demographic data about the organization's work force, existing levels of employee satisfaction, the state of relations between management and employees, and the effectiveness of employee communication. The uniqueness of research in this form of PR is, of course, the focus on information gathering about the work force itself.

Both impact and output objectives are generally used in employee relations programs. Impact objectives include such desired outcomes as increasing employee knowledge of organizational matters and eliciting favorable employee attitudes and behaviors toward the organization. Output objectives are the efforts of practitioners to recognize employee contributions, distribute employee communications effectively, and otherwise enhance the impact objectives.

Programming for employee relations may include catchy themes; special events such as training seminars, special employee campaigns or programs, or social events for employees; and controlled media such as house publications, bulletin boards, displays, meetings, and a variety of electronic means of communication.

Evaluation of employee communication should refer back to each stated objective. Methods of assessment may include such specialized techniques as network analysis, duty studies, observational studies, or the ICA communication audit. Finally, follow-up surveys are a popular means of evaluating attitudinal and behavioral objectives.

Each element of the ROPE process should be tailored for the particular situation, as we will see in this chapter's cases.

Employee Relations Cases

In the wake of business reversals, a loss of assets, a downsizing of its work force, and the survival of a hostile takeover attempt, the Bank of America sought to counteract low employee morale and dissatisfaction by reinstating a dividend with a surprise presentation of shares of stock to every employee who had participated in the turnaround effort. Exhibit 4–1a is the schedule of the Special Award Program. Exhibit 4–1b is the special issue of the bank's newsletter that describes the awards event and gives employees' reactions to it.

Case 4–1   Surprise Stock Awards to Employees

Bank of America NT & SA, San Francisco, CA

The Background

From 1985 to the end of 1987, Bank of America lost 1.8 billion dollars. It suspended the dividend, sold prime assets including its headquarters building, lost senior executives and public confidence, reduced the number of employees, and fought off a hostile takeover attempt.

A new management team began to engineer a massive restructuring and, as 1989 approached, recovery was in sight. Yet, as the management team turned its attention from crisis management to regrowing the company, it found employee morale to be extremely low — and a major stumbling block to achieving critical goals still ahead.

A bankwide survey of employees found that only 53% were satisfied with the recognition they received for doing a good job. Only 32% agreed that senior management had a sincere interest in their satisfaction and well-being. Managers at all levels of the company were among the most negative.

Executive management and the board of directors asked Communications for help in transforming this low morale into renewed confidence, buy-in, and productive performance. The challenge was to find a dramatic way to communicate to employees management's deep appreciation of employees' hard work, loyalty, and contributions.

Within the bank, top-secret planning had begun in order to reinstate the dividend on February 6, 1989, pending approval by

Courtesy Bank of America

the board. Corporate Communications knew this announcement would send a powerful message to the public and employees that Bank of America was once again strong and stable. Communications proposed using the occasion of "D-Day" (Dividend Day) as the right moment to convey to employees management's caring and appreciation.

Design

A small project team was quickly assembled to brainstorm ideas. Communications then proposed that management and the board present shares of stock to every employee who was, and continued to be, part of the company's turnaround effort. Bob Beck, head of Corporate Human Resources, enthusiastically agreed and brought the proposal before the bank's Managing Committee. They embraced the idea and asked for analysis on feasibility, eligibility, cost, and timing for delivery of the awards.

In early January 1989, the Committee gave final approval to the proposal to award ten shares of stock to each eligible employee. They also added an extra vacation day in 1989 for each employee and cash awards to those who were newcomers or part-time workers. Every bank employee and manager—specifically the 50,000 employees and 3,000 unit managers located in seven states and 44 countries around the world—would be the beneficiaries of this award.

Communications Strategy

A communications strategy was designed to gain maximum impact. It had these elements:

- Keep the awards absolutely secret until the moment of announcement.
- Hold surprise staff meetings and give each employee a letter from CEO Tom Clausen announcing the award and thanking him or her.
- Stage these meetings simultaneously worldwide to gain the maximum impact from this as a "major event."
- Hold these meetings on February 8th—two days after "D-Day"—to link the award to this corporate accomplishment, while allowing breathing space between the announcements.

- Follow up immediately through bank publications and video with feedback on positive reactions from employees.
- Arrange a second morale-boosting celebration one month later to hand out the actual stock certificates.

Execution

- Three thousand information packages were assembled in strictest secrecy. These included the announcement letter from CEO Clausen, instructions to the manager, Q & A's, and suggested remarks by the manager.
- Human Resources managers were briefed in confidence and 21 "country managers" were informed whose units had works councils or union contracts that required prior notification.
- A massive, specially handled mail delivery put the packages on managers' desks for opening ONLY on February 8, at 8 A.M. Pacific Daylight Time.
- A phone tree was launched the night before to alert every manager to the package's arrival. Electronic messages were sent to managers offshore.
- On February 8, employees in bank units worldwide met with their managers. Each was given a letter from Tom Clausen. Tom praised the employees for their efforts and announced that they would receive this special award of ten shares of stock and an extra day off.
- Phone calls were made immediately to employees throughout the company to gather reactions.
- A special edition of *NewsFront*, the employee newsletter, was produced overnight and distributed to every employee the next day. It featured quotes gathered from the phone calls.
- One month later, managers gathered staff together for a celebration and handed out the certificates and checks. This two-stage approach increased the impact. We covered these events in *NewsFront* and our bankwide video, *BankAmerica Report.*

Results

- The surprise was total. The response was overwhelming.
- Thousands of employees sent "thank you" cards, letters, and banners to Tom Clausen in appreciation of this special award.
- A phone survey after the announcement showed:
  - Virtually 100% of managers and employees viewed this award to be a major morale booster.
  - The fact that the award was stock rather than cash made a much deeper impact on employees. It said, "You have a real stake in our company. You're part of our future."
- The awards received positive press coverage. Employees even called local papers to brag about what "their bank" had just done for them.

Cost

Staff time and printing costs were approximately $50,000 for Corporate Communications, Corporate Agency, and Human Resources. The cost of the awards was close to $20 million dollars. This covered 500,000 shares valued at $20.75, the cash awards, and the corporation's paying for the initial federal and state withholding tax, national taxes offshore, and processing costs.

Conclusion

Although no precise correlation can be made between the awards and subsequent corporate performance, by the end of 1989 profits soared to $1.1 billion—the most in Bank of America's 85-year history, and the largest of any U.S. bank in 1989.

On January 22, 1990, CEO Tom Clausen told employees, "You prevailed. You produced. You proved your quality—in 1989 as in no other year in this corporation's history. I hope you are as proud of your accomplishments as I am."

The distance between success and failure is often covered by faith in the future. For Bank of America, that faith was displayed in 10 shares of stock.

Exhibit 4–1a   Special Award Program

CONFIDENTIAL

Special Award Program

Communications Strategy and Distribution Process

MONDAY, FEBRUARY 6, 1989

1. International: Brief three Human Resources Managers (John Cammidge, Jose Luis Gaglairdi, and Tom Bianchi),so they can begin to prenotify country managers whose units have works councils or union contracts that require prior consultation or notification before such a program can be implemented. This is 21 countries.

TUESDAY, FEBRUARY 7

1. NewsFront distributed with announcement and details of the reinstatement of the dividend.

2. U.S. packages go into Interbranch mail for Wednesday morning arrival. Packages timed according to U.S. time zones not to be opened before the San Francisco announcement.
   o   International packages go via courier for delivery within 2 to 3 days.

3. Special Tom Clausen letter delivered to all Senior Vice Presidents and above.

4. Electronic message sent, where possible, to domestic managers to alert them that a special package (without details of the content) will arrive on Wednesday, requiring immediate action upon arrival.

5. Meet with Human Resources Group/Division Directors to finalize communications/distribution, to ensure all employees receive the Tom Clausen letter on Wednesday AM, with maximum impact for the program.

6. Phone tree throughout the day notifies key managers/distribution contacts of special packages (without details of the content) to arrive on Wednesday, requiring immediate action upon arrival.

7. International: Prenotifications will continue where required.

WEDNESDAY, FEBRUARY 8 – ANNOUNCEMENT DAY

1. Electronic messages sent in the morning worldwide to country heads and managers.

(February 1, 1989; 1:15 PM)

Courtesy Bank of America

2. Packages delivered to managers in all domestic units.
   - o Packages include: Tom Clausen letter, manager instructions and processing information, Questions and Answers, Roster/Tax Certification Sheet, and Tax Information Sheet.
   - o Managers hold staff meetings to give employees Clausen letter. For most employees, this will be the first announcement of the award program.
   - o Managers follow up individually with each employee with the processing for the awards.

3. No press releases are planned, but Public Relations Officers have standby media information prepared in case of need.

4. International: 8:00 AM PST, Electronic Message goes to 40 locations with a single message to the country manager responsible for in-country announcement to all locations and all units, including hosted units such as BASE, CCES, Private Banking, Legal, and Audit.
   - o There will be two versions: one for the 30 locations where stock will be given, and a second version for the 10 locations where cash awards will be made in lieu of stock.
   - o In 4 locations in the Middle East and Africa, we have a total of 10 IA's at non-bank entities. These people will be individually notified of the program either by telephone or telex by John Cammidge as quickly as practical.

5. International: Impact of notification at 8:00 AM, San Francisco time.
   - o 5 PM – Continential Europe   o 4 PM -- U.K.
   - o 1 PM – Argentina, Brazil   o 12 Noon -- Venezuela, Chile
   - o 11 AM – Peru, Ecuador

   It may not be possible to announce prior to close of business without earlier release.

THURSDAY, FEBRUARY 9

1. NewsFront distributed worldwide with details of the awards.

2. International: Middle East and Asia locations will announce at open of business day on Thursday, February 9.
   - o We are finalizing the holiday closure schedule for branches because the week of February 6 is Chinese New Year in Asia and Pre-Lent holidays in Latin America. Between 2 and 5 branches will not be open on February 8. A large number, some unionized locations, will be closed February 6, so prenotification of appropriate people may be difficult, and therefore delay the announcement by a few hours.

FOLLOW UP

1. Small event staged at San Francisco Main Office, allowing photo opportunity of CEO delivering first stock awards to employees.

(February 1, 1989; 1:15 PM)

Exhibit 4–1b   Special Edition of the Bank's Newsletter

NewsFront
BankAmerica Corporation

Special Edition

Vol. 4, No. 9   For BankAmerica employees worldwide   February 9, 1989

'Extraordinary effort' is recognized
Clausen announces special award to over 50,000 BankAmericans

Chairman Tom Clausen announced yesterday that BankAmerica's Board of Directors, recognizing the "extraordinary effort," has authorized a special one-time award to all eligible employees who were part of the 1988 earnings achievement at the companies comprising BankAmerica Corporation.

Eligible employees will receive 10 shares of BankAmerica common stock or a cash award, and an extra paid day off. Employees' initial federal and state income tax withholding on the award also will be paid.

In letters delivered worldwide to all eligible employees, Clausen said the one-time award was "in recognition of the extraordinary effort you turned in—when nothing less than an extraordinary effort would do...."

In 1988, BankAmerica earned $726 million—its third best year in history—and closed with a record-breaking quarter, earning $265 million in the fourth quarter.

More than 50,000 employees will receive BankAmerica stock which will

be issued March 1. Employees will be registered as owners on that date.

Senior vice presidents and above are not eligible for the stock or cash awards.

Neither are employees who received a stock option or restricted stock award from BankAmerica in either 1987 or 1988. However, both groups will get the extra day off this year.

Employees should get their stock certificates or cash awards during the first two weeks of March.

Clausen reiterated that BankAmerica's recovery "is due to the hard

work of employees at the many companies making up the corporation. You 'own' the recovery." That's why, he explained, stock was given to most salaried employees.

Clausen said, "We want to encourage BankAmericans to be owners of the corporation. This award strengthens that ownership and recognizes the value you are building in the company."

Although the corporation posted its first annual profit in four years, Clausen again reminded employees of the job ahead. "We are significantly stronger and have good momentum," he said. "But there is still a great deal of work to be done—to reduce our costs relative to our competitors, to increase our revenues, and to continue to provide high levels of customer service."

Clausen emphasized, as he said in his letter to employees, "The members of our senior management team are immensely proud of your achievement and very grateful for the hard work and loyalty you have given to benefit BankAmerica. This award reflects that."

Employees' reaction to the award: surprise and pleasure

BankAmericans were surprised and pleased at the news of the special one-time award.

Here is a sampling of some of their comments:

E.J. Stewart, administrative assistant, San Diego Regional Commercial Banking Office: "It's fantastic. I think it's going to be a great employee morale booster. Sell the stock? Are you kiddin'. This is going to be a long-term hold."

Kathy Stern, credit support officer, Warner Center Regional Commer-

cial Banking Office, Woodland Hills: "A great gift! It made my morning."

Alison Fleming-Stewart, manager, Preferred Banking, Monterey Main: "I think it's wonderful. I've been with the bank for 19 years and I think this is one of the most significant actions that senior management has taken. This is the frosting on the cake."

Mel Harrah, area manager's secretary, San Diego Coastal area management group, La Jolla: "I was so thrilled and surprised. I've been with the bank 20 years and I've never seen

anything like it. It makes you feel good."

Jim Bracco, merchant teller, Cupertino Branch: "It's great. When you see Tom Clausen, please thank him for me."

Sandra Gardner, Mortgage Warehouse Lending, California Real Estate Industries Division, San Francisco: "We're completely delighted. It's very nice that the contributions of the ordinary workers of the corporation have been recognized."

Gloria Teper, corporate safety
See back page

Reaction *From front page*

specialist, Corporate Human Resources, Los Angeles: "It's a very representative way to recognize BofA employees, particularly considering how much the stock has risen in value. And I think the day off is great too."

Ed Hain, senior Preferred Banker, Diamond Bar Branch: "This morning it's rainy and cold—a nasty day in the Los Angeles area. Everyone came in looking glum, until our manager got us together and broke the good news. It turned the frowns to smiles and put a lot of warmth in the branch."

Leslie Soderlund, senior administrative secretary, Preferred Banking, Stanford Branch: "It's always nice to be recognized and rewarded for hard work. But I'm most impressed that Mr. Clausen cared enough about us to do this. What am I going to do with my stock? I didn't own any until this. I might just buy more now."

Jim Marquis, manager of Sacramento Regional Proof Centers, "Very nice action to take. Right time too. It means a lot to all of us but it's especially important to the employees who day in and day out keep this bank going."

Sam Nervino, manager, Belmont Branch: "Our staff was surprised, to say the least. I think it's a great shot in the arm for the troops' morale."

Cynthia Ruiz, paralegal, Legal Department, San Francisco: "I'm delighted, and I'm happy for the bank. It was a nice gesture on the part of Tom Clausen and our Board of Directors."

Bruce Dierkes, Tulare Commercial-Agribusiness Banking Group, Visalia: "I'm simply impressed . . . wasn't expecting something like this so soon. I thought maybe something like this would happen a bit later, but this was truly a surprise. It was also nice that everybody got something across the board."

Linda Smith, manager, Support Services, Legal, New York: "It's a wonderful gesture by management to recognize the contributions of its employees. It's especially apropos that they reward us by giving us a stake in the company and its future."

Debbie Ray, secretary, Project Management, Concord: "One of my girlfriends called and said, 'Well, I guess I'll stay with the bank!' I've heard employees singing, 'We're in the Money!' "

Steve Yotter, Remote Financial Services, San Francisco: "A unique and innovative approach in recognizing every employee's contribution to the recovery."

Beck answers questions about award

EVP Bob Beck, responsible for Human Resources, provided some additional information about the one-time awards.

The following are excerpts from an interview with NewsFront:

NewsFront: When will employees receive their stock or check?

Beck: You should receive your stock certificate or check during the first two weeks of March.

NewsFront: What do employees have to do to receive their award?

Beck: In order to receive the award, each eligible employee must sign and date a roster and tax certification sheet, which is being circulated by unit managers. The managers should return the sheets as soon as possible, but no later than February 21, to Corporate Agency #9506.

NewsFront: What if an employee missed the meeting explaining the award?

Beck: Employees who were unable to attend their manager's presentation should contact their manager for more information.

NewsFront: When can an employee take the additional Personal Choice Day?

Beck: It must be taken in 1989, subject to the usual scheduling process in your unit.

NewsFront: When will the stock be issued?

Beck: The stock will be issued as of March 1, 1989. That will also be the day that we value the stock for tax purposes.

NewsFront: Why are we waiting until March 1?

Beck: The March 1 date will give us the time we need to make sure that the entire process goes smoothly for everyone.

This distribution of BankAmerica shares to employees worldwide represents the first time that we have done something like this on such a vast scale. We will be preparing and distributing more than 50,000 stock certificates around the world. The stock must be

Paula Maxwell, assistant manager, San Francisco Branch Support Center: "The last time we held a centerwide staff meeting we had to announce some cutbacks and redeployments. Needless to say most people were very nervous. There was an enormous sigh of relief after Mr. Clausen's letter was read. The awards were just thrilling to all of us. People loved the personal choice day as much as the stock or cash."

issued on an individual basis in the correct name of each employee receiving it. Also, there are varying legal and tax requirements for both the company and individuals, and we want to be sure that we fully comply with these.

We knew that this would not be an easy task when we decided to do it, but we wanted to provide special recognition for the efforts of employees, and we wanted to thank them.

NewsFront: Will employees who receive the stock award also get dividends?

Beck: The dividend declared on Monday is payable to stockholders of record on February 23. The stock awards will be issued on March 1. However, as owners of this stock, employees are entitled to all common stock shareholder benefits and will be paid any dividends declared after March 1.

NewsFront: Can this new stock be combined with BankAmerishare stock?

Beck: No. Under the terms of the BankAmerishare plan, only payroll contributions can be accepted. The plan cannot accept contributions of property such as stock.

NewsFront: How should employees safeguard the certificate?

Beck: Your stock certificate is a valuable document. You should give it the same protection as any of your valuables by keeping it in a safe place.

NewsFront: What if it's lost?

Beck: If your certificate is lost, stolen, or mutilated, you can get it replaced by writing to Corporate Agency, Attention Lost Stock #9118, P.O. Box 37002, San Francisco, CA 94137. It will cost you 2 percent to 3 percent of the current market price to have it replaced, using a bond purchased through an insurance company.

NewsFront: What if an employee leaves the company? Does he or she get to keep the stock?

Beck: When you receive the stock it is fully yours. If you leave the company after that date, stock issued to you will still be yours.

NewsFront: What if you want your spouse's name on the certificate? How is this accomplished?

Beck: If you want to add another person's name to the certificate, just complete the reverse side of the certificate, have your signature "guaranteed" and forward it with a letter to Corporate Agency #9506, P.O. Box 37002, San Francisco, CA 94137.

For internal use only • Editor: Tim Gartner • Associate Editor: Don Kington • Published weekly by Corporate Communications #3631 • WHQ, San Francisco • 622-4088

EXEC 599 2/89

In moving its headquarters from Virginia to Florida, the American Automobile Association (AAA) conducted an aggressive internal communications program to maintain high morale, retain a qualified work force, and continue the high quality of its customer service during the transition period. Exhibits 4–2a, 4–2b, and 4–2c are from AAA's Transitions booklet.

Case 4–2	**AAA on the Move**

American Automobile Association, Heathrow, FL

The Background

In 1986, President James B. Creal of the American Automobile Association (AAA) informed employees at the Virginia-based national headquarters that a study of alternatives for accommodating corporate growth, including long-distance relocation, would soon begin. Subsequently, AAA announced plans to develop a new complex in Orlando, Florida, and for the next several years, "move news" dominated employee concerns.

To maintain high morale, retain a qualified work force, and continue quality customer service during the transition, AAA conducted an aggressive internal communications program on relocation commencing with that initial announcement in 1986, accelerating through 1989, and climaxing with a special open house at the new facility in 1990.

Research

To identify issues of particular concern to employees, AAA and corporate relocation consultants, Moran, Stahl & Boyer (MS&B):

- Conducted confidential employee surveys on job concerns, housing, community preferences, financial and family considerations, and other issues
- Held "Managing Relocation Change" workshops to solicit feedback on relocation's impact on employee attitudes, turnover, productivity, and communication

---

Courtesy American Automobile Association

- Interviewed management to ensure AAA's corporate culture and employee loyalty would be preserved after the move

Planning

The AAA communications program was designed to communicate frequently, substantively, and effectively to all employees and their families on move developments, persuade most to relocate, and assuage those who did not. To accomplish this, AAA planned to:

- Open a fully staffed AAA relocation center
- Publish a relocation bulletin, an illustrated guide of the new headquarters facility, a move brochure outlining financial and other assistance, and related items
- Sponsor employee and family briefings
- Schedule Orlando familiarization tours for employees and spouses (before personal move decisions were made)
- Issue timely updates from the AAA president
- Host an employee and family open house upon completion of the new facility

Execution

The communications program featured *Orlando Relocation News*, the *Personal Assistance Program* booklet, employee/family dinners with video introductions of central Florida, and lobby and cafeteria displays that included an architect's model of the new building, a daily Orlando temperature reading, and photographs of construction progress. The AAA employee newsletter, *Highlights*, and internal magazine, *Interchange*, contained stories about the move.

Special attention was directed to providing *tangible* evidence to dispel and prevent move rumors. This was accomplished through the wide use of actual construction photographs, briefings, video, and direct, written statements by the president and in *Relocation News*.

Other materials were offered through a full-time, on-site relocation office. Employees took familiarization tours of central Florida and received briefings by local business and community leaders. To acquaint employees with the Orlando area, the AAA Cartography Department prepared a series of resource maps identifying cultural and recreational sites, schools, hospitals, and housing.

On arrival at the new building, each employee received a "Goodwill Ambassador's" kit, an "I survived the move to Orlando" T-shirt, and a candy jar with the same sentiments, at his or her workstation. All employees and their families received personal invitations, with a "thank you" theme, to an open house complete with entertainment, refreshments, and souvenir photographs.

Evaluation

Success can be measured by the 296 employees, 54 percent of those eligible, who moved the 865 miles. This figure—nearly 25 percent above the national corporate relocation average—and the fact that only 6 employees returned to Virginia are indications that the communications effort fostered a positive response to and realistic expectations about the move.

The long-term relocation communications budget was $250,000. Actual costs were $240,918, $138,399 of which was spent on production of the 35-minute relocation video and employee and family dinners. Qualitatively, AAA Human Resources reported that satisfactory employee morale was sustained during the transition, and business line operations continued with no measurable degradation in service and no increase in customer complaints.

Finally, in September, nearly 1,000 AAA employees and their families attended the headquarters open house, which culminated the American Automobile Association's successful relocation.

Exhibit 4–2a   Cover from AAA's *Transitions* Booklet

Courtesy American Automobile Association

Exhibit 4–2b   Excerpt from AAA's *Transitions* Booklet

AAA's relocation from Falls Church, Va., to Heathrow, Fla., is much more than a simple change of address. It signals a major transition—a new era that will change the face of AAA into the 1990s and beyond.

It promises to be an exciting era full of challenge and opportunity for continued growth and success–for the organization *and* for you.

This brochure will help smooth your personal transition to a new workplace and new community.

The move marks yet another major transition for AAA–about half of the staff at Heathrow come from Falls Church, with appreciable AAA experience. The other half will be new employees, with no AAA experience. This mix of old and new in every department and at every level –management and non-management –creates a healthy combination of freshness and stability.

Also among co-workers at Heathrow are administrative em-

new operating efficiencies and ensure even better service to AAA clubs and 31 million AAA members. Lower housing costs and taxes provide a quality, affordable lifestyle.

This association has never been content to merely keep up with the times. To remain the dominant leader in our industry will require excellence of each of us and the continued dedication and hard work that got AAA where it is today.

The time is right. The location is

A LETTER TO ASSOCIATES

T R A N S I T I O N S

ployees of AAA Florida relocating from Miami. Like headquarters employees, they leave familiar homes and neighborhoods to live and work with new neighbors and co-workers in new surroundings.

We believe employees will find Central Florida an outstanding working and living environment. AAA's state-of-the-art office facilities are designed to enrich time spent at work, which should increase productivity, bring about

right. All the needed elements are in place for exciting new transitions.

AAA's new headquarters facility is important, but not as important as *you,* AAA's most important asset. Thank you for your commitment to make the most of this bright new era in AAA history.

J. B. Creal

President
American Automobile Association

Courtesy American Automobile Association

Exhibit 4–2c   **Excerpt from AAA's *Transitions* Booklet**

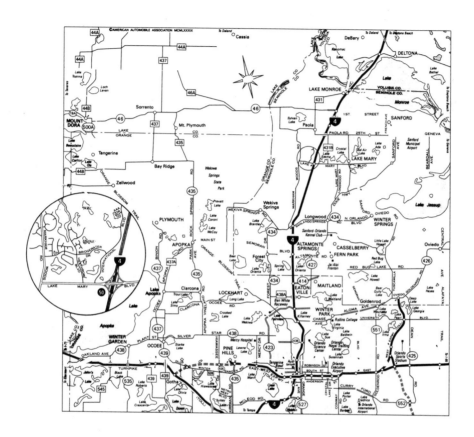

Courtesy American Automobile Association

Member Relations

Membership organizations include trade associations, professional associations, labor unions, interest groups, social and religious organizations, and thousands of other groups, large and small, which dot the societal landscape. Each has a need for communication between its officers and members. This process is called *member relations*.

Research

Research in member relations includes the client, the opportunity or problem, and the member audiences to be targeted for communication.

Client Research. As a prerequisite for the member relations program, the practitioner needs a thorough understanding of the membership organization conducting the program. The precise nature of the organization, its purpose, its headquarters organization and personnel, its financial status, its reputation with the general public and especially with its own members, its present and past public relations practices, and its public relations or image strengths and vulnerabilities will be part of the organizational profile the practitioner must construct.

Opportunity or Problem Research. As in all other forms of public relations, the second research objective of member relations is a determination of the reason for conducting the program. Will it be a long-range, proactive program, or will it address a particular problem? The expenditure necessary for the program should be thoroughly justified at this point.

Audience Research. Identification of audiences to be targeted for communication is the last of the three aspects of research in member relations. Member publics can be categorized into six groups:

Organization employees
  Headquarters management
  Headquarters nonmanagement (staff)
  Other headquarters personnel
Organization officers
  Elected officers
  Appointed officers
  Legislative groups
  Boards, committees

Organization members
  Regular members
  Members in special categories, such as sustaining, emeritus, students
  Honorary members or groups
Prospective organization members
State or local chapters
  Organization employees
  Organization officers
  Organization members
  Prospective organization members
Related or other allied organizations

Member relations research, then, consists of an examination of the client or organization conducting the program, the opportunity or problem that necessitates the program, and the member audiences targeted for communication.

Objectives

Impact and output objectives are used in member relations and, as in other forms of public relations, objectives should be specific and quantitative as far as possible.

Impact Objectives. For member relations, impact objectives consist of the desired outcomes of informing or modifying the attitudes and behaviors of the members of an organization. Some examples are:

1. to increase members' knowledge of organizational developments, policies, or activities (by 50 percent during the current year)
2. to engender (30 percent) more favorable member attitudes toward the organization (during the months of October and November)
3. to stimulate desired behavior modification among the organization's membership (by 30 percent during the next six months)

Impact objectives, in member relations, as in all types of communication, should be developed carefully for they are the standard against which the success of a program will be evaluated.

Output Objectives. Output objectives in member relations refer to the distribution or execution of essentially controlled forms of communication. Some examples are:

1. to prepare and distribute membership communications on a regular basis
2. to prepare and execute membership conventions, seminars, and other meetings on a timely basis

Programming

Programming for member relations includes theme and messages, action or special event(s), controlled media, and the use of effective communication principles. These factors are the same for member relations as for employee relations except for the types of action or special event(s) and the types of communication used.

Actions or special events for member relations concentrate on conventions, seminars, conferences, and similar meetings. The headquarters management of an organization has an obligation to schedule and execute such gatherings for the membership.

Other actions on the part of the headquarters officials of an organization usually include the promotion of industry research, preparation of industry statistics and data, development of professional standards and ethical codes, development of in-service education and training for members, and promotion of standards of safety and efficiency among the members or in the industry.

Member communications are limited to controlled media. These usually consist of newsletters and other member publications, reports, industry brochures, pamphlets, and other printed materials, some of which can be distributed to the members' clients. For example, the American Dental Association publishes dental care brochures for patients, and the American Heart Association prints materials for individuals who want to lower their levels of cholesterol.

Uncontrolled media in the form of news releases about employees or members are often considered part of the internal communication program. Strictly speaking, however, such communication falls into the category of external media relations.

Principles of effective communication are the same in member relations programs as in other forms of public relations.

Thus, programming for member relations shares many similarities with that for employee relations.

Evaluation

Evaluation of member relations directs attention back to the objectives established for such programs.

Success for programs may be directly linked to the objectives — informational, behavioral, and/or attitudinal — stated at the outset of a program. Was there favorable reaction from the membership? Did the number of members increase or decrease? Have requests for membership information increased?

Summary

Member relations is communication between the officers (management) of a membership organization and its members.

Research in member relations focuses on the demographics, information levels, attitudes, and behaviors of the organization's membership. A complete member profile should be constructed through such research, with special attention to the typical member's attitudes and behaviors toward the organization itself.

Both impact and output objectives are used in member relations. Impact objectives include the desired programmatic outcomes of favorable member attitudes and behaviors toward the organization. Output objectives catalog desired PR practices, such as effective planning, preparation, and distribution of member communications.

Programming for member relations usually includes such events as conventions, conferences, seminars, and such actions as promotion of industry research, preparation of industry statistics and data, and general promotion and development of the industry or profession represented by the membership. Commonly used forms of communication are member publications, reports, printed materials, audiovisual materials, and meetings.

As in other forms of public relations, evaluation consists of measuring stated objectives through surveys, observation, or other appropriate means suggested by the objectives themselves.

Readings on Internal Communications

Employee Relations

Conrad, Charles. *Strategic Organizational Communication: Cultures, Situations, and Adaptation.* New York: Holt, Rinehart & Winston, 1985.

D'Aprix, Roger. *Communicating for Productivity.* New York: Harper & Row, 1982.

Employee Annual Report: Purpose, Format, Content. Chicago: Ragan Communications, 1984.

Farinelli, Jean L. "Motivating Your Staff." *Public Relations Journal* 48 (March 1992): 18ff.

Gonring, Matthew. "Communication Makes Employee Involvement Work." *Public Relations Journal* 47 (November 1991): 40ff.

Harris, Thomas E. *Applied Organizational Communication: Perspectives, Principles, and Pragmatics.* Hillsdale, NJ: Erlbaum, 1992.

How to Prepare and Write Your Employee Handbook. New York: AMACOM, 1984.

Kreps, Gary L. *Organizational Communication.* New York: Longman, 1986.

McCathrin, E. Zoe. "Beyond Employee Publications: Making the Personal Connection." *Public Relations Journal,* 45 (July 1989): 14–20.

McPhee, Robert D., and Phillip K. Tompkins. *Organizational Communication: Traditional Themes and New Directions.* Beverly Hills, CA: Russell Sage Foundation, 1985.

O'Connor, James V. "Building Internal Communications." *Public Relations Journal* 46 (June 1990): 29–33.

"Restructuring: Good and Bad News for Employee Communications." *Public Relations Journal* 45 (April 1989): 6–10.

Reuss, Carol, and Donn Silvis, eds. *Inside Organizational Communication,* 2d ed. New York: Longman, 1985.

Member Relations

"Association Public Relations" (special issue). *Public Relations Quarterly* 37 (Spring 1992).

Career Guide to Professional Associations: A Directory of Organizations by Occupational Field, 2d ed. Cranston, RI: Carroll Press, 1980.

Cutlip, Scott M., Allen H. Center, and Glen M. Broom. "The Practice: Trade Associations, Professional Societies, and Labor Unions." In *Effective Public Relations,* 6th ed. Englewood Cliffs, NJ: Prentice-Hall, 1985, pp. 500–16.

Encyclopedia of Associations. Detroit: Gale Research Co., published annually.

Fraser, Edith A. "Association Public Relations: The State of the Art." *Public Relations Journal* 37 (October 1981): 18–21, 30.

Pace, Patricia Ewing, and Jo Culbertson. *Successful Public Relations for the Professions.* Edwardsville, KA: Professional Publishing Co., 1982.

The ICA Audit

Goldhaber, Gerald M., and Donald P. Rogers. *Auditing Organizational Communication Systems: The ICA Communication Audit.* Dubuque, IA: Kendall/Hunt, 1979.

Member Relations Cases

The U.S. Chamber of Commerce represents a major segment of the U.S. business community and develops policy recommendations on domestic and international issues critical to U.S. business. The Chamber's extensive program of communications includes print, broadcast, and interpersonal methods designed to inform both members and the population at large. Exhibit 4–3a is an excerpt from Helping Your Business Thrive. *Exhibit 4–3b is taken from* Your Trade Group Probably Joined the U.S. Chamber — You Should Too. *Exhibit 4–3c is from "GAIN — Grassroots Action Information Network."*

Case 4–3	**The Member Relations Program of the U.S. Chamber of Commerce**

Compiled by Adam Konowe, associate producer of BizNet, U.S. Chamber of Commerce, Washington, DC

Recognizing the need for a central organization to define the business community's views to Congress, President William H. Taft took the first step toward forming the United States Chamber of Commerce at a meeting of more than 700 businesses and trade association representatives in Washington, DC, in April 1912. The initial membership comprised 82 businesses, trade associations, and state or local chambers of commerce. Headquarters for the Chamber were built in 1922 across Lafayette Park from the White House, one of the most strategically valuable sites in the country.

Today, the U.S. Chamber maintains its eminent position as the world's largest business federation, with more than 215,000 members representing a broad spectrum of the business community. This diversity, as well as depth, is key to the continued success of the Chamber. While most of the nation's largest companies are active members, more than 96 percent of the members have fewer than 100 employees and 85 percent have 25 employees or less. Chamber members come from each state and represent every major classification of American business — manufacturing, retailing, services, construction, wholesaling and finance — with more than 10,000 members in each group.

Courtesy U.S. Chamber of Commerce

Research

As a membership organization, the U.S. Chamber of Commerce listens very closely to its membership. Through meetings, mailings, and surveys, members communicate their views. These exchanges provide information vital to volunteers and to the board of directors. The Chamber looks to help define policy on domestic and international issues critical to American business. Once a policy is developed, Congress, the White House, the regulatory agencies, the courts, and countries around the world are informed of the business community's recommendations on legislative issues and government policies.

A majority of these proposals originate in the U.S. Chamber's committees and councils. These specialized groups, comprised of member representatives from firms of every size, type, and geographic area, study the technical details of issues and judge their impact on business. A proposed policy statement is then submitted to the board of directors, the body that sets final policy positions. The board debates committee recommendations and adopts new policy positions by a majority of at least two-thirds. Interpretations of existing policy merely require a simple majority.

In addition to the standing policy committees, a special council representing small business interests exists to advise the board directly. The U.S. Chamber also has bilateral and multilateral councils working to improve the international climate for trade and investment abroad. And though any member may submit a proposed policy directly to the board, the proposed policy must be "national in character, timely in importance, general in application, and of significance to business and industry." Thus, single industry or specific company issues are excluded.

Objectives

As America's principal advocate for the business community, the U.S. chamber is dedicated to championing the principles of private enterprise. Its mission is to "advance human progress through an economic, political, and social system based on individual freedom, incentive, initiative, opportunity, and responsibility." Thus, the Chamber works on behalf of its members on a wide range of critical issues including economic growth, the federal budget, health care, America's work force, technology, infrastructure, removing barriers to doing business, and the global marketplace. In the Chamber's major areas of concern — domestic, economic, and international policy — more than 50 full-time experts in three policy units help advocate policies upon which this nation's enterprise system was built, consistent with the federation's mission.

Through a series of nationwide meetings held every two years, members help craft a National Business Agenda comprising those issues that matter most to business. The agenda, the ultimate statement of the federation's objectives, is then formally presented to government agencies, Congress, and the administration by members at the National Business Action Rally in Washington, DC.

Programming

The U.S. Chamber of Commerce has an extensive communications program. The entire range of print, broadcast, and interpersonal methods are utilized to bring timely and topical information to the members and the population at large.

To enhance Chamber efforts before policy makers, four separately funded affiliate organizations have been founded. Because today's courts shape policies and interpret laws that affect business, the National Chamber Litigation Center (NCLC) gives business a voice in the judicial arena. The National Chamber Foundation (NCF) is a public policy research arm that anticipates trends and conducts studies on emerging issues. Established as the business representative in the National Endowment for Democracy, the Center for International Private Enterprise (CIPE) encourages the growth overseas of private enterprise organizations and principles. Finally, the Center for Workforce Preparation and Quality Education (CWPQE) helps local and state chambers identify and implement strategies for community-wide education reform.

Chamber policy is implemented by nearly 70 staff specialists who are helped by thousands of members serving as activists in the Chamber's Grassroots Action Information Network (GAIN). GAIN empowers the members through a comprehensive, state-of-the-art communications network. Regardless of size or industry, individual businesses and business groups can receive information on select issues, participate in instantaneous calls to action, and access Congress directly. But GAIN is only one of the many member services offered by the U.S. Chamber.

Through its publications, the Chamber provides the inside track on the people and events that affect business decisions. *Nation's Business*, the Chamber's monthly magazine, has a circulation of more than 850,000 and is read by more than 2.5 million people, a majority of whom are senior business executives. Also printed exclusively for members is *The Business Advocate*, a bi-monthly publication that relates Chamber's programs and positions on public policy issues. Distributed to over 700 newspapers, the "Voice of Business" columns written by the Chamber president focus attention on breaking issues that affect economic growth and the business community.

The Chamber's telecommunications facilities and division, known collectively as BizNet, has been acclaimed as the finest of its kind in the nation. Since 1979, the flagship television program, "It's Your Business" has kept millions of American viewers informed about vital business and economic issues. The award-winning program is seen nationwide on more than 140 stations and is available overseas via the USIA's Worldnet satellite system.

The Chamber also produces the country's only news program focusing on small business owners and entrepreneurs. "First Business" airs every weekday from 6:30 to 7:00 A.M. Eastern and Pacific times (5:30 A.M. Central time) on the USA Network, the nation's most watched cable television network. It, too, is carried overseas by Worldnet.

Special broadcasts are also produced for internal audiences. Live and taped programs addressing key policy issues are received by members around the world. The Chamber's Quality Learning Services Division conducts special seminars on various elements of quality performance and leadership aimed at businesses with 50 or fewer employees. The sessions, featuring the most prominent experts on quality, are broadcast live by satellite, permitting interaction with audiences throughout the country.

Enrollment in the Institutes for Organization Management represents a six-year commitment to strengthen leadership, management, interpersonal, and communication skills. The institute holds a variety of annual one-week courses individually designed for chamber or association executives. Over 2,200 executives a year attend these programs at sites around the country, receiving college and continuing education credit in addition to enhancing vital decision-making skills.

ConSern: Loans for Education enables members to offer employees and their families an attractive benefit free of administration or financial responsibility. The program provides long-term, competitive financing for the various costs of obtaining an education without any liability to the participating companies. So far, over $500 million has been loaned to member employees and their families.

Members can receive research and development expertise through ChamberTech, which provides access to 100,000 federal lab employees in 650 labs nationwide. The Federal Laboratory Consortium for Technology Transfer is also available to assist members in solving technical, manufacturing, design, research, and regulatory issues.

The U.S. Chamber's international programs respond to the critical need for global, economic, and business interdependence in U.S. enterprise. The federation shapes legislative and regulatory policies at home and abroad that lower barriers and open competition. A network of 11 bilateral councils around the world complement the Chamber's efforts in the United States by producing agreements and shaping trade policies that improve business conditions in other countries. This network and 65 American Chambers of Commerce Abroad (AmChams) provide the Chamber with the ability to communicate on key economic and commercial issues. Closer to home, the International Division Information Center provides one-on-one assistance with questions regarding trade policy, export promotion, and services, as well as regional concerns and market opportunities. Hot lines and special publications provide up-to-date information on key actions affecting business, including export controls as well as bilateral and multilateral trade agreements.

Evaluation

The success of the Chamber's programs, and of the federation itself, is contingent on the accurate measurement and implementation of member input. All of the programs listed above have opportunities for member feedback built in to the process. For example, reader surveys are used in *Nation's Business* and *The Business Advocate*, telephone and on-line responses are solicited by all the broadcast operations, and GAIN uses a combination of all these methods as well as sending follow-up reports to members to explain the outcome of a program and the impact they have made.

The success of any federation rides on its ability to accurately represent the opinions and interests of its members over an extended period of time. In a sense, programming initiatives begin as well as end with evaluation of member opinion. It is this refined constant process of self-examination and improvement that has given the U.S. Chamber of Commerce a reputation for unyielding leadership for more than 80 years.

Exhibit 4–3a   Helping Your Business Thrive

THE UNITED STATES CHAMBER OF COMMERCE

A WEALTH OF RESOURCES TO MEET YOUR NEEDS

HELPING YOUR BUSINESS THRIVE

When you join the U.S. Chamber, you hire us to serve as your advocate in Washington — making your voice heard on the critical issues affecting the business community. But our efforts don't stop there. We function as your business adviser, providing needed information to give you every competitive advantage in the marketplace. Here's just a sampling of the valuable resources and benefits available to you as a member of the U.S. Chamber of Commerce.

Courtesy U.S. Chamber of Commerce

RESOURCE GUIDES

To help you choose among the many benefits of your U.S. Chamber membership, a variety of resource guides are free to you as part of your membership investment. Among them are:

Membership Participation Guide
An overview of the benefits and services available to you.

A Guide to U.S. Chamber of Commerce Communication Tools
A comprehensive listing of publications and services.

U.S. Chamber Staff Specialists
A list of issue specialists who can provide you with information, opinion and analysis on legislation, regulations, and other programs.

U.S. Chamber International Publications
To assist you in competing for trade and investment opportunities.

PERIODICALS

As a member, you automatically receive two vital resources: **Nation's Business,** published monthly, and The **Business Advocate**, published bi-monthly. These magazines are an invaluable source of information on federal legislation and regulations that affect you. In addition to forecasts on government action and economic trends, **Nation's Business** offers practical how-to information on running a business. Both magazines include regular surveys, used to direct U. S. Chamber policy decisions and to inform Congress of your views. Some other periodicals include:

U.S. Chamber Watch on Small Business Legislation and Regulation

National Business Agenda Report and its Legislative Supplement

Economic Outlook

Global Climate Newsletter

PUBLICATIONS

Have you ever wondered where to turn when you're trying to decipher new laws? Or who can help when you're looking for ways to lower costs or expand your customer base? The U.S. Chamber offers specialized publications to give you detailed information and help clarify the issues. Here's just a sampling:

Health Care 101: The Basics of Reform

What Business Must Know About The Americans With Disabilities Act: Compliance Guide

Concerns of Small Business

The Small Business Resource Guide

Risk Management: A Small Business Primer

OSHA: An Employer's Handbook

100 Ways to Cut Legal Fees and Manage Your Lawyer

Analysis of Workers' Compensation Laws

Employment Law: A Checklist

Employee Benefits Survey Data

The National Business Agenda

The North American Free Trade Agreement: What It Means for U.S. Business

A Strategy Handbook: Helping Small Businesses Through Chambers of Commerce

Guide to Municipal Solid Waste Management for Communities and Businesses

Managing Chemicals Safely

Making Your Family Business Outlast You

HOW-TO BROCHURES

The U.S. Chamber also offers easily understood "How-To" brochures as part of your membership investment. They contain tips on how to comply with new regulations and information about opportunities for your business. Here is a sampling of titles:

How to Obtain Small Business Financing

How to Sell to the Federal Government

How to Manage Risk and Control Your Insurance Costs

How to Expand Your Market through Exporting

How to Obtain Good Legal Advice and Control Your Legal Costs

How to Comply with The Americans With Disabilities Act

How to Comply with the Civil Rights Act of 1991

How to Communicate with Your Congressional Representatives

How to Comply with the OSHA Hazard Communication Standard

How to Locate Information for Your Family Business

OTHER MEMBER BENEFITS

GAIN
Grassroots Action Information Network

The U.S. Chamber created GAIN to keep you better informed and to help you have a real impact on legislation that affects your business. Our powerful grassroots network uses advanced technology to make it easier for you to communicate your views to members of Congress and the administration, as you attend to your day-to-day operations. The system is constantly expanding to meet our members' needs in many different ways, such as developing member to member networking opportunities.

ConSern
Loans for Education

Employee benefits are important tools for hiring and retaining good employees, but they can be expensive. That's why the U.S. Chamber makes the ConSern loan program available to members, at very little cost. It's a valuable benefit you can offer your employees and their families. And, as an employer, you have no liability for the loans, and no administrative hassles.

Quality Learning Services
Training via Satellite

The U.S. Chamber provides quality management training, educational and information services to help you run your business. Seminar series are available by satellite to U.S. Chamber members, either directly or through your local or state chamber, for a minimal fee. The sessions are also available on videocassettes.

ChamberTech
R&D Expertise

As a member of the U.S. Chamber, you can draw upon the resources of 100,000 Federal lab employees in 650 labs nationwide to help you in the development of new products, processes and technologies. The U.S. Chamber provides you with access to the Federal Laboratory Consortium for Technology Transfer to assist you in solving technical, manufacturing, design, research or regulatory problems.

IDIC
International Division Information Center

This U.S. Chamber service provides one-on-one assistance, answering member questions about trade policy, export promotion, export services and regional concerns. Hotlines and specialized publications keep you up-to-date on key actions affecting business, such as export controls and the North American Free Trade Agreement. And, they provide you with essential information about markets around the world.

Your Trade Group Probably Joined The U.S. Chamber

© U.S. CHAMBER OF COMMERCE
The world's largest federation of businesses, chambers
of commerce, and trade and professional associations.
1615 H Street, N.W., Washington, D.C. 20062-2000
(800) 638-6582 (In Maryland (800) 352-1450)

YOU SHOULD TOO

MS 1027   5/93

Courtesy U.S. Chamber of Commerce

If you are a member of your trade or professional association, congratulations. It shows that you are involved in the issues that face your business and you work hard to meet the standards of your industry. You know business must work together. It also shows you know a smart investment when you see one.

Here's another smart investment—The United States Chamber of Commerce.

The U.S. Chamber is the nation's leading business association with 215,000 member businesses, large and small, across the country. We also have hundreds of member trade and professional associations that probably include yours.

Why would your association join an association? And why should you join the U.S. Chamber?

The U.S. Chamber of Commerce is an outstanding complement to your trade or professional association membership. Take a look at all that we have to offer your business:

LEADERSHIP

The U.S. Chamber was created in 1912 when President Taft called for a *single*, strong voice for American business. Since then, we have grown stronger every year to become the nation's largest and most respected business federation. That means that when the Chamber speaks to the nation's legislators and decision makers, the *unified* voice of American business is heard and respected.

AUTHORITY

Your association works to help you with issues specific to your business. The U.S. Chamber keeps you on top of the national broad-based issues. The Chamber has over 50 specialists covering issues from health care and the federal budget to regulatory reform and export promotion. If an issue is important to business, you can bet the U.S. Chamber is involved. Few other organizations have the resources to keep you informed and represented on such a wide range of issues.

We are prepared to defend your interests long before the issues become headline news. That kind of authority means that we are ready when critical battles begin and you can be confident that your voice is being heard.

DETERMINATION

One of the keys to the respect the Chamber has earned in Washington is its reputation for staying with an issue, for not folding under to special interests or unproductive compromise.

It's that kind of determination that produces the Chamber's outstanding victories, including reforming the payroll tax deposit system, increasing the availability of credit for small business, and reducing federal regulations. From start to finish, the U.S. Chamber fights for legislation favorable to your business.

CLOUT

The Chamber's principal strength is its large, active membership base. The Chamber's advanced Grassroots Action Information Network—GAIN—uses powerful technology to coordinate direct action by members. On any issue, Chamber members in every congressional district directly influence federal legislators. In addition, the Chamber leads numerous coalitions of businesses and organizations that work together for common goals. The results are impressive. Each year, the U.S. Chamber achieves numerous victories. Each success translates into huge savings for the business community.

But our reach doesn't stop at our nation's borders. The U.S. Chamber is one of the most respected business organizations around the world, as well. We have 66 American Chambers abroad, covering the world's major markets. Our presence in foreign countries protects our nation's interests, and that makes your economic environment at home even stronger.

AND THERE'S MORE

We are committed to helping your business grow. Our "How To" brochure series helps you comply with complex rules and regulations. Chamber television programs give you the latest business news. *Nation's Business* magazine provides valuable management ideas. And U.S. Chamber ConSern: Loans for Education lets you offer your employees and their families low-cost, long term education loans with *no* liability for you or your business.

Membership in the U.S. Chamber earns a huge return. You'll be better informed on the issues that affect your business, you'll receive vital information on how to make your business even more successful, and your voice will help influence the decisions made on Capitol Hill.

Now that's a good investment.

Exhibit 4–3c   GAIN — Grassroots Action Information Network

Members of the U.S. Chamber of Commerce now have an important new opportunity to become real players in influencing legislation affecting the business community and the national economy. GAIN, the *Grassroots Action Information Network*, makes this all possible. Participation is open to all U.S. Chamber members who are actively committed to furthering American free enterprise.

GAIN is a new service that combines strategic grassroots action with state-of-the-art technology. GAIN empowers the Federation — our members — in a vital new way. By providing them with the information they need *and* the means to act, they easily can become active and make a difference in the issues that affect them.

Regardless of size or industry, individual businesses *and* business groups can now benefit from a national grassroots network with all of these special features:

❑ insightful updates on issues that individual members *select*
❑ wide-reaching, *instantaneous* calls-to-action
❑ *direct* avenues of communication with Congress

INSIGHTS ON IMPORTANT BUSINESS ISSUES

Participants select the GAIN issues in which they want to become involved. The U.S. Chamber has the unmatched resources to track these important issues and to update GAIN participants on key developments. Participants learn how issues affect them through:

● The *National Business Agenda Report* and *Legislative Supplement.* These GAIN newsletters summarize key developments in the legislative priorities of American business.
● Single-issue updates. These "play-by-play" reports are easy to read and free of specialized jargon.
● Access to issue specialists at the Chamber. Our specialists can share inside information and thoughts on the business issues of the day.

Associations and chambers of commerce that participate in GAIN can take advantage of these GAIN resources to provide additional services to their own members.

❑ CALLS TO ACTION

"Action calls" alert participants whenever it becomes urgent to contact members of Congress. The action calls are made via telephone, fax, or mail, depending on the circumstances and on the preferences of the individual GAIN participant. As swiftly as action calls are made to GAIN participants, members of Congress can hear from their constituents. *New* members of Congress, as well as many re-elected ones, are listening more intently than ever to those voices from back home.

❑ DIRECT COMMUNICATION WITH CONGRESS

The issue updates that GAIN participants receive equip them to communicate effectively with their members of Congress when called to action. *Some* action calls are "interactive," using a sophisticated, yet easy-to-use telephone-based system. GAIN participants receive a carefully-timed telephone call with a message from the U.S. Chamber urging the participant to contact Congress on a specific issue. Then, for example, GAIN participants can:

● be connected directly to the office of their members of Congress,
● send a telegram, or
● write a personalized letter to their members of Congress.

Whenever GAIN participants are asked to take action on a given issue, a follow-up report will explain the outcome and let participants know what kind of impact they've made. Participants also will be given the voting records of members of Congress. Constituents can thus hold members of Congress more accountable for their actions.

If you are a member of the U.S. Chamber of Commerce, we invite you to participate in GAIN. Please call us at 202/463-5604 or complete and mail the attached form today.

GAIN
GRASSROOTS ACTION
INFORMATION
NETWORK

U.S. Chamber of Commerce Federation

★ ★ ★ ★ ★ ★ ★ ★ ★ ★ ★ ★ ★ ★ ★ ★ ★ ★ ★ ★

Please complete and mail or fax this form today!

Yes!

Please send me more information on becoming a GAIN participant.

U.S. Chamber of Commerce
Office of Membership
Grassroots Management
1615 H Street, N.W.
Washington, D.C. 20062-2000

Fax: 202\463-3190

Name:_____
Title:_____
Business/Organization:_____
_____
Business Address:_____
_____
City:_____
State:_____ Zip:_____
Telephone No:_____

RF03

Courtesy U.S. Chamber of Commerce

*An unlikely broad-based alliance of consumer, safety, law en-
forcement, and insurance industry organizations, Advocates
for Highway and Auto Safety, lobbies for effective highway
safety legislation and policies at both the national and state
level. Communication within this curious but effective coalition takes several forms. Exhibit 4–4a is an excerpt from the
newsletter,* The Safety Advocate. *Exhibit 4–4b is a sample
"Report to the Board," Exhibit 4–4c is an "Action Alert," and
Exhibit 4–4d is a photograph of an Advocates' Capitol Hill
press conference.*

Case 4–4

Communicating with a Coalition: Advocates for Highway and Auto Safety

by Katherine R. Hutt, APR, Director, Public Affairs for
Advocates for Highway and Auto Safety, Washington, DC

It was U.S. newspaper editor Charles Dudley Warner who coined
the phrase "politics makes strange bedfellows," and although he
wrote it in his garden in 1870, he could have been describing the
leading public affairs trend of the 1990s. No longer are organizations or companies operating in a vacuum or limiting their political
networks to traditional trade associations. Coalitions are the key
to successful legislative efforts, whether in Washington or in state
capitals across the country.

This is certainly true in the highway safety arena, and no
stranger bedfellows can be found than the property and casualty
insurance industry and the Ralph Nader–inspired consumer
groups who make up the effective and successful organization
Advocates for Highway and Auto Safety.

After years of working together informally on highway safety
issues and battling about almost everything else, the insurance
industry and the consumer movement came together in late 1989
to launch Advocates, a broad-based alliance of consumer, safety,
law enforcement, insurance and agents organizations working together to lobby for effective highway safety legislation and policies
at national and state levels.

Courtesy Advocates for Highway and Auto Safety

Advocates institutionalized an uneasy but already successful alliance of groups with widely different motivations but virtually identical interests: reducing motor vehicle injuries. Motor vehicle crashes are the number one killer and disabler of children and young adults. In 1992, nearly 40,000 people were killed and another 4.5 million injured on our nation's roadways. The cost to society for these crashes was more than $137 billion.

Property and casualty insurance companies want to reduce highway deaths and injuries, as well as auto fraud and theft, to decrease the amount of claims they pay and thereby help stem the rising cost of insurance for consumers and businesses. As an industry that takes a lot of hits in the court of public opinion, they also want to be good corporate citizens and be viewed as caring about the issues that matter to their primary public, their customers. The consumer movement, with its own various incarnations and personalities, saw a chance to improve its effectiveness by teaming up with logical, although unlikely, corporate allies who had vastly greater resources.

Structure, Funding and Policy Development

The idea for Advocates was to bring together all the various organizations with an interest in highway safety, form a new nonprofit organization and develop adequate resources to properly fund an aggressive advocacy and public affairs effort. The organization's Board of Directors is comprised of organizations and is evenly split between the "insurance side" (currently eight large property and casualty insurance companies, two insurance trade associations and two insurance agents associations) and the "consumer side" (currently four consumer, five public health, and three safety/law enforcement groups).

This shared, equal leadership helps ensure the integrity of the group to its various audiences. It is one of the ways that Advocates differs from some other coalitions that have been criticized for being "front" organizations for a particular industry with only marginal consumer representation.

Although Advocates' leadership is shared equally, funding comes from the insurance side only. The budget is about $1.3 million per year and the organization has a staff of nine, including specialists in government relations and lobbying, public relations, regulatory affairs, safety, and law. It is based on Capitol Hill in Washington, D.C.

Under the group's Bylaws, leadership on the board is split between two co-chairs, and even the committees are made up of equal numbers from both sides of the board, under shared leadership. All issues are brought before the board and must be agreed to by both sides before being added to the policy agenda. Advocates works only on safety issues and not, for instance, on issues such as auto insurance rates or fuel economy. Examples of areas in common are: auto safety standards, occupant restraint laws (safety belts, motorcycle helmets, child safety seats, air bags), anti-impaired driving laws, motor vehicle theft and fraud, speed related issues (including radar detector bans), truck safety, and consumer protection issues (bumper quality, consumer disclosure matters). For issues of controversy, like fuel economy, the rule is "agree to disagree."

Action

Advocates' goal is to leverage influence by working within existing coalitions and bringing the strength of the organization's members to the effort, whether at the state or federal level. Its staff and committee members have developed an extensive network of contacts in nearly every state, including thousands of citizen activists, legislators, state and local government officials, business leaders and others.

Each year, the staff and Program Committee develops a program plan based on anticipated legislative action, which is then approved by the board. Proposed activities are prioritized with approximately equal weight given to federal and state issues (although the Board allows considerable leeway in implementation of the plan, to give the organization the flexibility needed to respond to ever-changing political climates).

At the state level, a local official, legislator or local activist often will approach Advocates and ask for assistance with a particular piece of legislation. If no local coalition exists, Advocates helps organize one that parallels the national group's diversity. Occasionally, Advocates also make a small grant to enhance grassroots efforts.

At the Congressional level, the Member of Congress initiates the contact, or Advocates' staff approach them to suggest working together on an issue. Advocates is well known among members and staff of key transportation committees in both parties and on both sides of Capitol Hill.

Recruiting interested groups beyond Advocates' formal membership is the second step here, as well. In both state and federal endeavors, Advocates often staffs the effort, providing organizational, communications and lobbying support.

Advocates has also developed the usual system of media contacts in Washington and around the country, including transportation and consumer reporters, editorial page editors, and assignment editors.

Communications Tools

Communicating with diverse audiences—*and inspiring them to action*—requires different types of communications tools. Advocates has three primary public documents and two major internal communications tools.

A periodic newsletter, *The Safety Advocate*, reports on the organization's various activities at the state and federal level. It does not attempt to serve as a comprehensive record of the highway safety field, as there are several other publications that already do a fine job of this. It is designed to inform and motivate those with an interest in Advocates' issues. The 12-page, two-color newsletter is written by the staff, and layout is done in-house using desktop publishing (photos, spot color, and other graphic elements are added by the printer). *The Safety Advocate* is complimentary, and it is automatically sent to everyone in Advocates' database of federal, state, and local contacts, as well as members of Congress, the media, and other interested parties (total circulation: approximately 6,000).

An annual *Progress Report* serves a similar function and is circulated to most of those who receive the newsletter. It is a 12–16 page statement of accomplishments to, again, inform and motivate those in Advocates' sphere. Written by the staff, designed by a professional graphic artist, and produced in a format similar to corporate annual reports (photographs, graphics, color cover), it is Advocates' most eye-catching publication.

These two publications are also widely distributed at five to ten trade shows that Advocates attends each year, and are a key way to inform safety advocates, legislators, and the media of the organization's work.

The third public document is Advocates' *Policy Statements*, a summary of the organization's positions on a range of issues. Organized by topics such as "Occupant Protection," "Federal Safety Legislation," and "Consumer Protection and Information," the publication summarizes each issue and declaration of belief in one to three paragraphs. Changes or additions to the statements must be made by the board of directors; however, the statements are worded broadly enough to give the staff discretion to act quickly on specific legislative or regulatory issues, or to respond to the media.

Two internal documents have a very limited circulation. The "Report to the Board" is a 2–4 page compilation of the staff's activities of the week, including the progress of any pending legislation. It is published in-house on a weekly basis and mailed to board members and their key staff (approximately 50 total recipients). It gives this critical audience a short, easy-to-read bulletin of important information and keeps them up to date on the extensive work being done. The report also serves as documentation and an orderly, chronological record of activities.

Advocates' most crucial publication is also its primary method of generating legislative support: an "Action Alert" is a call to action on a specific issue (usually a piece of pending state legislation). These one-page messages are issued only when needed and are vital to mobilizing the resources of the organization's members.

Typically, an "Alert" would be generated when a bill has been introduced in committee in a state legislature. The "Alert" includes critical information, such as the bill number, a summary of its contents, the "political landscape," the committee of jurisdiction, needed action (letters, calls, telegrams, and so forth), and members' names, addresses, and fax numbers. Follow-up "Alerts" may be issued as the bill progresses through the legislative process.

"Alerts" are produced in-house and distributed by broadcast fax (a service provided by commercial vendors), and the staff is well versed in quick response and immediate turnaround. It is often the case that an "Action Alert" is issued within hours of when the staff first learn of a need. Basic circulation is identical to the "Report to the Board," but additional recipients are added depending on the issue and what coalitions are in place to respond.

All of these communications tools have one thing in common: they are brief and to the point. Representatives of Advocates' member-organizations already have full agendas, and the group cannot afford to waste the time of its staff or its members with unnecessary reading or, worse, insufficient or fruitless action.

Conclusion

Advocates has been extremely successful at lobbying for improved highway and auto safety legislation at both the state and federal levels. Bringing together diverse organizations with a unified commitment has helped break the gridlock on numerous issues that had been stalled for years.

One prime example is air bags, which the auto industry opposed for more than 20 years. Thanks to the mobilization of an enormous coalition of support from dozens of organizations that support auto safety, dual air bags will be required in all cars, vans and light trucks by the end of the decade (and, in fact, most automakers are ahead of schedule—90% of 1994 model cars will offer one or two air bags).

If it is true that the proof is in the pudding, then this unusual coalition works and works well. Although no formal communications audit has been done, the board members and their staff are periodically questioned as to how the group's communications tools meet their needs, and changes have been made in response to those suggestions.

Coalitions have special needs and require a different approach to internal communications than traditional trade, social, or charitable organizations. But the benefits are well worth the effort. Coalitions can prove beyond the shadow of a doubt the old axiom that "the whole is greater than the sum of its parts." Advocates for Highway and Auto Safety is proud to have brought together such a diverse group of organizations and companies to work for such worthy goals as saving lives and reducing injuries on our nation's highways.

Exhibit 4–4a   **Excerpt from *The Safety Advocate***

The Safety Advocate

Spring 1993
Vol. 4, No. 1-2

Published by Advocates for Highway and Auto Safety -- a broad-based alliance of consumer, safety and law enforcement groups and insurance and agents organizations working together to promote effective highway safety legislation, standards, policies and programs at national and state levels to reduce deaths, injuries and economic costs associated with motor vehicle crashes, fraud and theft.

"Children at Risk" Campaign Seeks to Close Gaps in State Child Occupant Protection Laws

Advocates has teamed up with the National SAFE KIDS Campaign to launch the "Children at Risk" Campaign, an effort to improve child passenger safety by calling for emphasis on injury prevention as a cornerstone of health care reform.

The principal objective of the Campaign is to close the gaps in state child safety seat and safety belt laws so that all children under the age of 16 are required to buckle up. Other goals are outlined in a 10-point "Wish List" of action for federal and state governments and the private sector.

Although all states have a child safety seat law, 43 states have gaps, according to research by the Insurance Institute for Highway Safety (IIHS). An IIHS study found that only seven states (Alaska, California, Maine, Michigan, Oregon, Rhode Island and Washington) and the District of Columbia have no gaps in child restraint coverage from birth to age 15. An American Academy of Pediatrics study came to similar conclusions.

Motor vehicle crashes are the leading cause of death and disabling injury for children and young adults. In 1991, nearly 2,000 children under age 16 died as passengers in motor vehicle crashes.

More than two dozen organizations have signed on to the "Children at Risk" Campaign, which was kicked off at a press conference in Chicago on March 16th, during the Lifesavers Conference. Transporta-
(continued on page 11)

U.S. DOT SECRETARY FEDERICO PENA examines a Chrysler integrated child safety seat, part of a display on innovative technologies, during the kick-off event for the "Children at Risk" Campaign. Advocates' Deputy Executive Director Jacqueline S. Gillan and the Hon. John Cullerton, Illinois State Senator, look on. (Photo by Jim Carlson Photo/Imaging.)

High Risk Driver Bill Targets Younger, Older Drivers, Repeat Offenders

The High Risk Driver Act of 1993, introduced in Congress by Senators John C. Danforth (R-MO) and J. James Exon (D-NE), will help address the problem of categories of drivers over-represented in motor vehicle crashes -- the youngest and oldest drivers on our roadways, and repeat offenders.

Drivers at both ends of the age scale have significantly higher crash rates than other drivers. Those between ages 16- and 20-years-old represent only 7.4 percent of licensed drivers, but were involved in 15.4 percent of fatal crashes and more than 20 percent of single-vehicle crashes in 1991.

Per mile driven, elderly drivers have higher fatal crash rates than drivers in any other age group except teenagers. Fatal crash rates per licensed driver begin to increase at age 75. However, fewer older people have licenses and they drive fewer miles, on average, than other drivers.
(continued on page 5)

Courtesy Advocates for Highway and Auto Safety

Advocates for Highway and Auto Safety

777 N. Capitol St. NE, Suite 410
Washington, D.C. 20002
Phone 202/408-1711
FAX 202/408-1699

Board of Directors

Co-Chairs:

D. Richard McFerson, Nationwide Insurance

Andrew McGuire, Trauma Foundation

Insurance/Agents Organizations:

August P. Alegi, GEICO

Patricia Borowski, Natl. Association of Professional Insurance Agents

Herman Brandau, State Farm Insurance

Elizabeth White Call, Independent Insurance Agents of America

John Conners, Liberty Mutual Insurance

Dale S. Hammond, Travelers Insurance

Sonja Larkin-Thorne, ITT Hartford Insurance

Rodger S. Lawson, Ph.D., Alliance of American Insurers

Gerald Maatman, Kemper Natl. Insurance

Robert Vagley, American Insurance Association

Marie T. van Luling, Aetna Life and Casualty

Consumer/Safety Organizations:

Stephen Brobeck, Consumer Federation of America

Joan Claybrook, Public Citizen

Clarence Ditlow, Center for Auto Safety

Donald Friedman, MCR Technology Inc.

Jay R. Halfon, New York Public Interest Research Group

Ralf Hotchkiss, Wheeled Mobility Center/San Francisco State University

Janine Jagger, M.P.H., Ph.D., Head Injury Foundation/University of Virginia

Robert J. King, Mothers Against Drunk Driving (MADD)

Robert F. Larkin, M.D., FACEP, American College of Emergency Physicians

Stephen Teret, American Public Health Association

Hubert Williams, Police Foundation

Staff

Judith Lee Stone, President and Executive Director

Jacqueline S. Gillan, Deputy Executive Director

Sangita Chari, State Legislative Assistant

Gerald A. Donaldson, Ph.D., Assistant Director for Highway Safety

Katherine R. Hutt, APR, Associate Director for Public Affairs & Editor, *The Safety Advocate*

Henry M. Jasny, Counsel

Stephanie Lewis, Secretary/Receptionist

Kathleen M. McNamara, Special Assistant/Office Manager

Carol Stroebel, Associate Director for Federal Affairs

Kyle J. Zimmer, Associate Director for State Affairs

President's Column

Home Movies and Family Memories

by Judith Lee Stone

We recently received in our office two very touching audio-visual programs made by mothers who love their children. That wouldn't be unusual, of course, except that these mothers are passionate in both their pursuit of highway safety and their gratitude for successes in the field.

The first was a charming home video of the first year in the life of Thomas James Hanrahan of Albuquerque, New Mexico. Included was footage of his baptism, his first steps, his birthday party -- all the usual moments that proud parents capture on tape, that grandparents watch repeatedly and that the rest of us smile at politely.

But T.J.'s parents have more reason than most to be joyous. An air bag saved the life of his mother, Debbie, before she even knew she was pregnant. Walking away from a horrible crash was miracle enough for Debbie, but a few weeks later she and her husband, Michael, found out about the second miracle -- the baby they thought they'd never have was on the way, and he was fine thanks to the air bag and safety belt that had kept Debbie safe.

So, along with baby steps and other "firsts," T.J.'s story includes an appearance in a national commercial for Allstate Insurance ("We're alive...Debbie and T.J. Hanrahan"), his induction as the youngest member of Advocates' "Saved by the Air Bag" Club, and participation in Ralph Nader's awards dinner honoring the inventors and technical pioneers of the air bag.

The second presentation was heartbreaking. It was a slide show developed by Kristen Micheletti of Bloomington, Illinois, about her crusade to close the loopholes in that state's child safety seat law. Kristen's baby daughter, Michelle, was killed in a crash just moments after her grandmother took the crying infant from her car seat. At the time, Illinois's child safety seat law only applied when a parent was driving; in fact, a bill to change that provision had been defeated days before.

We came to know Kristen through Illinois State Senator John Cullerton, who introduced the bill Kristen worked to pass. The slide show was developed for legislators in Springfield, and Kristen's message doesn't spare your emotions. She chose to include slides of the crash site, the crumpled car, Michelle's obituary and even her funeral.

Every time Kristen tells her story, she relives the most painful days of her life. She does it for Michelle, for the other children who might be saved, and for the baby brother Michelle never knew. And she's agreed to be the spokesperson for the "Children at Risk" Campaign (*see story on page 1*).

One of our most difficult but most important jobs is helping those who've lost a loved one to channel their grief into action. They are the clearest voices calling out for change. Their messages and the faces of their children are the reasons we do what we do.

Advocates salutes the many victims who have assisted us over the past three years in our efforts to pass state and federal legislation to improve highway safety. These citizen lobbyists have a story to tell that puts faces on statistics and puts hope in political debate. ◊

If you would like to be on the mailing list of *The Safety Advocate*, please send your business card or name and address to:

The Safety Advocate
Advocates for Highway & Auto Safety
777 N. Capitol St., N.E.
Suite 410
Washington, D.C. 20002

Exhibit 4–4b   "Report to the Board"

ADVOCATES
FOR HIGHWAY
AND AUTO SAFETY

Sample   Abridged from Week of October 11, 1993

State Activities:

Continued efforts on behalf Massachusetts safety belt bill: worked with coalition members to assess support, compile vote count and strategize on efforts; issued "Action Alert;" prepared and sent letters to all state Senators urging support; pitched editorial to *Boston Globe*. Bill was pulled from vote on senate floor and may be taken up as early as Monday, October 18th.

Discussed Illinois motorcycle helmet strategy with potential bill sponsor.

Accepted invitation to testify at Illinois hearing on drunk driving bill.

Met with several Wisconsin emergency physicians to discuss status of effort to establish state safety coalition.

Began identifying organizations and individuals for membership in possible drunk driving coalition in South Carolina.

Continued preparations with MADD for joint press conference in mid-November to release results from second "Rating the States."

Federal Activities:

Met with staff of House Public Works and Transportation Committee to discuss truck safety issues and hazardous materials legislation.

Discussed transportation appropriations conference with Senate staff.

Began preparation of draft comments on three FHWA dockets: standards for load securement; intermodal container securement criteria; and implementing regulations for Intermodal Safety Transportation of Containers Act of 1992.

Followed-up on potential safety belt story with reporter from NBC's "Now with Tom Brokow and Katie Couric."

Coalition Activities:

Participated in annual meeting of American College of Emergency Physicians; at exhibit booth, gathered names from 600+ attendees for grassroots efforts in support of safety belt and all-rider motorcycle helmets.

Discussed agenda for upcoming quarterly meeting of Coalition for Consumer Health & Safety and prepared materials for meeting.

777 North Capitol Street, NE, Suite 410, Washington, DC 20002   Tel: 202-408-1711   Fax: 202-408-1699

Courtesy Advocates for Highway and Auto Safety   **161**

Exhibit 4–4c   "Action Alert"

ADVOCATES
FOR HIGHWAY
AND AUTO SAFETY

ADVOCATES ALERT

ILLINOIS

OCTOBER, 1993

ALERT: The "Children at Risk" Campaign is a coalition of health, safety, children's advocacy, law enforcement and business organizations working together to improve child passenger safety by closing the gaps in state safety belt/child safety seat laws. State Senator John Cullerton has introduced a bill, S.B. 1124, that would effectively eliminate the one remaining gap in the Illinois safety belt and child restraint laws--it will require **all** children age 6 and older to wear safety belts in all seating positions. Currently, the law requires only those children sitting in the front of the vehicle to wear them.

SITUATION: The bill will be considered in the next legislative session, which convenes January 12, 1994. Please contact members of the Illinois General Assembly and urge their support of S.B. 1124.

TALKING
POINTS:
- Motor vehicle crashes are the number one killer and disabler of children and young adults. In 1991, nearly 2000 children under age 16 died as passengers in motor vehicle crashes.

- Only ten states and the District of Columbia have no gaps in child restraint coverage (Alaska, California, Georgia, Maine, Michigan, Oregon, Rhode Island, Vermont, Washington, and West Virginia).

- Making this minor amendment to Illinois' safety belt law will close the final gap in occupant protection laws for children and will save lives.

NEED: Write or call your state senators and representatives, and ask them to support Sen. Cullerton's bill, S.B. 1124.

FOR MORE INFORMATION, CALL: Advocates for Highway and Auto Safety
(202) 408-1711.

777 North Capitol Street, NE Suite 410 Washington, DC 20002 Tel: 202/408-1711 Fax: 202/408-1699

Courtesy Advocates for Highway and Auto Safety

Exhibit 4–4d   **Advocates' Capitol Hill Press Conference**

Advocates for Highway and Auto Safety often join with members of Congress or state legislators in promoting highway and auto safety issues to the media and the general public. Press conferences usually include medical, public health, or law enforcement officials who bring professional expertise to issues, as well as survivors or family members of victims who can tell the personal stories behind the statistics. *(Photo by Marvin T. Jones and Associates, courtesy Advocates for Highway and Auto Safety.)*

Courtesy Advocates for Highway and Auto Safety

Chapter 5   **Community Relations**

One of the most important audiences an organization has is its community, the home of its offices and operations. Maintaining good relations with the community usually entails management and employees becoming involved in and contributing to local organizations and activities. In addition, the organization may communicate with the community in other ways, such as distributing house publications or meeting with community leaders.

Solving community relations problems may follow the usual sequence of research, objectives, programming, and evaluation.

Research

Research for community relations includes investigation to understand the client, the reason for the program, and the community audiences to be targeted for communication.

Client Research

Client research for community relations concentrates on the organization's role and reputation in the community. What is its level of credibility? Have there been significant community complaints in the past? What are the organization's present and past community relations practices? What are its major strengths and weaknesses in the community? What opportunities exist to enhance community relations? These questions provide a helpful framework for a community relations program.

Opportunity or Problem Research

Why have a community relations program in the first place? Considering the cost and benefits involved, this is a question worthy of detailed justification. The public relations practitioner should assess problems the organization may have had with community groups and make a searching analysis of community relations opportunities. Many organizations conduct ongoing proactive community relations as a form of insurance against any sudden problem requiring a reactive public relations solution.

Audience Research

The final aspect of community relations research consists of carefully identifying audiences to be targeted for communication and learning as much about each audience as possible. Community publics can be subdivided into three major groups: community media, community leaders, and community organizations. These categories can then be further subdivided as shown in Exhibit 5–a.

Exhibit 5–a   **Community Publics**

Community media
  Mass
  Specialized
Community leaders
  Public officials
  Educators
  Religious leaders
  Professionals
  Executives
  Bankers
  Union leaders
  Ethnic leaders
  Neighborhood leaders

Exhibit 5-a
(*continued*)

Community organizations
    Civic
    Business
    Service
    Social
    Cultural
    Religious
    Youth
    Political
    Special interest groups
    Other

In conducting community relations programs, it is important for the practitioner to develop contact lists of journalists, community leaders, and organizations.

The media contacts list will be similar to those discussed in Chapter 3, on media relations. These lists should include the type and size of audience reached by each media outlet in the community, the type of material used by each outlet, the name and title of appropriate editors who handle organizational news, and deadlines.

The list of community and organization leaders should be equally thorough. It should include the name, title, affiliation, address, and telephone number of all important community leaders. These data should be categorized according to occupational fields, such as public officials, educators, media people, or religious leaders. In addition to a listing of leaders alone, there should be a list of organizations that includes frequently updated names of officers, their addresses, and telephone numbers.

Research for community relations, then, consists of investigation of the client, the reason for the program, and the target audiences in the community.

Objectives

Impact and output objectives for community relations, like those for other forms of public relations, should be specific and quantitative.

Impact Objectives

Impact objectives for community relations involve informing the community audiences or modifying their attitudes or behaviors. Some examples are:

1. to increase (by 30 percent this year) community knowledge of the operations of the organization, including its products, services, employees, and support of community projects
2. to promote (20 percent) more favorable community opinion toward the organization (during a specified time period)
3. to gain (15 percent) greater organizational support from community leaders (during a particular campaign)
4. to encourage (20 percent) more feedback from community leaders (during the current year)

Output Objectives

Output objectives consist of the efforts made by the practitioner to enhance the organization's community relations. Some illustrations are:

1. to prepare and distribute (15 percent) more community publications (than last year)
2. to be (10 percent) more responsive to community needs (during this year)
3. to create (five) new community projects involving organizational personnel and resources (during this calendar year)
4. to schedule (five) meetings with community leaders (this year)

Thus, both impact and output objectives are helpful in preparing community relations programs. They serve as useful and necessary precursors to programming.

Programming

Programming for community relations includes planning the theme and messages, action or special event(s), uncontrolled and controlled media, and using effective communication principles.

Theme and Messages

The theme and messages for community relations are situational and grow out of research findings related to the organization, the reason for conducting the program, and the existing and past relationships with the targeted community audiences.

Action or Special Event(s)

Actions and special events most often associated with community relations are:

1. an organizational open house and tour of facilities
2. sponsorship of special community events or projects
3. participation of management and other personnel in volunteer community activities
4. purchase of advertising in local media
5. contribution of funds to community organizations or causes
6. meetings with community leaders
7. membership of management and personnel in a variety of community organizations — civic, professional, religious
8. participation of management and workers in the political affairs of the community — service in political office and on councils and boards

Involvement of the organization, its management, and its other personnel in the affairs of the community is the most significant aspect of a community relations program. With this kind of link to the community, there should be relatively smooth community relations, with few or no surprises.

Uncontrolled and Controlled Media

In the communications part of a community relations program, the practitioner should think first of servicing community media outlets with appropriate uncontrolled media, such as news releases, photographs or photo opportunities, and interviews of organizational officers with local reporters.

The use of controlled media, on the other hand, should include sending copies of house publications to a select list of community leaders. The practitioner should also help the organization develop a speakers bureau, and publicize the availability of organizational management and expert personnel to address meetings of local clubs and organizations. It is also appropriate to target community leaders on a timely basis for selected direct mailings, such as important announcements or notices of organizational involvement in community affairs.

Both uncontrolled and controlled media in the community relations program should be focused on the eight types of community involvement listed earlier. These are the heart of the program.

Effective Communication

Three principles of effective communication deserve special attention in community relations programs.

First, the targeting of opinion leaders or community leaders for communication is crucial to the success of such a program. The leadership provides the structure and substance of the community itself.

Second, group influence plays a substantial role in effective community relations. Organizations exercise varying degrees of cohesiveness and member conformity. The community relations program must cultivate community groups, their leaders, and their memberships. The effective speakers bureau is a primary means for accomplishing this.

Finally, audience participation is highly significant. Targeted community media, leaders, and groups can be encouraged to participate in the client's organizational events. Most important, the client should reach out to the community by sponsoring attractive activities.

Evaluation

If the objectives of the community relations program have been phrased specifically and quantitatively, their evaluation should be relatively easy. The success of a program should be directly linked to its attainment of the objectives stated at the program's outset.

Summary

Research for community relations assesses the organization's reputation and its existing and potential problems with the community. Targeting audiences usually includes a detailed analysis of community media, leaders, and organizations.

Impact objectives for community relations are such desired outcomes as informing or influencing the attitudes and behaviors of the community. Output objectives consist of a listing of public relations efforts to enhance the organization's relations with the community.

Programming concentrates on organizational involvement with the community through sponsorship of events, employee participation in community activities, contributions to community causes, meetings, and the like. The uncontrolled media used in community relations are aimed at servicing local journalists with appropriate news releases, photographs, and interviews with organizational officers. Controlled media usually include house publications, speakers bureaus, and appropriate direct mailings to community leaders.

Evaluation of stated objectives uses methods appropriate to the type of objective. Impact objectives are usually measured by a survey or other appropriate quantitative methods, while output objectives may call for simple observation of whether the desired output was achieved.

Readings on Community Relations

Aiken, Michael, and Paul E. Mott, eds. *The Structure of Community Power*. New York: Random House, 1970.

Baker, W. R. "Houston Takes the Bus." *Public Relations Journal*, December 1985), pp. 33ff.

Bickerstaffe, George. "What Companies Are Doing to Make Themselves Good Neighbors." *International Management*, May 1981, pp. 30ff.

"Community Relations and Internal Communications" (entire issue). *Public Relations Journal*, February 1980.

"Community Relations: A Necessary Ingredient in Cleanups." *Environmental Manager* 3 (April 1992): 3–7.

Dyer, Sam. "The Story of a Community Relations Fiasco." *Public Relations Quarterly* 38 (Summer 1993): 33–35.

Harper, W. A. "A Rationale for Effective Community Relations." *New Directions for Institutional Advancement*, March 1982, pp. 3ff.

Kelly, D. C. "Decentralized Community Relations." *Public Relations Journal*, February 1984, pp. 23ff.

Kipps, H. C. *Community Resources Directory*. Detroit: Gale, 1984.

Kruckeberg, Dean, and Kenneth Starck. *Public Relations and the Community: A Reconstructed Theory*. New York: Praeger, 1988.

Lowengard, Mary. "Community Relations: New Approaches to Building Consensus." *Public Relations Journal* 45 (October 1989): 24–30.

Putman, Bryan. "How to Build a Community Relations Program." *Public Relations Journal* 36 (February 1980): 29–33.

Wandersman, Abraham. "A Framework of Participation in Community Organizations." *Journal of Applied Behavioral Science* 1 (1981): 27ff.

Williams, Joe, ed. *World-Class Community Relations*, Vol. II. Bartlesville, OK: Joe Williams Communications Books, 1988.

Yarrington, Roger. *Community Relations Handbook*. New York: Longman, 1983.

Community Relations Cases

A major problem with the opening of Oriole Park at Camden Yards, the new home of the Baltimore Orioles baseball team, was persuading fans to utilize public transportation rather than their cars to attend the games. The Maryland Stadium Authority conducted a campaign to educate baseball fans about the available public transportation options. Exhibit 5–1a is a news release providing a "game plan" for getting to Camden Yards. Exhibit 5–1b is a photograph of the stadium itself.

Case 5–1   ## Route, Route, Route for the Home Team

Maryland Stadium Authority, Baltimore, MD, with Trahan, Burden & Charles, Inc., Baltimore, MD

The Background

Oriole Park at Camden Yards, the new home of the Baltimore Orioles baseball team, was opened in April 1992 by the Maryland Stadium Authority. As the most important economic development project planned for Baltimore in the 1990s, complete operational success was demanded by political and business leaders, the media and the community at large. Heading a consortia of four organizations (including the Baltimore City and Maryland state departments of transportation and the Baltimore Orioles), the Maryland Stadium Authority retained Trahan, Burden & Charles (TBC) to design and implement a public relations campaign to address one aspect of the ballpark's opening—transportation access.

The campaign was not geared toward selling a product (the Orioles), but instead, selling the most effective means to reach the product. Impact studies indicated that without cooperation from fans, commuters and other area residents in utilizing public transportation, the entire downtown community and interstate highway system would be affected by major traffic congestion and parking problems on the dates of the Orioles' 81 home games. Baltimore, however, had a history of limited public transportation use, particularly among individuals matching the demographics of the average Oriole fan and season ticket holder. This issue was compounded by two circumstances: 1) the introduction of Central Light Rail—a mode of transportation totally foreign to potential

Courtesy Maryland Stadium Authority

users that held its inaugural run Opening Week and, 2) a lack of parking spaces available at the ballpark. Due to enormous season ticket sales, taxpayers had paid for a stadium parking lot that planners later realized would be insufficient to handle parking for regular ticket holders.

Research

Research was compiled from a variety of sources and analyzed by TBC with the client consortia:

Other Major League Cities: TBC investigated other downtown ballparks in the major leagues with similar traffic and parking conditions (Toronto, Atlanta, Seattle).

JFX Campaign: TBC gave detailed study to a similar transportation access campaign undertaken in Baltimore in the 1980s during the reconstruction of the city's major north/south expressway.

Traffic and Parking Feasibility Studies: 1985 Baltimore Memorial Stadium Modernization Study; 1985 Baltimore Stadium Study; 1986 New Stadium Site Evaluation; 1986 Stadium Access Study; 1990 Maryland Stadium Authority Camden Yards Master Plan; 1992 Downtown Parking Analysis.

Public Transportation Research: An analysis of ridership statistics including demographics; construction plans; and transit schedules of transportation options for Camden Yards: Light Rail (new); MARC commuter rail from Washington, DC (expanded schedule); Express Park-and-Ride bus (expanded schedule); downtown metro line (existing); regular transit bus service (existing).

Planning

Planning began with the establishment of two major objectives for the campaign: 1) to educate members of the community about the transportation options available for traveling to and from the ballpark and downtown, and 2) to seek community members' cooperation in utilizing public transportation services and preferred alternative driving routes for the ballpark and downtown. Using fear as the main propelling agent, TBC recommended a campaign for Camden Yards that simultaneously lowered expectations and motivated Orioles fans and others traveling downtown to think in advance, to think wisely and to be prepared for congestion. With the client, TBC identified two target audiences:

1) Orioles fans traveling to the ballpark, particularly season ticket holders (primary), and 2) others traveling downtown for business or leisure activities (secondary). After identifying these audiences, five primary messages were established: 1) plan ahead, 2) there are great public transportation choices other than your car, 3) If you drive, don't use major thoroughfares, use secondary "back door" routes, 4) park at a distance and walk, 5) come early, stay late, and take advantage of downtown retail and dining offerings. With a budget of $200,000, TBC set out to determine the most cost-effective means of delivering the campaign messages. The agency started by identifying media partners, businesses, and others willing to donate or trade time and space. The major components of the campaign were then determined: an aggressive media relations effort that included a kick-off media event, editorial board meetings, an exhaustive roster of radio/sports talk show interviews, and a final Opening Week press conference; presentations to community groups; a 30-second television PSA appearing in the Baltimore/Washington market; a map/brochure; and multiple uses of signage at/on parking garages, metro/buses and transit stations. A campaign theme "Route, Route, Route for the Home Team" was developed based on the popular baseball song, and an early February launch date was planned to coincide with the unofficial beginning of the baseball season—Spring Training.

Objectives

The stage was set. Orioles fans had 38 years to develop favorite routes and parking locations for the old Memorial Stadium, where the use of public transportation was less than 2 percent. TBC had 2 months to gain the community's support and educate fans from Baltimore, Washington and beyond about the best route to the new ballpark. A goal of 15 percent nonauto ridership (10 percent public transportation; 5 percent charter bus) had to be met to allow for the distribution of an anticipated 13,750 cars to 5,000 on-site parking spots and 20,000 available downtown spaces.

Execution

The campaign implementation required the utmost cooperation among TBC, each member of the client consortia, and other city and state services. Meetings were held weekly from Nov. 1991 to

May 1992 for consensus-building purposes. Flexibility was key throughout the planning and execution of the campaign. Creative and operational decisions required constant adjustments due to changing construction schedules, rail access negotiations and political pressures from government leaders. One of the greatest challenges came three days prior to Opening Day when the Stadium Authority's transportation head and spokesperson for the campaign left for a family emergency. TBC personnel, trained as backups, stepped in to coordinate and conduct the majority of the transportation-related media interviews during Opening Week. TBC was in the unique position of being the client and the agency.

Evaluation

The campaign was an overwhelming success as goals were exceeded in every instance and the community's concerns about transportation access were quickly eliminated. Three months into the season, non-auto ridership averaged 22 percent and was as high as 35 percent for major games such as Opening Day. By midseason, traffic control officers were reduced and parking garages dropped prices due to the low number of fans driving to games. Non-auto ridership lowered to 19 percent at the end of the year as fans became more accustomed to driving routes, but the campaign's goal of 15 percent was still exceeded and traffic and parking problems were kept to a minimum. Much of the campaign's success was attributed to the media relations blitz engineered by TBC which generated nearly $650,000 worth of newspaper and magazine news coverage (broadcast not monitored due to budget). The *Baltimore Sun* delivered the ultimate compliment the day after Opening Day when its headline read: *Traffic? What Traffic?*

ROUTE, ROUTE, ROUTE, FOR THE HOME TEAM!

FOR IMMEDIATE RELEASE
February 24, 1992

For Further Information
Contact: Brent Burkhardt
              410-347-7500

ORIOLES FANS ENCOURAGED TO MAP OUT A GAME PLAN FOR '92, AND ROUTE, ROUTE, ROUTE FOR THE HOME TEAM

A public information campaign was launched today by the Baltimore City Department of Transportation, the Baltimore Orioles, the Maryland Department of Transportation and the Maryland Stadium Authority to assist baseball fans in picking the best way to get to Oriole Park at Camden Yards.

With a little over a month to Opening Day, April 6, Orioles fans are encouraged to plan ahead and to begin mapping out a game plan to reach the new ballpark in downtown Baltimore.

Oriole Park at Camden Yards will be served by a variety of new transit options that will operate for every game.

- **Metro** from Northwest to downtown's Lexington Market and Charles Center stations (8,000 free parking spaces along route).

- **MARC** trains from Washington, D.C. and other locations to Camden Station at the ballpark and Penn Station north of downtown (shuttle service between Penn Station and the ballpark).

- **Park-and-Ride** express buses from 13 metropolitan locations to the ballpark.

- **MTA bus** service with 24 regular routes passing within walking distance of the ballpark.

And Baltimore's newest form of mass transit,

- **Light Rail** from north central Baltimore County/City to the Pratt Street and Camden Yards stops at the ballpark.

-more-

PRESS RELEASE

Courtesy Maryland Stadium Authority

Route, Route, Route, page two

"No other ballpark in America can match the mass transportation services we are providing to Orioles fans," said Ronald Hartman, administrator of the Mass Transit Administration. "Whether individuals live in Owings Mills, Essex, Annapolis, Washington, D.C., or Southeastern Pennsylvania, there are transit services available to get them to the park in a quick, efficient manner."

Many of these transportation services will take fans directly to Oriole Park at Camden Yards and literally stop at the main entrances.

"One of the advantages of the ballpark's central location is its proximity to mass transportation services," said Bruce Hoffman, executive director of the Maryland Stadium Authority. "The distance from the MARC Station, Light Rail stops and bus staging areas to the park's entrance will be shorter than the distance from home plate to the right field foul pole. We think fans will agree that transit is the most convenient way to reach the park."

Stadium Authority and transportation officials hope that anywhere from 15 to 30 percent of the people headed to Oriole Park at Camden Yards will take mass transportation.

Those who choose to drive to the ballpark are being encouraged to stay off the main highways and to consider taking alternative "back door" routes. Transportation officials suggest that fans, especially those driving from the north, west and east, avoid such routes as I-95, I-395, Russell Street and Martin Luther King, Jr. Boulevard. Roads such as Route 40 from the west and east, I-83 from the north, and the major north/south city streets are included among the suggested alternative routes.

Highway message signs throughout the region and travelers advisory radio

-more-

(530 AM) will provide current driving and parking information to fans traveling to the game.

The parking resources for Oriole Park at Camden Yards include more than 35,000 parking spaces located on site and throughout downtown. Based on parking surveys, it is known that approximately 25,000 of those spaces will be available for an average game. Parking in many downtown lots and garages is expected to be more convenient than the parking at the on-site (General Parking) lots south of the ballpark.

The main parking recommendation for fans driving from the north, west or east is to park downtown at a distance and walk to the ballpark. Those who do are likely to find lower rates and less congestion and will enjoy a quicker trip to and from the park. MTA shuttle buses will operate along the Pratt/Lombard Street and Eutaw/Paca Street corridors. Fans parking near Howard Street can take Light Rail directly to the park. Parking operators have been encouraged to charge a flat, pay-as-you-enter rate. Downtown garages and lots will display signs with the Oriole bird.

Main on-site General Parking is located in Lots D & E south of Hamburg Street. It includes more than 2,600 spaces that are ideal for fans coming to the ballpark from the south.

The rate for on-site General Parking is $5. Downtown parking garages and lots in close proximity to the park are expected to charge similar prices.

"It's a new ballgame," said David Chapin, an official of the Maryland Department of Transportation who has worked with the Stadium Authority on transportation access. "At Memorial Stadium fans had 38 years to

-more-

Route, Route, Route, page four

develop their favorite routes to the stadium. We want people to start thinking about how they're going to reach the new park, now, before Opening Day."

The theme of the transportation access campaign, developed by Baltimore's Trahan, Burden & Charles Advertising & Public Relations, Inc., is "Route, Route for the Home Team." It will include radio, television, print and transit advertising as well public relations components. A special map/brochure containing driving, parking and transit information has been developed for fans and will soon be available at Orioles' ticket outlets, MTA stations and transit vehicles, downtown merchants, libraries and other outlets.

"Last season, the Orioles didn't finish first on the playing field, but they did finish first in support from Governor Schaefer, Mayor Schmoke and the business community," said Robert Aylward, vice president of business affairs for the Orioles. "Hundreds of individuals have worked long and hard on these transportation access plans. We appreciate their efforts and know our fans will too."

For information on mass transportations services, fans may call 410-539-5000 (Baltimore area), 410-760-4554 (Annapolis toll-free) and 1-800-543-9809 (in Maryland and Washington, D.C.). For information on MARC train service, call 1-800-325-RAIL.

Exhibit 5–1b   **Photograph of Camden Yards**

Courtesy Maryland Stadium Authority

Sybron Chemicals, Inc., experienced severe image erosion in both its home community and state following an accidental release of a noxious chemical and a processing accident that seriously burned three workers. The company developed a community relations program that targeted neighbors, local officials, environmental groups, and the press as priority audiences. The campaign involved these audiences in a truly interactive program that included a variety of communication methods. Exhibit 5–2a consists of excerpts from an early issue of Sybron's community newsletter explaining the company's extensive neighborhood survey. Exhibit 5–2b is a brochure explaining Sybron's new Prompt Inquiry and Notification System (PINS).

Case 5–2   ## Sybron Chemicals, Inc. — A Case Study in Community Relations

Sybron Chemicals, Inc., Birmingham, NJ, with Holt, Ross & Yulish, Edison, NJ

Introduction

This is a turn-around story. The story of how a chemicals manufacturing plant, operated by Sybron Chemicals, Inc., the nation's leading manufacturer of water purification resins, lost the confidence of its neighbors and community and how, in an atmosphere of fear, this resulted in public demands that it be investigated and possibly closed. It is the story of how a new commitment to corrective action and communications resulted in a complete turn-around, in just seven months, with state regulators praising Sybron's actions as a model for the entire chemical industry.

Background

12:15 AM–October 14, 1988. An accidental release of a noxious chemical ultimately results in the evacuation of about 60 nearby residents and widespread fear and concern. Although it follows all required notification procedures, Sybron receives widespread bad publicity. Due to this and previous complaints about odors

Courtesy Sybron Chemicals, Inc.

and lack of information, several neighbors and a U.S. Senator call for a state and federal crack-down. To compound Sybron's problems, one month later, a processing accident seriously burns three workers. Concerns are rampant.

Holt, Ross & Yulish is retained on October 18th, four days after the incident. HR&Y immediately forms a project team with Sybron's key management to begin to develop a strategy to identify and address the concerns of the community and to restore public confidence in Sybron's operations.

Research

HRY's initial investigations promptly identified (1) odor abatement; (2) process safety; (3) facilities upgrade; and (4) improved communications as the main issues with urgent priorities. While Stone & Webster, an independent engineering consulting firm, substantively attacked odor and safety problems, HR&Y and its affiliate, the Environmental Affairs Institute, designed and supervised a public opinion survey of Sybron's neighbors. Rather than using phone surveys, 300 one hour in-home interviews provided in-depth information on the real concerns, knowledge, expectations, needs, and views of area residents. This survey provided a firm basis for strategic planning and action programs.

Planning

Objective

To quickly halt, stabilize, and turn around the deteriorating community, political, and media perceptions of Sybron. Create and maintain a positive, constructive, and continuing relationship with various audiences. Gain recognition of Sybron's efforts to redress these problems and become accepted as a responsible, trusted "good neighbor."

Strategy

Take immediate, effective, and credible action regarding each of the concerns identified by neighbors, local officials, and state regulatory officials. Regularly report on substantive efforts, progress, and intended actions to neighbors, local officials, environmental groups, and the press.

Execution

(1) The in-home opinion surveys constitute the initial highly effective communications action by Sybron. Kitchen table and living room interviews ease fears and anger, encourage communications, and also present information about Sybron and its operations. They prove to neighbors that Sybron is really committed to listening and responding with action. (2) Sybron team members speak out publicly on all aspects of plant operations. (3) All neighbors receive quarterly Sybron Community Update newspapers dealing with facts and issues. (4) The Prompt Inquiry and Notification System (PINS), a revolutionary computerized 24-hour phone system, which allows neighbors to get instant information about the plant, and which calls them at home if there is a problem, is developed, tested, and installed. (5) The first Sybron "Open House and Plant Tour" is well attended. (6) The Sybron Neighborhood Involvement Council is formed in September of 1989.

Evaluation

Evaluating the "success" of a community relations program is always a challenge. Our accompanying videotape shows many of the elements of the turn-around success. Positive press coverage, negligible complaints, considerable praise by former critics are some indicators. For example, the Commissioner of the New Jersey Department of Environmental Protection placed the system in operation and praised Sybron's ingenuity, declaring the program a model of effectiveness. And there are the extraordinarily positive results from our follow-up opinion survey of neighbors. Highlights include:

- 87% of Sybron's neighbors now feel more secure about Sybron;
- 91% are confident that PINS will enable Sybron to notify residents of problems at the plant;
- 74% believe the Neighborhood Involvement Council is useful;
- 97% believe that Sybron has improved communication with its neighbors.

Exhibit 5–2a   Community Update

Community Update
SYBRON CHEMICALS INC.

VOL. 1, NO. 2   FEBRUARY 1989

NEIGHBORHOOD SURVEY RESULTS PROVIDE INPUT FOR PINS START-UP

Background Information

In December 1988, Sybron Chemicals Inc. had a survey conducted of residents in the immediate vicinity of its manufacturing plant on Birmingham Road in Birmingham, New Jersey, Burlington County. The purpose of the survey was twofold: 1) to determine the specific concerns of residents living in close proximity to the plant and 2) to find out what those individuals considered to be the best means for the company to communicate with them on both a routine and incidental basis.

SCI presented the findings of the survey to the Pemberton Township Environmental Commission on Wednesday, January 25, 1989. According to Steve Adler, SCI Vice President of Human Resources, who made the presentation, "The survey provided very valuable input which will help us to address a variety of objectives, including the need for us to do a much better job of communicating with our neighbors".

The survey is an important step in implementing Sybron's previously announced plan to provide its neighbors with a fast and efficient notification system that would address community needs and desires. This is "PINS", the Prompt Inquiry and Notification System.

Sybron retained the Environmental Affairs Institute (EAI) to design and conduct the survey as well as to make the PINS an operational reality.

EAI conducted house-to-house interviews of approximately 550 households. Virtually every residence within a mile-and-a-half radius of the Birmingham plant was visited.

Lavonne Johnson of the Environmental Affairs Institute (far right) interviews Ronald and Stephanie Klinger, with their daughter, Abigail, of Mobile Estates in Pemberton, for a survey conducted for Sybron Chemicals Inc. The survey was conducted in December in conjunction with SCI's development of its Prompt Inquiry and Notification System (PINS), a 24-hour "hot-line" the company will use to notify area residents of important plant-related incidents or events. About 300 neighbors were interviewed for the survey.

Phase I of the survey was conducted on December 3, 4 and 5 and Phase II was conducted on December 10 and 11. Further efforts were made to offer special interviews, such as mail-in questionnaires for residents who did not have time to be interviewed.

Although several visits and other attempts were made to reach each resident, some were not home when interviewers called. Some did not respond to communications or refused to be interviewed. This resulted in a reduced number of actual interviews conducted.

Approximately 300, 45-minute interviews were completed out of an estimated total of 550. The accuracy of this survey is projected to be within 2%.

Focus of Survey Questions

The survey questions focused on five major areas:

1) local awareness of who the company is and what it actually does

2) awareness of and about perceived odors emanating from the plant

3) awareness of and about the state of nearby Rancocas Creek and Sybron's releases of treated wastewater to it

4) exploration of neighbors' interest in communications from and about SCT on a routine and continuing basis and ways to improve SCI's community activities and relations

5) identification of neighbors actual notification concerns, what they want to be notified about and communications preferences.

Summary of Survey Findings

The principal findings of this survey are as follows:

Recognition Highest
Among Nearest Neighbors
Recognition of the Company's name was substantially higher among Phase I partici-

(continued on page 5)

Highlights of Survey Results

- 83% know what SCI is, and 70% feel that the Company is a valuable member of the Community
- 68% never or seldom smell odors
- 68% were not aware that SCI releases only treated wastewater to Rancocas Creek
- 78% think that SCI should do more to communicate with its neighbors, and 68% favor establishment of a Neighborhood Advisory Committee
- 87% signed up for the Prompt Notification and Inquiry System, and 93% wish to be notified at any time (24 hours per day) of serious situations

---

Courtesy Sybron Chemicals, Inc.

NEIGHBORHOOD SURVEY RESULTS PROVIDE
INPUT FOR PINS START-UP
(continued from page 1)

pants (those neighbors closest to the plant) than among those interviewed in Phase II.

92% of residents surveyed in Phase I had heard of Sybron and 45% knew it is a chemical plant, while 41% did not know what the company does. Among Phase II respondents, 62% had heard of Sybron and 42% knew what it was. But almost two-thirds (65%) had no idea what the company manufactures and how its products are used.

Community Values SCI

Asked if they considered SCI to be a valuable member of the community:
70% of the respondents said yes. Asked how the company could improve its community standing, however, 78% either didn't know or had no opinion.

Neighbors Want Better Communication

A strong consensus felt that the company should improve its methods of communicating with its neighbors. 78% said SCI should do more to communicate about what it does.

Many (45%) even suggested to interviewers that a newsletter or brochure would help achieve this objective. A majority of respondents (55%) expressed a strong desire to know more about operations.

Proposed Neighborhood Committee Seen as Helpful

Asked if SCI should play a more active role in the community through a Neighborhood Advisory Committee, formed to permit neighbors to communicate and plan programs directly with SCI's management, 68% of respondents felt such a group would be effective and helpful.

Awareness Levels of Water Treatment Plant Vary

Asked if they knew of any wastewater treatment plants in the area, 68% of Phase I respondents said yes while 23% said no. Conversely, only 31% of the Phase II respondents knew of such a facility, while 67% did not.

Most Neighbors Seldom Smell Odors

Nearly half the residents in Phase I (45%) said they could tell the difference between odors from SCI's facility and the local Municipal Utilities Authority (MUA) treatment plant, while most in Phase II (69%) could not.

Most in Phase I, however (51%) said they seldom smelled anything; 26% said they often smelled odors; and 9% said they always did. In Phase II, 41% said they **never** smell anything.

Residents Have Differing Concerns about Odors

Some expressed concern or fear when they smelled odors; 44% said "yes" and 43% said "no".

But, most said they would be less concerned if they knew what the smell was and that it presented no health problem (61%).

A strong consensus (62%) felt that SCI and MUA should form a joint team to examine odor and possible solutions

Wastewater Treatment Mandate Eases Concerns Over Releases

Most Phase I respondents (63%) were aware that SCI normally releases wastewater to Rancocas Creek, while most in Phase II (72%) did not. A majority (68%) did not know that only treated wastewater is released. A majority of respondents (62%) said they were less concerned when informed that the company only releases treated wastewater which must meet DEP water quality standards.

Majority of Respondents Sign Up for Notification System

Respondents were almost unanimous in their conviction that SCI should notify its neighbors by telephone in the event of an incident at the plant.

88%, respectively, agreed, citing the speed and effeciency of telephone communications.

However, 42% of the respondents also cited their desire for a back-up system, such as a Civil Defense siren or door-to-door notification, to augment the telephone program.

Resident Say Local Officials Should Play Active Role

Almost all respondents felt SCI and the Pemberton Township Emergency Planning Committee, or Central Dispatch, should work jointly to develop the proposed emergency notification system.

Asked what other organizations should be involved in the development of the system, some Phase I respondents cited emergency services (15%), state and federal regulatory agencies (11%) and local government (18%). A large number (47%), however either did not know or had no opinion.

37% said they would be willing to commit time to a community group to help develop and implement the system.

Health, Safety Cited as Key Factors for Notification

A strong consensus of neighbors (78%) said they would feel more secure if the Prompt Inquiry and Notification System were already in operation.

A majority (59%) would want to be notified only about serious accidents which could affect health and safety.

Majority Sign Up for Notification Program

Neighbors were almost unanimous (93%) in their desire to be notified about a serious incident affecting community health and safety at any time of the day or night, 24 hours a day.

— 5 —

Steve Adler, SCI Vice President of Human Resources, displays a copy of the Neighborhood Survey Results, which were reported to the Pemberton Township Environmental Commission on January 25. The survey findings will assist the Company in implementing its Prompt Inquiry and Notification System during February.

The vast majority of respondents (87%) signed up for the free Prompt Inquiry and Notification System at the conclusion of their interview.

SCI also presented an initial action plan to respond to the survey findings. According to Adler, "We will be working hard to improve and expand communications with our neighbors, the community, local officials, and the press." Among the steps that will be taken are: publication of "Community Update", more attendance at local meetings, exploring plans for neighborhood advisory groups, implementation of PINS, and aggressively pursuing ways to reduce or eliminate sources of odor problems.

HOLIDAY FOOD BASKET PROGRAM
(continued from page 2)

Through the efforts of 26 employees from all departments and operations, SCI was able to collect food donations from all areas of the facility, package the food for distribution, and then (in teams of 2 or 3 employees) personally deliver the food baskets to each recipient. "We were also very pleased to have Terry Lee Wagner and Donald Fonda, family members of Randy Fonda, helping with the program. Donald Fonda, who dressed up as Santa Claus, gave the program the perfect finishing touch," said Steve Adler.

Everyone who volunteered to help with the program experienced a great sense of satisfaction in being able to personally see the response from those who received the food baskets. Additionally, it was an opportunity for many employees, from all levels within the company, who would ordinarily have no work-related contact, to join together in support of a worthy cause, and develop a greater sense of camaraderie. This also benefits SCI's operations.

Each food basket contained a wide variety of staples and canned goods, along with dairy and baked items. Some of the items provided were low salt/low sugar and smaller sizes, in keeping with the needs of many senior citizens.

Exhibit 5–2b   The PINS System

SYBRON CHEMICALS INC.
introduces

PINS

THE
"PROMPT INQUIRY and
NOTIFICATION SYSTEM"

INQUIRY HOT-LINE
894-0400

Courtesy Sybron Chemicals, Inc.

PINS is a computerized, telephone based communications system which both takes and makes calls to neighboring subscribers, providing them with pre-recorded phone messages on the current status of plant operations.

PINS is being used by Sybron to provide a 24 hour telephone communications resource neighbors can use to find out about events or incidents at Sybron's manufacturing facility on Birmingham Road in Pemberton. These telephone reports will be recorded and updated frequently by a Sybron official.

The PINS communications system consists of two separate computerized systems. One is called INQUIRY, which handles incoming calls from neighbors, and the other is called NOTIFICATION, which will be used by Sybron to automatically call subscribing neighbors to tell them about significant situations which may have occurred at the plant. Here's how they work and will be used.

INQUIRY

The INQUIRY system can be called by a subscriber at any time. Several calls can be taken by the system at the same time to minimize busy signals.

The call will be answered and a recorded message will be played telling briefly about the status of plant operations at that time. The message will also include the time of the recording and name of the individual recording the message. The INQUIRY HOT-LINE number is 894-0400.

At the end of the message each caller will have an opportunity to leave their own message, up to one minute in length. Neighbors using INQUIRY can report about odors or any situation they feel appropriate. They can also leave their name and number if they want to be contacted. Plant personnel will periodically check INQUIRY for messages which are left and, if required, will return calls as soon as they can. Experience operating the system will allow us to minimize our response time.

INQUIRY information will include messages about:

the status of the plant during each work shift

occasional community/or neighborhood public service messages

reports and facts about significant incidents which have occurred at the plant

unusual situations, such as odors, of which Sybron is aware

additional updates on special situations or events

NOTIFICATION

This companion system handles outgoing calls to subscribers. The computerized telephone system has been programmed with the phone numbers and residence locations of each subscriber. Using NOTIFICATION, the company will be able to simultaneously call the now over 300 subscribing neighbors to the PINS program in about 20 minutes.

If the line is busy or there is no answer, PINS will retry several times later. If there is an answering machine on the line, part of the PINS message may be lost since it is given as soon as a phone is connected. However, subscribers can then call the INQUIRY number to hear a report on the situation.

NOTIFICATION will only be used to report serious situations, such as those with a potential public health or safety impact which may have occurred at the plant and for occasional system test messages. Neighbors who completed the survey and signed up for PINS overwhelmingly said they wanted to be contacted only if there was a serious situation at the plant, and that they be contacted anytime of the day or night. That is the basis of the NOTIFICATION system.

In 1988, Macomb Community College, Warren, Michigan, won support from voters for millage and bond issue ballot proposals, both essential to the survival of the college. When both tax issues expired in 1992, the college conducted another campaign for their renewal. Exhibit 5–3a is a news release announcing the bond proposal for the November ballot. Exhibit 5–3b is a news release pointing out that it would be the students who would profit most from successful passage of the bond issue. Exhibit 5–3c is a newspaper advertisement used in the campaign. Exhibit 5–3d is a direct mail piece from the program, and Exhibit 5–3e is a photograph of Democratic candidate Bill Clinton at a college town meeting.

Case 5–3   **Funding Education in an Antitax Environment**

Macomb Community College, Warren, MI

Background

For 40 years, Macomb Community College has served the residents of Macomb County. During this time the College has grown from 87 to more than 28,000 in student enrollment. Since the mid-1970s, declining federal and state aid, skyrocketing health care costs and needs to establish new educational programs have forced the College to ask taxpayers for additional financial support.

In 1988, the College won support from voters for two separate ballot proposals (a millage & bond issue), which secured $32 million in new resources for the institution. Both tax issues expired in 1992 and needed to be renewed. A property tax freeze and a severe budget crisis in the State of Michigan meant that the College's financial position was further eroded. Renewing the two proposals was even more critical—and an even bigger challenge—in this predominantly anti-tax community of blue-collar traditions.

Research

Existing data and original research were used to develop major campaign strategies:

Courtesy Macomb Community College, Warren, MI

Research	Findings	Resulting Strategies
Telephone Survey of 400 residents/ Spring	Taxes viewed as #1 problem by residents	Emphasize renewal means no new taxes
Research Report on past renewal elections in Macomb County	Voters will support renewals before increases	Emphasize the word renewal
	More than 91% have passed in Macomb County	
Focus Groups	Can't ignore special groups (i.e., Seniors and likely voters)	Target literature to them; use them to test ballot language
Previous elections analysis	Simple message is needed to pass	"No New Taxes" message
Telephone Survey of 400 residents/ Fall	Major jump in concern for unemployment	Link education to stable employment

Planning

- Goals: 1. To establish that a "yes" vote would not raise taxes.
  2. To significantly increase support of voters in Macomb County's largest city, Warren (pop. 144,000)
  3. To successfully renew two ballot proposals (a millage & bond issue).

- Strategies: (1) Conduct a high-visibility public information campaign displaying MCC's commitment to providing residents with quality education while reinforcing the theme that support of the proposals will not raise taxes. (2) Reinforce the value of higher education.

- Target Audiences: Those who make the decision (voters), those who have a direct stake in the success of the institution (employees, students, alumni, vendors, donors, county decisionmakers and business owners), and those who influence discussion on ballot proposals in the county (senior citizen groups, ethnic groups and the media).

- Message: Passage of the proposals will not raise taxes.
- Budget: Ballot proposal public information program:
    $61,000
    Related recruitment activities: $29,500

Execution

- Clinton/Bush Visits — In 1988, more than 97 percent of those attending a presidential event on an MCC campus supported the proposals. MCC again followed the strategy of inviting the two main candidates in the 1992 presidential election to campus. Bill Clinton visited the College twice, while George Bush came to MCC once during the last month of the campaign. More than 15,000 voters came to campus during the visits. MCC students and staff actively worked the crowd to distribute millage literature. Local and national media attention was focused on MCC.
- Endorsements — Endorsements from 25 community, business, media, labor, education and professional groups provided third party credibility. Their names were printed in literature and used in speeches. A citizens' group called Moving Macomb Forward Committee, which formed during previous campaigns, organized again to endorse and advocate for the proposals.
- Media Relations — Utilizing a combination of news releases, interviews, on-campus events and other media activities, the College was able to convey the message that renewal of the ballot proposals would not increase taxes, evidenced by endorsements for the proposal from one of the major Detroit area newspapers, the county's daily newspaper and a very important chain of weekly newspapers (12 of which are in Macomb County cities).
- Speaker's Bureau — The College proactively sought strategic speaking engagements to targeted groups such as civic organizations, student and senior citizen groups. Speeches about the proposals were made to more than 170 organizations, reaching more than 5,500 people.
- Targeted Communities — Warren, Michigan, the largest community in Macomb County, had held the most opposition in the past to MCC issues. With that in mind, the College

hired a private consultant to give special attention to this city. The consultant arranged for literature and speeches to be delivered to special civic, social, ethnic and senior citizen groups within this community. Special interviews also were arranged for the College president with Warren's two weekly newspapers.

- Survey News Conference — Because of past voting patterns in presidential elections, Macomb County is considered a bellwether community. The news media and the political parties themselves look to Macomb County for information about how the rest of America will vote. The College took advantage of this situation and added presidential voter opinion questions to its bi-annual survey. The results were released at a news conference, which focused attention on the College.

- Voter Registration — A voter registration drive sponsored by the College and the Detroit Free Press resulted in more than 550 new students, staff and resident registration. The drive focused attention on the upcoming election date and information on the drive was included in a newspaper column. Several student organizations and local businesses volunteered to register voters and spread the word.

- On Campus — Student involvement again played a key role in the campaign. A theme message, "60 Seconds of Straight Facts," spelled out exactly what the proposals meant to MCC and reminded students to vote. Posters were put up in every classroom (356) and on bulletin boards and walls throughout all three campuses. The same message was featured in a small tabletop display piece that was placed on lounge, cafeteria and other tables throughout campus. It also was used on a bookmark that was distributed to students. The College president also offered MCC's south and center campus students a special presentation called "60 Minutes of Straight Talk," which explained the proposals. Students organized a "chalk blitz" and covered all campus sidewalks with a vote message the week before the election.

- Internal Communications — A steady flow of ballot proposal information ran in 15 bi-weekly issues of the internal newsletter, mailed to 1,800 full and part-time employees. Campaign buttons were distributed twice with fact sheets to all employees. The College President personally solicited support from faculty, managers, union leaders and other staff.

- Print Collateral — Letters were mailed to target audiences announcing the ballot proposals; buttons, posters and fact sheets were distributed at special events, extensive coverage was placed in the alumni magazine and legislative newsletter, and a new newsletter to students was created.

- Higher Education Week — Held three weeks before the election, this week of special events celebrated the value of higher education. Activities included MCC trustees riding in a local Columbus Day Parade, a transfer fair for students considering moving on to a four-year college or university, a high school and college fair for students interested in attending MCC, four newspaper ads that highlighted education in the community, a teleconference on leadership in the '90s, and various student activities throughout the three campuses.

- Essay Contest — For the fifth year in a row, MCC and the county's daily newspaper sponsored the annual "Why I Want a College Education" essay contest for junior and senior high school students. More than 450 students from 40 county high schools (the most ever to compete) submitted essays for an opportunity to win a $75 U.S. Savings Bond and a college dictionary. Winners were honored at a reception during Higher Education Week.

Evaluation

The campaign successfully achieved its goals:

1. Voters in the August primary election approved the millage renewal by a vote of 46,718 to 39,945. The bond renewal failed by a narrow margin. It was placed on the November general election ballot and passed by a vote of 153,049 to 130,774.

2. Overall performance in the City of Warren improved dramatically. The "yes" vote on the bond issue was increased by six percent from the August primary to the November general.

3. In a post-election telephone survey, voters recognized the campaign message that a "yes" vote would not raise taxes by a two to one margin (Yes 52.5%, No 23.0%, DK/NA 24.6%).

The $90,500 investment in this community relations program netted $32 million in new resources for the College!

Exhibit 5–3a   News Release Announcing the Bond Proposal

105-92

News Release

Macomb
Community
College

Catherine B. Ahles
Vice President for
College Relations
14500 Twelve Mile Road
Warren, Michigan 48093-3896
(313) 445-7244

FOR IMMEDIATE RELEASE

August 21, 1992
Contact: Bob Rini
445-7051

MCC Bond Proposal Will Be On November 3 Ballot

On Tuesday, August 18, the Macomb Community College Board of Trustees approved the placement of a funding proposal on the November 3 ballot. The proposal seeks reauthorization to sell $15.9 million in bonds to finance the renovation of College facilities and the replacement of equipment. It would not increase the current tax rate

The bond proposal first appeared on the August 4 ballot along with a request to renew a one-third mill levy for four years. The millage supports the continued operation and development of the College's University Center. At the University Center, Macomb County residents can earn bachelors degrees through partnerships with senior colleges and universities. Voters approved the renewal, 46,024 to 39,640. The bond proposal was defeated 43,139 to 40,587.

"We have no choice but to ask voters to reconsider our request to sell bonds," said Daniel McCafferty, chairperson of the College's Board of Trustees. "We need the community's help if our institution is to keep pace with the educational needs of both students and the businesses that hire them."

McCafferty and other College administrators believe the defeat of the bond proposal was due, in part, to low voter turnout and confusion between bonding and millages.

- more -

Courtesy Macomb Community College, Warren, MI

"Issuing bonds is a common practice for public institutions but it is not as easy to explain as a millage," said McCafferty. "When a house needs extensive repairs, its owner will often take out a home equity loan. A bond is to a public institution what a loan is to an individual. Except, the interest rate for a bond is much less than what it is for a loan. For financing special projects that are not covered by an institution's general fund and require a large cash outlay, issuing bonds is the most prudent and practical way to go."

Special projects not covered by Macomb's general fund include removal of underground storage tanks, overhauling of ventilation systems, upgrading of lighting systems and installation of a telephone registration system. Many of these projects, which would be financed by the sale of bonds, are required by new state and federal regulations for air quality and environmental safety.

"We're not asking for luxuries. We're not asking for an increase in taxes. We're asking for the means to provide students with a quality education," said McCafferty. "We want the best for Macomb students. We hope the community feels the same."

Macomb Community College is one of the nation's leading community colleges. With an emphasis on student success, the College offers a variety of educational opportunities for updating occupational skills, exploring new careers, or preparing for transfer to a four-year college or university. The recently opened University Center at Macomb Community College offers bachelors degrees in 15 programs.

# # #

Exhibit 5–3b   News Release About Bonds' Benefits for Students

NR 145-92

News Release

Macomb
Community
College

Catherine B. Ahles
Vice President for
College Relations
14500 Twelve Mile Road
Warren, Michigan 48093-3896
(313) 445-7244

FOR IMMEDIATE RELEASE

November 4, 1992
Contact: Catherine B. Ahles
445-7244

Students Profit Most
From MCC Bond Continuation
Victory

"Students choosing Macomb Community College for their
education were the winners in tonight's election," said
College President Albert L. Lorenzo, following passage of
Macomb's bond continuation proposal in yesterday's general
election. Unofficial results place the margin of victory for
the proposal at 149,191 to 127,600, with 100 percent of the
precincts reporting.

The proposal asked voters to authorize the College to
borrow $15.9 million through the sale of general obligation
bonds. The College had recently paid off a loan for a like
amount and was in the position to borrow more without raising
the current tax rate. The bond sale will maintain the
average homeowner cost of about $1.69 a year after property
tax credits and federal income tax deductions.

"Passage of the ballot proposal preserves the
integrity of this institution and protects the community's
investment," said Lorenzo. "It enables the College to
continue to adapt so that it can meet the changing
educational needs of Macomb County residents."

Projects to be funded by the bond sale include the
expansion of the computer curriculum, installation of a
telephone registration system, compliance with state
environmental quality and safety standards, improvements in
handicapped access, and replacement of classroom furniture
and equipment.

"Many of our buildings are nearly 30 years old," noted
Lorenzo. "Just like a house, they will only increase in

value if they are taken care of." The money borrowed through
the bond sale, he added, will enable the College to protect
the community's investment.

"Macomb County residents have proven again that they
support this College and the ideal of accessible education,"
said Lorenzo. "We appreciate that support and credit it for
Macomb's reputation as a quality institution."

Macomb Community College is one of the nation's leading
community colleges. With an emphasis on student success, the
College offers a variety of educational opportunities for
updating occupational skills, exploring new careers, or
preparing for transfer to a four-year college or university.
The recently opened University Center at Macomb Community
College offers bachelors degrees in 15 programs.

\#

Exhibit 5–3c   Campaign Newspaper Advertisement

NO INCREASE IN TAXES

Macomb Community College
Equipment Replacement and Facilities Renovation
Bond Continuation Proposal

(near the end of your ballot)

✔ a <u>YES</u> vote will NOT increase your taxes. You will continue to pay what you pay now — about $1.69 a year for the average Macomb County taxpayer.

✔ a <u>YES</u> vote will allow the College to borrow the money needed to buy up-to-date teaching equipment, repair classrooms and protect your $220 million investment in Macomb Community College.

✔ a <u>YES</u> vote will make your community college better able to educate you, your children, and your neighbors for LIFETIME employment.

✔ a <u>YES</u> vote will create a safer community college with better lighting and security.

✔ a <u>YES</u> vote will NOT raise your taxes.

 ✔ **YES NOV. 3**

Paid for by the Moving Macomb Forward Committee, 54367 Queens Row, Shelby Township, MI 48316

Courtesy Macomb Community College, Warren, MI

Exhibit 5–3d   Direct Mail Piece

MOVING MACOMB FORWARD COMMITTEE

You can count on me to help pass Macomb Community College's
Millage Renewal Proposal and Bond Continuation Proposal by:

_____ Voting YES on August 4

_____ Endorsing the proposals

_____ Sending reminder to vote cards to friends and neighbors

_____ Working a voting precinct on August 4

_____ Identifying speaking engagements

_____ Using my name in printed material or newspaper advertising

_____ Reminding my family and friends to VOTE YES on
August 4

_____ Wearing a button that says "Vote YES August 4"

_____ Stuffing envelopes

_____ **MAKING A CONTRIBUTION OF** _____
(Please make check payable to Moving Macomb Forward
Committee)

Mailing Address:

NAME_____

ADDRESS_____

CITY/ZIP_____

PHONE_____(HOME)_____(BUSINESS)

Please return to: Moving Macomb Forward Committee
54367 Queens Row
Shelby Township, MI 48316

54367 Queens Row   Shelby Township, MI   48316

Courtesy Macomb Community College, Warren, MI

Exhibit 5–3e   Photograph of Democratic Candidate Bill
                      Clinton at a College Town Meeting

Courtesy Macomb Community College, Warren, MI

Chapter 6   Public Affairs and Government Relations

In the last 10 or 15 years many U.S. corporations have subsumed what was formerly known as government relations within the broader enterprise now called public affairs. To add further semantic confusion, the U.S. government in the early 1980s decreed that the term *public affairs* would replace *public information* in all its departments and agencies.

Our principal concern here will be with how the enactment of legislation is influenced. This process includes the creation of political coalitions, direct and indirect lobbying, political action and political education activities, communication on political issues, and political support activities.

Research

The research process of public affairs includes investigation of the practitioner's client or organization, the opportunity or problem that accounts for the need for communication — including the important area of issues management — and the audiences to be targeted for public affairs programs.

Client Research

Client research for public affairs is similar to that for other forms of public relations. Background information about the client or organization should be obtained, including its personnel, financial status, and reputation, especially with government and community audiences. The practitioner should pay particular attention to past and present relations with the government and the community, along with any particular client strengths or weaknesses in these areas. Finally, the practitioner should catalog all opportunities for profitable communication with government or community audiences.

Opportunity or Problem Research

In public affairs programs, the process of issues management can make assessment of the client's opportunity or problem much easier. *Issues management* consists of listing and giving priority to all issues of interest to the client and then determining options and strategies for dealing with them. This process includes assessing political risks and monitoring social and political developments of concern to the client at the local, state, national, and international levels. An examination of each of these areas on a priority basis is a useful means of targeting the client's public affairs program.

Audience Research

The final aspect of research for public affairs consists of identifying target audiences, the necessary data regarding each one, and the methods of research necessary to obtain this information.

Public affairs programs target three audiences: community publics, government, and ancillary publics — this last group consisting of client allies, constituents of legislators, and media that reach both of them. Community publics were examined in the preceding chapter (see Exhibit 5–a). Government publics can be considered at the federal, state, county, or city level; they and the ancillary publics are listed in Exhibit 6–a.

Data necessary for understanding members of the legislative branches of government include officials' voting records on issues of concern to the client; their general attitudes or past and present reactions to the client; the size, location, and general demographics of their voting constituencies; their committee assignments; and their general interests and areas of expertise. Government officials in the executive branch may or may not hold elective office; this is their single most important characteristic. Beyond that, the nature and authority of the offices they hold, along with as much background about them as possible, should prove helpful. For officials in both legislative and executive positions, of course, the highest priority information about them is their degree of involvement with each issue or piece of legislation affecting the client, along with their stand and how they are expected to vote.

Methods of gathering information about government officials are usually nonquantitative. Voting records or accomplishments are public knowledge and easily accessible. Beyond that, conducting surveys among officials is usually not feasible. Thus, the practitioner must rely on other sources of information, such as conversations with staff people, the officials' past behavior, and their public statements regarding issues of concern to the client.

Research on the ancillary publics listed in Exhibit 6–a is also of considerable value. Allies of the client must be identified and cultivated with the goal of building a coalition. The home districts, communities, and constituents of legislators must also be identified and studied. Finally, mass and specialized media for reaching constituents and client allies should be identified, and media contacts lists should be prepared, as discussed in Chapter 3.

Exhibit 6–a   **Government and Ancillary Publics**

Government Publics

Federal
  Legislative branch
    Representatives, staff, committee personnel
    Senators, staff, committee personnel
  Executive branch
    President
    White House staff, advisers, committees
    Cabinet officers, departments, agencies, commissions
State
  Legislative branch
    Representatives, delegates, staff, committee personnel
    Senators, staff, committee personnel
  Executive branch
    Governor
    Governor's staff, advisers, committees
    Cabinet officers, departments, agencies, commissions
County
  County executive
  Other county officials, commissioners, departments

City
    Mayor or city manager
    City council
    Other city officials, commissions, departments

Ancillary Publics

    Allies
    Constituents of legislators
    Media
        Mass media
        Specialized media
          Trade
          Allied organizations' publications
        Constituent media

Objectives

As in other forms of public relations, objectives for public affairs programs should be specific and quantitative.

Impact Objectives

A sampling of impact objectives for public affairs includes such statements as:

1. to increase knowledge of the client's activities and field of operations among legislators (by 50 percent during the current year)
2. to create or enhance favorable attitudes toward the client among officials (by 30 percent before the February vote)
3. to influence a favorable vote on a bill (by 30 members of the House of Representatives during the current session)

Output Objectives

Output objectives represent the effort of the practitioner without reference to potential audience impact. Such objectives might use such statements as:

1. to make oral presentations to 30 lawmakers
2. to distribute printed information to 45 lawmakers

Programming

Public affairs programming includes the same four planning and execution elements used in other forms of public relations: (1) theme and messages, (2) action or special event(s), (3) uncontrolled and controlled media, and (4) principles of effective communication.

Theme and Messages

Always be aware that government audiences may be the most knowledgeable and sophisticated of all audiences for public relations communication. For this reason, the use of catchy themes or slogans may not be helpful; at times they can even be counterproductive. When addressing public affairs programming to ancillary audiences, however, more traditional use of themes or slogans may be appropriate. Messages, of course, should be carefully coordinated with the program objectives and actions or special events.

Action or Special Event(s)

Public affairs programming, like other forms of public relations, is structured around actions and special events. The practitioner should review the types found in Exhibit 2–c.

The actions unique to public affairs programming are:

1. fact finding
2. coalition building
3. direct lobbying
4. grassroots activities (indirect lobbying)
5. political action committees
6. political education activities
7. communications on political issues
8. political support activities

Fact Finding. Information gathering is an important aspect of public affairs. It includes attendance at openly conducted hearings, generally scheduled by both the legislative and executive branches of government when considering legislation or regulations. This monitoring function is indispensable for all public affairs programs.

In addition to monitoring hearings, fact finding often includes exchanging information with government officials, representatives of trade associations or interest groups, and other sources of reliable data. Fact finding may also include entertainment, since the relaxed atmosphere of most social gatherings can be conducive to exchanging information.

A final aspect of fact finding is the reporting of data and findings to the client, along with recommendations for appropriate responses.

Coalition Building. It is useful to organize groups or individuals with a common interest in the passage or defeat of legislation or regulations. Such coalitions can be much more effective in attaining goals than groups or individuals working alone. Coalitions can pool such resources as staff time, legal help, and printing and mailing costs. Working together, they can set priorities and devise operational strategies more effectively. In brief, the building of coalitions is one of the most important and effective tactics in public affairs.

Direct Lobbying. The two "core" activities of public affairs are direct and indirect lobbying. In direct lobbying, the practitioner contacts legislators or officials who can influence the passage or defeat of a bill or proposed regulation. It is an overt advocacy process, although it takes the sometimes subtle forms of information exchange and hospitality.

Information exchange includes providing the lawmaker or official with data about the client's field of interest and the effect the proposed legislation or regulation would have on this field. The practitioner, or lobbyist, usually makes an authoritative oral presentation, including the publicity potential for the legislator or official and the potential interest or impact of the proposals on constituents. These two aspects — *publicity value* and *constituent interest* — strike the most responsive chords in the ears of legislators or officials. They should always be central to a public affairs presentation. In addition to presentations, the practitioner usually offers the official a sample draft of the proposed legislation or regulation that incorporates the views of the client. Finally, information exchange may include providing authoritative testimony or offering witnesses for the hearings that are usually held in conjunction with proposed legislation or regulations. The practitioner often writes the testimony that is usually given by the client or the chief executive officer of the client's organization.

The second form of direct lobbying is still more subtle than information exchange. It involves offering *hospitality* to the legislator or agency official. The days of mink coats, yachting trips, weekends in hunting lodges, and the like have passed. Legislators and agency officials are now afraid of the ubiquitous investigative journalist, constantly in search of wrongdoing in high places. Nonetheless, hospitality still plays an important role in public affairs, or, more particularly, in lobbying. Lawmakers and agency officials often accept invitations to social functions sponsored by influential associations or corporations. These social gatherings provide a relaxed and conducive atmosphere for the subtle conduct of the business of public affairs.

Grassroots Activities. Indirect lobbying, or grassroots activities, is the second of the two core aspects of public affairs. This form of indirect lobbying involves mobilizing support for or opposition to proposed legislation or regulations at the state or local level, especially in the home districts of elected legislators. In the case of government departments or agencies, this grassroots level may be the location where a large agency is considering constructing or closing an installation that will profoundly affect the local economy.

Grassroots activities include working with national, state, or local mass media; the use of interpersonal communication; and the orchestration of direct mail or letter writing campaigns to bring constituent pressure on legislators or officials.

The grassroots use of the mass media includes publicizing the client's position in national, state, or local media, demonstrating that this position will be beneficial to the media audience. This action is usually performed in cases where an elected official is in opposition to the client's position or is uncommitted. The practitioner, on behalf of the client, will use all feasible forms of media, including paid advertising, to generate news coverage about the situation. If the legislator has taken a stand contrary to that of the client's, the media messages will call attention to that, to voting records, and to the harm such a position will bring to the constituency. Care must be taken not to engage in overkill in this endeavor. In some cases, besieged legislators have also used the media, successfully portraying themselves as the victims of "fat-cat lobbyists."

A second effective type of grassroots activity is the use of various forms of interpersonal communication at the national, state, or local level. This includes targeting key groups of opinion leaders in the home districts of legislators and getting expert and highly credible representatives of the client's viewpoint invited to their meetings, conferences, or conventions as guest speakers.

In addition to addressing important grassroots audiences, the client can meet with key executives at breakfast, with editorial staffs of newspapers, or with small groups of community leaders.

Dyadic interactions may include interviews and meetings with key public officials, executives, and/or union leaders.

Interpersonal communication, then, in the form of speeches, small group meetings, or dyadic interactions can be a highly useful form of grassroots activity.

Finally, grassroots activities culminate in the orchestration of mass-mailing campaigns at the national, state, or local level. These mailings are planned to bring pressure directly on legislators or officials. They can be orchestrated by small or large membership groups, associations, or other affected groups. The National Rifle Association is the membership group that uses mass mailing most effectively to influence the course of national legislation. The NRA boasts the ability to mobilize its membership within 24 hours to flood Congress with enough constituent mail to shape the course of gun legislation.

Of the two public affairs core methods, grassroots activities usually prove more effective. These actions — working with mass media, interpersonal communication, and direct mail campaigns — can provide legislators and other officials with unmistakable evidence regarding the will of the electorate.

Political Action Committees.   Political action committees (PACs) are an outgrowth of the reform in federal election campaign practices that followed the Watergate scandal. A PAC is a group established for the purpose of contributing an organization's money toward the election of political candidates. The Federal Election Commission permits PACs to contribute a maximum of $5,000 per candidate per election. Thus, PACs may contribute a total of $10,000 to a candidate who is in both a primary contest and the general election.

Since their inception in the mid-1970s, PACs have enjoyed phenomenal growth. Each year PACs provide funds to several thousand candidates for federal office. Such money may be solicited (but not coerced) from an organization's employees. Large groups, such as the banking and finance industry, labor unions, and the insurance industry, have the resources of hundreds of PACs at their disposal. Of course, PAC money can be used collectively for candidates who support legislation favorable to an entire industry.

The use of such funds to support the campaigns of elected officials guarantees access to those officials. Thus, PACs have become a significant force in public affairs.

Political Education Activities. During the past 20 years, corporations have increasingly attempted to politicize their employees. They issue newsletters on the major political issues confronting given industries along with the company's positions on these issues. Employees are instructed in the methods of grassroots lobbying: writing letters to legislators, taking action through membership groups, or visiting legislators in their home district offices. Moreover, some large organizations provide their employees with political education seminars. Elected officials and candidates are invited to corporate headquarters, where they make presentations and meet groups of employees. In return, the officials are often given honoraria, usually in accordance with legally allowable limitations. Political education activities, then, play an increasingly important role in the conduct of public affairs programs.

Communications on Political Issues. Corporations communicate on political issues chiefly through advocacy advertising and targeted communications, such as direct mail to community leaders or special audiences.

Advocacy advertising has become increasingly popular since the early 1970s, when Herbert Schmertz, vice president for public affairs of Mobil, decided that major media outlets seemed interested only in condemning large oil companies for their alleged role in the creation of the gasoline shortages of the day. Schmertz abandoned the use of news releases and other uncontrolled media to give the oil companies' side of the controversy. Instead he began to buy advocacy advertising space in the nation's most prestigious newspapers and later bought time on cooperative broadcast networks. Schmertz's success in calling attention to his corporation's political views gave rise to a boom in the corporate use of advocacy advertising. Today it is impossible to read the editorial section of the Sunday edition of a major metropolitan newspaper without encountering myriad advocacy ads. Their proliferation has probably diminished their effectiveness, but they remain a major vehicle for corporate communication on political issues.

Political communications can also be aimed at community leaders or occupational groups. Professors of communication, for example, are frequently the recipients of slick reprints of speeches by the chief executive officers of television networks and other corporations. These reprints are only one of many forms of mailings to community leaders and members of various professions.

Political Support Activities. A final public affairs action is the support a corporation, association, or other organization offers an incumbent legislator or a candidate. Some organizations offer free media training, with expert consultants hired for the occasion. Guidance in effective public speaking, group communication management techniques, and other interpersonal communication skills are also offered. Some organizations provide volunteers to work on political campaigns. Finally, political support can be offered in the form of expertise and other services needed for orchestrating election campaign events such as fund-raisers and testimonial dinners. Donations of facilities, recruiting celebrities to appear at the events, and any number of other services can be offered.

Like other forms of public affairs activities, political support can assure access to the officeholder at a later time.

Uncontrolled and Controlled Media

The practitioner's communication with public officials must largely be direct and interpersonal. The lobbyist or practitioner of public affairs uses uncontrolled media at the grassroots level. However, all forms of controlled media can be used both in direct contact with lawmakers and in grassroots communication with constituents. In general, then, the uniqueness of public affairs communication lies in the interaction that occurs directly with lawmakers and officials. To be effective, it should emphasize interpersonal, preferably one-on-one, communication.

Effective Communications

The communication flow in public affairs is best described as triangular (see Exhibit 6–b). The flow is targeted ultimately at lawmakers, in the legislative branch, or at regulation-makers, in the executive branch. Thus, communication is generally initiated from the private sector and flows appropriately toward those two targets. In many cases, however, communication is initiated in the executive branch. Presidents, governors, and mayors may lobby their respective legislative branches for the passage or defeat of a law. Sometimes officials in the executive branch lobby a particular audience in the private sector to bring pressure on the legislative branch. Legislators often refer to this as "going over their heads to the people." Some U.S. presidents have been particularly fond of this form of lobbying.

Exhibit 6–b   **A Public Affairs Communication Model**

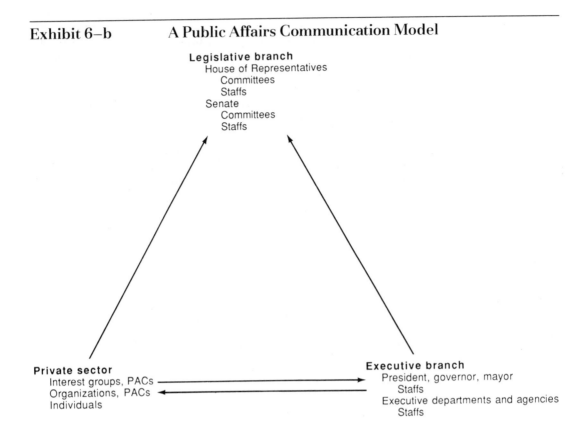

The nine principles of effective communication discussed in Chapter 2 all apply in public affairs. Of special concern, however, is *selective exposure.* Public affairs, more than other forms of public relations, deals with legislation and regulations that are controversial. Therefore, it is important that the practitioner categorize the targeted receivers based on their agreement or disagreement with the public affairs messages. As suggested in Chapter 2, the terms that coincide with the Likert scale can be useful in this process. Thus, targeted legislators or other officials should be rated as "positives," "somewhat positives," "undecideds," "somewhat negatives," or "negatives." The selective exposure principle is applicable in this situation. The practitioner should thus begin persuasive efforts with the positives. Next, to be targeted are the somewhat positives, then the undecideds, and last, if at all, the somewhat negatives. The pure negatives have hardened attitudes against the practitioner's cause and should not be targeted for communication. To communicate with those strongly opposed to the message is usually counterproductive; it simply makes them more determined and sometimes more active in their opposition.

Thus, the selective exposure principle of effective communication bears reiteration because of its special significance in public affairs. All other principles of effective communication should also be observed. Each one can contribute to the success of public affairs programs.

Evaluation

In public affairs, the measurement of impact and output objectives is somewhat different from the general methods of assessment presented in Chapter 2.

Evaluating Impact Objectives

There are two differences in the measurement of impact objectives for public affairs. First, message exposure, message comprehension, and message retention are not measured in the same way. The primary target audiences for public affairs are legislators and officials. The media, however, are used essentially to reach the *constituents* of these public officials. And though the officials themselves are usually media sensitive, message exposure in public affairs usually refers to *constituent* exposure.

The second difference in the measurement of impact objectives is that surveys or other quantitative methods of research cannot be used with the primary target audiences because legislators and officials will not usually take the time to respond to such PR surveys. Thus, nonquantitative measurements of message exposure and message retention are used in assessing the results of informational objectives.

Message comprehension, of course, can be measured, as usual, by the application of readability formulas. This will give the practitioner an indication of the *potential* for comprehension, not actual audience comprehension, which can be measured using nonquantitative research methods.

These same generalizations are applicable to attitude and behavioral objectives. Surveys among the primary audience are generally impossible, so the practitioner must rely on the nonquantitative research methods discussed earlier in this chapter—voting records or accomplishments, conversations, use of the practitioner's materials, and public statements by the targeted legislators or officials. At the grassroots level, of course, surveys are useful and should be employed to evaluate the impact objectives.

Evaluating Output Objectives

The practitioner needs to evaluate both forms of public affairs objectives. Output objectives can be measured through counting presentations and materials and through making qualitative value judgments. This is especially important in public affairs since surveys are impractical with the primary audiences. Evaluation of public affairs, then, ultimately focuses on observing the voting behavior or actions of legislators and other public officials. The practitioners in this chapter's cases accomplished all of their stated objectives remarkably well. In addition to informing their various targeted audiences, they also met their legislative or regulatory goals.

Summary

Research for public affairs concentrates on problem assessment through issues management and on identifying and understanding target audiences. Audiences are usually in the legislative or executive branch of government, at various levels. Information about these officials consists of voting records, accomplishments, and public stands on issues.

Impact and output objectives are both useful in public affairs. Impact objectives consist of providing the target audience with information or influencing its attitudes or behavior, in this case, voting behavior. Output objectives catalog the practitioner's communication efforts without reference to the desired impact.

The most essential activities in public affairs programming are fact finding, coalition building, direct lobbying, grassroots (indirect) lobbying, the use of political action committees, political education, communications on political issues, and political support activities. Of special significance in lobbying is the principle of selective exposure. Lawmakers to be lobbied should be categorized as "positives," "somewhat positives," "undecideds," "somewhat negatives," or "negatives." The positives through the undecideds should be targeted for lobbying; the somewhat negatives should be targeted with caution, and the negatives, not at all.

Evaluation is not the same for public affairs as for other forms of public relations. Media exposure or placement does not ensure contact with legislators, and legislators and officials are often unresponsive to PR surveys. Nonquantitative measurements of impact objectives are thus more useful. Output objectives, of course, are measured by the same means as usual — observation and quantification. The ultimate means of evaluation in public affairs, however, is the voting behavior of the target audience.

Readings on Public Affairs

Altschull, J. Herbert. *Agents of Power: The Role of the News Media in Public Affairs.* New York: Longman, 1984.

Bernays, E. L. "Operatives and Lobbyists vs. PR Professionals." *Public Relations Quarterly*, Summer 1985, pp. 27ff.

Berry, J. M. *The Interest Group Society.* Boston: Little, Brown, 1985.

Brown, James K. *Guidelines for Managing Corporate Issues Programs.* New York: The Conference Board, 1981.

Chase, Howard. *Issues Management: Origins of the Future.* Stamford, CT: Issues Action Publications, 1984.

Clark, Joe. "Business-Government Relations: Opening the Systems." *Business Quarterly*, Summer 1985, pp. 82ff.

Dominguez, George. *Government Relations: A Handbook for Developing and Conducting the Company Program.* New York: Wiley, 1982.

Gabriel, Edward M. "The Changing Face of Public Affairs in Washington." *Public Relations Quarterly* 37 (Winter 1992): 24ff.

Gollner, Andrew. *Social Change and Corporate Strategy: The Expanding Role of Public Affairs.* Stamford, CT: Issues Action Publications, 1984.

Heath, Robert L., and Richard A. Nelson. *Issues Management — Corporate Policymaking in an Information Society.* Beverly Hills, CA: Russell Sage Foundation, 1986.

"Issues Management in Public Relations" (special issue). *Public Relations Review* 16 (Spring 1990).

Lammers, Nancy, ed. *The Washington Lobby.* Washington, DC: Congressional Quarterly (annual publication).

Lusterman, Seymour. *Managerial Competence: The Public Affairs Aspects.* New York: The Conference Board, 1981.

Masterson, John. "Looming Legislative Shake Up to Alter Public Affairs Practice." *Public Relations Journal*, 48 June 1992, pp. 12ff.

Nagelschmidt, Joseph S. *The Public Affairs Handbook.* New York: AMACOM, 1982.

Pedersen, Wes. *Winning at the Grassroots: How to Succeed in the Legislative Arena by Mobilizing Employees and Other Allies.* Washington, DC: Public Affairs Council, 1989.

Sabato, L. J. *PAC Power: Inside the World of Political Action Committees.* New York: Norton, 1985.

Tate, Sheila. "Prescriptions to Avoid Disaster in Washington." *Public Relations Quarterly* 37 (Spring 1992): 24ff.

Wise, Jim. "Tracking Legislation." *Public Relations Journal*, 45 (September 1989), pp. 43–44.

Public Affairs Cases

As one of only three states without a dedicated transportation fund and with its funding from federal aid and bonds soon to expire, New York faced a worsening future of crumbling highways and collapsing bridges. The Crisis Program of New York, a public information group representing the state's construction industry, successfully educated New Yorkers, legislators, and the governor regarding the need for a dedicated transportation fund. Exhibits 6–1a and 6–1b are print advertisements used in the program. Exhibit 6–1c contains excerpts from a campaign brochure, and Exhibit 6–1d contains part of a campaign newsletter.

Case 6–1

New York's Road to Repair: Creating a Dedicated Transportation Fund

The Crisis Program/The Road Information Program, Albany, NY, with Ketchum Public Relations, Washington, DC

Situation

New York's highway system is not a pretty picture. Roads and bridges are crumbling, traffic congestion is worsening, and an already old system is growing older. Funding for road and bridge improvements comes mainly from federal aid and bonds that expire in early 1993. These monies have barely allowed New York to keep pace with a backlog of improvement needs.

Until this summer, New York was one of only three states that had no dedicated transportation fund. While the need for a dedicated fund had long been evident, so had the need to increase taxes to fuel the fund. However, the often heated legislative debate over tax hikes — plus Governor Mario Cuomo's opposition to dedicated funding — prompted support for voter-approved bonds for almost 10 years. As the state's budget gap widened and debt service ballooned by 1990, the public would not tolerate another transportation bond. With time running out, lawmakers had to find another source to fund the repair of New York's roads and bridges.

The Crisis Program (TCP) of New York, a public information group representing the state's construction industry, labor, and other business concerns, sought the creation of a stable transportation funding mechanism. Early in 1990, TCP asked Ketchum and

Courtesy The Crisis Program

its client, The Road Information Program (TRIP), a nonprofit highway transportation research organization in Washington, DC, to help build support for an adequate, permanent, and dedicated transportation fund in New York.

Research

TRIP, a long-established information resource, studied New York's road and bridge funding, the system's condition, how much money was needed, and how much was available for improvements. A public opinion survey, conducted by Apogee Research of Bethesda, Maryland, further showed that most New Yorkers wanted highway improvement to be one of the top priorities of the state's 1991 legislative session. This extensive research helped form the basis for TCP's messages.

Planning

The program objective was to focus public pressure on New York's lawmakers to make a firm decision on funding in 1991. Ketchum's strategy called for TCP to alert New Yorkers, primarily through the news media, as to the severity of the state's road and bridge problems and that funding for improvements was in jeopardy. The defined progressive goals were:

- To establish the need for increased and guaranteed highway funding
- To educate New Yorkers as to the general scope of the problems
- To show that New Yorkers are tired of poor roads and traffic jams — *they are willing to pay a higher gas tax as long as the revenues are dedicated to highway improvements*
- To continue to inform New Yorkers about the full impact of road and bridge failure

Strategy

Communicating strategies included:

- Localizing information specific to the state's different regions
- Releasing findings shortly before key political and legislative events
- Using officials and opinion leaders to promote highway funding needs.

Ketchum developed the following messages from TRIP's and Apogee's research:

- Almost half of New York's roads and bridges need improvements
- Overcrowding is putting more stress on an aging system
- Growing needs can barely be met with current funding
- Driving on ailing, crowded roads costs motorists money, wastes their time, and threatens their safety
- Inadequate highway funding is hampering New York's economic development
- New Yorkers want their roads and bridges fixed immediately

The audiences were:

- Consumer, business, and political media
- Business leaders, owners, and managers
- Community leaders and activists
- Motorists and voters
- Governor Cuomo and state legislators

The 18-month program was budgeted at $500,000 for public relations services, advertising, and expenses. Approximately 70 percent of the program was dedicated to public relations efforts and 30 percent was dedicated to advertising.

Execution

From June 1990 through July 1991, TCP made its most aggressive communication effort ever. Without formally lobbying New York's legislators. Ketchum launched for TCP a multilevel public information program supported by TRIP studies and other tenable research.

Ketchum's diverse media communications, based largely on data collected and analyzed by TRIP presented TCP as a credible resource on New York's highway transportation needs. Media events included:

- Press conferences and briefings: Five reports on New York's state and county highway needs and economic development were released at more than 30 press conferences and briefings from New York City to Buffalo. Ketchum timed conferences to draw attention to hearings and key legislative action. A "Report Card" study was released less than one week before Governor Cuomo's 1991 "State of the State" address, prompting his call for creation of a dedicated transportation fund.

- Public affairs talk shows: Ketchum booked approximately 50 TV and radio interviews in which TCP and TRIP spokespersons spoke at length about New York's transportation woes.
- Editorials: Major newspaper editorials, based on TCP releases, demanded the creation of a dedicated fund. Ketchum also wrote guest editorials for TCP that further clarified the state's needs.

Legislative contact was made in the form of public information. Not established as a lobbying group, TCP addressed lawmakers by educating them about the state's road and bridge needs. TCP's efforts included:

- Legislative testimony: Ketchum used TRIP findings to write TCP's testimonies before the New York State Assembly Committee on Transportation. TCP maintained an ongoing dialogue with legislators working toward the fund's creation.
- Lobbying tools: While TCP couldn't lobby, it could help lobbyists and TCP supporters with creative resources. Various lobbying tools were developed to draw legislators' attention to key transportation issues.

Other aspects of the program were:

- Advertising: This was used to guarantee delivery of TCP's messages, unchallenged by editorial interpretation. Provocative newspaper ads and an Albany billboard told citizens and lawmakers that New York was being threatened by the potential failure of its roads and bridges. Ads were created by Ketchum Advertising in New York, an Albany political cartoonist, and TCP staff.
- Communicating with "influentials": This was essential to building the support of New York's community, business, and

labor leaders. TCP spoke to dozens of groups statewide, distributing New York pocket highway fact cards and newsletters created by Ketchum, as well as other informative materials. Ketchum also produced two promotional videos to tell TCP's story and explain New York's highway needs. The videos debuted at TCP's 1990 and 1991 fund-raising dinners and have been used subsequently for the group's marketing efforts.

Evaluation

Our ultimate goal was met—history was made on July 23, 1991, when Governor Mario Cuomo signed into law a bill creating New York's first dedicated transportation fund. Supported by an increase in the state's Petroleum Business Tax and other driver-related user fees, it will pump $1.2 billion annually into the state's transportation system. It was Governor Cuomo who, in his "State of the State" address, reversed his long-standing opposition to dedication and provided leadership for the bill's passage. At the signing ceremony, Governor Cuomo publicly praised TCP's efforts in helping to create the legislation.

Widespread media coverage carried TCP's message to all levels of the state's society. Unsolicited newspaper editorials and legislators' news releases supporting dedicated funding were written based on TCP reports. At least 350 media placements included *The New York Times, The Albany Times Union, The Buffalo News,* WINS-AM and WOR-AM in New York City, and almost every local TV news program statewide. More than 1,400 citizens contacted TCP's office during its campaign, asking how they could support road and bridge improvement.

For almost a decade, legislative action on permanent transportation funding was stymied by differences of opinion. With Ketchum and TRIP's help, TCP spotlighted the problem, spurring lawmakers to ensure the preservation and improvement of New York's infrastructure.

Exhibit 6–1a   Print Advertisement

Break a campaign promise.

New York needs a dedicated highway fund.

We know you promised not to raise taxes. We admire the fact that you're standing by your convictions. Unfortunately, you're also standing by and watching New York's roads and bridges crumble away to nothing.

The time has come to finally do something about it. With the state budget on the table, let's finally bite the bullet and implement a statewide dedicated highway fund to help maintain, repair and improve our aging infrastructure.

New York needs it. New Yorkers want it. A recent survey shows that New York State residents would be in favor of a dedicated highway fund, even if it means higher taxes.†

So break a campaign promise that the voters want you to break.

For a change.

The Crisis Program. Let's put New York back together.

†Source: New York Transportation Survey, Apogee Research, Inc. Washington, D.C.

Exhibit 6–1b   Print Advertisement

If you don't think there's a problem with our roads and bridges you may need to have your head examined.

With all the pot holes, broken pavement, rusting girders and congestion, navigating your way around New York's ailing roads and bridges can be more than annoying. It can be downright dangerous.

What's more, the number of roads and bridges in such poor condition is reaching epidemic proportions. According to the New York State Department of Transportation, statewide, 48% of our bridges are structurally deficient. And 40% of all state maintained roads are in dire need of repair.

The time and money to repair and renovate our aging infrastructure is rapidly running out. What is Albany doing? Good question. Especially when a sound highway maintenance program with dedicated funding is vital to our future.

Let the decision makers know where you stand. Because if you don't we may be putting something far more valuable than our roads at risk.

For more information send us the coupon. Or call 1-518-452-1782.

The Crisis Program. Let's put New York back together.

> **Please send me the facts**
> on how we can deal with New York's aging infrastructure.
> Name_____
> Address_____
> City _____ State ____ Zip _____
> Phone_____ Fax _____
>
> The Crisis Program
> Box 12129, Albany, NY 12212
> 1-518-452-1782

THE CRISIS PROGRAM

VAL'TESS COUPON WILLIAMS

Exhibit 6–1c   Campaign Brochure

THE CRISIS PROGRAM
P.O. BOX 12129
ALBANY, NY 12212

"No matter where you live in New York State, your odds

ROAD CLOSED

are 50-50 that you will

be on a deficient bridge — every time you drive your car."

BRIDGE CLOSED

BULK RATE
U.S. POSTAGE
PAID
Permit No. 882
Albany, NY

Courtesy The Crisis Program

Imagine...

... if we heard a report that
half of our school buses were deficient.
We certainly wouldn't let our children ride them.
But we don't have an alternate road system
and we can't avoid the bridges.

We must fix the problem now!

The Crisis Program has been designed to alert
New Yorkers to the condition of their highways
and enlist their support in demanding a safer system.

The Crisis Program asks for your support in getting
the message across. For more information on how
you can help, please contact us at:

THE CRISIS PROGRAM
P.O. Box 12129 • Albany, New York • 12212
Phone 518 452-1782

New York can no longer afford to defer costly repairs, rehabilitation and maintenance that our roads and bridges desperately need. If our lawmakers do not develop new policies to fund these infrastructure projects *now*, we will pay an exorbitant, needless and tragic price for decades to come.

FACTS

- 40% of NY's state-owned roads are in poor or fair condition.

- 48% of NY's bridges are structurally deficient.

- NYS highway system ranks 11th nationally in size and carries the 4th largest traffic volume.

- NYS has the 3rd largest number of licensed motorists and the 4th largest number of registered vehicles in the U.S.

- NY's roads are among the oldest in the nation. Many NY bridges are older than average design life of 40 - 60 years.

- NYS is 1 of 3 states in the nation that *does not* have a separate state highway fund with dedicated revenues to repair its infrastructure (New York, Alaska, Rhode Island).

- NYS's highways are funded by 3 main sources:
    - 40% - Federal
    - 40% - Bond Act (expires in FY 1992)
    - 20% - N.Y.S. General Fund

- NYS's gasoline excise tax is 8¢ per gallon, has not changed since 1972 (2nd lowest in nation, lowest in northeast).

Subway column embedded in retaining wall.

Exhibit 6–1d   Campaign Newsletter

TCP Update

Volume 2, No 2 - August, 1991

The Crisis Program · P.O. Box 12129 · Albany, N.Y. · Phone 518-452-1782 · FAX 518-456-1198

CUOMO SIGNS DEDICATED HIGHWAY FUND BILL: TCP EFFORTS PAY BIG DIVIDENDS

Governor Mario M. Cuomo made history on July 23 when he signed into law a bill creating New York's first dedicated highway fund.

Governor Mario M. Cuomo signed into law a bill that will create a dedicated highway fund in New York State. The new law is expected to generate nearly $1.2 billion a year for improvement of the state's aging transportation infrastructure.

Both Governor Cuomo and Transportation Commissioner Franklin White praised the efforts of The Crisis Program, AGC, NYRIC, AAA, the County Highway Superintendents Association and organized labor as having been critical to the establishment of the historic legislation. "New York learned a painful lesson. That deferring the upkeep of its infrastructure during difficult fiscal times only increases the burden on future generations," Cuomo said at a ceremony in a sweltering Department of Transportation garage. "This legislation is a major step forward in securing the future of New York's highway rehabilitation efforts. By dedicating funds solely to the upkeep of our roads and bridges, we will ensure a continuing commitment to meeting our transportation needs."

Under the legislation, money from the state's gas tax, petroleum business tax, gross receipts tax and other fees paid by New York motorists will be dedicated to the fund beginning April, 1993. Use of the dedicated fund for highway improvements will begin upon the depletion of monies from New York's latest transportation bond issue, the $3 billion "Rebuild New York" package approved by voters in 1988. In 1983, voters approved a $1.25 billion transportation bond issue.

The legislation also provides for more than $340 million in state aid for local highway projects over the next two years. Earlier this year, there was much doubt about the availability of such funds because of the state's persistent budget problems.

Cuomo called the bill a "triumph of cooperation between *(continued on page 2)*

1

CUOMO SIGNS DEDICATED HIGHWAY FUND BILL
(continued)

the legislative and executive branches'' as sponsors of the landmark legislation, Assembly Transportation Committee Chairman Michael Bragman and Senate Transportation Committee Chairman Norman Levy, looked on.

"This law will eliminate the need for major transportation bond issues," Assemblyman Bragman said. "When the fund becomes active, New York State taxpayers can look forward to a 'pay-as-you-go' approach to meeting the state's transportation infrastructure needs."

"This legislation is a cornerstone of the goal of meeting our future funding of the capital needs both upstate and downstate," Senator Levy commented. "Up to 75 percent of the state's annual needs for the next capital program for state-owned highways and bridges will be in place....Today is not the conclusion; it's the beginning. The best is yet to be, and the best ᵕ yet to come."

The ceremony also included the signing of legislation that establishes a separate dedicated mass transit fund, although the Governor and the legislature were unable to agree on how much of the money should go to highways and how much to mass transit. They have promised to reach an agreement by year's end.

2

TCP WELCOMES NEW PRESIDENT

Thomas Longe

There's no doubt about it, Tom Longe is crystal clear on The Crisis Program's mission. "We have to make the public aware that they are going to benefit from highway improvements in the long run," said TCP's new president in a recent issue of <u>The Low Bidder</u>. The five-year AGC board member officially became TCP's president on April 1.

Longe, who is chief operating officer of D. A. Collins Construction Company, Inc., in Mechanicville, is well-known for his straightforward, shoot-from-the-hip style. As the "Rebuild New York" bond program nears its end, Longe has made the push for a dedicated highway fund TCP's primary focus.

(continued on page 3)

Cuomo Tips Hat to TCP - The Crisis Program president Tom Longe, left, and executive director Dan McCormack, center, joined Governor Mario M. Cuomo who praised TCP's role in the historic creation of New York's dedicated highway fund.

The discovery of minuscule traces of dioxin in its paper mill sludge product, BYPRO, created a problem for the Mead Corporation. For several years, Mead had used BYPRO as a substitute for missing topsoil in mine reclamation in southeast Ohio. Based on its research and analysis, Mead sought to communicate the negligible threat from BYPRO and to win state approval and public support for its use. Exhibit 6–2a is a Mead Paper position overview on BYPRO. Exhibit 6–2b is an excerpt from a Mead brochure on BYPRO.

Case 6–2   ## Mead's Sludge Management Program

Mead Corporation, Chillicothe, OH, with Edward Howard & Co., Akron, OH

Large parts of southeast Ohio look like the surface of the moon. Strip mining has left them barren and pitted, creating one of the state's most difficult environmental problems. Working with the Ohio Department of Natural Resources and the U.S. Department of Agriculture, Mead Paper had come up with what everyone thought was an ideal solution: Use paper mill sludge as a substitute for missing topsoil in mine reclamation.

Paper mill sludge produced by Mead's Chillicothe, Ohio, operations—known as Mead BYPRO—is loaded with nutrients essential for plant life. Its use in mine reclamation provided the state with a low-cost alternative to topsoil and Mead a practical method for disposing of the byproducts of the paper making process. Then came the discovery of minuscule traces of dioxin—a toxic chemical compound—in the BYPRO. This presented Mead with a major public affairs challenge: how to convince a skeptical public that BYPRO is safe and a benefit, not a threat.

This entry demonstrates how Mead combined a comprehensive scientific risk assessment with a strong environmental public relations program to produce a win-win solution for the state, the people of Ohio, environmentalists and the Mead Corporation.

Research

The research function assumes even greater than normal importance in the practice of environmental public relations. In the case of Mead's BYPRO, research data and scientific analysis on dioxin

Courtesy Mead Corporation, Fine Paper Division

was a foundation for the communications program. Research included a search of the literature on dioxin and health risks from every perspective — the EPA, the FDA, the Center for Disease Control, trade and industry publications, the American Paper Institute, information from environmental activist groups and publications as diverse as "Rachel's Hazardous Waste News" and "Environmental Toxicology and Chemistry." Extensive searches of electronic data bases through NEXIS and a comprehensive review of technical libraries were conducted. Interviews with authoritative sources ranging from leading toxicologists to several county directors of health were held. Additional research was done on other dioxin cases including Love Canal, Times Beach and Agent Orange.

To better understand local concerns and issues, research included a review of media coverage on BYPRO and other environmental matters. Publications by local environmental groups were analyzed. Research also included interviews with local public officials and opinion leaders.

The research clearly showed that dioxin at the levels contained in BYPRO — the low parts per trillion — was not a risk to public health or the environment. However, a review of all previous communication activities showed that little hard information on the dioxin content of BYPRO, or the almost infinitesimal risk involved, had been communicated by Mead or the State of Ohio. The net result showed that only a carefully-framed program of risk communication which dealt squarely with citizens' concerns could allay their fears and win acceptance for the program.

Planning

Three goals were established: (1) gain broad support for the use of BYPRO; (2) secure State approval of its use; and (3) increase landowners' willingness to use it. Based upon the research, three messages were developed. They were: (1) that scientific data and expert opinion showed negligible threat from the use of BYPRO in reclamation; (2) environmental benefits greatly exceeded any risk; and (3) Mead had acted in a way that earned the public's trust.

The program sought to open a dialogue with concerned citizens, to hear their views and to share information on Mead's BYPRO program, underlining Mead's reputation for honesty and corporate responsibility, and the company's economic and social contributions to the area for more than a century. The program strategy focused on a seven-county area using a mix of communications vehicles but emphasizing face-to-face contact with key media and opinion leaders. Communication strategy required that the tone of the program be positive and matter-of-fact in dealing with public concerns without getting bogged down in scientific jargon.

Mead needed to muster support of all those who had a stake in the company's operations in the area and to communicate with a variety of public interest groups and interested organizations. Careful monitoring of all opinion on the issue through the eyes and ears of Mead personnel and stakeholders was essential to respond to both problems and opportunities. Activities were planned to support legal work aimed at resolving litigation and in obtaining state government approval for wider applications of BYPRO.

Measurement of the program's success was Mead obtaining a permit from Ohio EPA to apply BYPRO, and then the amount of BYPRO put to use.

Execution

Work began in July 1987 and continued through 1990. Total budget for the entire program was approximately $150,000, including less than $5,000 for advertising. Major elements, aimed primarily at the people of southeast Ohio, their government, business and civic leaders and the local news media, consisted of:

- Three position papers — on dioxin, the need for mine reclamation and the social and economic benefits of Mead's presence in southeast Ohio.
- Visits to newspapers in the seven-county area to brief the editorial staff on the issues at hand.
- A pamphlet explaining BYPRO's benefits to landowners and the general public.
- Formation of a citizens advisory council which became a key factor in settling early litigation.
- "An idea so good it can't miss" background release on BYPRO and strip mine reclamation.
- "Small creatures thrive in BYPRO" news release on a scientific study showing how mice thrived at a BYPRO reclamation site.

- Newspaper ads announcing a 1-800 BYPRO hotline.
- Q and A on BYPRO for answering hotline and to hand out in response to inquiries.
- Letter to 1-800 hotline callers.
- Letter to community leaders with basic release.
- Hunting and fishing release on forest and wildlife management on Mead lands.
- Economic impact release on having Mead in the area.
- Media tour of Mead's Broken Arrow reclaimed strip mine, site.
- Ohio EPA and Department of Natural Resources directors tour of Broken Arrow.

Evaluation

The program succeeded in gaining the support of the majority of people in the seven-county area, including many public officials and community leaders who had previously remained silent. They came to agree with Jackson County Health Commissioner Dr. Carl Greever who said the environmental benefits of BYPRO far outweighed the "infinitesimal" risk that accompanied using it.

The program achieved its two measurable goals. (1) Public understanding and endorsement of the BYPRO program was the key to the Ohio EPA approving a five-year extension of Mead's sludge management plan in mid-1989 and in 1990 sharply expanding the program to include active as well as abandoned strip mines. (2) In 1990 — its first year of operation — the program successfully reclaimed more than 400 acres of strip mined land and saved the State of Ohio and landowners thousands of dollars in topsoil costs. Additionally, Mead's savings are estimated at hundreds of thousands of dollars. With tens of thousands of acres in need of reclamation, the program appears to have many years of success ahead of it.

The real winners were the people of southeast Ohio. When presented all the facts, they made the right decision, proving that a company that communicates responsibly on environmental issues can — and will — be heard. As such, Mead's BYPRO program holds important lessons for all environmental communications.

Exhibit 6–2a   Mead Paper Position Overview on BYPRO

<u>MEAD PAPER POSITION OVERVIEW</u>

8/31/87

<u>Dioxin in Mead Paper Mill Wastewater Sludge -- A Perspective</u>

Since 1979, Mead Paper has cooperated with the Ohio Department of Natural Resources in a strip mine land reclamation program using the mill's waste water sludge. The program, carefully planned and administered, has been remarkably successful and widely acclaimed. It has been a clear and exemplary response to the federal mandate to recover and recycle natural resources.

Since trace amounts of the chemical dioxin were discovered in Mead's sludge in 1985, however, not only has the successful strip mine land reclamation program been sidetracked, but questions concerning both public safety and the propriety of Mead Paper's actions in the matter have been raised.

The company has seen a growing amount of public misunderstanding, misinformation and speculation on the issue. In such instances, Mead Paper feels it must speak out to defend its record and integrity as a company as well as to attempt to separate fact from fiction, and put the emotion-laden dioxin issue in perspective.

Achieving a balanced understanding of the issue is critical. Several factors, however, make this difficult at best:

• the degree of general public fear and lack of understanding regarding dioxin;

• the complex and subjective nature of assessing risk to human health;

• the extremely technical nature of research data addressing the subject; and

Courtesy Mead Corporation, Fine Paper Division

• public perceptions and attitudes stemming from sensational prior events such as the U.S. military's Agent Orange spraying, the Times Beach, Missouri contamination, Love Canal and similar episodes.

Beyond the technical factors that bear on dioxin and the land reclamation program, Mead Paper wants to put its statements and actions on the matter in perspective as they relate to company philosophy and policy.

Mead Paper has acted and will continue to act with the public interest and welfare as top priority. The company operates with a keen sense of corporate responsibility and feels a deep obligation to the public trust. In no case has it allowed or will it allow business motives or any other influence to dictate actions or policy that could reasonably be seen as unlawful, unethical, or threatening to the health or well-being of the public. And it intends to vigorously defend its integrity and good name against attempts to discredit them.

In supporting the use of sludge in strip mine land reclamation, Mead Paper has absolutely no intent to degrade the environment or ask anyone to put up with a possible threat to his or her well-being. To do so just wouldn't make sense by any measure. Although use of sludge for land reclamation does have economic benefits to Mead in terms of cost avoidance, the real winners of the reclamation program are the people of southeast Ohio. The known health dangers, pollution, unsightliness and loss of productivity of thousands of acres of barren, lifeless land far eclipse what an increasing majority of scientific data and expert opinion show is little if any risk from almost undetectable amounts of dioxin.

Given the notoriety of the subject of dioxin and other toxic chemicals, however, it's natural to question the advisability of applying waste water sludge containing dioxin -- no matter how miniscule the amount -- in rural strip mine land reclamation programs, even if they are approved and coordinated by appropriate state regulatory agencies and departments. Might there be a risk to health?

To answer that question, Mead Paper has devoted considerable technical and administrative resources to examine scientific and other relevant expert data and opinion. It has reviewed exhaustive research encompassing every known relevant scientific paper on the issue, including a report compiled by an independent firm commissioned by the National Council of the Paper Industry for Air and Stream Improvement, Inc. It has taken the initiative to involve as well as cooperate fully and closely with all pertinent government agencies. It has also commissioned and funded its own original research and data acquisition by an independent firm on the question and related areas. Only then, after the most conservative and cautious evaluation, has Mead Paper arrived at the following positions:

1. The preponderant majority of current scientific data and opinion support the position that the trace dioxin-class contaminants in Mead sludge, particularly in this land reclamation application, pose an infinitesimally small risk to human and animal life, if one at all. A small number of scientific and individual opinions exist that take exception to this statement in varying degrees. But they are isolated and not supported by equivalent opinion and research. Mead Paper is convinced that given the total sum of fact and expert

opinion, reasonable persons will find the risks posed by the trace contaminants in Mead sludge negligible, even if there were no merit to the reclamation program.

2. The potential risk posed by Mead sludge, even when considered in the most conservative, questionable and worst case scenarios, is orders of magnitude smaller than risks posed by other threats common in everyday life from other sources, both natural and artificial. For example:

- We are much more likely to come in contact with more pervasive and overall larger amounts of dioxin from more numerous, common and nearby sources such as municipal incinerators, automobile exhaust, municipal waste water treatment, possibly even forest fires and wood stoves;

- We face exposure to other toxic chemicals and agents, often just as potent as dioxin, that are pervasive in our society and lifestyles. They include the very food we eat, such as alcohol, peanut butter, corn, mushrooms, fried/grilled meats, coffee, preserved meats, potatoes, artificial sweetners and colors, and much more;

- We are surrounded by other threats to public health and safety, such as natural ionizing radiation, sunlight, automobile and air travel, accidents, etc.

3. The risk posed by Mead sludge is also dwarfed by the serious, widespread and well-documented environmental damage and threat to safety and health caused by erosion and flash flooding, as well as by acid mine runoff at the strip mine sites being reclaimed.

Today we are confronted with risks and threats, both known and unknown, throughout our society. We must judge and react to each -- no matter what their nature -- not as isolated, individual questions, but from a broad perspective and in terms of relative risks and benefits. Since assessing risk to humans usually requires extrapolation of data from one set of conditions to another, in many instances the science of toxicology simply cannot provide the unequivocal answers we would like to have. So the choices we have are seldom, if ever, black or white, right or wrong. Rather we must decide which alternative presents the best, safest and most prudent overall choice with the minimum risk. This choice can often be a difficult and complex one to make, but one that nevertheless must be made.

In the case of dioxin, however, large amounts of research data have been compiled. And we're continually getting more. Those data enable the following statement to be made with a relatively high degree of confidence and scientific support: "The application of Mead Paper sludge containing minute amounts of dioxin for strip mine land reclamation presents at worst only a very small risk, and certainly one that is negligible relative to the many other risks that we choose or are forced to accept daily." And as each new piece of research is added, that confidence grows even stronger.

###

You could build a house on it,

hunt on it,

or even play golf on it.

Mead BYPRO® is a natural byproduct of the paper manufacturing process. It is produced as sludge and is composed of cellulose (wood) fibers, clay and lime, as well as nitrogen and phosphorous, nutrients which are essential for plant growth.

Next to dwindling supplies of topsoil, it is the best material available to reclaim the hundreds of thousands of acres of abandoned strip mined land identified as needing some form of reclamation by the Ohio Department of Natural Resources.

BYPRO® is available at no cost to strip mine owners or local communities through federal and Ohio Department of Natural Resources abandoned mined land reclamation programs.

It is abundantly available. Mead Paper in Chillicothe produces hundreds of tons of BYPRO® daily.

Inherent properties make it an excellent material for reclaiming strip mine sites. On sites where it has been tried since 1979, applications of BYPRO® have promoted vigorous plant growth, neutralized the soil and minimized erosion, while reestablishing the natural habitat for wildlife.

What you should know about BYPRO®

In May 1987, the Ohio Environmental Protection Agency concluded that Mead BYPRO® is safe for strip mine application. The question before the EPA was whether trace levels of a substance known as dioxin were of concern to human health or the environment. The EPA, Ohio Department of Health and others concluded that these levels are safe when BYPRO® is used according to the guidelines issued by the Ohio EPA.

The dioxin appears in minute quantities—in the low parts per trillion. For comparison purposes, 1 part per trillion is roughly equivalent to 1 second in 32,000 years. At these extremely low levels, the overwhelming body of scientific evidence supports the use of BYPRO® in strip mine reclamation.

When questioned about the appropriateness of Ohio EPA's decision to allow use of BYPRO® for strip mine reclamation, Valdas V. Adamkus, U.S. Regional EPA Administrator in Chicago, said, ''It is the particular dioxin concentration of the sludge and the application rate that are critical, and Ohio has addressed these factors in its decision.''

The levels in BYPRO® are approximately 100 times less than the 1,000 parts per trillion that the U.S. EPA and the Centers for Disease Control in Atlanta use as a threshold for concern for dioxin in soil in residential areas.

How BYPRO® is applied

Another advantage of BYPRO® is that nothing has to be done once it is applied. It is not necessary to add fertilizers or other chemicals to the site. BYPRO® contains all of the essential nutrients for developing and maintaining plant life. Its high lime content neutralizes acid found at strip mine sites. Its clay and cellulose content allows it to retard runoff and to stabilize steep slopes.

The application process begins when a team of specialists from the Ohio Department of Natural Resources inspects the abandoned strip mine site and develops an engineering plan for reclaiming the land. Once the plan is approved, the project is put out for bids. An independent contractor is hired by the state to regrade and recontour the land, truck in BYPRO®, spread it and plant grass.

What seems like a lot of BYPRO®—about 100 tons per acre—actually becomes a relatively thin, 2-1/4-inch layer when spread. That is all that is necessary to support vegetation and return the land to its naturally fertile condition.

Strip mine reclamation—a top Ohio priority

The reclamation of abandoned strip mine acreage became a top state priority in 1972 with the passage of what was then the nation's most comprehensive strip mine reclamation law. Mead BYPRO® has become an important ingredient in the reclaiming efforts as a substitute for dwindling supplies of topsoil.

Seventy percent of Ohio's coal production is achieved by strip mining. More than 370,000 acres of land have been identified as being in need of some form of reclamation. With so many acres to be restored, and 180,000 acres given top priority, it is apparent that sources of topsoil are limited and will become increasingly difficult to obtain.

By the late 1970s, paper mill sludge was recognized as a potentially effective and inexpensive alternative to soil for reclamation. Mead Paper's Broken Arrow site, once considered one of the three worst strip mine sites in the state before it was acquired by Mead and reclaimed as a demonstration project, has been transformed into a model of what reclamation can do.

Toward a greener Ohio

The potential risk posed by BYPRO®, even when considered in the most conservative scenarios, is many times smaller than risks posed by other threats common in everyday life from other sources.

The general population is much more likely to come in contact with larger amounts of dioxin from more numerous, common and nearby sources— municipal incinerators, automobile exhaust, and possibly forest fires and wood burning fireplaces.

Most people face daily exposure to other toxic chemicals and agents, often just as potent as dioxin— including the very food they eat—peanut butter, corn, mushrooms, fried meats, coffee, preserved meats, potatoes, and artificial sweeteners and colors.

The risk posed by BYPRO® is like most other questions involving risks. Decisions must be based on which alternative presents the best, safest and most prudent overall choice with the minimum risk. The risk must then be weighed against the benefits obtained.

For Mead BYPRO®, it is a choice between the insignificant risk of almost undetectable traces of dioxin and the multiple known risks of acid mine drainage, erosion and flash flooding that strip mines present. It is like comparing the choice between opening a door to leave a burning building or choosing to stay behind because of the possible risk of contracting a contagious disease upon touching the door handle to get out.

Few would choose the second alternative. For strip mine owners and families living close to abandoned strip mines, the benefits far outweigh the risks.

Without alternative resoiling materials, such as BYPRO®, programs to reclaim the strip mines will be severely limited because of lack of suitable material to do the job.

What is dioxin?

Dioxin is a generic term for a family of some 75 chemical compounds known as polychlorinated dibenzo-p-dioxins. A useless and once obscure organic substance, it has acquired worldwide recognition as being among the most potent toxic substances known. But research data on its effects have varied widely when human and animal exposures were compared.

Adverse effects of relatively high doses of dioxin on laboratory animals have been clearly established. However, no human death—or even a serious illness—has been attributed to dioxin in the four decades of toxicological records compiled on the substance. None of the many studies directed at dioxin's effects on human health has demonstrated or even suggested that it causes severe chronic human effects. Studies of effects on wildlife from exposure to levels of dioxin similar to those found in BYPRO® have shown no adverse effects.

Concern about dioxin has mushroomed in the past decade. This concern has been furthered by rapidly developing technology that allows the measurement of trace levels of dioxin. This technology has allowed the measurement of dioxin in many materials where it previously could not be detected. Simply because dioxin can now be detected in these materials does not mean that it is harmful. This is where the science of "Risk Assessment" must be used along with the knowledge of scientists worldwide.

The most recent findings on the effects of dioxin have shown that its toxicity may be less than believed in the past. In fact the U.S. EPA, which has taken the most conservative regulatory approach to dioxin in the world, has announced that it is considering reducing its earlier risk assessment of how harmful dioxin is to human health and the environment.

Paper mill sludge— the byproduct of paper manufacturing

Paper mill sludge is the natural byproduct of pulp and paper manufacturing. It is significantly different from other sludges, with a composition primarily of cellulose (wood) fiber, clay, lime and such nutrients as nitrogen and phosphorus. It contains no pathogens and is very low in concentrations of heavy metals like lead and cadmium.

In cooperation with Ohio State University, Mead found an excellent use for sludge in reclamation of abandoned strip mine sites in Southeastern Ohio. Because of its fibrous nature and associated cohesiveness, this sludge retards rain runoff and erosion. It neutralizes acid strip mine runoff and provides essential nutrients for vegetation.

Demonstrations of the benefits of using Mead sludge for strip mine reclamation over a six year period were so successful that it was renamed BYPRO® to reflect the beneficial use of an otherwise unwanted waste material. It was considered by many experts to be the answer to Ohio's severe abandoned strip mine land problem.

The discovery of dioxin in pulp and paper mill sludges, in 1985, was a surprise to Mead and the paper industry, which neither manufactures nor uses dioxin in its processes. No dioxin had been detected in testing of several pulp and paper mill sludges as recent as a year before. But new technology had been developed which was capable of detecting dioxin in the parts per trillion range.

When it was first discovered that dioxin might be present in Mead sludge, Mead voluntarily suspended the mine reclamation program and began an extensive process of testing BYPRO® to determine what levels, if any, of dioxin were present. These tests showed very low levels of dioxin. Subsequent risk assessments conducted by independent scientists indicated that the risks of continued use of BYPRO® on strip mines were inconsequential.

Based on these results, a Sludge Management Plan was prepared by Mead and submitted to the Ohio EPA. In May 1987, the EPA, in conjunction with the Ohio Department of Health, concluded that BYPRO® was safe for such applications and granted permission for its use in seven Southeastern Ohio counties.

A caretaker of Ohio forests

Mead Corporation has been a caretaker of Ohio forests for years, owning about 112,000 acres in 10 Southern Ohio counties. That's an area roughly equal to a fourth of Ross County, Ohio's second largest county.

The company conducts an active program to be a good steward of these priceless natural resources. That effort has been recognized.

In 1987, the Ohio Department of Natural Resources notified Mead Corporation that it was inducted into its Friends of the Forest program.

To protect central Florida from flooding after hurricanes, the state and federal governments "channelized" the Kissimmee River. When completed in the 1970s, both the beautiful river and all its environmental and ecological values were lost. A public outcry demanded return of the river's natural beauty and accompanying wetlands. The South Florida Water Management District determined that restoration, along with flood control benefits, was possible. To obtain congressional authorization and funding, the district conducted information campaigns statewide, among river residents, and at the federal level among members of Congress. Exhibit 6–3a is a Public Input Survey/Questionnaire with results of the questionnaire. Exhibits 6–3b and 6–3c are news releases announcing public meetings, and Exhibit 6–3d is a photograph of the Kissimmee River, both old and restored.

Case 6–3   ## Seeking Congressional Authorization to Restore a Florida River

South Florida Water Management District, West Palm Beach, FL

The Background

The Kissimmee River was once a 103-mile-long river that meandered a snaking course through central Florida. The graceful river provided a home for hundreds of species of wading birds, waterfowl, and winter migratory birds; created excellent fishing waters; and gave birth to more than 43,000 acres of wetlands.

To protect central Florida from flooding in the aftermath of devastating hurricanes of the 1940s, the state and federal governments chose to "channelize" the Kissimmee. At the time, this seemed the best method to quickly drain floodwaters from central Florida. Channelization took nearly 10 years to complete. By the early 1970s, the serpentine Kissimmee was transformed into a 56-mile-long, 30-foot-deep canal, renamed C-38. Not only was a beautiful river lost, but so were virtually all of the environmental and ecological values that accompanied the river. Channelization resulted in long-term degradation of the natural environment and the loss of many acres of wetlands.

Courtesy South Florida Water Management District

Almost immediately, public outcry was heard to return the river's natural flows and oxbows. Environmentalists and three successive Florida governors supported restoration. The South Florida Water Management District — a regional water management and environmental agency — elected to explore the possibilities of river restoration. Throughout the 1980s, the district conducted meticulous research projects in Florida and California to see if restoration could be achieved. Scientists developed physical and mathematical models and on-site demonstration projects. This research clearly showed restoration was possible, with virtually all environmental values returning, while flood control benefits would be maintained.

With this good news in hand, the challenge before the water district was to obtain congressional authorization for river restoration. The project was estimated to cost $380 million and would take 20 years to complete. The district sought a 50/50 cost-sharing arrangement with the state and federal government splitting the costs. The U.S. Army Corps of Engineers — which originally straightened the river — would conduct the construction project to restore it.

Research

Scientific research through the 1980s showed restoration could be successfully achieved by filling in the channelized river — allowing water to return to original river floodplains and oxbows — and by raising the elevation of several upper lakes to increase water storage. This extensive research helped form the basis of the district's messages to the public and to state and federal officials. Once the restoration was proved scientifically possible, a public opinion survey in 1989 showed support from river area residents for restoration.

Analysis of editorials, news articles, TV news clips, and petitions showed vast, yet unfocused, support for restoration throughout the state of Florida.

Further interviews with river residents and legislators revealed a minority group of people who opposed the restoration, for reasons that included the cost, disruption of lifestyle, and/or concern that the restoration project wouldn't work.

Planning

The district's public affairs campaign involved two efforts: first was to create a supportive constituency in Florida, which was needed for state funding, and for Congress to support the project.

Second was obtaining the necessary federal support in the form of congressional authorization.

To generate state support, the district elected to launch an extensive media campaign from 1989 to 1991 to inform citizens of the latest results of Kissimmee River restoration research. The public also had to be willing to accept the $380 million estimated cost—with half to come from the state.

Target groups included environmentalists, river residents, residents throughout Florida since the Kissimmee is a state resource, elected officials, and news media.

In 1992, the district would focus its efforts on winning congressional authorization. This included meeting with members of Congress and their aides, meetings with federal agency staff members, closely following the progress of the legislation, and continuing to keep the restoration issue alive and in the spotlight at the state and national levels.

Execution

The district conducted a mass media campaign to educate the public on the specifics of the river restoration project. The cornerstone tool was a 30-minute district-produced video entitled "Run River Run." The $64,000 video traced the history of the river from prechannelization days and explained why it should be returned to its original form. The video was broadcast on public TV throughout the state and was made available to schools and community groups. Three years after its original production, many groups still are requesting copies of the video. The district also produced news releases, brochures, and booklets, held press conferences on the river banks, conducted site tours, and held editorial board meetings. The result was widespread public education and support for this unique project. This allowed the district governing board to endorse the project, support needed for the federal effort.

Special attention had to be given to a select group of river residents who would be affected by the restoration, with a small number losing their homes. An opposition group called Residents Opposing Alleged Restoration (ROAR) formed. In the early 1990s, several hundred people were against restoration. In 1993, less than 50 were still vocalizing their opposition. This was due to the district governing board slightly modifying the river backfilling plan in early 1992 and the personal attention the district's government and public affairs staff gave to residents.

Once state support was secured in 1991, the district spent most of 1992 soliciting federal support. The program objective was to keep key congressional members and aides educated on the river restoration project, so they would keep the needed authorization language in the bill. Throughout 1992, the district conducted a letter-writing campaign, briefed members of Congress and aides on the scientific merits of the program, provided tours and briefings, and followed the progress of the 1992 Water Resources Development Act which authorized the restoration.

Evaluation

In October 1992, the district's ultimate goal was met. The 1992 Water Resources Development Act was passed in the final hours of Congress, an omnibus water projects bill authorizing the Army Corps of Engineers to move ahead with restoration activities. In December, President Bush signed the bill into law. Federal and state support had been secured for the most ambitious river restoration project ever attempted in the world. An early grassroots campaign was crystallized into a very focused effort, which will now result in the return of a natural Florida river and all of its environmental values. This accomplishment has placed the state of Florida and country in a position of global leadership in the restoration of aquatic resources.

Exhibit 6–3a   **Public Input Survey/Questionnaire Results**

From four public meetings held during late June 1989, a public opinion survey was conducted. The surveys were taken after the program presentations and discussion periods were complete. The public meetings were held in Kissimmee, Sebring, Okeechobee and West Palm Beach on successive nights. The total number of respondents for all locations was 104.

The questionnaire and a graphical summary of the responses follow. It is acknowledged that the sampling provided at public meetings may not represent the public at large because of the complexity of the issues and the general interest of the restoration; however, it is instructive to note that many demographic backgrounds were represented. Effort was made to assure that scientific surveying techniques were observed. Each attendee received one questionnaire and there was generally no repeat attendance at subsequent meetings by given individuals.

Courtesy South Florida Water Management District

Instructions: With a dark pencil, blacken the box that indicates your response to each item. If you choose not to make a response, leave all the boxes blank for that item. Mark only one box for each item unless otherwise instructed.

Part I: Demographics (Please mark the appropriate box(es) for each category)

1. Age
- ☐ 24 years or younger
- ☐ 25 - 34 years
- ☐ 35 - 44 years
- ☐ 45 - 54 years
- ☐ 55 - 64 years
- ☐ 65 years or older

5. Sex
- ☐ Male ☐ Female

2. Education
- ☐ 8th grade or less
- ☐ 9th - 12th grade
- ☐ 1 - 2 years of college
- ☐ 3 - 4 years of college
- ☐ 5 years or more of college

3. Years lived in Florida
- ☐ 2 years or less
- ☐ 3 - 5 years
- ☐ 6 - 10 years
- ☐ 11 - 15 years
- ☐ 16 - 20 years
- ☐ 21 - 30 years
- ☐ 31 - 35 years
- ☐ 36 - 40 years
- ☐ 41 years or more

4. Employment/Occupation
- ☐ Manufacturing
- ☐ Education
- ☐ Government
- ☐ Beef Cattle
- ☐ Dairy
- ☐ Other Agriculture
- ☐ Guide Service
- ☐ Boat Sales/Service
- ☐ Marina
- ☐ Medical
- ☐ Construction
- ☐ Insurance
- ☐ Real Estate
- ☐ Finance/Banking
- ☐ Retail
- ☐ Restaurant
- ☐ Homemaker
- ☐ Retired
- ☐ Other

6. Household income
- ☐ $10,000 or less
- ☐ $10,001 - $20,000
- ☐ $20,001 - $30,000
- ☐ $30,001 - $40,000
- ☐ $40,001 - $50,000
- ☐ $50,001 - $99,999
- ☐ $100,000 or more

7. Total value of real estate holdings
- ☐ Do not own any real estate
- ☐ $50,000 or less
- ☐ $50,001 - $100,000
- ☐ $100,001 - $250,000
- ☐ $250,001 - $500,000
- ☐ $500,001 - $1,000,000
- ☐ $1,000,001 o more

8. County location(s) of residence and employment.
- ☐ Orange
- ☐ Osceola
- ☐ Polk
- ☐ Highlands
- ☐ Okeechobee
- ☐ St. Lucie
- ☐ Martin
- ☐ Glades
- ☐ Lee
- ☐ Hendry
- ☐ Palm Beach
- ☐ Collier
- ☐ Broward
- ☐ Dade
- ☐ Monroe
- ☐ Other

9. Indicate types (more than one if applicable) of real estate property owned by you or members of your household.
- ☐ Do not own real estate property
- ☐ Personal residence within city limits
- ☐ Personal residence outside city limits
- ☐ Residential rental property
- ☐ Commercial (non-Ag) property
- ☐ Farm or ranch of 100 acres or less
- ☐ Farm or ranch of 101 - 500 acres
- ☐ Farm or ranch of 501 - 1,000 acres
- ☐ Farm or ranch of 1,001 - 5,000 acres
- ☐ Farm or ranch of 5,001 acres or more

Part II: "Quality of Life"

10. Indicate the "quality of life" that you now enjoy
- ☐ Poor ☐ Needs some improvement ☐ Acceptable ☐ Outstanding ☐ No opinion

11. Indicate any change in "quality of life" over the last 40 years or since you have lived in Florida.
- ☐ Significant changes have occurred that caused great decline
- ☐ Some changes have occurred that caused some decline
- ☐ There has been no change
- ☐ There has been improvement and decline
- ☐ Some changes have occurred that caused some improvement
- ☐ Significant changes have occurred that caused great improvement.

12. If your "quality of life" has declined or improved, indicate what (more than one if applicable) partly or wholly caused the changes.
- ☐ No changes
- ☐ Pollution
- ☐ Inflation
- ☐ Tourism
- ☐ Higher taxes
- ☐ Roadways
- ☐ Population growth
- ☐ Utility services
- ☐ Cost of living
- ☐ Environmental degradation
- ☐ Public education system
- ☐ Crime and law enforcement
- ☐ Real estate appreciation
- ☐ Management of water resources
- ☐ Loss of recreational facilities

Part III: Management of Water Resources

13. Select the priority by which you feel the following should be water resources management goals.

Low	Medium	High	
☐	☐	☐	a. Safeguard water quality
☐	☐	☐	b. Provide drainage of open land
☐	☐	☐	c. Protect aquatic environments
☐	☐	☐	d. Control the use of surface water
☐	☐	☐	e. Guarantee navigation
☐	☐	☐	f. Control the use of ground water
☐	☐	☐	g. Drain swamplands
☐	☐	☐	h. Provide irrigation water supplies
☐	☐	☐	i. Provide municipal water supplies
☐	☐	☐	j. Restore damaged wetlands
☐	☐	☐	k. Provide flood protection
☐	☐	☐	l. Provide recreational facilities

For items 14 - 22 darken the box that describes your response to each statement.

Significant Damage	Slight Damage	No Impact	Slight Improve.	Significant Improve.	
☐	☐	☐	☐	☐	14. The environment in central and southern Florida has been impacted by management of water resources.
☐	☐	☐	☐	☐	15. Flood protection in central and southern Florida has been impacted by management of water resources.
☐	☐	☐	☐	☐	16. Navigation in central and southern Florida has been impacted by management of water resources.
☐	☐	☐	☐	☐	17. Drought protection in central and southern Florida has been impacted by management of water resources.
☐	☐	☐	☐	☐	18. The Kissimmee River Flood Control Project has impacted flood protection.
☐	☐	☐	☐	☐	19. The Kissimmee River Flood Control Project has impacted aesthetic, fish, and wildlife values.
☐	☐	☐	☐	☐	20. The Kissimmee River Flood Control Project has impacted navigation.
☐	☐	☐	☐	☐	21. The Kissimmee River Flood Control Project has impacted wetland drainage.
☐	☐	☐	☐	☐	22. The Kissimmee River Flood Control Project has impacted drought protection.

23. How many major hurricanes have you experienced while living in Florida?

☐ None ☐ 1 ☐ 2 ☐ 3 ☐ 4 ☐ 5 ☐ 6 or more

For items 24 - 29, darken the box that describes your response to each statement.

Strongly Agree	Agree	No Opinion	Disagree	Strongly Disagree	
☐	☐	☐	☐	☐	24. The Kissimmee River/Floodplain should be restored to its pre-canal condition.
☐	☐	☐	☐	☐	25. In a significantly altered ecosystem, such as the Kissimmee River/Floodplain, it is not prudent to undertake an expensive restoration effort.
☐	☐	☐	☐	☐	26. If the Kissimmee River had not been channelized, the present floodplain ecosystem would not be very different than it was in 1950.
☐	☐	☐	☐	☐	27. The cost of any restoration effort should be shared by the South Florida Water Management District, the State of Florida, and the Federal Government.
☐	☐	☐	☐	☐	28. Good water management for fish and wildlife is good water management for mankind.
☐	☐	☐	☐	☐	29. There have been enough technical studies conducted in order to make sound decisions regarding the restoration of the Kissimmee River/Floodplain.

30. How much do you feel a restored floodplain ecosystem in the Kissimmee valley would be worth to each Florida resident?

☐ $1 or less ☐ $1 - $5 ☐ $5 - $10 ☐ $10 - more

21. Would you support the use of some tourism tax revenues to help fund any Kissimmee River restoration program?

☐ Yes ☐ No

(Please do not mark in this space)

Survey Location Key: ☐ 1 ☐ 2 ☐ 3 ☐ 4 ☐ 5 ☐ 6 ☐ 7 ☐ 8 ☐ 9

B-3

Kissimmee River Restoration Survey
Part III. Management of Water Resources
13. Priority of Water Management Goals

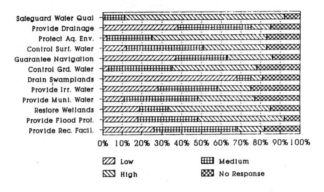

Kissimmee River Restoration Survey
Part III. Management of Water Resources
14-17. Impact of Managing Water Resources

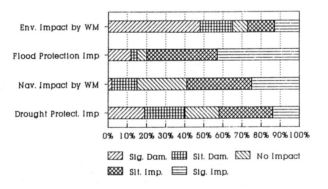

Kissimmee River Restoration Survey
Part III. Management of Water Resources
18-22. Kissimmee River Project Impacted:

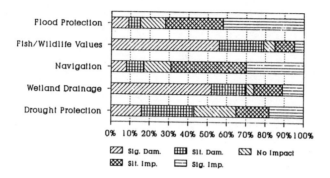

▨ Sig. Dam.	▦ Slt. Dam.
▧ Slt. Imp.	▤ Sig. Imp.
◺ No Impact	

Kissimmee River Restoration Survey
Part III. Management of Water Resources
23. No. of Major Hurricanes Experienced

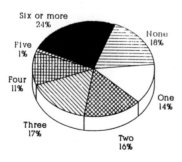

Kissimmee River Restoration Survey
Part III. Management of Water Resources
24-29 Concerning the Restoration:

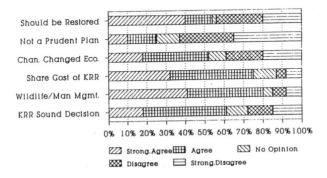

Should be Restored
Not a Prudent Plan
Chan. Changed Eco.
Share Gost of KRR
Wildlife/Man Mgmt.
KRR Sound Decision

0% 10% 20% 30% 40% 50% 60% 70% 80% 90%100%

Strong.Agree   Agree   No Opinion
Disagree   Strong.Disagree

Kissimmee River Restoration Survey
Part III. Management of Water Resource
30. Worth of Restored Floodplain/person

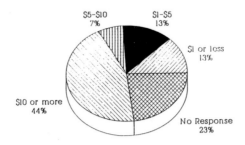

$5-$10
7%

$1-$5
13%

$1 or less
13%

$10 or more
44%

No Response
23%

Kissimmee River Restoration Survey
Part III. Management of Water Resources
31. Support use of Tourism Tax Revenues

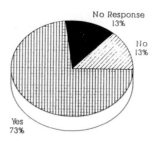

No Response
13%

No
13%

Yes
73%

Kissimmee River Restoration Survey
Survey Locations

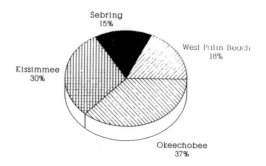

Sebring
15%

West Palm Beach
18%

Kissimmee
30%

Okeechobee
37%

Exhibit 6–3b   News Release Announcing Public Meetings

Protecting South Florida's Water Resources for 40 Years
1949-1989

South Florida Water Management District

P.O. Box 24680 • 3301 Gun Club Road • West Palm Beach FL 33416-4680 • (407) 686-8800 • FL WATS 1-800-432-2045

NEWS RELEASE

For more information, contact:

Office of Communications   June 19, 1989
Ann Overton or Cathy Anclade

PUBLIC MEETINGS TO DISCUSS KISSIMMEE RIVER RESTORATION

The South Florida Water Management District has scheduled four public meetings to discuss the status of the Kissimmee River restoration project.

All meetings start at 7 p.m. The schedule is as follows:

Monday, June 26, Kissimmee --	Agricultural Center, 1901 E. Irlo Bronson Memorial Hwy. (intersection of U.S. 192 and U.S. 441)
Tuesday, June 27, Sebring --	Agri-Civic Center, 4509 W. George Blvd. (faces U.S. 27 North)
Wednesday, June 28, Okeechobee --	Civic Center, 1750 U.S. 98 North (across from airport)
Thursday, June 29, West Palm Beach --	John I. Leonard High School, 4701 10th Ave. N., Lake Worth

Kent Loftin, manager of the District's Kissimmee restoration project, and Dr. H.W. Shen of the University of California at Berkeley will speak at the meetings. Shen, a world-renowned expert in sedimentation and environmental river mechanics, is under contract to the District to develop physical and computer models to examine the effects of existing and proposed restoration efforts on the river.   He will make his final recommendations on the restoration to the District's Governing Board late this year.

These meetings will provide a general update on the Kissimmee restoration and

(MORE)

Courtesy South Florida Water Management District

Exhibit 6–3c   News Release Announcing Public Meetings

Protecting South Florida's Water Resources for 40 Years
1949-1989

South Florida Water Management District

P.O. Box 24680 • 3301 Gun Club Road • West Palm Beach, FL 33416-4680 • (407) 686-8800 • FL WATS 1-800-432-2045

NEWS RELEASE

For more information, contact:

ANN OVERTON
SFWMD
OFFICE OF COMMUNICATIONS

Office of Communications   October 18, 1989
Ann Overton or Cathy Anclade

FINAL ROUND OF PUBLIC MEETINGS SCHEDULED TO DISCUSS
KISSIMMEE RIVER RESTORATION

The South Florida Water Management District has scheduled three public
meetings to evaluate the final alternatives for the planned restoration of the
Kissimmee River.

All meetings start at 7 p.m. The schedule is as follows:

THURSDAY, NOVEMBER 2, Kissimmee --   Agricultural Center, 1901 E. Irlo
                                            Bronson Memorial Highway (next to
                                            rodeo grounds)

FRIDAY, NOVEMBER 3, Okeechobee --   Civic Center, 1750 U.S. 98 North
                                            (across from airport)

MONDAY, NOVEMBER 6, West Palm Beach --   SFWMD auditorium, 3301 Gun Club Road

On Wednesday, November 8, the District's Governing Board will discuss the
various plans for the river restoration during the workshop session of its
monthly meeting.

The final restoration alternatives have been developed through the cooperative
efforts of District staff, led by Kent Loftin, project manager, and Professor
H.W. Shen of the University of California, an international expert in

(MORE)

Courtesy South Florida Water Management District   253

Exhibit 6–3d   **Photograph of Kissimmee River, Old and Restored**

Courtesy South Florida Water Management District

Chapter **7**

Investor and Financial Relations

Corporations that sell shares to the public must conduct a specialized form of public relations with the investment, or financial, community. Investor and other financial relations cannot be managed in the same aggressive manner that characterizes other forms of public relations. The U.S. Securities and Exchange Commission (SEC) prohibits the promotion of corporate stock under certain circumstances, and it has detailed regulations regarding the issuance of annual and quarterly reports and the timely disclosure of all information that will affect the value of publicly traded corporate shares.

How, then, does our four-stage process apply to this highly specialized form of public relations?

Research

Investor relations research includes investigation of the client, the reason for the program, and the audiences to be targeted for communication.

Client Research

The public relations practitioner needs to focus first on the company's past and present financial status, its past and present investor relations practices, and its strengths, weaknesses, and opportunities specifically related to the financial community.

Opportunity or Problem Research

The second area of research involves assessing the need for a program of financial public relations. Most corporations engage in ongoing investor relations programs that may involve routine communication with the financial media, the annual report to shareowners, the annual meeting, as well as miscellaneous meetings with and tours for shareowners. When problems develop with particular publics, special programs may be devised reactively. Thus, the need for the program should be clearly justified and explained in this phase of research.

Audience Research

Finally, research for investor relations involves identification of key audiences or groups that make up the financial community:

Shareowners and potential shareowners

Security analysts and investment counselors

The financial press
   Major wire services: Dow Jones, Reuters Economic Service, AP, UPI
   Major business magazines: *Business Week, Fortune* — mass circulation and specialized
   Major New York City newspapers: *The New York Times, The Wall Street Journal*
   Statistical services: Standard and Poor's, Moody's Investor Service
   Private wire services: PR News Wire, Business Wire

Securities and Exchange Commission

Objectives

Investor relations objectives, both impact and output, should be as specific and as quantifiable as possible.

Impact Objectives

Impact objectives for investor relations include informing investor publics and affecting their attitudes and behaviors. Some examples are:

1. to increase the investor publics' knowledge of significant corporate developments (by 40 percent during the current year)

2. to enhance favorable attitudes toward the corporation (by 30 percent this year)
3. to create (40 percent) more interest in the corporation among potential investors (during this year)
4. to raise (20 percent) more capital through the investor relations program (by our deadline of December 1)
5. to receive (45 percent) greater responses from shareowners and other targeted investor publics (during the next fiscal year)

Output Objectives

In investor relations, output objectives constitute the distribution and execution of program materials and forms of communication. For example:

1. to distribute corporate news releases to 12 major outlets among the financial media
2. to make 18 presentations to security analysts during the months of March and April

Public relations directors often prefer to use output objectives exclusively. These clarify public relations actions and are much simpler to evaluate than impact objectives.

Programming

As in other forms of public relations, the element of programming for investor relations includes planning the theme and messages, the action or special event(s), the uncontrolled and controlled media, and the use of effective principles of communication in program execution.

Theme and Messages

The theme and messages for an investor relations program will be entirely situational. Such programs usually provide assurances of credibility and attempt to enhance relations between the company and the financial community.

Action or Special Event(s)

Actions and special events unique to investor relations include

1. an annual shareowners' meeting
2. an open house for shareowners or analysts
3. meetings with members of the financial community
4. special seminars or other group meetings with analysts
5. special visits to corporate headquarters or plant tours for analysts and shareowners
6. presentations at meetings or conventions of analysts, in and outside of New York City
7. promotional events designed to enhance the company's image in the financial community

Uncontrolled and Controlled Media

Uncontrolled media most frequently used in investor relations include:

1. news releases or feature stories targeted to the financial and mass media
2. CEO interviews with the financial and mass media
3. media relations with key members of the financial press to stimulate positive news coverage of the company and its activities

Controlled media most often found in investor relations programs are:

1. printed materials for shareowners, including the annual report, quarterly and other financial reports, newsletters, magazines, special letters, dividend stuffers, and announcements
2. company promotional films or videos
3. CEO and other corporate officers' speeches to key audiences in the financial community
4. company financial fact books, biographies and photographs of corporate officers, special fact sheets, and news releases
5. shareowner opinion surveys
6. financial advertising

Several examples of uncontrolled and controlled forms of communication are included with the cases in this chapter.

Effective Communication

The most relevant communication principles for investor and financial relations are source credibility and audience participation.

Much of the effort of the investor relations program is directed toward enhancing the credibility of the corporation inside the financial community. The financial media, security analysts, shareowners, and potential shareowners must have a favorable image of the corporation. To accomplish this, organizations have changed their stock offerings from over-the-counter to the American or the New York Stock Exchange; have upgraded their printed materials, incorporating designs to convey a more "blue-chip" image; and have stepped up presentations to security analysts. Thus, corporate credibility must always be a paramount concern.

Audience participation is also a vital aspect of such programs. Prospective shareowners, financial media people, security analysts, and others targeted for communication are invited to as many corporate functions as possible. The ultimate form of "audience participation," of course, is the actual purchase of shares in the company.

Evaluation

Evaluation of investor relations programs should be goal oriented, with each objective reexamined and measured in turn. Although there is a great temptation to cite analyst reports about the company and the company's performance, especially its stock's price/earnings (P/E) ratio, these measures may not be related to investor relations programming, or there may be other intervening variables that overshadow the influence of such programming.

Summary

Research for investor relations aims at understanding the publicly owned company's status in the financial and investment community, the need for communicating with that community, and the makeup of that community as a target audience. The audience components are shareowners and potential shareowners, security analysts and investment counselors, the financial press, and the Securities and Exchange Commission.

Both impact and output objectives are used in investor relations. Impact objectives are oriented toward informing or influencing the attitudes and behaviors of the financial community, while output objectives cite distribution of materials and other forms of programming as desired outcomes.

Programming for investor relations usually consists of such actions and events as annual shareowners' meetings, an open house for shareowners, special meetings with analysts or other members of the financial community, and promotional events designed to enhance the company's image in the financial community. Uncontrolled and controlled media used in investor relations include news releases, interviews, printed literature, audiovisual materials, and/or speeches directed to targeted segments of the financial community.

Evaluation of investor relations should return to the program's specific, stated objectives and measure each one appropriately. Some practitioners attribute enhancement of the corporation's P/E ratio to the efforts of the investor relations program. However, the presence of intervening variables should always be suspected in such cases.

Readings on Investor and Financial Relations

Cluff, Susan. "Going Public: A Step-by-Step Guide for Communicators." *Communication World*, December 1984, pp. 17ff.

"Corporate Public Relations" (special issue). *Public Relations Quarterly* 36 (Fall 1991).

Davids, Meryl. "How Now, IR?" *Public Relations Journal* 45 (April 1989): 15–19.

Denmarsh, Robert I., and Francis R. Esteban. "How to Produce a Credible Annual Report." *Public Relations Journal* 44 (October 1988): 35–36.

Goldman, A. I. "How to Develop an Investor Relations Program." *Financial Executive*, July 1982, pp. 26ff.

Graves, Joseph. *Managing Investor Relations*. Homewood, IL: Dow Jones-Irwin, 1982.

Investor Relations: A Practical Guide for NASDAQ Companies. Washington, DC: National Association of Securities Dealers, 1982.

Johnson, Johnnie, and Win Neilson. "Integrating IR and Other Public Relations." *Public Relations Journal* 46 (April 1990): 26–29.

Mahoney, William F. *Investor Relations: The Professional's Guide to Financial Marketing and Communications*. New York: New York Institute of Finance, A Division of Simon & Schuster, 1991.

Marken, G. A. "Does Your Management Know the Language of Take-over?" *Public Relations Quarterly*, Winter 1985, pp. 14ff.

McMullen, Melinda. "IR: Staying on Top in the '90s." *Public Relations Journal* 46 (April 1990): 30–31.

Nichols, Donald R. *The Handbook of Investor Relations*. Homewood, IL: Dow Jones-Irwin, 1989.

The SEC, the Securities Market and Your Financial Communications. New York: Hill and Knowlton, 1985.

Seely, Michael. "Investor Relations at the Crossroads." *Public Relations Journal* 39 (April 1983), pp. 21–24.

Taggart, Phillip W., and Roy Alexander with Robert M. Arnold. *Taking Your Company Public: Red Lights and Green Lights For a Go/No-Go Decision*. New York: AMACOM, 1991.

Thompson, C. R. "How to Plan Successful Financial Presentations." *Public Relations Journal* 39 (April 1983), pp. 25–27.

Walton, Wesley, and Charles P. Brissman. *Corporate Communications Handbook: A Guide for Managing Unstructured Disclosure in Today's Corporate Environment*. New York: Clark Boardman, 1988.

Winkelman, Michael. "Takeover-Fever Fever." *Public Relations Journal* 41 (May 1985), pp. 22–24.

Investor Relations Cases

*After its initial public offering, Quantum Health Resources
delivered powerful, well-targeted investment messages and
built a strong following among investment professionals. The
results of its investor relations program during its first full
year as a public company included a market value increase of
115 percent. Exhibits 7–1a, 7–1b, and 7–1c are news releases
about the company's financial standing. Exhibit 7–1d is an excerpt from the company's Chronicare flyer.*

Case 7–1   Helping Good Guys Come in First

Quantum Health Resources, Inc., Orange, CA, with
The Financial Relations Board, Chicago, IL

Background

Taking a company public is a formidable task. And there is little
an uninitiated executive can do to prepare for the insatiable information demands he or she will receive from the investment community, media, regulatory agencies and shareholders. Frequently,
these newly public companies and their CEOs turn to IR counsel
to build sustainable interest in their company's stock.

Quantum Health Resources is a case in point. Even with a CFO
well seasoned in the IR needs of public companies, management
sought counsel from The Financial Relations Board shortly after
its initial public offering. The primary objectives of its initially
modest program were to:

- identify and communicate the company's investment appeals
- initiate and sustain those market actions designed to fully
  value the company's stock
- establish policy and procedures for managing all required
  public disclosure.

Over the course of the first year, management learned how to
go beyond perfunctory earnings releases and acquisition announcements. They learned to negotiate the rocky shoals of public
controversy by having to come to grips with:

- emotionally-charged editorials about the business of chronic
  disorders

Courtesy Quantum Health Resources

- unwarranted price volatility precipitated by external market forces
- civil litigation over the company's very right to exist.
- contradictory advice regarding how much or how little to say in the public arena about company operations; what constitutes inside information; how to fulfill SEC rule 10b-5 regarding "good faith forecasts and forward looking disclosures" without falling victim to predatory attorneys and plaintiffs who use public companies to practice *legal extortion* in the form of frivolous class action suits.

Situation

Quantum Health Resources is a young, well-run company with solid investment appeals. It provides home health care regimens and support services to individuals affected by long-term genetic protein deficiencies—a highly competitive industry subject to rapid changes in technology, active cost containment efforts, government regulation, limited product supply from orphan drug manufacturers and has a limited operating history.

Research

Research took five forms:

- an assessment of each disease state served by Quantum, including charitable foundations
- surveys of current and past stockholders to determine perceptions about the stock
- telephone interviews with industry analysts and other investment professionals
- continuous peer analysis to measure key ratios and other performance comparisons
- empirical research into the market impact of voluntary and mandatory disclosure

Assessment of disease states, foundations and professional opinions about Quantum sought to identify hidden political agenda and exposed any investment weaknesses in Quantum's position. Peer analysis provided tangible and unbiased measures of the program's effectiveness. Empirical research formed the basis for policy counsel.

Planning

In the Planning Phase, explicit objectives were established:

- double company's market value from $160 to $320 million
- improve liquidity by 10% through increased institutional ownership
- sustain a 35.0X price/earnings multiple
- add 150 new followers among investment professionals
- increase market makers from 8 to 15
- generate 4 market research reports
- use face-to-face meetings and conference calls ahead of media to accomplish goals.

The investment message was targeted at analysts, institutional investors, brokers, current stockholders and the financial media and stresses the company's:

- rapid growth and long-term profitability
- leadership position in chronic disorder niche markets and related medical fields
- continued development of patient/physician loyalty
- strong cost-control programs and productivity enhancements through Chronicare™
- acquisition strategy to grow to $1 billion with our appreciable dilution in stockholder equity.

Execution

The program incorporated the following elements:

- eight major analysts/broker meetings, 8 one-on-one meetings in large financial communities
- visits to 30 financial communities by FRB investment community contacts
- award winning annual report, corporate summaries, direct mail and other financial documents
- speaking engagements at major conferences, panel and industry forums
- crisis communications plan

- modest media campaign, limited to 6 interviews in financial and trade press
- an ongoing communications program to strengthen stockholder relations
- quarterly conference calls to roughly 45 key analysts and other close followers.

Media note: We conducted extensive interviews with executives and PR directors whose companies are past casualties of the CBS investigative news program *60 Minutes* to learn how its producers select stories to be aired and what strategies have proved most successful in avoiding unwanted coverage. These actions were taken in response to a thinly veiled editorial by Morley Safer in *The New York Times*, titled "Blood Money" which seemed to indicate a story was in the works which might involve Quantum. By using patients loyal to Quantum, the company indirectly guided the *60 Minutes* investigation away from the expense of treating hemophilia and helped focus attention on the plight of the chronically ill—notably hemophiliacs, and the need for some form of national health care for those with long-term disabilities. No mention was ever made of Quantum during the 10-minute segment on *60 Minutes*.

Evaluation

Despite the recessionary economy and investment disfavor faced by biotech, health care and other medical service stocks in 1992, market action was nothing less than spectacular. The company weathered several crises, including major disruptions in its investment category and still managed to exceed every performance objective set for itself. The program received high marks from the financial community and individual investors and the company's president and CEO, Doug Stickney, was named entrepreneur of the year by *Inc. Magazine*.

Financial Results

- market value climbed by more than $180 million to $343.2 million
- institutional ownership grew to 69 — 25 new positions were opened in fourth quarter 1992

- price/earnings multiple stood at 37.0X — the highest in its peer group
- registry of sell-side professionals who closely follow the company reached 175 names
- NASDAQ market makers currently stands at 16
- 6 research reports were written and issued, 2 are pending publication
- FRB arranged 8 analyst meetings and 8 private meetings in 1992 and hosted 5 conference calls.
- in its first full year as a public company, Quantum's stock outperformed the Dow Jones Industrial Average, S&P 500, the NASDAQ Composite and by all common measures was the most successful stock in its peer and industry category
- program cost: $132,925
- return on investment: 1,375%

Research

Program research took five forms:

- an assessment of each disease state served by Quantum, including associated charitable foundations
- surveys of current and past stockholders to determine perceptions about the stock
- telephone interviews with industry analysts and other investment professionals
- continuous peer analysis to measure key ratios and other performance comparisons
- empirical research into the market impact of voluntary and mandatory disclosure

The *primary* purpose of the Research Phase was to: (1) assess current interest in Quantum Health Resources among health care analysts, money managers and senior brokers; (2) assess near-term interest in the company among institutional investors; (3) uncover positive and negative perceptions about the stock and its industry; and (4) assemble a body of evidence and professional consensus on which to base sound public and investor policies that will serve the company well over time.

Key elements in this portion of the investor relations program were:

- An in-depth study of the disease states served by Quantum Health Resources (hemophilia, immunodeficiency disorders and alpha-antitrypsin), including a visit to the National Organization for Rare Diseases (NORD) and each of the charitable foundations associated with these genetic diseases to assess their political agenda, their working relationship with Quantum, assess their militancy and potential exposure of stockholders to action by the foundation, and quantify each disease state in terms of its physical and economic impact on the individual and the nation's health care system.

- Discussions with Quantum's top executives to gather feelings about their business, the likelihood of government intervention in the pharmaceutical industry and to determine their impressions of current feelings among Wall Streeters toward the company and its industry.

- A review of comments by analysts and institutional brokers who attended Quantum's IPO road show or subsequent analyst meetings within the past six months to understand investment attitudes toward the company and its industry.

- Field trip surveys by FRB's investment community contact staff in 30 major metropolitan areas to identify new and continuing interest in Quantum Health Resources. Field trips were followed by detailed commentary from those canvassed.

- Telephone surveys of stockbrokers who currently or in the past have recommended Quantum's stock to determine (1) their level of understanding of off-site health care, (2) their satisfaction with the stock's performance and (3) to whom they recommended the stock.

- Discussions with executives and PR directors whose companies are past casualties of the CBS investigative news program *60 Minutes* to learn how its producers select stories to be aired and what strategies have proved most successful in avoiding unwanted coverage. These actions were taken in response to a thinly veiled editorial by Morley Safer in *The New York Times*, titled "Blood Money" which seemed to indicate a story was in the works which might involve Quantum.

Planning

The Planning Phase centered on refining the investment appeals to offset or mitigate negative perceptions about Quantum's stock; more closely defining target audiences, including current stockholders whom we wished to retain; choosing the delivery vehicles to put our message into the target's hand; and develop the means of measuring results to insure we are on target with our desire to:

- double company's market value from $160 to $320 million
- improve liquidity by 10% through increased institutional ownership
- sustain a 35.0X price/earnings multiple
- add 150 new followers among investment professionals
- increase market makers from 8 to 15
- generate 4 market research reports
- use face-to-face meetings and conference calls ahead of media to accomplish goals.

Major elements in the Planning Phase included:

- Gain management's full endorsement on performance objectives, target audiences, methodologies and budget and a commitment to meet with shareholders, the Street and the press.
- Develop media policy guides and training manuals for all management levels and implement a training program, to be administered at national and regional staff meetings.
- Organize a nationwide account team capable of producing program deliverables on time and on budget, to include: program manager, certified stock analyst, media specialists and calling officers for Street contact.
- Produce intelligibly written documents and oral presentations detailing the complexities of self-administration of infusion therapies at home; i.e., what it is, how it works, quality of life issues, and for whom such therapies are best suited.
- Create multiple audience screens to identify those individuals capable of helping us meet our objectives.
- Organize eight major analysts/broker meetings in key financial communities for face-to-face contact and with appropriate follow-up.

- Maximize executive efficiency by promoting one-on-one meetings with key analysts and brokers as business travel schedules permitted.
- Use direct mail to augment financial and trade media in reaching investment professionals.
- Actively track and report on results, refine the process on an ongoing basis and repeat until all objectives are met.

Execution

Execution Phase was greatly enhanced by the research and detailed planning phases that preceded it, making it easy to carry out program recommendations. This staged process helped clearly define Quantum's investment appeals. Details regarding each element of the program are found below:

- **Corporate Summary** — This six-page document was updated twice during the year. It is written in language that facilitates broker understanding and selling of the company as an investment. It also served to educate the financial press by providing background information on each of the disease states served by Quantum and on the company's operations.

- **Analyst Presentation** — Organized along the same lines as the corporate summary, this presentation provides greater detail and depth to the investment story. Over the course of eight analyst/broker meetings and investment banking conferences, the presentation was revised each time in response to post-meeting follow-up calls and quarterly financial updates.

- **Analyst/Broker Meetings** — FRB hosted eight meetings in six of the largest financial centers in the country. These included: New York, Boston, Chicago, Minneapolis, Los Angeles and San Francisco.

- **One-on-One Analyst Meetings** — Using business travel schedules, FRB booked senior management into meetings with analysts, fund and money managers and other "opinion makers" in the investment community. Piggy-backing investor relations activities on other business trips increased IR exposure at little or no cost.

- **Quarterly Conference Calls** — Teleconferencing key followers the day of important news releases provided analysts with immediate access to senior management, the chance to probe behind the numbers and gave management the opportunity to explain non-recurring distortions.

- **Direct Mail Campaign** — Direct mail proved well suited to the IR program: audiences were easily targetable; results were immediate; and respondents provided the opportunities for future mailings. The mailings were used to appeal to brokers and analysts to follow the company and recommend it to clients.

- **Media Campaign** — In the course of the program, FRB determined that the company's CEO was willing to support a limited media effort. This resulted in selective use of media, most notably *Inc.* magazine and live air time on CNBC-FNN and Bloomberg.

  Media note: By using patients loyal to Quantum, the company indirectly guided the *60 Minutes* investigation away from the pharmaceutical expense of hemophilia and helped focus attention on the plight of the chronically ill — notably hemophiliacs, and the need for some form of national health care for the chronically ill. No mention was ever made of Quantum during the 10-minute segment.

- **Article Reprints** — As stories appeared in the press and on the air, they were reprinted or taped and sent on a regular basis to the company's current financial list, to stockholders and used in the direct mail campaign.

- **Stockholder Relations** — To boost shareholder commitment, all communications were carefully crafted to be educational and financially informative; NIRI voted Quantum's annual report best in its industry.

Evaluation

Gain in Market Value	$182,500,000
Program Cost	132,925
Return on Investment	1,375%

In its first full year as a public company, Quantum Health Resources achieved one of the best performances of any nationally traded biotech or health care stock in 1992. The company weathered several crises, including major disruptions in its investment category, deflected a potentially negative story on *60 Minutes*, and still managed to exceed every performance objective set for itself. The program received high marks from the financial community and individual investors and the company's president and CEO, Doug Stickney, was named entrepreneur of the year by *Inc.* magazine.

- market value climbed to $343.2 million from $160.7, a 115% increase
- the number of institutional owners grew to 69 from 45, a gain of 53%
- price/earnings multiple stood at 37.0X, the highest in its peer group
- the registry of close followers of the stock reached 175 names
- market makers doubled to 16 from 8
- 6 research reports were written and issued, 2 are pending publication
- Quantum's stock outperformed the Dow Jones Industrial Average, S&P 500 and NASDAQ Composite by wide margins; by all common measures Quantum was the most successful stock in its peer and industry category

Exhibit 7–1a   News Release

Quantum
Health Resources

NEWS RELEASE

790 The City Drive South. Suite 400. Orange. CA 92668   (714) 750-1610   Fax (714) 750-3235

FOR IMMEDIATE RELEASE: February 17, 1993

CONTACT:

Douglas H. Stickney	**OR** **William James Nicol**
Chairman, Chief Executive Officer	**Senior Vice President and**
and President	**Chief Financial Officer**
Quantum Health Resources, Inc.	**(714) 750-1610**
790 The City Drive South, Suite 400	
Orange, California 92668	**Gary Strong or Kathy Brunson**
(714) 750-1610	**The Financial Relations Board**
	(312) 266-7800

QUANTUM HEALTH RESOURCES, INC.
Reports Record 1992 Revenues, Earnings

ORANGE, CA, February 17, 1993. Quantum Health Resources, Inc. (NASDAQ-QHRI) today reported record revenues and earnings for the year ended December 31, 1992.

Year to date and fourth quarter results for 1992 were reduced by the previously-announced settlement, in the fourth quarter, of litigation brought against Quantum and certain of its officers, directors, employees and others by Caremark, Inc., ("Caremark") in April 1991. The Company's cost of the settlement was $1.85 million, which resulted in an after-tax charge of approximately $1.1 million, or $.08 per share, against net income for the fourth quarter of 1992. Year to date and fourth quarter results for 1991 have been restated to account for the April 28, 1992 acquisition of Factor Care Plus, Inc. as a pooling of interests.

Revenues increased 46% to $118,258,500 compared to $80,770,000 in 1991. Net income for the year just ended increased to $9,256,200, or $0.67 per share, from $5,526,100, or $0.44 per share, in 1991.

In the fourth quarter of 1992, revenues increased 48% to $34,790,200 from $23,507,900 in the same period last year. Net income was $1,974,500, or $0.14 per share, compared to $1,893,000, also $0.14 per share, in the fourth quarter of 1991.

Commenting on the year just ended, Douglas H. Stickney stated, "We are extremely proud of our 1992 results. Were it not for the litigation settlement, which we are very pleased to have finally behind us, our 1992 operating income for the year and fourth quarter would have been $15.4 million and $4.7 million, respectively, reflecting gains of 93% and 82% over the prior year."

((MORE))

Courtesy Quantum Health Resources

Quantum Health Resources, Inc.
February 17, 1993
Add One

"Quantum's ability to produce consistent quarterly earnings growth is most directly attributable to the broadening acceptance of our Chronicare™ service model by physicians who refer patients affected by long-term chronic disorders and by the payors who subsidize the cost of care for those patients," Stickney said. "This model provides Quantum with the means to understand and respond to the special problems facing chronically ill patients, their families and the clinical professionals and payors supporting them.

"Quantum initially developed its Chronicare model to honor its commitment to people affected by hemophilia. By keeping its promises to these patients, families, providers and payors, Quantum has been able to successfully transfer the model to other chronic disorders, most notably genetic emphysema (AAT) and primary immunodeficiency disease (PIDs)," said Stickney. "In the future, the Company will seek other chronic disorders to which the Chronicare service model may be applied."

Quantum has maintained an extremely strong balance sheet featuring over $30 million in cash and no debt. At December 31, 1992, the Company operated 18 licensed branches and 16 sales and service offices. The Company expects to transition several of these offices to licensed branches during 1993.

Pursuant to its previously announced letter of intent, the Company recently executed a Stock Purchase Agreement to acquire The I.V. Clinic, Inc. ("IVC") in exchange for approximately 1.4 million shares of Quantum common stock. Consummation of this transaction is pending completion of IVC's financial audit for the year ended December 31, 1992, which is anticipated prior to February 28, 1993. The acquisition will be accounted for as a pooling of interests.

IVC, founded in 1988, provides a broad array of pediatric and adult home infusion therapies and services to individuals affected by chronic and non-chronic disorders, from three licensed pharmacies located in Dallas, Fort Worth and Houston, Texas. IVC's unaudited revenues for the 12 months ended December 31, 1992, were approximately $19 million.

Quantum Health Resources, Inc., is a national provider of therapies and support services to individuals affected by chronic disorders requiring lifelong therapy. Quantum's Chronicare service is designed to provide therapies and services that enable patients and their families to manage the patient's condition with greater independence, address psychosocial issues related to the disorder and manage the financial burden of the cost of care.

Quantum Health Resources, Inc.
February 17, 1993
Add Two

QUANTUM HEALTH RESOURCES, INC., AND SUBSIDIARIES
SUMMARY STATEMENT OF INCOME

	Year Ended		Three Months Ended	
	12/31/92	12/31/91 [1]	12/31/92	12/31/91 [1]
REVENUES	$118,258,500	$80,770,000	$34,790,200	$23,507,900
OPERATING INCOME [2]	13,578,100	8,007,200	2,861,300	2,594,800
NET INCOME [2]	$ 9,256,200	$ 5,526,100	$ 1,974,500	$ 1,893,000
Earnings per share [2]	$ 0.67	$ 0.44	$ 0.14	$ 0.14
Weighted average shares outstanding	13,833,000	12,537,000	13,934,000	13,650,000

[1] Restated to account for the 4/28/92 acquisition of Factor Care Plus, Inc., as a pooling of interests.

[2] Year and quarter ended 12/31/92 include the Company's cost of the settlement of litigation with Caremark, which reduced operating income, net income and earnings per share by $1,850,000, $1,110,000 and $0.08, respectively.

Quantum Health Resources, Inc.
February 17, 1993
Add Three

QUANTUM HEALTH RESOURCES, INC., AND SUBSIDIARIES
SELECTED CONSOLIDATED FINANCIAL DATA
(in thousands, except per share data)

	Year Ended				Three Months Ended			
	12/31/92		12/31/91		12/31/92		12/31/91	
	Amount	%	Amount	%(1)	Amount	%	Amount	%(1)
Consolidated Statement of Income Data:								
Revenues:								
Hemophilia	$ 81,623	69.0%	$57,787	71.5%	$23,769	68.3%	$16,276	69.2%
AAT/PIDs	17,894	15.2	8,708	10.8	5,897	16.9	2,932	12.5
Other disorders	18,742	15.8	14,275	17.7	5,124	14.8	4,300	18.3
Total revenues	118,259	100.0	80,770	100.0	34,790	100.0	23,508	100.0
Less—Operating costs:								
Cost of products sold	60,485	51.1	42,671	52.8	18,081	52.0	12,086	51.4
Branch personnel costs	15,322	13.0	10,687	13.2	4,441	12.8	2,961	12.6
Other branch costs	9,172	7.8	6,711	8.3	2,691	7.7	2,117	9.0
Provision for uncollectible accounts	5,825	4.9	4,738	5.9	1,521	4.4	1,343	5.7
Branch contribution to earnings	27,455	23.2	15,963	19.7	8,056	23.1	5,001	21.3
Less—Corporate costs:								
General and administrative expenses	12,027	10.2	7,956	9.8	3,344	9.6	2,406	10.2
Settlement of Caremark litigation	1,850	1.5	—	—	1,850	5.3	—	—
Operating income	13,578	11.5	8,007	9.9	2,862	8.2	2,595	11.1
Other, net	1,181	1.0	904	1.1	285	0.8	352	1.5
Income taxes	5,503	4.7	3,385	4.2	1,172	3.3	1,054	4.5
Net income	$ 9,256	7.8%	$ 5,526	6.8%	$ 1,975	5.7%	$ 1,893	8.1%
Earnings per share	$ 0.67		$ 0.44		$ 0.14		$ 0.14	
Weighted average shares outstanding	13,833		12,537		13,934		13,650	

	12/31/92	12/31/91 (1)
Consolidated Balance Sheet Data:		
Cash and equivalents	$30,720	$28,617
Current assets	82,610	62,952
Total assets	87,773	65,926
Liabilities	18,913	13,707
Stockholders' equity	$68,860	$52,219

(1) Restated to account for the 4/28/92 acquisition of Factor Care Plus, Inc., as a pooling of interests.

Exhibit 7–1b   News Release

NEWS RELEASE

790 The City Drive South. Suite 400. Orange. CA 92668   (714) 750-1610   Fax (714) 750-3235

<u>FOR IMMEDIATE RELEASE</u>: February 26, 1993

CONTACT:

Douglas H. Stickney   OR   William James Nicol
Chairman, Chief Executive Officer   Senior Vice President and
 and President   Chief Financial Officer
Quantum Health Resources, Inc.   (714) 750-1610
790 The City Drive South, Suite 400
Orange, California 92668   Gary Strong or Kathy Brunson
(714) 750-1610   Financial Relations Board, Inc.
                                                           (312) 266-7800

QUANTUM HEALTH RESOURCES, INC.
ANNOUNCES COMPLETION OF ITS ACQUISITION OF
THE I. V. CLINIC, INC.

ORANGE, CA, February 26, 1993. Quantum Health Resources, Inc. (NASDAQ-QHRI) announced today that it has consummated its acquisition of The I.V. Clinic, Inc. ("IVC") in exchange for 1,386,681 shares of Quantum common stock. The acquisition will be accounted for as a pooling of interests.

IVC, founded in 1988, provides a broad array of pediatric and adult home infusion therapies and services to individuals affected by chronic and non-chronic disorders from three licensed pharmacies located in Dallas, Fort Worth and Houston, Texas. IVC's audited revenues for the 12 months ended December 31, 1992 were $18,787,918.

Quantum Health Resources, Inc. is a national provider of therapies and support services to individuals affected by certain long-term chronic disorders requiring lifelong therapy. Quantum's Chronicare™ service is designed to provide therapies and services that enable patients and their families to manage the patient's condition with greater independence, address psychosocial issues related to the disorder and manage the financial burden of the cost of care. The Company is headquartered at Nexus City Square, 790 The City Drive South, Suite 400, Orange, California 92668.

Courtesy Quantum Health Resources

Exhibit 7–1c   News Release

Health Resources

NEWS RELEASE

790 The City Drive South. Suite 400. Orange. CA 92668   (714) 750-1610   Fax (714) 750-3235

FOR IMMEDIATE RELEASE: April 28, 1993

CONTACT:

Douglas H. Stickney
Chairman, Chief Executive Officer
 and President
Quantum Health Resources, Inc.
790 The City Drive South, Suite 400
Orange, California 92668
(714) 750-1610

OR   William James Nicol
Senior Vice President and
Chief Financial Officer
(714) 750-1610

Gary Strong or Kathy Brunson
The Financial Relations Board
(312) 266-7800

QUANTUM HEALTH RESOURCES, INC.
REPORTS SUBSTANTIAL INCREASE IN FIRST QUARTER REVENUE,
OPERATING INCOME; NONRECURRING COSTS OF TEXAS ACQUISITION
PARE NET INCOME

ORANGE, CA, April 28, 1993. Quantum Health Resources, Inc. (NASDAQ-QHRI) today reported revenues and net income for the first quarter ended March 31, 1993. The Company also released restated prior period financial statements which reflect its February 25, 1993 acquisition of The I.V. Clinic, Inc. and its two 75%-owned subsidiaries ("IVC"), a Texas provider of pediatric and adult home infusion therapies and services to individuals affected by chronic and nonchronic disorders. This transaction has been accounted for as a pooling of interests.

For the 1993 quarter, revenues increased by $13,476,100, or 47%, to $42,294,700. Operating income, which bore $927,000 in nonrecurring merger transaction costs relating to the IVC acquisition, increased $668,700, or 16%, over the 1992 quarter; before such costs, the increase would have been 37%. Net income, however, decreased slightly to $3,209,000, compared to $3,290,200 for the first quarter of 1992. This decline was primarily attributable to several factors, all relating to the IVC merger. The restatement of the prior year first quarter produced a much lower effective income tax rate since a significant portion of IVC's earnings were generated by an S Corporation not subject to federal income taxes; the 1992 quarter also included revenues and operating income that pertained to an IVC business relationship that was mutually terminated at the end of that quarter. At the same time, the most recent quarter included transaction costs relating to the conclusion of the IVC merger. Earnings per share declined slightly from $0.22 to $0.21 for the same reasons.

Commenting on the quarter just ended, Douglas H. Stickney stated, "Although the accounting conventions relating to poolings of interests and income taxes cloud the comparisons, I believe we had a very strong first quarter compared to the year ago and trailing quarters. Revenues were up significantly and operating income, when adjusted for the fourth quarter's litigation settlement and this quarter's transaction costs, reflected solid gains as well. Gross margin is also tracking as expected from the fourth quarter.

((MORE))

Courtesy Quantum Health Resources

"There are several important considerations in assessing these operating results. First, IVC's revenue and earnings contributions to the comparable period in 1992 included a traditional home I.V. therapy relationship it chose to discontinue at the end of that quarter—a decision with which we wholeheartedly concur. Moreover, IVC's historical financials for the 1992 quarter reflect only a 14% effective tax rate due to the S Corporation status of a significant portion of IVC's earnings. Second, our 1993 figures include the one-time merger transactions costs.

"A better analysis of our performance can be made in this and subsequent periods this year by excluding the 1993 merger transaction costs and assessing an equivalent pro forma tax rate of approximately 40% for both the 1992 and 1993 periods.

"As the notes to the attached Summary Statement of Income indicate, from an earnings per share standpoint, the use of an equivalent pro forma tax rate alone would convert the quarterly performance from a modest decline to a modest improvement, resulting in a comparison of $0.20 this year to $0.19 for the first quarter of 1992. The prior period also includes an extra $0.02 relating to the discontinued traditional I.V. business relationship discussed above. Further, this year's first quarter bears a rounded $0.04 in merger transaction costs. From that perspective, an apples-to-apples comparison is much more indicative of our strong first quarter 1993 performance—$0.24 this year compared to $0.17 last year.

"We are tremendously pleased with the IVC acquisition and our combined results," concluded Mr. Stickney. "IVC has, in one step, gained us a major position in the southwest marketplace as well as some unique insights into new disease categories. We believe we are now even better-positioned for the future."

Quantum Health Resources, Inc., is a national provider of therapies and support services to individuals affected by chronic disorders requiring lifelong therapy. Quantum's Chronicare™ service is designed to provide therapies and services that enable patients and their families to manage the patient's condition with greater independence, address psychosocial issues related to the disorder and manage the financial burden of the cost of care.

((MORE))

279

Quantum Health Resources, Inc.
April 28, 1993
Add Two

QUANTUM HEALTH RESOURCES, INC., AND SUBSIDIARIES
SUMMARY STATEMENT OF INCOME
(Unaudited)

	Three Months Ended	
	3/31/93	3/31/92 [1] [4]
REVENUES	$ 42,294,700	$ 28,818,600
OPERATING INCOME[2]	4,952,300	4,283,600
NET INCOME	$ 3,209,000	$ 3,290,200
EARNINGS PER SHARE	$ 0.21	$ 0.22
Weighted average shares outstanding	15,403,800	15,159,700
SUPPLEMENTAL PRO FORMA DATA[3]:		
NET INCOME	$ 3,084,000	$ 2,928,100
EARNINGS PER SHARE	$ 0.20	$ 0.19

SELECTED BALANCE SHEET ITEMS

	3/31/93	12/31/92 [1]
CURRENT ASSETS	$ 83,301,200	$ 88,598,500
TOTAL ASSETS	$ 90,264,600	$ 94,591,400
LIABILITIES	$ 14,138,600	$ 21,125,900
STOCKHOLDERS' EQUITY	$ 76,126,000	$ 73,465,500

[1] Restated to account for the February 25, 1993, acquisition of The I.V. Clinic, Inc. ("IVC") as a pooling of interests.

[2] Operating income for 1993 quarter included $927,000 of nonrecurring merger transaction costs pertaining to the acquisition of IVC which are not deductible for income tax purposes. These charges reduced net income and earnings per share by $552,000 and $0.036 per share, respectively, in the first quarter of 1993.

[3] Supplemental pro forma data reflects the combined net income of the Company and IVC, adjusted by a pro forma increase in income tax expense for financial reporting purposes on certain S Corporation earnings of IVC which had not been subject to federal income taxes prior to the acquisition, using the Company's blended effective income tax rate for the respective periods.

[4] Operating results for 1992 quarter included revenues and operating income attributable to one of IVC's then-largest business relationships which was discontinued, by mutual agreement, on March 31, 1992, in conjunction with IVC's decision to shift its strategic emphasis to patients affected by chronic disorders. Revenues, operating income and earnings per share (reported and pro forma) generated from this relationship approximated $1.5 million, $0.4 million and $0.02 per share, respectively, in the 1992 quarter.

Exhibit 7–1d   **Excerpt from Chronicare Flyer**

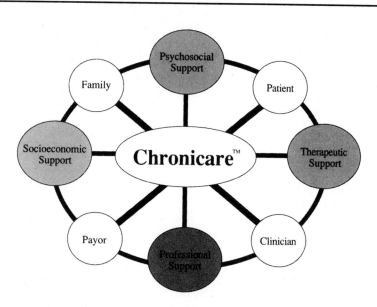

Q**uantum Health Resources** is a national organization dedicated to understanding and meeting the specialized needs of persons affected by chronic disorders such as:

- Alpha$_1$-Antitrypsin Deficiency (Genetic Emphysema)
- Hemophilia and Related Coagulation Disorders
- Primary Immune Deficiencies
- Autoimmune/Polyneuropathy Disorders
- Cystic Fibrosis

C**hronicare**™ services for these patients include:

- Protein Replacement Therapies, such as Prolastin®, Factors 8 & 9 and IVIG
- Concomitant I.V. Therapies, including Antibiotics, Nutrition, GCSF and Pain Management
- Concomitant Oral Medications such as Bronchodilators, AZT, Corticosteroids, Enzymes, etc.
- Third Party Payor Services
- Family Support Groups
- Professional Educational Seminars
- Foundation, Registry and Association Support
- Professional Services: Clinical Pharmacy & Nursing, Respiratory Therapy, Nutritional Support and Psychosocial Counseling

Quantum
Health Resources

For local branch locations or information about Chronicare,™ call Quantum Health Resources at (800) 477-1610.

Courtesy Quantum Health Resources

Its 1992 investor relations program successfully positioned the nonbeer businesses of the Adolph Coors Company as ACX Technologies, a diversified technology company that quickly became one of the "hottest stocks on Wall Street." Exhibit 7– 2a consists of excerpts from an ACX Technologies brochure.

Case 7–2   ACX Technologies 1992 Investor Relations Program

ACX Technologies, Golden, CO

Research

In May 1992, the board of directors of Adolph Coors Company agreed in principle to spin off the nonbeer business of Coors in order to allow better access to capital sources to finance growth, enhance managerial flexibility, and permit investors, lenders, and other constituencies to better evaluate the separate businesses. On December 27, 1992, the spin-off was finalized and the distribution to stockholders of shares in the new company was completed. Initially, the new company, ACX Technologies, Inc., was unknown and had no Wall Street following. The company, with the assistance of its investment banker, helped create interest in the company and its shares through an aggressive investor relations campaign. The company first examined thirty-five public companies within five industry peer group categories and compared these companies with ACX Technologies. As a result of this study, it was decided to emphasize the proprietary technology which was involved in the manufacturing of many of the products produced by the company. With its unique aluminum mini-mill process, high-performance consumer packaging, and advanced technical ceramic products business segment, along with several research and development businesses, ACX Technologies believed it should be considered a Diversified Technology company. This peer group has the advantage of attaining the highest price/ earnings multiple next to the aluminum companies.

Courtesy ACX Technologies

Planning

The following goals were set for the company:

- Establish ACX Technology as a Diversified Technology company because of the unique technologies employed. This category had the greatest price/earnings multiple of the industries examined.

- Create a personality or identity so that ACX Technologies would not be perceived as still being in the shadow of Coors, its former parent.

- Identify the target audience in terms of sell-side analysts most likely to be interested in covering the company and institutions concerned with investing in the stock based on their investment parameters.

- Establish third-party credibility through media placements and independent research reports from brokerage firms.

- Have an orderly market in the stock once it began trading.

Execution

Planning for the launch of the new company began in early October. Several investor relations communications vehicles, such as a fact sheet, a seven-minute corporate video, and a slide show were created. A logo was developed, along with news release stationery and various "give aways" such as coffee mugs, pens, memo paper, and luggage tags, all with the ACX logo on them. A press kit folder containing camera-ready logo sheets, bios on top management, along with the fact sheet and appropriate news releases was prepared for the media. ACX management received media training and participated in meetings with sell-side analysts and the media. Company management also met with analysts in New York City and in Chicago, including several prestigious analysts on the *Institutional Investor* All-American Research Team. The meetings included large brokerage houses with vast retail coverage, such as Donaldson, Lufkin & Jenrette, First Boston Corporation, Merrill Lynch & Co. Inc., Morgan Stanley Group, Inc., Paine Webber Inc., Prudential Financial, and Salomon Brothers Asset Management. More formal meetings were arranged in December in a half-dozen other cities around the country, as well as a New York City media tour.

Evaluation

The spin-off launch of ACX Technologies has been viewed by many analysts and money managers as one of the most successful they had seen. Third-party credibility for ACX Technologies came quickly, with extensive local and national business media coverage, including the *Wall Street Journal* and *Business Week*. Sample headlines included: "Coors spin-off ACX starting off on fast track." Analysts' acceptance of ACX Technologies on the two-week financial tour was very positive, as shown by the December 29, 1992, "soft soundings" of those individuals. Also, five research reports were in the process of being prepared. They included reports by Bear, Stearns & Co. Inc., C. J. Lawrence, Inc., Dillon, Read & Co. Inc., Merrill Lynch & Co. and The Robinson-Humphrey Company, Inc. The target audience was identified as both sell-side and buy-side analysts. Meetings have taken place with these individuals, and they are now on the company's mailing list. ACX Technologies was successfully accepted as its own company, with its own personality and style based on media stories, preliminary research reports, and soft-soundings. As the *Rocky Mountain News* article of December 16, 1992 stated: "A new Fortune 500 company has been born in Colorado. Adolph Coors Co.'s spin-off of its ceramics, packaging, aluminum and technology businesses into ACX Technologies, Inc. is the talk of Denver equities circles." ACX Technologies was effectively positioned as a Diversified Technology company, based on media stories, preliminary research reports and soft-soundings.

STOCK PRICE HISTORY	
DATE	OPENING PRICE
December 10, 1992	$10.75
	CLOSING PRICE
December 10, 1992	$15.50
End of December 1992	$21.75
End of January 1993	$27.25
End of February 1993	$28.50

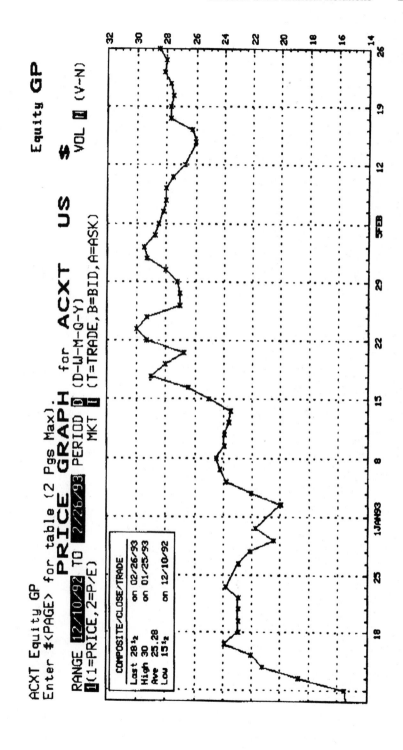

Exhibit 7–2a   **Excerpts from ACX Technologies Brochure**

Winter 1992

★ HEADQUARTERS

■ GRAPHIC PACKAGING
   CORPORATION

✳ GOLDEN ALUMINUM
   COMPANY

● COORS CERAMICS
   COMPANY

▼ DEVELOPMENTAL
   COMPANIES

FOREIGN OPERATIONS (not shown):   Glenrothes, Scotland (Ceramic Manufacturing Plant)
                                  Thun, Switzerland (Bauener Engineering)

ACX Technologies is a new,

Fortune 500-sized Company, which applies

innovative technology in the manufacture

of superior industrial products.

HIGHLIGHTS

■ ACX Technologies manufactures value-added materials and products with unique or special properties for industrial markets worldwide. Its products include: high-impact, moisture-resistant packaging; advanced ceramics; and aluminum rigid container sheet.

■ ACX Technologies will be spun-off in late December 1992 as an independent, innovative technology company.

■ ACX Technologies utilizes environmentally sound, technically advanced manufacturing processes.

■ ACX Technologies is committed to focusing on earnings growth.

■ ACX Technologies manages a portfolio of seasoned core businesses that provide base earnings, as well as growth potential. The Company has a solid balance sheet and a high asset value.

NASDAQ: ACXT	
Stock Distribution Date:	Dec. 27, 1992
Est. Shares Outstanding:	12,537,000
Est. Shareowners of Record:	6,000
Pro Forma 3rd Quarter 1992	
Book Value Per Share:	$31.65

Pro Forma 3rd Quarter 1992	
Total Assets:	$625,833,000
Current Ratio:	1.6
1991	
Net Sales:	$543,503,000
Operating Income:	$8,897,000
Net Income:	$1,345,000

Courtesy ACX Technologies

TECHNOLOGIES

EMPLOYS APPROXIMATELY 4,200 FULL-TIME
EMPLOYEES, INCLUDING 3,000 IN MANUFACTURING
AND 1,200 IN RESEARCH AND DEVELOPMENT,
ENGINEERING, AND SALES AND ADMINISTRATION.

PRODUCTS/MARKETS

Graphic Packaging Corporation

HIGH-PERFORMANCE value-added folding carton and flexible packaging for major manufacturers of beverages, bar soaps, concentrated detergents, snack foods, photographic paper, pet food and other products. The folding carton market is a $5 billion industry. The flexible packaging market is a $13 billion industry. Both markets have grown at consistent, moderate rates, with higher growth expected in certain niches (e.g., bar soaps, concentrated detergents, microwave dinner entrees and snack foods such as soft cookies).

Coors Ceramics Company

IN BUSINESS for more than 70 years, Coors Ceramics is the largest U.S. manufacturer of advanced technical ceramics, producing a wide range of product lines for thousands of structural and electronic applications. Industry data indicates substantial growth in the 1990s for the U.S. and world markets in the advanced technical ceramics industry.

Golden Aluminum Company

FORMED IN 1980, Golden Aluminum manufactures aluminum rigid container sheet (RCS) used by its customers to make can ends, lids, tabs and bodies for aluminum beverage and food use. The RCS market in North America has experienced moderate but consistent growth for the past several years with higher growth rates expected for international markets.

LOOKING TO THE FUTURE

R&D and Developmental Companies

GOLDEN TECHNOLOGIES is the company's R&D vehicle for the development of promising new technologies and is the parent company of the developmental companies. Golden Technologies intends to focus on commercializing promising technologies that have the potential for high profitability and significant growth.

287

TECHNOLOGY

USING COMPOSIPAC™ a patented packaging technology developed internally, Graphic Packaging's folding cartons are manufactured with high-quality graphics and have enhanced moisture and air protection properties that preserve the integrity of the product inside. The use of a printed film allows recycled paperboard to be used while providing superior package graphics.

COORS CERAMICS continues to develop exciting new materials and new technologies, including automobile air-bag initiators, pressure sensors and fiber-optic connectors. The company has also developed zirconia and silicon carbide-based ceramic products and is developing other materials to complement its conventional alumina-based product lines.

GOLDEN ALUMINUM'S patented continuous-cast technology uses a higher proportion of recycled material and less energy than any other RCS process. In 1984, Golden Aluminum began manufacturing operations at its Ft. Lupton, Colorado, rolling mill. This facility proved, on a small scale, the commercial viability of its continuous block casting process to manufacture RCS end and tab stock using primarily used beverage can scrap.

GOLDEN TECHNOLOGIES uses a proprietary process to manufacture Bio-T, a biodegradable solvent replacement for chlorinated hydrocarbons. Another new technology is the development of advanced electronic modules that are used in military and industrial applications.

RECENT DEVELOPMENTS

RECENTLY COMPLETED and planned upgrades to printing, bag making and lamination equipment will enable Graphic Packaging to extend sales into personal care products and expand sales in existing flexible packaging markets, such as photographic and chemical packaging. A total quality management program is used to improve product quality and lower manufacturing costs.

THE COMPANY HAS COMPLETED a plant modernization program begun in 1988 that involved the construction of a number of new facilities and the modernization of several others. The company recently signed multi-year cooperative agreements that give Coors Ceramics exclusive rights to study and develop certain technology owned by the U.S. Department of Energy.

IN 1991, the company completed construction of its San Antonio rolling mill which is now in the start-up phase. This state-of-the-art mill is designed to manufacture RCS for food and beverage can bodies. The company has also entered into a joint venture with an Australian company to investigate the feasibility of constructing a 230 million pound annual capacity aluminum rolling mill in Australia.

GOLDEN TECHNOLOGIES has acquired the equipment and technology to research and develop low-cost, thin panel solar energy modules. The company is also involved in the co-development of a proprietary technology for the application of biodegradable polymers.

CHALLENGES

AS THE COMPANY BEGINS to become a more significant player in the value-added packaging market, managing its growth and maintaining high-quality standards will be the major challenges. Competition is also a factor, with large suppliers dominating the folding carton segment and numerous suppliers in the flexible packaging segment.

THE COMPANY INTENDS TO BUILD ON its success in industrial markets by continued materials development and strategic international growth. International players and competition from manufacturers of lower cost alternative materials continue to challenge the ceramics industry.

THE SAN ANTONIO MILL is targeted to complete the qualification process, for certain customers, in early 1993. The worldwide aluminum RCS market is highly competitive and dominated by large multinational integrated producers.

FINDING COMMERCIALLY VIABLE, untapped markets or utilizing new technologies is a high-risk, high-reward business. Some of these ventures will not succeed. Most will take years to develop.

OPPORTUNITIES

MANAGEMENT EXPERIENCE

GRAPHIC PACKAGING is targeting selected market segments which are expected to grow more rapidly than the overall industry. Individual products such as bags and pouches, and roll stock products such as labels, overwraps and lidding, used in medical, personal care, food, coffee and detergent products are Graphic Packaging's primary targets. Potential new product development efforts are expected in sift proof cartons, linerless cartons and liquid containment packages and environmentally friendly packaging innovations.

DAVID H. HOFMANN, 54, has been president and chief executive officer of Graphic Packaging since October of 1989. He has more than 25 years of industry experience.

CERAMICS IS A MATERIAL OF THE FUTURE because of its inherent properties which include corrosion and wear resistance, hardness, non-conductivity and extreme temperature resistance. New applications and markets in the U.S. and abroad are being developed.

JIM WADE, 52, has been president and chief operating officer of Coors Ceramics since 1992 and 1991, respectively. He has more than 30 years of industry experience, having started his career with Coors Ceramics in 1959.

GOLDEN ALUMINUM'S FOCUS is to expand market share in North America and enter international markets where growth opportunities are greatest. When fully operational, the San Antonio plant will nearly triple the company's aluminum sheet capacity.

JOSEPH S. LAMB, 48, has been president and chief executive officer of Golden Aluminum since 1982. He has more than 25 years of industry and business experience.

THESE DEVELOPMENTAL COMPANIES are working on several technologies that could become substantial future business opportunities.

DEAN A. RULIS, 45, president of Golden Technologies, has more than 25 years of engineering and business experience. He has held numerous positions in project management, facilities management and engineering.

SUMMARY FINANCIAL RESULTS

(Dollars in Thousands)	1991	1990	1989
Net Sales			
Graphic Packaging Corporation	$188,141	$155,809	$136,848
Coors Ceramics Company	180,146	179,796	166,227
Golden Aluminum Company	95,996	113,445	94,173
Developmental Companies	76,956	69,866	69,570
Corporate and R&D[1]	2,264	2,313	—
Total	$543,503	$521,229	$466,818
Operating Income (Loss)			
Graphic Packaging Corporation	$17,185	$ 9,804	$ 772
Coors Ceramics Company	1,983	2,214	14,802
Golden Aluminum Company	6,346	16,322	9,110
Developmental Companies	(4,805)	(3,394)	(7,897)
Corporate and R&D[1]	(11,812)	(8,998)	(1,906)
Total	$ 8,897	$ 15,948	$ 14,881
Assets			
Graphic Packaging Corporation	$109,831	$102,800	$110,961
Coors Ceramics Company	167,330	147,915	151,175
Golden Aluminum Company	252,691	194,152	93,702
Developmental Companies	83,640	80,832	65,760
Corporate and R&D[1]	27,459	50,736	1,159
Total	$640,951	$576,435	$422,757
Capital Expenditures			
Graphic Packaging Corporation	$ 11,217	$ 4,187	$ 3,114
Coors Ceramics Company	26,668	14,356	32,960
Golden Aluminum Company	67,552	83,236	15,826
Developmental Companies	7,314	14,938	5,154
Corporate and R&D[1]	266	1,936	—
Total	$113,017	$118,653	$ 57,054

Note (1) Corporate and Research and Development's (R&D) operating results include allocated corporate charges from the parent company and the historical results of certain efforts to develop and commercialize new technologies. Corporate and R&D assets include cash and cash equivalents and certain property, plant and equipment.

Consolidated Net Sales
(Dollars in Millions)

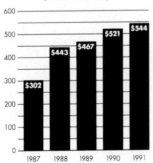

1991 Net Sales by Business

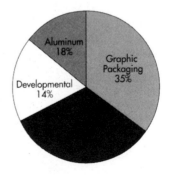

A lingering malaise caused by, among other reasons, a "flat" yield curve, pegged the share price for Asset Investors Corporation at half its book value through all of 1990. This problem seemed destined to persist into 1991 despite healthy earnings, a 24 percent annual cash dividend, and a five-year total annual return to stockholders of 32 percent. Research revealed that the complexity of the company's business and a negative industry image deterred interest in the stock by the investment community. Given these circumstances, the company mounted a major investor education program that made its business less esoteric and positioned it as a high-performance exception to its industry. Exhibits 7–3a and 7–3b are news bulletins about the company's financial position.

Case 7–3

Asset Investors Corporation Broadens Investment Appeal by Educating Investors

Asset Investors Corporation, Denver, CO, with The Financial Relations Board, Chicago, IL

The Background

Asset Investors Corporation helped establish the collateralized mortgage obligation (CMO) residuals industry in 1986 — an industry that fell out of investment favor in 1989–1990. This New York Stock Exchange-listed stock dropped from a high of $19.25 per share in 1987 to a low of $5.37 in 1989 and hovered at $8.00 through much of 1990. Negative investor sentiment seemed destined to persist well into 1991 despite a healthy earnings recovery, a 24 percent annual dividend yield on a AAA-rated portfolio, and a five-year total annual return to stockholders of 32 percent.

In this context, the investor relations issues became:

1. Identify those issues preventing investors from buying Asset Investors' stock
2. Find means to overcome the roadblocks to stock ownership
3. Separate Asset Investors from its industry's negative image
4. Broaden stock support and secure an appropriate price/earnings ratio

Courtesy Asset Investors Corporation

Research

Research efforts took four forms:

1. An ongoing program of discussion and contact with financial industry analysts
2. A series of discussions with stockbrokers who currently or previously recommended Asset Investors stock
3. A survey of current and past stockholders to determine positive and negative perceptions about the stock
4. A series of detailed questions, asked of each group, to determine the level of understanding of interest rate arbitrage (the principle behind Asset Investors' business)

These efforts brought several facts to light:

- Few investment professionals and even fewer stockholders understood interest rate arbitrage and how Asset Investors earned its income
- In some cases, this lack of knowledge (specifically the stock's potential volatility) had led to unsuitable investments by individuals and brokers
- This lack of understanding caused other investment professionals and individuals not to invest in something that "looked too good to be true"
- No distinction was being made between Asset Investors and other real estate investment trusts (REITs) despite significant fundamental distinctions between them
- Any new interest in the stock would require extensive documentation and marketing effort

Objectives

Asset Investors and The Financial Relations Board concluded that the primary goal of the 1991 investor relations program was to educate both individual and professional investors. All efforts were to be directed at:

1. Explaining the business of CMO residuals and eliminating misconceptions

2. Differentiating the company from other REITs
3. Providing investment suitability guidelines for brokers
4. Encouraging the use of this new knowledge to assess the company's investment merits

Specific goals were:

- Introduce Asset Investors to 150 prequalified, high-producing retail brokers and 50 institutional managers who would follow and recommend the stock
- Attract a cadre of independent high net worth investors capable of taking large share positions
- Generate high profile national press coverage and speaking engagements that would aid the education process
- Solidify support among current stockholders

Execution

The program incorporated the following elements:

- Ten major analysts/broker meetings in large financial communities
- Visits to 30 financial communities by FRB investment community contacts
- A corporate summary fact sheet targeted at retail brokers and sophisticated independent investors
- A direct mail campaign targeted at select high-volume brokers and affluent independent investors
- Speaking engagements and panel and industry forums
- An extensive media campaign, including bylined articles and interviews in the financial press, national business publications, television, radio, and selected trade journals
- An ongoing communications program to strengthen stockholder relations
- A telephone-activated data retrieval system for distributing company information via fax

Concurrent to these activities, FRB conducted lengthy interviews for clues as to how to improve presentation and written materials at every point in the program.

Evaluation

The program received high marks from the financial community and individual investors. Results included:

- Professional investment interest in the company by 174 registered representatives, 35 portfolio managers, 16 analysts, and 5 research directors
- More than 200 high net worth investors being added to the company's following
- Two pending research reports
- Two investment banks entered preliminary discussions on how to raise $50 to $200 million in new equity, which would double the company's size

Media played an important role in achieving these results. Asset Investors received extensive coverage because of its willingness to educate and guide reporters through the intricacies of CMO residuals. Interviews were conducted with and coverage appeared in *Barron's, The Wall Street Journal, Dow Jones News Wire, Reuters, Chief Executive Magazine, Personal Investing News, Institutional Investor, Financial World, Wall Street Transcript,* Business Radio Network, CNBC-FNN, and WCIU-Channel 26 in Chicago.

A reporting problem was also resolved. For years, the business wires (Dow Jones and Reuters) had a policy of only reporting GAAP net income on quarterly corporate earnings. The exclusion of tax income in the third quarter, 1991, earnings broadcast by Dow Jones and Reuters precipitated a $1.50 per share price drop in 40 minutes — a 9.4 percent loss in market value equal to $21 million. FRB efforts resulted in (1) a fuller disclosure and broadtape story on the company and (2) a change in Dow Jones, Reuters, and Bloomberg reporting policies on real estate investment trusts; the wire services now report not only GAAP net income, but tax income and cash dividends as well for the REIT industry.

The program's tangible results were greater than projected:

- Price per share rose 103 percent to $15.00
- The company's price earnings ratio jumped 66 percent, a four year high
- Average daily trading volume was up 31 percent to 17 million shares per month

Research

The purpose of the Research Phase was four-fold: (1) Assess current interest in Asset Investors among financial industry analysts, money managers and senior brokers; (2) Assess near-term interest in the company among high net worth investors; (3) Uncover positive and negative perceptions about the stock and its industry; (4) Determine whether or not investors (professional or individual) truly understand Asset Investors' business.

Key elements in this portion of the investor relations program were:

- In-depth study of CMO-residuals, including: how income is generated through interest rate arbitrage; their value as an industry; performance characteristics; performance over time; comparative assessments of Asset Investors' competitors.

- A review of written reactions by all analysts/brokers who had attended Asset Investors analyst meetings within the past two years to fully understand investment community attitudes toward the company.

- Discussions with Asset Investors' two principal executives to determine their impressions of current feelings among Wall Streeters toward the company and its industry.

- An extensive national survey of key buy-side (institutional) and sell-side (retail) analysts to assess overall interest in the stock and to classify major players in terms of potential or continuing investment interest in Asset Investors.

- Field trip surveys by FRB's investment community contact staff in 30 major metropolitan areas to identify new and continuing interest in Asset Investors. Field trips were followed by detailed commentary from those canvassed.

- Telephone and direct mail surveys of stockbrokers who currently or in the past have recommended the stock to determine (1) their level of understanding of CMO residuals, (2) their satisfaction with the stock's performance and (3) to whom they recommended the stock.

Key findings in this portion of the investor relations program were:

- Almost universally, the professional investment community found CMO-REITs of little interest because of the volatility of the stock, the complexities behind interest rate arbitrage and a lack of conviction that Asset's high yields were sustainable.

- Those brokerage houses that had touted REITs in their halcyon days had suffered major losses and had been barraged by lawsuits from disgruntled investors; there was little desire on their part to repeat the exercise.

- Because REIT income is untaxed at the corporate level, it must be taxed at the stockholder's personal income level; this requires additional tax work for some portfolio managers and others, a deterrent to investment even at the highest yields.

- High net worth investors, were very interested in the company's high yields (particularly in today's declining rate environment); however, a lack of understanding about CMO residuals or bad experience with them were major investment deterrents.

- Substantial numbers of investors were not truly suitable for the stock but were lured to it by its high yields; little understanding of the investment risks made them vulnerable to unexpected fluctuations in dividend payments and stock price.

- Few investors understood the differences between equity, mortgage and hybrid REITs and generally lumped them together in terms of investment appeals; the 1990 bankruptcy of a major mortgage REIT helped sour the industry.

- Long-term investors were more than satisfied with the stock's high dividend payout and 32 percent total annual return on the investment; those no longer in the stock either had sold for profit taking purposes or suffered substantial losses in the stock.

- Literature, research or even current financial press on the industry was woefully lacking, and none of what did exist was very successful in explaining how or why CMO-REITs even exist.

- Asset Investors' own literature and presentations were difficult to follow; most of it had the feel of a legal document and offered few readily-understandable comparisons to other segments of the financial industry.

- The general and financial press had only a superficial knowledge of CMO-REITs and were no better off than most uninformed investors about the investment characteristics of these securities; little editorial interest existed.

Planning

If Asset Investors expected to resolve the issues uncovered in the research, or if it expected to identify itself as a special investment opportunity (separate from its general industry), and if it expected to broaden its investment support, it had to persuasively educate all audiences about its value as an investment, the risks involved and how to manage those risks.

The Planning Phase centered on finding ways to remove real or perceived roadblocks to owning Asset Investors' stock and developing support for the stock to secure an appropriate price earnings ratio. Specifically we needed to: (1) Introduce Asset Investors to 150 retail brokers and 50 institutional managers who would recommend the stock; (2) Attract a cadre of 200 or more independent high net worth investors capable of taking large share positions; (3) Generate high profile national press coverage and speaking engagements that would aid the education process; (4) Solidify support among current stockholders.

To accomplish these objectives we needed to: (1) Create an educational investment appeals message; (2) Selectively distribute this message and materials to targeted audiences; (3) Actively seek feedback on these efforts. Major elements in the Planning Phase included:

- Gain management's full endorsement of the education concept, an agreement to stay the course throughout 1991 and an unwavering commitment to the time obligations required to meet with shareholders, the Street and the press.

- Organize a nationwide account team capable of producing program deliverables on time and on budget, to include: program manager, certified stock analyst, media specialists and calling officers for Street contact.

- Produce intelligibly written documents and oral presentations detailing CMO-residuals in the simplest possible terms; i.e., what it is, how it works, its potential rewards, its investment risks, and for whom such an investment is best suited.

- Create multiple audience screens to identify those individuals capable of helping us meet our objectives.

- Organize ten major analysts/broker meetings in key financial communities for face-to-face contact and with appropriate follow-up.

- Maximize executive efficiency by promoting one-on-one meetings with key analysts and brokers as business travel schedules permitted.

- Use direct mail to augment FRB's list of 30,000 investment professionals and develop an outside source of high net worth investors.

- Launch a broad media and platform campaign using the CEO as spokesperson for the company for highest possible audience visibility.

- Actively track and report on results, refine the process on an ongoing basis and repeat until all objectives are met.

Execution

Execution Phase was greatly enhanced by the research and detailed planning phases that preceded it, making it easy to carry out program recommendations. This staged process helped clearly define Asset Investors' core business and identify its investment appeals. Details regarding each element of the program are found below:

- **Corporate Summary** — This eight-page document was drafted in language that facilitated broker understanding and selling of the company as an investment. It also served to educate the financial press by communicating CMO-residual industry basics. A great deal of space is devoted to describing exactly what it is the company does and where its investment risks lie. By simplifying the complexity of the client's business, the summary helped spark interest among sophisticated high net worth investors and their financial advisors. The summary has two unique features. First, for retail brokers and other investment professionals, it suggests for whom the stock is most appropriate: (1) Investors who can buy and hold for longer periods of time, or (2) Investors with actively traded accounts who closely follow interest rate trends. Second, the summary makes compelling financial comparisons between Asset Investors and its largest competitors. Call to brokers yielded reactions such as, "the best document available on CMO residuals," and "[the AIC summary] has helped enormously in selling this type of high yield/high risk investment."

- **Analyst Presentation** — Organized along the same lines as the corporate summary, this presentation delves into the financial intricacies of the company and provides greater detail and depth to the investment story. This higher level of analytical analysis was possible due to pre-meeting efforts to "school" attendees in company basics prior to the meeting. Over the course of ten analyst/broker meetings, the presentation was revised four times in response to post-meeting follow-up calls among those that attended.

- **Analyst/Broker Meetings** — FRB hosted ten meetings in six of the largest financial centers in the country. These included: New York, Boston, Chicago, Minneapolis, Los Angeles and San Francisco.

- **One-on-One Analyst Meetings** — Using business travel schedules, FRB booked senior management into meetings with analysts, fund and money managers and other "opinion makers" in the investment community. Piggy-backing investor relations activities on other business trips increased IR exposure at little or no cost.

- **Quarterly Conference Calls** — Teleconferencing key followers the day of important news releases provided analysts with immediate access to senior management, the chance to probe behind the numbers and gave management the opportunity to explain anomalies or non-recurring distortions.

- **Direct Mail Campaign** — Direct mail proved well suited to the IR program: (1) audiences were easily targetable, (2) results were immediately measurable, (3) respondents provided the opportunities for future mailings. The lists used for this portion of the campaign included: (1) American Association of Individual Investors, (2) *Financial World*, (3) *Individual Investor*, (4) *Registered Representative*, (5) *Today's Investor*, (6) *Wall Street Games*, and (7) FRB's own list.

The mailings were used (1) to appeal directly to brokers and analysts to follow the company and recommend it to clients and (2) to spark interest in the stock among sophisticated high net worth investors and their financial advisors. The mailing contained the corporate summary, a Q&A interview reprinted from *Personal Investing News* and a business reply card.

- **Media Campaign** — In the course of the program, FRB determined that the company's two principal officers were willing to support a high visibility media effort, over and above what had been planned for the year. [It should be noted here that since 1989 the company had shied away from the press due to a rash of negative articles that had appeared in the Denver press.] In short order, FRB's Chicago and New York media executives landed a series of exceptional interviews and articles for the company, a process that has continued unabated since March, 1991.

One media note: For years Dow Jones, Reuters and the business wires have had a policy of only reporting GAAP net income on quarterly corporate earnings. Their exclusion of *tax income* in the company's third quarter earnings broadcast caused Asset Investors' per share price to drop $1.50 in 40 minutes — a 9.4% loss in market value equal to $21 million. Efforts by FRB resulted in (1) a reissue of the earnings release with fuller disclosure, (2) a broadtape story on AIC, and (3) a change in Dow Jones and Reuters reporting policies on real estate investment trusts, i.e., in the future the wire services will report all salient including: GAAP net income, tax income and cash dividends for the REITs.

- **By-Lined Articles** — By-lined articles are one of the best ways to air investment appeals from the company perspective. Two such articles were written, predictably using the program's "investor education" approach.

- **Article Reprints** — As stories appeared in the press and on the air, they were reprinted or taped and sent on a regular basis to the company's current financial list, to stockholders and used in the direct mail campaign.

- **Speaking Engagements** — FRB approached trade associations and professional organizations for platform opportunities; Investment Management Institute organized a complete program on CMO-REITs, chaired by the company's CEO.

- **Stockholder Relations** — To boost shareholder commitment, all communications were carefully crafted to be educational and financially informative.

- **Annual Report Proposal** — The 1991 Annual Report (due off the press in April) takes industry education to a prominent level.

- **Consulting** — Identified two firms willing to investigate how to raise $50 million to $200 million in new equity, effectively doubling the size of the company.

Evaluation

Results of the 1991 investor relations program for Asset Investors speak for themselves.

The original objectives were to: (1) Find the means to overcome roadblocks to Asset Investor stock ownership; (2) Differentiate the company from other REITs; (3) Introduce the company to 150 pre-qualified, high-producing retail brokers and 50 institutional managers who would follow and recommend the stock; (4) Attract a cadre of independent high net worth investors capable of taking large share positions; (5) Generate high profile national press coverage and speaking engagements that would aid the education process; (6) Solidify the support among current stockholders; all aimed at (7) Broadening stock support to secure an appropriate price/earnings ratio.

Claiming that the "educational approach" used in this program *proved* itself successful has to be considered subjective; however, the documentation used here to illustrate the achievement of all measurable goals should be sufficient to support the claim. Documentation includes:

- Independent statistical reports that show broadened investor sponsorship
     103 percent increase in share price
     66 percent increase in the company's price/earnings ratio
     31 percent increase in average daily trading volume
     14 percent increase in institutional holders
     9 percent increase in individual holders

- Surveys that show more than 58 percent of the 300 investment professionals who attended meetings have begun recommending or have begun regular coverage of the stock. In addition, the direct mail program attracted 174 registered representatives, 35 portfolio managers, 16 analysts, 5 research directors, and more than 200 high net worth investors to the stock.

- Feature articles from *Barron's, The Wall Street Journal, Dow Jones News Wire, Reuters, Chief Executive Magazine, Personal Investing News, Institutional Investor, Financial World, Wall Street Transcript,* Business Radio Network, CNBC-FNN and WCIU-Channel 26 in Chicago.

- Performance comparison that clearly indicates the company managed to separate itself from its poor industry image, as indicated by its total return performance when compared with the REIT industry as a whole.

NEWS BULLETIN RE:

Asset Investors Corporation
3600 South Yosemite Ste. 1000
Denver, Colorado 80237

TRADED: NYSE (AIC)

From: *The Financial Relations Board, Inc.*

Financial Relations Board. Inc. serves as financial relations counsel to this company. is acting on the company's behalf in issuing this bulletin and receiving compensation therefor. The information contained herein is furnished for information purposes only and is not to be construed as an offer to buy or sell securities.

For Further Information:

AT THE COMPANY:	AT FRB CHICAGO:	AT FRB NEW YORK:
Spencer I. Browne	Gary Strong	Scott Snyderman
President & CEO or	875 N. Michigan Ave.	675 Third Avenue
Michael H. Feinstein	Chicago, IL 60611	New York, NY 10017
Executive Vice President	(312) 266-7800	(212) 661-8030
(303) 793-2703		

FOR IMMEDIATE RELEASE
THURSDAY, DECEMBER 5, 1991

ASSET INVESTORS CORPORATION INCREASES REGULAR QUARTERLY

DIVIDEND TO 75 CENTS PER SHARE AND DECLARES A YEAR-END 1991

SPECIAL DIVIDEND OF 5 CENTS PER SHARE

DENVER, CO, December 5, 1991 -- Asset Investors Corporation (NYSE: AIC) today announced its board of directors had declared a regular quarterly dividend of 75 cents per share for the fourth quarter of 1991 and a year-end 1991 special dividend of 5 cents per share. These dividends are payable on December 27, 1991 to stockholders of record on December 16, 1991.

The 75 cent per share regular quarterly dividend represents a 25 cent per share increase over the Company's 50 cent per share dividend paid for the fourth quarter of 1990 and a 5 cent per share increase over the 70 cent dividend paid for the third quarter of 1991. The Company's $2.70 in dividends per share declared in 1991 are 46 percent higher than the $1.85 in dividends per share paid by Asset Investors in 1990.

Spencer I. Browne, president and chief executive officer of Asset Investors, commented, "The increase in the regular quarterly dividend and the addition of the special

-MORE-

Asset Investors Corporation

Add One

dividend are attributable, among other things, to increases in tax income due to additions to the Company's portfolio of CMO residual interests and lower short-term interest rates. With the payments of these dividends, Asset Investors will have paid in excess of $143,400,000, or $11.45 per share, in aggregate dividends since the Company's inception in December 1986."

Asset Investors Corporation is a real estate investment trust that generates income from a portfolio of ownership interests in the issuances of collateralized mortgage obligations (CMOs) and other mortgage-related assets.

-30-

**For Additional Information on Asset Investors Corporation,
VIA FAX, No Cost - Dial 1-800-PRO-INFO, Code #016**

NEWS BULLETIN RE:

Asset Investors Corporation
3600 South Yosemite Ste. 1000
Denver, Colorado 80237

TRADED: NYSE (AIC)

From: *The Financial Relations Board, Inc.*

Financial Relations Board. Inc. serves as financial relations counsel to this company, is acting on the company's behalf in issuing this bulletin and receiving compensation therefor. The information contained herein is furnished for information purposes only and is not to be construed as an offer to buy or sell securities.

For Further Information:

AT THE COMPANY:	AT FRB CHICAGO:	AT FRB NEW YORK:
Spencer I. Browne	Gary Strong	Scott Snyderman
President & CEO or	875 N. Michigan Ave.	675 Third Avenue
Michael H. Feinstein	Chicago, IL 60611	New York, NY 10017
Executive Vice President	(312) 266-7800	(212) 661-8030
(303) 793-2703		

FOR IMMEDIATE RELEASE
WEDNESDAY, MARCH 4, 1992

ASSET INVESTORS CORPORATION DECLARES

FIRST QUARTER DIVIDEND OF 50 CENTS PER SHARE

DENVER, CO, March 4 -- Asset Investors Corporation (NYSE: AIC) today announced its board of directors had declared a quarterly dividend of 50 cents per share payable on March 31, 1992 to stockholders of record on March 16, 1992.

The first quarter dividend represents a decrease of 5 cents per share from the 55 cents per share dividend declared for the first quarter of 1991. The decrease results from an anticipated reduction in first quarter 1992 REIT income as a result of a record level of refinancings which have increased significantly the level of mortgage prepayments of the Government National Mortgage Association (GNMA), Federal National Mortgage Association (FNMA) and Federal Home Loan Mortgage Corporation (FHLMC) Mortgage Collateral underlying the Company's CMO residual interests. The Company anticipates that a portion of its 1992 first quarter dividend will be from previous years' undistributed income.

Spencer I. Browne, President and Chief Executive Officer, stated, "We are continuing to implement our CMO residual acquisition program in order to mitigate the adverse effects on REIT income attributable to record levels of mortgage prepayments during the past six months. With the increased return of principal from our portfolio of CMO residuals, Asset Investors already has acquired or committed to acquire $10 million in new CMO residuals since the beginning of 1992. These new acquisitions were priced to yield the Company 27 percent."

Asset Investors Corporation is a real estate investment trust that generates income primarily from a portfolio of ownership interests in the issuances of collateralized mortgage obligations (CMOs) and other mortgage-related assets.

-30-

For Additional Information on Asset Investors Corporation,
BY FAX, No Cost -- Dial 1-800-PRO-INFO, Code #016

Courtesy Asset Investors Corporation

Chapter **8**   **Consumer Relations**

A development almost as significant to business as the Industrial Revolution has been the "Age of the Consumer." This emphasis on consumerism began with the establishment of the National Consumer's League in 1899. It received added impetus with the establishment of the Consumers Union and the publication of *Consumer Reports* in 1936. The creation of government regulatory agencies such as the Food and Drug Administration (FDA) and the Federal Trade Commission (FTC) added to the movement's impact, and consumerism finally came of age with the installation of a consumer affairs adviser in the White House during the presidency of John F. Kennedy.

Today, no corporation can ignore the need for a fully functioning program in consumer relations, or, as it is often known, consumer affairs. The ROPE process model is a useful means of preparing and executing a consumer relations program.

Research

Research for consumer relations includes investigation of the client, the reason for the program, and the consumer audiences to be targeted for communication.

Client Research

In the case of consumer relations, client research will be centered on the organization's reputation in its dealings with consumers. How credible is the organization with activist consumer groups? Has it been a frequent target of their attacks? What are its past and present consumer relations practices? Does it have a viable program in place? What are its major strengths and weaknesses in this area? What opportunities exist to enhance the organization's reputation and credibility in consumer affairs? The answers to these questions will provide a reasonably complete background for further development of a consumer relations program.

Opportunity or Problem Research

Explanation and justification of the need for a consumer relations program is part of the research process. The need grows out of the client research phase in determining past and present dealings with consumers. If problems already exist, a reactive program will be necessary. If there are no problems with consumers at the moment, the practitioner should consider preparing a proactive program. The organization's "wellness" in its relations with consumers should be made a matter of priority concern to management.

Audience Research

The final aspect of research consists of identifying and examining audiences to be targeted in a consumer relations program. These audiences usually include:

Company employees
Customers
  Professionals
  Middle class
  Working class
  Minorities
  Other
Activist consumer groups
Consumer publications
Community media — mass and specialized
Community leaders and organizations

Information about the customer groups and activist consumer groups should be of particular interest. Their attitudes and behaviors toward the company and their media habits are especially important.

Objectives

Consumer relations programs may use both impact and output objectives.

Impact Objectives

Some likely examples of impact objectives are:

1. to increase consumers' knowledge about the company's products, services, and policies (by 30 percent during the current year)
2. to promote (30 percent) more favorable consumer opinion toward the company (before December 1)
3. to stimulate (15 percent) greater participation in the company's consumer relations programs (this year)
4. to encourage more positive feedback (20 percent) from consumer groups to the company's programs (in the coming year)

Output Objectives

Output objectives for consumer relations involve the practitioner's measurable communication efforts with targeted audiences:

1. to distribute (10 percent) more consumer publications during the period June 1–August 31
2. to develop three employee consumer seminars for this fiscal year
3. to meet with five important consumer groups during the next six months
4. to prepare and distribute recipes for using the product to 12 major food editors in the state during the campaign

Programming

Programming for consumer relations includes planning the theme and messages, action or special event(s), uncontrolled and controlled media, and effective communication principles to execute the program.

Theme and Messages

The theme and messages will grow out of the consumer relations situation and will reflect research findings and objectives for the program.

Action or Special Event(s)

Organizational actions and special events in a consumer relations program generally include:

1. advising management and all employees about consumer issues
2. developing an efficient consumer response system
3. handling specific consumer complaints through a customer relations office
4. creating a company ombudsman, whose role is the investigation and resolution of complaints
5. maintaining liaison with external activist consumer groups
6. monitoring federal and state regulatory agencies and consumer legislation that might affect the company
7. developing emergency plans for a product recall
8. establishing a consumer education program, including meetings, information racks with printed materials on product uses, training tapes on product uses, celebrity endorsements and tours, and paid advertising on consumer topics
9. holding employee consumerism conferences, seminars, and/or field training

These actions and events form the basis of a thorough consumer relations program.

Uncontrolled and Controlled Media

Community, and sometimes state or national, media should be targeted for appropriate news releases, photo opportunities or photographs, interviews, and other forms of uncontrolled materials reporting the company's actions or events in consumer affairs.

Controlled media for a consumer relations program usually include printed materials on the effective use of the company's products or on health, safety, or other consumer-oriented topics. In addition, specific printed materials are developed for meetings, conferences, and other special events. Audiovisual materials, such as training tapes and films, are often used as vehicles for consumer education. The cases included in this chapter illustrate a variety of forms of both uncontrolled and controlled media.

Finally, interpersonal communication should play a significant role in any consumer relations program. Ideally, the company can employ a consumer affairs spokesperson whose tasks may include conferring with consumer groups, addressing community organizations, or even representing the company in mass media appearances, including paid consumer advertising. Interpersonal communications should also be used generously in the company's consumer response system, its customer relations office, and other meetings and conferences in the consumer relations program.

Effective Communication

The principles of special interest for effective communication in consumer relations are source credibility, two-way communication, and audience participation.

A major purpose of consumer relations programs is credibility enhancement. Consumers are increasingly quality-conscious in their purchases of goods and services. To cite one prominent example, U.S. automobile manufacturers have suffered a loss of public confidence and credibility in comparison with the high quality standards of their Japanese competitors. Because of this stiff overseas competition, the U.S. companies have been forced to improve their quality controls, their warranties, and their treatment of consumers in general. Once lost, corporate credibility is difficult to rebuild, but effective programs in consumer relations can be a decisive factor in that rebuilding process.

Two-way communication and audience participation go hand in hand in consumer relations. There can be no substitute for direct, interpersonal communication in some situations. The proper treatment of consumers demands that their grievances be heard and, in most cases, personally resolved. The most effective consumer education programs are those that go beyond mere distribution of literature on store information racks. The best programs involve the consumer personally in meetings, interviews, conferences, and/or other interpersonal presentations that allow audience feedback and participation.

Evaluation

There are no surprises and nothing out of the ordinary in the evaluation of consumer relations programs. The practitioner uses the previously discussed methods to evaluate the program's stated objectives.

Summary

Research for consumer relations concentrates on an organization's reputation with its consumers and on the reason for conducting a program of this kind. In some instances, the consumer publics are segmented, with different messages and media designed for communication with each group.

Consumer relations uses both impact and output objectives. Impact objectives propose outcomes that increase consumers' knowledge or influence their attitudes and behaviors. Output objectives propose outcomes in terms of measurable practitioner efforts without regard to impact.

Programming involves organizational actions such as advising management about consumer affairs, developing consumer-oriented programs, and/or holding meetings or conferences about consumerism. Communication for consumer relations includes uncontrolled, controlled, and interpersonal formats, although the use of controlled printed materials is often emphasized. But interpersonal communication is increasingly being used.

Evaluation, as in other forms of public relations, consists of discovering appropriate measurements for the program's stated objectives.

Readings on Consumer Relations

Austin, Nancy K. "Managing the Service Edge: How a Few Smart Companies Deliver What Customers Want." *Working Women*, July 1992, pp. 26ff.

Baher, Connie. "Keeping Your Customers Satisfied." *Small Business Reports*, February 1992, pp. 16ff.

Cespedes, Frank V. "Once More: How Do You Improve Customer Service?" *Business Horizons*, April 1992, pp. 58ff.

Farber, Barry J., and Joyce Wycoff. "Relationships: Six Steps to Success." *Sales & Marketing Management*, April 1992, pp. 50ff.

Finkelman, Dan, et al. "Making Customer Satisfaction Efforts Pay Off." *Telephony*, March 30, 1992, pp. 20ff.

Fornell, Claes. "A Method for Improving Customer Satisfaction and Measuring Its Impact on Profitability." *International Public Relations Review* 15 (1992): 6ff.

Haney, Camille, and Keith S. Collins. "Consumer Relations," in *Experts in Action: Inside Public Relations*, 2nd ed., edited by Bill Cantor. New York: Longman, 1989.

Lesly, Philip. "Consumer Relations," in *Lesly's Handbook of Public Relations and Communications*, 4th ed., edited by Philip Lesly. New York: AMACOM, 1991.

Liebmann, Wendy. "The Changing Consumer." *Vital Speeches*, April 15, 1992, pp. 409ff.

Raphel, Murray. "Customer Service Doesn't Work Anymore." *Direct Marketing*, July 1992, pp. 38ff.

Sjoberg, Goran. "Customer Satisfaction and Quality Control: What's in It for Public Relations Professionals?" *International Public Relations Review* 15 (1992): 5ff.

"Targeting Black Consumers." *Public Relations Journal* 47 (February 1991): 20ff.

Thompson, Gary W. "Consumer PR Techniques in the High Tech Arena." *Public Relations Quarterly* 37 (Winter 1992): 21–22.

Trudel, Mary R. "Consumer Marketing Synergy: PR Comes of Age." *Public Relations Quarterly* 36 (Spring 1991): 26ff.

Consumer Relations Cases

To call attention to the steel industry's commitment to recycling, the American Iron and Steel Institute developed the Steel Recycling Partnership program with a consortium including national environmental, trade, and industry organizations. Partnership programs were established in Washington, DC, and other cities, including Sacramento, CA; Tallahassee, FL; Columbus, OH; London and Toronto, Ontario; and Raleigh, NC. Exhibit 8–1a is an excerpt from the brochure, "Major Attractions." Exhibit 8–1b is a news release from the Steel Recycling Partnership.

Case 8–1   Steel Recycling Partnership

American Iron and Steel Institute, Washington, DC, with Ketchum Public Relations, Pittsburgh, PA

The Background

Today's steel industry, operating in our increasingly environmentally conscious society, faces a challenging paradox — while it produces America's most recycled material, legislative and government decision-makers, as well as the general public, are largely unaware of the steel industry's current recycling efforts.

There is increasing concern for the recyclability of products and packaging. Consumers are demanding it; and federal, state, and local governments are either introducing recycling and solid waste management legislation or have already enacted regulations of varying types. From the steel industry's perspective, this groundswell of activity represents an opportunity for steel to be recognized as a preferred material for a variety of product applications, particularly containers.

Research

Gordon S. Black Research was commissioned to conduct a two-phased research study to confirm that perceived issues about the steel industry were correct and to conduct qualitative research where responses were recorded, tabulated, and analyzed. The research included the use of focus groups and open-ended surveys to ascertain attitudes as well as telephone and mail surveys to

Courtesy American Iron and Steel Institute

quantify attitudes and provide a basis for action. Media, academics, government, customers, investment bankers, and the general public were targeted for this research.

The findings of this research included the fact that the best educated and most affluent respondents in the general public survey gave the steel industry the lowest ratings in regard to recyclability and environmental compatibility. In the government sector, only 29 percent pay a great deal of attention to news about steel, only 35 percent believe steel is important to the economy, and, on the whole, steel was not believed to be recyclable or beneficial for the environment.

In addition to these findings, awareness studies in specific markets were conducted by the Steel Can Recycling Institute. Also, annual studies conducted by leading packaging trade journals cited steel as one of the least recyclable packaging materials. This research indicated a *need* for a program that reached our target audiences with the important messages of steel's environmental compatibility, recyclability, and packaging benefits.

Planning

To demonstrate the steel industry's commitment to actively promoting and building awareness of the steel container's packaging and recycling benefits, Ketchum Public Relations developed the "Steel Recycling Partnership" program. Sponsored by the American Iron and Steel Institute (AISI), the campaign was designed to increase awareness and educate consumers as well as individuals who influence packaging and recycling decisions throughout the country.

Objective

The objective of the program was to:

- Raise awareness of and promote increased steel recycling to drive the steel can recycling rate toward the industry's overall 66 percent recycling rate.

Audience

The program's target audiences were:

- Legislators
- Government officials
- Municipal officials
- Grocery trade

- Environmentalists
- Consumers
- Customers
- Media

Strategies

To accomplish these objectives, our strategies were to:

- Build coalitions for third-party support and credibility
- Influence legislation on recycling, deposits, or packaging restrictions/bans in favor of steel containers by focusing on steel's environmental compatibility.

Execution

The program was designed to give the steel industry an opportunity to "partner" with environmental, trade, and industry organizations to achieve common recycling and solid waste management goals. The Steel Recycling Partnership became a consortium of steel industry representatives and steel can producers and users as well as solid waste management, recycling, and environmental organizations. Steel Recycling Partnership members include major, national environmental and trade organizations, including Keep America Beautiful, National Recycling Coalition, Food Marketing Institute, National Soft Drink Association, National Grocers Association, and others.

With the support of these partners, the steel industry began a multiyear, nationwide public education program, featuring program kickoff events, promotional tie-ins, and television advertising, to build awareness and promote steel can recycling. The theme of the program was "Major Attractions," to reinforce the fact that because steel is magnetic, it can easily be separated from the solid waste stream.

The Steel Recycling Partnership was launched in Washington, D.C. After the national launch, Steel Recycling Partnerships were formed in key markets where important steel recycling legislation was pending or where local steel recycling programs needed assistance. These cities included Sacramento, California; Tallahassee, Florida; Columbus, Ohio; London and Toronto, Ontario; and Raleigh, North Carolina.

To launch the Steel Recycling Partnership in each market, a similar format was developed and implemented. To reach the media, Steel Recycling Partnership information kits were mailed to local and national media outlets. Follow-up was conducted to place interviews and generate media attendance at the event.

Legislators, public officials, media, and members of government and business communities were invited to a breakfast briefing. A local television anchor served as master of ceremonies. Other speakers included the representatives of the American Iron and Steel Institute and the Steel Can Recycling Institute, local legislators, and steel industry spokespeople. A special video, which contained messages about steel's recyclability and the companion television commercial, was produced and previewed at the briefing. A display with all types of steel containers, recycling bins, and informational graphics was arranged in the room. After the event, follow-up letters and Steel Recycling Partnership informational materials were sent to all invitees. To further communicate steel recycling messages, AISI aired a steel recycling commercial for six weeks in the Washington, D.C., area. And, to reinforce the recycling messages that were initiated at the briefing and through the advertising, follow-up mailings were conducted in each market to both event attendees and non-attendees.

Evaluation

Postprogram research was conducted in three of the six markets to determine the effectiveness of the Steel Recycling Partnership in generating awareness and educating key audiences about the benefits of steel recycling. To measure awareness levels among attendees and non-attendees of this program, research, in the form of phone interviews, was conducted several weeks after the program by an independent research company that was contracted by Ketchum. For the Washington, D.C., market, the awareness and attitudes survey yielded valuable findings and indicated success. Awareness of a steel recycling program was very high, with nearly one-half, 48 percent, of all respondents claiming to be aware of a program promoting steel recyclability.

Importantly, the perceived main messages of the meeting were the promotion of steel recycling; awareness of steel recycling advertising and public relations; that steel is the most recyclable material; and general education regarding steel recycling. Overall, the reaction to the program was very positive with 62 percent rating it either excellent or very good. Attendees rated the program more positively, 73 percent, than non-attendees, 55 percent.

In Sacramento and Columbus, consumer research studies, via phone calls and a national tracking device, were conducted in June 1991 and then again after the Steel Recycling Partnership events in 1992. This research revealed significant scores of success. Specifically, more than half of the respondents became aware that steel cans are 100 percent recyclable. And there was a clear increase in the number of consumers (in Columbus, from 52 percent in 1991 to 64 percent in 1992, and in Sacramento, from 40 percent in 1991 to 63 percent in 1992) who believed that steel food cans are recyclable packaging.

Since the inception of the Steel Recycling Partnership, the steel can recycling rate has risen from 24.6 percent to 34 percent. In the first year of this program, more than 100 organizations and associations became members of the Steel Recycling Partnership on both the national and local levels. Nearly 800 legislative, recycling, and steel industry representatives attended the Partnership events. More than 5,000 legislative, recycling, and steel industry representatives were invited to and received information about the Partnership program.

Significant media coverage was generated, including 9 television interviews, 15 radio interviews, and over 20 in-market print stories. Highlights included the "Today" show with Willard Scott, an editorial in the *Columbus Dispatch*, and a one-half hour public affairs show in Raleigh.

THE STEEL RECYCLING PARTNERSHIP PRESENTS

A COLLABORATIVE EFFORT THAT IS MAKING A DIFFERENCE

The Steel Recycling Partnership (SRP) is proof that great things can happen when everyone works together. We're a consortium of individuals, groups and organizations dedicated to helping communities all across North America recycle more steel cans. This cooperative effort is aimed at contributing to solid waste solutions at the national, state and local levels. Members include steel producers, canmakers, recyclers, grocers, environmental groups and others with a stake in steel recycling.

OUR STORY BEGINS...

In 1988, the steel industry made a significant commitment to expanding its container recycling efforts.

Courtesy American Iron and Steel Institute

OUR OBJECTIVE

The SRP awareness and promotion programs are built on the strength of steel's traditional recycling leadership. The combined efforts of the AISI, SCRI and our partners through the SRP have consistently driven steel can recycling rates higher, toward the industry's overall 66 percent recycling rate. Today, one out of every three steel containers is recycled, and the goal is to recycle two of every three by 1995. With momentum building — whether it's steel cans being added to more local curbside programs or steel being magnetically separated at additional solid waste processing plants — we're well on our way to reaching that goal and maximizing the recycling of today's steel can.

THE MAJOR ATTRACTION

Launched nationally in September, 1991, in Washington, D.C., the program was introduced to legislators, public

officials, media, members of government and the business community. To further communicate steel recycling messages, AISI produced a steel recycling commercial, and it was broadcast for six weeks on television stations in the Washington, D.C., area.

Since that time, the Steel Recycling Partnership has reached five additional North American markets across the continent. Similar kickoff receptions and television advertising were initiated in Sacramento, California; Tallahassee, Florida; Columbus, Ohio; London and Toronto, Ontario; and Raleigh, North Carolina. In each market, the Steel Recycling Partners' efforts were reinforced by local chapters of their organizations as well as by other relevant community constituencies.

The campaign's theme, "Major Attractions," promotes what is probably steel's greatest recycling attribute — the material's unique magnetic property, which enables magnetic separators to efficiently and economically remove all steel from the solid waste stream, making it the easiest of materials to retrieve for recycling.

THE SUCCESS OF THE PARTNERSHIP

To date, more than 100 organizations and associations are members of the Partnership; nearly 800 legislative, recycling and steel industry representatives have attended Steel Recycling Partnership events; and over 5,000 legislative, recycling and steel industry representatives have been served by the Partnership in one way or another.

News coverage ranged from newspaper stories to radio and television interviews about the Steel Recycling Partnership in each of the six markets. Highlights include the *Today* show with Willard Scott, an editorial in the COLUMBUS DISPATCH and a half-hour public affairs television show in Raleigh.

But the best measure of the Partnership's success was a sharp increase in the steel can recycling rate. With a goal of 66 percent by the year 1995, the industry was well on its way in the United States with a 34 percent recycling rate in 1991. That's a gain of 38 percent over the 1990 rate of 24.6 percent. And, in Ontario, the steel can recycling rate grew to 50 percent in 1991.

In the coming months, the Steel Recycling Partnership will expand its reach into more key markets.

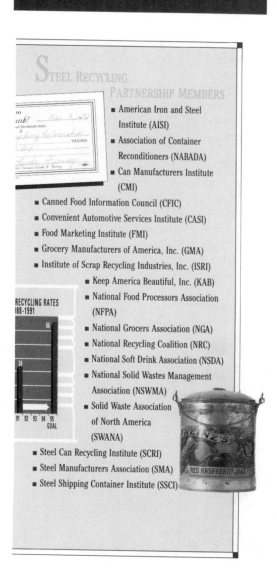

STEEL RECYCLING PARTNERSHIP MEMBERS

- American Iron and Steel Institute (AISI)
- Association of Container Reconditioners (NABADA)
- Can Manufacturers Institute (CMI)
- Canned Food Information Council (CFIC)
- Convenient Automotive Services Institute (CASI)
- Food Marketing Institute (FMI)
- Grocery Manufacturers of America, Inc. (GMA)
- Institute of Scrap Recycling Industries, Inc. (ISRI)
- Keep America Beautiful, Inc. (KAB)
- National Food Processors Association (NFPA)
- National Grocers Association (NGA)
- National Recycling Coalition (NRC)
- National Soft Drink Association (NSDA)
- National Solid Wastes Management Association (NSWMA)
- Solid Waste Association of North America (SWANA)
- Steel Can Recycling Institute (SCRI)
- Steel Manufacturers Association (SMA)
- Steel Shipping Container Institute (SSCI)

RECYCLING RATES
1988-1991

66

34

91 92 93 94 95
              GOAL

Through the American Iron and Steel Institute (AISI), the Steel Can Recycling Institute (SCRI) was established to serve as the information and technical resource that would help drive the effort. The industry's campaign began with education and awareness-building, targeted to a variety of constituents, while the SCRI quickly expanded the steel recycling infrastructure.

In 1991, the AISI and SCRI organized the SRP, creating a broad-based organization representing virtually every phase of the steel container's life cycle. The SRP's goal is to expand the initial effort with emphasis on leaders in business, government and local communities by providing the information and assistance necessary to make steel recycling part of *every* solid waste management and recycling program.

To learn more about the Steel Recycling Partnership and how to become involved in its activities, please contact either of the following organizations:

American Iron and Steel Institute
1101 17th Street, N.W.
Suite 1300
Washington, D.C. 20036-4700
(202) 452-7100

Steel Can Recycling Institute
Foster Plaza X
Pittsburgh, PA 15220
1-800-876-SCRI

Exhibit 8–1b   News Release

**STEEL
CAN
RECYCLING
INSTITUTE**

NEWS RELEASE

CONTACT:
Mary Norton or Cyndi Braun
Steel Can Recycling Institute
800/876-SCRI

FOR IMMEDIATE RELEASE

Steel Can Recycling Institute Becomes Steel Recycling Institute
Name Change Reflects Expanded Vision

NEW YORK, NY (May 19, 1993)... Promoting and sustaining steel can recycling has been the mission of the Steel Can Recycling Institute (SCRI) since its founding in 1988. Today, at the Annual Meeting of the American Iron and Steel Institute in New York, the steel industry announced an exciting development — the expansion of SCRI's focus to include all steel recycling.

Renamed the Steel Recycling Institute (SRI), the organization's expanded mission encompasses all steel products, including cans, cars, appliances, and construction materials.

"In 1988, about 15 percent of the steel cans were recycled in this country; in 1992, that number increased to more than 40 percent. This remarkable progress is due to the efforts of SCRI, in conjunction with growing recycling efforts across the United States," said David H. Hoag, chairman and chief executive officer of LTV Steel, who made the announcement. "Looking back on these tremendous advances in steel can recycling, the steel industry recognizes the need to promote greater awareness of the recyclability of all steel products. And this organization will get the job done."

Since the domestic steel industry requires old steel to produce new steel, steel is recycled over and over again into new steel products. Today's steel recycling efforts reflect a broad spectrum of steel products, from steel cans collected through curbside recycling programs to automobiles shredded at ferrous scrap yards.

"Most consumers do not realize that the steel industry is America's number one recycler, with an overall recycling rate of 66 percent. In fact, this industry has been recycling at above 60 percent for more than 20 years," said James B. Bruhn, chair of SRI and vice president of Weirton Steel Corporation. "We are excited by the dynamic progress made since SCRI's inception, and the timing is appropriate to bring the entire industry together into SRI. But as we go forward to escalate all steel recycling even further, we will not lose sight of our original goal for 1995, to recycle steel cans at the overall steel recycling level of 66 percent."

–OVER–

Steel Can Recycling Institute • Foster Plaza X • 680 Andersen Drive • Pittsburgh, PA 15220 • 800/876-SCRI

Recycled Paper

With its expanded mission, SRI will work to ensure a steady supply of recycled steel for the industry, as well as generate more awareness of the industry's overall recycling efforts. Through its seven regional offices, SRI will continue SCRI's ethic of "hands-on" activity, which includes working closely with all facets of the steel recycling infrastructure. At the same time, SRI will continue to promote and sustain steel can recycling.

"In the coming months, SRI will get the word out that every time you buy steel, you buy recycled. The reason for this is that the steel industry requires old steel to produce new steel," said William M. Heenan, Jr., president of SRI. "We're proud of the industry's recycling accomplishments, and we're dedicated to the recycling of all steel."

Recycling, reusing and reducing are all part of effective solid waste management programs. For this reason, in order to ensure a smooth transition without wasting resources, SRI will use up its preprinted materials before reprinting any items with its new name.

The Steel Recycling Institute, an industry association dedicated to promoting and sustaining steel recycling, is the primary information and technical resource for recyclers, municipalities, legislators, educators, businesses and other entities with an interest in steel recycling. Through its seven regional recycling offices, SRI works directly with city and county recycling coordinators and solid waste managers, recycling center operators, intermediate processors and end market buyers.

# # #

To stem the economic decline in its industry, the General Aviation Task Force initiated a program called the General Aviation Market Expansion (GAME) Plan. A central goal of the GAME Plan was to create positive consumer awareness of general aviation products and services, especially flight instruction and aircraft charter. The most interactive feature of the GAME Plan was National Learn-to-Fly Month, using actor Christopher Reeve as spokesperson. It involved flight schools across the country in an attractive consumer promotion. Exhibit 8–2a is a fact sheet on the Learn-to-Fly program. Exhibit 8–2b is a news release on the program, and Exhibit 8–2c is a photograph of Christopher Reeve as representative of the GAME Plan during National Learn-to-Fly Month.

Case 8–2   The General Aviation Market Expansion (GAME) Plan

The General Aviation Task Force, Alexandria, VA

Research

Secondary research accumulated from General Aviation industry associations identified factors contributing to the industry's near decade of sharp economic decline in the early 1980's: aircraft manufacturers halted successful, yet costly, flight instruction promotions, the Middle East oil embargo escalated retail fuel prices, inflation rose to double digits and thousands of striking air traffic controllers were fired. The downward spiral affected virtually every segment of the industry: flight schools, charter operators, manufacturers, fuel retailers, etc.

Original national research revealed (1) the opportunity: the industry lacked identity among consumers and (2) the approach: expand the industry's market by increasing consumer awareness of two entry points — charter and flight instruction. The research identified key target audience segments, attitudes and usage patterns within the two entry points.

Courtesy the General Aviation Task Force

Planning

We wrote a marketing communications plan with the following objectives:

1. **To build familiarity** with the term "General Aviation" among the general public. Identified key consumer audiences as (1) frequent business travelers (10+ trips per year, $50,000 HHI), and (2) potential flight instruction candidates (Age 20–39, $34,000 HHI).

2. **To create positive consumer awareness** of General Aviation products and services, specifically flight instruction and aircraft charter. (A toll-free number was established to respond to consumer requests for more information and served as a measurement of consumer awareness.)

3. **To increase utilization** of these services in order to benefit the entire General Aviation industry. (Annual reviews of industry economic barometers, i.e. pilot starts, fuel sales, aircraft shipments, hours flown, etc., measured industry utilization.)

4. **To enable/train General Aviation businesses** to market themselves and serve first-time General Aviation customers.

The **strategy** selected to achieve objectives was a three-year industry-wide marketing program, called The General Aviation Market Expansion (GAME) Plan. The program included national and local public relations, advertising, promotional events and direct marketing. More than 800 General Aviation companies fund the $2 million annual GAME Plan budget through voluntary contributions.

1988 and 1989 year-end analyses measured the effectiveness of the program and served as research for future planning.

Execution

Leaders of General Aviation businesses and associations initiated the program. The program is administered by individuals within existing General Aviation associations.

1. Beginning in July, 1988, **held Marketing Workshops** in 18 cities across the country. The workshops instructed CEOs and communications executives of General Aviation businesses to use the GAME Plan materials in their market.

2. **Created a Marketing Workbook** for participating companies that included step-by-step instructions on how to generate positive communications in the local market. The Workbook contained sections for each marketing area addressed in the Workshops.

3. **Sent Marketing Support Mailings** to participating companies on an ongoing basis. Mailings included marketing ideas such as direct mail suggestions, ready-to-use press releases and editorial slicks.

4. **Created a newsletter,** *Game Highlights,* to keep the industry informed on GAME Plan activities and to promote enthusiasm for the campaign.

5. **Created a General Aviation Taskforce Board of Directors** representing every segment of the General Aviation industry. The Board is the decision-making body for the GAME Plan, and provides credibility among the General Aviation industry. Board members serve as industry experts for the consumer media.

6. **Created a toll free number, (800) I-CAN-FLY,** to answer and fulfill requests for information about General Aviation services. Callers received brochures and were referred to the most appropriate General Aviation service provider.

7. **Held a national press conference** to announce the GAME Plan to the travel industry and general public. Sent a **Video News Release** via satellite to 750 television stations, and released the story to 3,000 publications via a news wire service and a press kit mailing. Provided promotion packets to local participating companies to generate news at the grassroots level. The packet included press releases and media relations tips.

8. **Produced a General Consumer Press Kit** that included press releases explaining the GAME Plan and fact sheets on General Aviation, Chartering and Careers in Flying. Distributed the press kits to 5,000 television, radio and print newsrooms around the country.

9. **Planned and conducted ongoing media relations** targeted at key audiences. Tailored the GAME Plan message to specific media groups such as the travel trade and business publications.

10. **Implemented National Learn-To-Fly Month** during June, using actor and pilot Christopher Reeve as spokesperson. The promotion included a national satellite media tour with Reeve and distribution of a Learn-To-Fly press kit to

2,000 newsrooms nationwide. Participating flight schools around the country were supplied promotion packets to generate local coverage. Pilot-oriented trade associations participated in the event as well.

Evaluation

1. **Earned approximately 122 million gross impressions** through national and local media relations efforts. Tracked media coverage valued at $5.5 million through clipping services and follow-up calls to media contacts. The agency estimates that for every dollar spent, the client netted $15 worth of coverage.

2. **A media database search conducted one year after the GAME Plan began produced 63 positive news stories** with the term "General Aviation" appearing in major publications such as the *Chicago Tribune, New York Times* and *Business Week.* (A similar search done more than eight months earlier turned up no stories using the terminology "General Aviation.")

3. **Media events such as the press conference** earned national exposure, including CNN's Travel Guide.

4. In **Post-Workshop surveys,** the majority of respondents rated the GAME Plan as "excellent" and the Workshops as "very informative." Informal research nine months later revealed higher marketing success rates among companies that sent employees to the Workshops than among companies that did not.

5. **Every segment of the General Aviation industry reported signs of improved business** in the first two quarters of 1989. This was tracked through associations representing each industry segment. Increases have been reported in air charter use, business aircraft, new business starts, business expansions and pilot starts (see below).

6. Following National Learn-To-Fly Month in June, **August student pilot starts increased 27 percent** over those processed in August 1988 — the highest year-to-date increase in nine years — and **September student pilot starts increased 33 percent** over those processed the previous year. (Figures provided by the Federal Aviation Administration.) Overall, **1989 pilot starts were up 10.5 percent of 1988.**

Exhibit 8–2a   **GAME Plan Fact Sheet**

AMERICANS TAKE TO THE SKIES
June is National Learn-To-Fly Month

Not so very long ago, flying a plane was a frivolous pursuit reserved for the very rich. Today, it's a way of life for hundreds of thousands of Americans. In fact, a recent study showed that more than 3.6 million Americans have the desire as well as the resources to take over the controls of the cockpit themselves, but have little idea of where to begin.

Throughout the month of June, actor and pilot Christopher Reeve will do his part to encourage more people to learn to fly. Reeve, a pilot for 14 years, will help kick off the nation's first National Learn-To-Fly Month by sharing his own experience as a pilot and shedding some light on the basics of learning to fly.

Learn-To-Fly Month is an effort organized by The General Aviation Taskforce, a non-profit group providing public education of flight instruction, as well as other aspects of General Aviation. The Taskforce's goal for June is to take the mystery out of learning to fly.

Why Learn to Fly?

Each year, more than 100,000 people in the United States take flying lessons to learn how to fly General Aviation aircraft. Some may say they have practical reasons for wanting to fly, but most are completely honest. They'll tell you they're flying for the fun of it...for the thrill, the challenge, the confidence and the freedom of it: the thrill of defying gravity and becoming one with the sky...the confidence of controlling a machine that moves through three dimensions -- not just two...the challenge of learning about the world above our heads...the air, the weather, radar and radio frequencies...the freedom of being "above it all."

All this makes flying fun as an activity -- but flying also makes having fun more efficient. Many trips that normally take a whole day by car can be made in half the time, or less, in an airplane.

Piloting your own plane also increases the number of destinations you can reach directly by air. In the United States, about 800 airports serve commercial airlines, but more than 12,000 airports are open to General Aviaton pilots.

- more -

Courtesy the General Aviation Task Force

Professionals and entrepreneurs alike have found the initial investment of time and money to learn to fly pays big dividends. Considering the high value of a top executive's time, learning to fly can be a prudent alternative to time-consuming and expensive commercial air travel.

Sales people who want to expand their business territories or doctors who need to reach patients in remote areas can reach their destinations and their professional goals faster with a pilot's license.

Learning to fly is not as costly or time-consuming as most people think. In fact, according to Reeve, "If you put in several hours a week, you can get your private pilot certificate in about six months at a cost of approximately $2,500 to $3,500. You've just got to make it a priority and get started." Once you earn your wings, airplane and flying clubs make flying fun and affordable, he says.

America Needs Pilots

Since more and more people are using the airways for commercial and business travel, there is a growing need for more pilots to carry the load. In the next decade the airlines are expected to hire between 52,000 and 62,000 new pilots. And currently, there are simply not enough pilots to keep up with that demand. Why? The massive numbers of pilots who were trained during wartime are now facing retirement and fewer pilots are being trained by the military today.

Who Can Learn to Fly?

Almost anyone can experience the excitement and freedom of piloting a plane. Although the average student pilot is 32 years of age, anyone 16 years old or older can learn to fly. The only other requirements are that you be in good health and that you are able to read, speak and understand English. There is no maximum age limit for piloting a plane because it's health, not age, that determines a person's ability to fly. In fact, the FAA requires everyone who wants to continue to be a pilot pass a routine medical exam every two years to insure that there are no medical problems which would interfere with the pilot's ability to fly.

Learn-To-Fly Month activities will continue through the month of June. People interested in finding a flight school can get information by calling 1-800-I-CAN-FLY.

# # #

For more information, contact The General Aviation Taskforce, (913) 236-7294.

Exhibit 8–2b   GAME Plan News Release

GENERAL AVIATION TASKFORCE • 6750 ANTIOCH RD. SUITE 100 • SHAWNEE MISSION, KS 66204 • (913) 236-7294

FOR IMMEDIATE RELEASE   June 1, 1989

CONTACT: Susan McCabe, (913) 236-7294

JUNE IS NATIONAL LEARN-TO-FLY MONTH
Actor, Pilot Christopher Reeve Is
Learn-To-Fly Month Spokesperson

Pilots and General Aviation organizations across the country have declared this June the first National Learn-To-Fly Month. The recently formed General Aviation Taskforce has launched the awareness campaign in an effort to rekindle America's love for flying. And they've asked actor and pilot Christopher Reeve to strike the match.

"Flying is the ultimate personal dream come true," says Reeve, who serves as the Learn-To-Fly Month spokesperson. "When you realize that learning to fly is relatively easy to do, fun to do -- that you don't have to be rich to do it and that it makes practical sense in your life, you're hooked. And this is one addiction that's good for you!"

A dedicated pilot for 14 years, Reeve's interest in flying developed early. He was fascinated with flying as a child, and began flying lessons with the first money he saved as an adult.

After earning his private pilot's license, Reeve later earned instrument and multi-engine ratings. He has logged nearly 2,000 hours of flying time. Reeve is the owner of a Piper Cheyenne II airplane, which he flies on many personal and business trips, including movie location shoots.

- more -

Courtesy the General Aviation Task Force

Reeve is one of more than 700,000 licensed pilots in this country who fly for recreation and business. "You don't have to be rich with a lot of time on your hands to learn to fly -- you just have to make it a priority," says Reeve.

"Most people think learning to fly is out of reach for them," says Thomas F. Comeau, chairman of The General Aviation Taskforce, the non-profit group sponsoring Learn-To-Fly Month. "Actually, getting a private pilot's license takes about six months, given a few hours a week, and costs between $2,500 and $3,500."

Comeau says most people begin learning to fly for the fun of it, but they soon learn the practical benefits of flying an airplane. "Business and professional people who travel regularly can gain tremendous control over their schedules by learning to fly," says Comeau.

Many people invest in flying lessons to make aviation a career. And there's never been a better time than now. The demand for commercial and corporate pilots is at an all-time high. The average pay for commercial pilots is $81,000 a year; corporate pilots are receiving an average $44,000 annually.

The country needs more career-oriented pilots, according to Comeau, who says a combination of factors point to an increasing need for civilian-trained pilots in the next decade: a burgeoning demand for pilots due to increasing commercial and corporate air travel, a reduced pool of military-trained pilots, and the escalating retirements of pilots trained during World War II and the Korean War. Learn-To-Fly Month may be the first step in helping to ease the potential shortage.

The General Aviation Taskforce also hopes that Learn-To-Fly Month will take the mystery out of learning to fly. A study they conducted recently found that more than 3.6 million people had an interest in learning to fly and believed they had the ability, but had no idea of where to begin.

To help those people get information, The Taskforce has established a toll-free number: 1-800-I-CAN-FLY. Callers will be referred to flight schools in their areas and will receive information about the procedures and requirements of flight instruction.

# # #

Exhibit 8–2c

Christopher Reeve, National Learn-to-Fly Month Spokesperson

Courtesy the General Aviation Task Force

In an effort to improve its product, Binney & Smith went directly to the consumers of its Crayola crayons, children aged 4 through 10. The children's suggestions were to include brighter, bolder colors in the Crayola box. The company obligingly introduced eight new hues, simultaneously "retiring" eight older "classics" to its newly created Crayola Hall of Fame, a ceremony that attracted adult protesters with sentimental attachments to the old colors. Sensing a media windfall, the company wisely encouraged the protest demonstration of its Hall of Fame ceremony. Thus, Binney & Smith's product renewal not only pleased consumers, it attained the highest level of media coverage of any campaign in the company's history. Exhibit 8–3a shows the artist's designs for the Crayola Hall of Fame. Exhibit 8–3b contains Crayola Hall of Fame plaque information. Exhibit 8–3c is the drawings for six "retired" colors. And Exhibit 8–3d is a photograph of protesters picketing outside the Hall of Fame ceremony.

Case 8–3	**Crayola Crayons New Color Launch**

Binney & Smith, Easton, PA

In the summer of 1990, after 18 months of research and planning, the first new Crayola crayon colors in 18 years were introduced. Results were spectacular. Media coverage of the color introduction spanned eight months and generated more than 600 million gross impressions. Sales surged by $6 million. Every major print media outlet covered the story including the *The Wall Street Journal, The New York Times, USA Today,* the *Washington Post,* the *Philadelphia Inquirer,* A.P., and U.P.I. TV coverage ranged from NBC Evening News to MTV. Awareness of the new colors was saturated without any advertising dollars having been spent against the introduction and interest in all Crayola products was elevated as a result of the campaign. The key to the success was a PR campaign that parlayed protesters into opportunities and leveraged the discontinuation of eight crayon colors to create awareness for eight new shades.

Research

In the summer of 1989, Binney & Smith conducted informal focus groups with children aged 4 through 10 in various locations

Courtesy Binney & Smith

around the country. The purpose of the research was consistent with a new company philosophy to become more attuned to the needs of the end users of our Crayola products — children. In the focus groups, kids were asked for suggestions on how they would improve or change our products to increase their appeal. Among other suggestions was the idea to include bolder, brighter colors in Crayola crayon assortments. This became the impetus for a marketing decision to introduce eight new, bolder, brighter colors.

Once the new colors were developed, they were given fun, upbeat names like wild strawberry, jungle green, and vivid tangerine. Additional focus groups were organized to obtain feedback. The results were unanimous. Kids strongly preferred the new colors. Further research was conducted to determine which eight colors could logically be removed to make room for the eight new hues. Colors were eliminated that were similar to other colors in our offering and that wouldn't create gaps in our color spectrum.

Cost effectiveness made a PR campaign the strongest option to communicate news of the color change. To launch the new crayon colors, extensive research was undertaken to create an accurate color history detailing time frames when existing colors were to be introduced or changed for use in the PR effort.

Planning

Crayola crayons historically had maintained a universally high awareness level and market share. However, it had grown increasingly difficult to generate any kind of excitement around the crayon category from a trade and consumer end. The introduction of eight new crayon colors could do both. In light of spending cuts and precommitted promotions, there were no funds available to advertise the new colors. Public relations became the only budgetarily viable means to generate awareness of the new colors. A budget of $20,000 was allocated for a program to create national awareness, leading to incremental sales increases at the back-to-school period in 1990. All program efforts would be developed and implemented by two media communications staff members who would spend time as needed to make the program successful. Results would be measured by media coverage, retail sales, and trade sales.

Our campaign was built around an emotional hook — the public's tremendous sentimental attachment to Crayola crayons. (This was well documented through thousands of letters and phone calls the company receives annually from consumers.) Rather than using the introduction of the new colors, which could fall by the wayside with the hoard of other "new product" stories pitched to the media, we focused our effort on the *retirement* of eight "classic" crayon colors. Media coverage of the story wasn't complete without also heralding the arrival of the new, contemporary shades. The culmination of our efforts was the enshrining of the retired colors in the Crayola Hall of Fame built at the company's Easton, Pennsylvania, headquarters for this campaign. This event also served to officially introduce the new colors. Efforts were focused during the summer, a normally slow news period, to build awareness for our Hall of Fame event that was executed in early August. The August time frame allowed us to impact back to school purchases. A low-cost press kit was used to disseminate information to the media and a b-roll satellite news feed of the Hall of Fame event was used to ensure national television coverage.

Execution

Because of the limited budget, a press kit was developed using art reproduced on the company's color copier. These copies were affixed to the front of white folders to create a slick, printed effect. Inside the kit were actual sample boxes of the new and outgoing crayon colors, color rubouts of the colors for easy comparison, a color history and appropriate background information and facts about Crayola products.

To reach important women's service magazines, which often work on three-month lead times, it was necessary that press information be sent in April to target coverage for their back-to-school issues. In June, media information was sent to the business editor of *USA Today* in hopes of developing a back-to-school piece with a business bent on the new colors. Within two days the story ran on page one, creating an avalanche of media interest. More than 200 media calls were fielded in the next 10 days. Coverage was national and extensive. Both the "Today Show" and CBS "This Morning" produced five minute segments on the color change in July. Additional coverage ran in every major metropolitan newspaper including *The New York Times,* the *Washington Post,* and the *Philadelphia Inquirer.*

In the aftermath, a groundswell of consumer reaction emerged in the form of phone calls, letters, and the formation of protest groups. It was decided to leverage this for further media value. After being screened by phone, names and phone numbers of the more interesting individuals and groups were fed to the media, which reacted with another wave of coverage. We felt that the intent of individuals protesting our crayon color change was so tongue-in-cheek and benign, and the benefit derived in the form of increased awareness for the new colors so great, that the opportunity far outweighed the slight risk that sales could be negatively impacted.

The Hall of Fame ceremony was set in the company's tour center where our maintenance department constructed the display at a nominal cost. Marla Wynne, Miss Pennsylvania and a local resident, unveiled the display while 150 local children watched the ceremony. Outside, pickets were invited to protest the ceremony, much to the media's delight. A PR newswire release 10 days earlier had alerted the media to the event and protesters' plans. An official retirement cake was cut by a seven-foot tall crayon character named Tip, while a fashion show performed by Bloomingdale's helped introduce the new colors in style. A b-roll news feed of the event was beamed out on a satellite within two hours of the ceremony to gain national television coverage.

Evaluation

The results of the new crayon color campaign far exceeded expectations. Initially, we believed that the bulk of our coverage would take place following the Hall of Fame ceremony just in time to drive back-to-schools sales. But intense early coverage created an unexpected phenomenon. Adults flocked to stores as early as June to hoard old boxes of crayons — as collectibles. This cleared retail shelves and prompted reorders. Prior to the Hall of Fame ceremony, we had already received coverage in almost every venue in the nation including coverage on NBC "Evening News" with Tom Brokaw! The Hall of Fame ceremony, while running simultaneous to the U.S. decision to enter the Kuwait fray, received excellent coverage. Covering the event live were CNN, three network affiliates from Philadelphia, AP, the *Philadelphia Inquirer*, the *Atlanta Constitution* and more than 20 others. The satellite b-roll newsfeed was aired 93 times in the top 30 ADIs with the estimated pick up nationally to be over 300. Later coverage appeared in *Time* magazine and *The Wall Street Journal.* In December, the new colors news was heralded as one of the year's top stories in the Associated Press and in *Parade* and *Life* magazine articles. Sales impact was staggering. A nearly $6 million incremental increase resulted, with no advertising support. Old product was cleaned off the shelves before the new had even hit the stock room. The trade was ecstatic. Consumer awareness was universal. The campaign is being touted as the most successful in the company's 88-year history and is currently being adapted for use by company subsidiaries in Canada and England under the direction of the U.S. based staff.

Courtesy Binney & Smith

Exhibit 8–3b   Crayola Hall of Fame Plaque Information

Crayola Hall Of Fame
Plaque Information

maize
INTRODUCED: 1949
RETIRED: 1990

A member of the yellow family, maize gets its name from Indian corn. It was frequently used to color the golden leaves of fall and is one of the University of Michigan's school colors A similar color found in the Crayola crayon family is goldenrod.

"Maize was as American as mom and Chevrolet...Apple pie came later."

Douglas
Age 42

---

raw umber
INTRODUCED: 1958
RETIRED: 1990

A member of the brown family, raw umber was especially popular for coloring tree trunks and branches. and is a frequently used color by professional artists. Similar colors found in the Crayola crayon family include sepia and brown.

"Whenever I drew me, I used raw umber."

Ebony
Age 6

---

violet blue
INTRODUCED: 1958
RETIRED: 1990

A member of the blue family, violet blue was ideal for coloring evening skies, blueberries and concord grapes. Similar colors found in the Crayola crayon family include blue violet, navy blue and blue.

Many suns have set with violet blue, the perfect color for twilights. Evening skies just won't be the same without her. Violet blue? I'll miss her too.
U.S. Congressman Don Ritter
R-15th

---

blue gray
INTRODUCED: 1958
RETIRED: 1990

A member of the blue family, blue gray was often a favorite of those coloring Confederate soldier's uniforms and mist on a cloudy morning. A similar color found in the Crayola crayon family is cadet blue.

"Blue gray is gone! How can you do Confederate soldier pictures and Civil War Pictures without it?"

Charlie Gibson
Co-Host ABC-TV's Good Morning America

Courtesy Binney & Smith

green blue
INTRODUCED: 1949
RETIRED: 1990

A member of the blue family, green blue was ideal for coloring lake water on a still summer day and peacock feathers. Similar colors found in the Crayola crayon family include turquoise blue and cerulean.

"Green blue was one of the best colors ever. Couldn't you retire carnation pink instead?

Jami
Age 11

---

lemon yellow
INTRODUCED: 1949
RETIRED: 1990

A member of the yellow family, lemon yellow has been relied on by many for coloring bright sunny days, the yellow in a rainbow and of course, lemons. Similar colors found in the Crayola crayon family include green yellow and yellow.

"We prefer to have one less lemon in our lineup."

Richard Gurin
President, Binney & Smith

---

orange red
INTRODUCED: 1949
RETIRED: 1990

A member of the red family, orange red was a favorite for coloring everything from cherry tomatoes to tabby cats. Similar colors found in the Crayola crayon family include red orange and red.

"Even though I love tabby cats and cherry tomatoes, its not their color that gives me the most pleasure. I'm color blind! Human beings have good ways of making do with what they have."

Fred Rogers
Mister Rogers'
Neighborhood

---

orange yellow
INTRODUCED: 1949
RETIRED: 1990
A member of the yellow family, orange yellow was a staple for creating warm sunsets and bananas for more than 40 years. Similar colors found in the Crayola crayon family include yellow and dandelion.

"Wonderful sunsets, that's what I used orange yellow the most for and I'll sure miss it. But please, don't ever change the Crayola name. I'm sort of attached to it!"
Crayola Collins
Age 82

Exhibit 8–3c   Drawings for Six "Retired" Colors

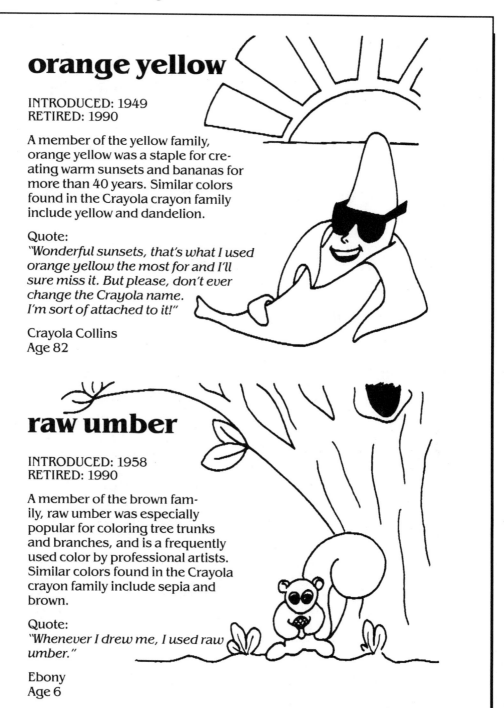

orange yellow

INTRODUCED: 1949
RETIRED: 1990

A member of the yellow family, orange yellow was a staple for creating warm sunsets and bananas for more than 40 years. Similar colors found in the Crayola crayon family include yellow and dandelion.

Quote:
"Wonderful sunsets, that's what I used orange yellow the most for and I'll sure miss it. But please, don't ever change the Crayola name. I'm sort of attached to it!"

Crayola Collins
Age 82

raw umber

INTRODUCED: 1958
RETIRED: 1990

A member of the brown family, raw umber was especially popular for coloring tree trunks and branches, and is a frequently used color by professional artists. Similar colors found in the Crayola crayon family include sepia and brown.

Quote:
"Whenever I drew me, I used raw umber."

Ebony
Age 6

Courtesy Binney & Smith

violet blue

INTRODUCED: 1958
RETIRED: 1990

A member of the blue family, violet blue was ideal for coloring evening skies, blueberries and concord grapes. Similar colors found in the Crayola crayon family include blue violet, navy blue and blue.

Quote:
"Many suns have been set with violet blue, the perfect color for twilights. Evening skies just won't be the same without her. Violet blue? I'll miss her too."

U.S. Congressman Don Ritter
Pennsylvania, 15th District

orange red

INTRODUCED: 1949
RETIRED: 1990

A member of the red family, orange red was a favorite for coloring everything from cherry tomatoes to tabby cats. Similar colors found in the Crayola crayon family include red orange and red.

Quote:
"Even though I love tabby cats and cherry tomatoes, it's not their color that gives me the most pleasure. I'm color blind! Human beings have good ways of making do with what they have."

Fred Rogers
"Mister Rogers'
Neighborhood"

green blue

INTRODUCED: 1949
RETIRED: 1990

A member of the blue family, green blue was ideal for coloring peacock feathers and lake water on a still summer day. Similar colors found in the Crayola crayon family include turquoise blue and cerulean.

Quote:
"Green blue was one of the best colors ever. Couldn't you retire carnation pink instead?"

Jami
Age 11

lemon yellow

INTRODUCED: 1949
RETIRED: 1990

A member of the yellow family, lemon yellow has been relied on by many for coloring bright sunny days, the yellow in a rainbow and of course, lemons. Similar colors found in the Crayola crayon family include green yellow and yellow.

Quote:
"We prefer to have one less lemon in our lineup."

Richard Gurin
President, Binney & Smith

343

Exhibit 8–3d   Protesters Picketing Outside Hall of Fame
Ceremony

Courtesy Binney & Smith

Chapter **9** **Relations with Special Publics**

Special publics are defined as those unique or distinctive groups with which an organization needs to communicate. These groups may be minority publics, such as African Americans, Hispanics, or Asian Americans. Practitioners should be aware of the extensive national, geographic, and ethnic subsets that exist within each of these broadly defined minority groups in the United States. For instance, practitioners might mistakenly lump all Hispanics together under the Mexican umbrella. For a Hispanic special event, they could employ a mariachi band and serve Mexican dishes. However, such treatment would easily offend Spaniards, Argentines, or Dominicans, all of whose home cultures differ sharply from one another and from that of Mexico, although all share Spanish as a common language. A similar mistake would be to treat Asian Americans as a singular group or, worse, to refer to them as Orientals. These Asian groups share neither common languages nor common cultural heritages. Many of them, in fact, have been enemies for centuries.

When dealing with a minority group with national origins outside the United States, practitioners would be well advised to consult in advance the embassy or consulate of that group's homeland and certainly the group's local leaders as well.

In addition to ethnic or national minority publics, practitioners may target for special communication such groups as women, students, educators, environmentalists, school-age children, the business community, municipal officials, or community physicians. The list of potential special publics can actually be extended to include all the segments of society.

The fastest growing and most significant of these special groups in the United States is the "senior citizen" segment of the population, a segment expected to double in size by the early 21st century. Age groupings such as 50–64 for the "active" seniors, 65–74 for the "less active," and 75-plus for the "elderly" are often used to describe subsegments of the senior citizen audience. These age groupings alone, though, are usually less useful in targeting senior audiences than are their organizational affiliations. Organizations such as the American Association of Retired Persons (AARP), the National Council on the Aging (NCOA), the National Hispanic Council on Aging, the National Council of Senior Citizens, the National Senior Sports Association, and the Gray Panthers have chapter networks and affiliate organizations that can be used to reach their members. Thus, the key to reaching a senior audience lies in cosponsorship of an event or project with an organization such as AARP or NCOA.

As with other forms of public relations, the four-part ROPE process model is a helpful format for preparing and executing programs that target special publics.

Research

Research for special programs includes investigation of the client, the reason for the program, and, most important, the distinctive audience to be targeted.

Client Research

Client research for an organization's relations with a special public should focus on the client's role and reputation with the particular audience. How credible is the organization with this public? Have there been significant complaints against it from this public in the past? What are its past and present communication practices toward this audience? What are its major strengths and weaknesses relative to this public? What opportunities exist to enhance its relations with this public?

Opportunity or Problem Research

Should a proactive public relations program be devised for this particular audience? Or has some problem arisen that must be addressed with a reactive program? Why should the organization communicate with this audience at all? Detailed answers to these questions will provide the necessary justification for the outlay of funds required for relations with a given special public.

Audience Research

Obviously, the practitioner should learn as much as possible about a special public. One way to do this is to regard such publics as differentiated communities. In community relations, practitioners address community media, community leaders, and community organizations. These same audience subsets may also be applicable in defining a special public:

Media utilized by this public
   Mass
   Specialized

Leaders of this public
   Public officials
   Professional leaders
   Ethnic leaders
   Neighborhood leaders
   Others

Organizations composing this public
   Civic
   Political
   Service
   Business
   Cultural
   Religious
   Youth
   Other

As in community relations, practitioners should develop special contact lists for the appropriate media and for the special public's leaders and organizations. These materials are indispensable in relations with a special public.

Objectives

Programs that target special publics can use both impact and output objectives; and, as in all other types of public relations, the objectives should be specific and quantitative.

Impact Objectives

Impact objectives represent the desired outcomes of informing or modifying the attitudes or behaviors of the special audience. Some examples include:

1. to increase the knowledge of the organization's minority-benefits program among members of this special public (by 50 percent before January 1)

2. to promote more favorable opinion (30 percent) toward the organization on the part of this special public (during the current year)

3. to stimulate greater participation (15 percent) in the organization's programs by this special public (during the summer months)

Output Objectives

Output objectives comprise the specific efforts to enhance relations with special publics. For example:

1. to prepare and distribute materials to (30 percent) of the Hispanic community in Washington (during the coming year)

2. to schedule four meetings each year with leaders of the Chinese community in Houston

3. to develop five new projects for African American instructors' use in their classrooms (during the current school year)

Programming

Programming for relations with special publics includes planning the theme and messages, action or special event(s), uncontrolled and controlled media, and effective communication principles in the program's execution.

Theme and Messages

Both the theme and messages should reflect the desired relationship between the organization and the targeted special public. They will also be an indicator of past and present relationships that exist between the organization and this public.

Action or Special Event(s)

Actions and special events should concentrate on the major interests of the targeted audience. The most successful actions and special events address the interests, needs, and problems of the particular target group. The special events in the cases in this chapter clearly meet this criterion.

Uncontrolled and Controlled Media

As mentioned earlier, representatives of both the mass and specialized media aimed at the special audience are an important segment of the audience itself. Uncontrolled media in the form of news releases, photo opportunities or photographs, feature stories, and/or interviews should be prepared in the language of the designated media; they should be directed to media outlets known to be used by this special public.

Controlled media should be prepared with all the cultural, language, ethnic, age, or other demographic specifications of the target public in mind. As with other publics, there can be no substitute for personal interaction in the effective execution of programs.

Effective Communication

Principles of effective communication are the same for special audiences as they are for most others. Extra care should be taken, however, in the matter of source credibility, which can be enhanced by the selection of a spokesperson from the same demographic group as the targeted audience.

In addition to source credibility, two-way communication and audience participation should also be given extra emphasis in relations with special publics.

Finally, the use of opinion leaders may be highly significant in relations with special publics, especially when the public is an organized ethnic or demographic group. In sum, all aspects of programming for relations with special publics are similar to those of community relations. The special public, in fact, can often be thought of as a community with its own media, leaders, and organizations.

Evaluation

The process of evaluating communications aimed at special audiences must take into account the program's objectives. Each one should be measured using previously discussed standards and methods.

Evaluation of special publics cases rely generally on the degree of participation by the target audiences and, in most instances, the amount of publicity generated by the program.

Summary

Research for programs that target special audiences focuses on the credibility of the client with a particular special public, along with the need or justification for the program. The audience itself can be analyzed using the same categories applicable to community relations—media, leaders, and organizations. Special audiences can usually be treated as communities, or subcommunities, in their own right.

Objectives for relations with special publics may be impact or output in nature. Impact objectives express desired outcomes, such as augmenting the public's knowledge or influencing its attitudes or behaviors. Without reference to impact, output objectives consist of practitioner efforts to execute the program.

Programming for special publics often uses the significant events of the public's ethnic or cultural past. Along with this, of course, the programming must also address the problems or potential problems of the special group. Although standard controlled and uncontrolled media are used in this form of public relations, there can be no substitute for two-way communication with such audiences. More than others, they need to know that the organization cares enough about them to include a personal touch.

As with other forms of public relations, the special program's stated objectives must be evaluated appropriately. In general, the level of participation by the targeted group and the publicity generated by the program are used as benchmarks of success.

Readings on Special Publics

"A New Agenda." *Working Women*, November 1992, pp. 55ff.

Becker, Lee B., et al. "Racial Differences in the Evaluations of the Mass Media." *Journalism Quarterly* 69 (Spring 1992): 124ff.

Bovet, Susan Fry. "Columbus Quincentenary Events Reflect America's Diversity." *Public Relations Journal* 48 (November 1992): 22.

Brimelow, Peter. "The Fracturing of America." *Forbes*, March 30, 1992, pp. 74ff.

Citrin, J., R. Reingold, and D. Green. "American Identity and the Politics of Ethnic Change." *Journal of Politics*, 1990, pp. 1124–1154.

Deutschman, Alan. "The Upbeat Generation." *Fortune*, July 13, 1992, pp. 42ff.

Dunn, Willim. "The Move Toward Ethnic Marketing." *Nation's Business* 80 (July 1992): 39ff.

Exter, Thomas G. "Middle-Aging Households." *American Demographics* 17 (July 1992): 63.

Frey, William H. "Boomer Magnets." *American Demographics* 17 (March 1992): 34ff.

Fry, Susan. "Reaching Hispanic Publics with Special Events." *Public Relations Journal* 47 (February 1991): 12ff.

Holland, James R. "Reaching Older Audiences." *Public Relations Journal* 47 (May 1991): 14ff.

Korzenny, Felipe. *Mass Media Effects Across Cultures.* Newbury Park, CA: Sage, 1992.

Levin, Gerald M. "Anthropologists in Adland: Researchers Studying Cultural Meanings of Brands." *Advertising Age* 63 (February 24, 1992): 3ff.

Light, Larry, and Joseph Weber. "Waking Up to a Major Market." *Business Week*, March 23, 1992, pp. 70ff.

List, S. K. "The Right Place to Find Children." *American Demographics* 14 (February 1992): 44ff.

"Mainstream Companies Address Hispanic Community's Needs." *Public Relations Journal* 47 (February 1991): 30.

Major, Michael J. "Dancing to a Different Drummer." *Public Relations Journal* 48 (November 1992): 20ff.

Mandel, Michael J., et al. "The Immigrants." *Business Week*, July 13, 1992, pp. 114ff.

Oberdorf, Meyera. "The Changing Role of Women in the 21st Century." *Vital Speeches*, October 1, 1992, pp. 751–54.

O'Hare, William P., and William H. Fry. "Booming, Suburban and Black." *American Demographics* 14 (September 1992): 30ff.

O'Neill, June. "The Changing Economic Status of Black Americans." *The American Enterprise*, September-October 1992, pp. 70ff.

Pol, Louis G., et al. "The Eight Stages of Aging." *American Demographics* 14 (August 1992): 54ff.

Schwartz, Felice N. "Women As a Business Imperative." *Harvard Business Review* 70 (March-April 1992): 105ff.

Thompson, Frederick G. "Reaching America's Aging Marketplace." *Public Relations Journal* 46 (February 1990): 28–30.

Westerbeck, Tim. "Suppliers Zero in on a Growing Hispanic Market." *Public Relations Journal* 48 (July 1992): 7ff.

Special Publics Cases

Concerned with shifting the solution to the solid waste issue from degradability to recycling, the Dow Chemical Company targeted a major audience of active consumers and decision-makers — high school students. To reach this audience, the "MTV generation," Dow mounted a touring road show consisting of music, excitement, and fast action, including skits, songs, and a game show involving audience participants. The show visited more than 100 high schools in major cities in the United States and Canada in 1990 and 1991. Exhibit 9–1a is a brochure about the Recycle This! show.

Case 9–1   ## Recycle This!

The Dow Chemical Company, Midland, MI, with Ketchum
Public Relations, Washington, DC

The Background

Increased awareness of solid waste issues dawned in the 1980s with landfills closing, the plight of the garbage barge, and local bans on nonbiodegradable packaging. With awareness came a barrage of information, much of it inaccurate.

Newspaper clips monitored by the Dow Chemical Company over an eight-month period from April to November, 1989, revealed that high school students were generating 50 percent of the negative news coverage on plastics in the waste stream. Students — active consumers and decision-makers — were calling for bans of plastics in their schools and communities, believing degradability to be the solid waste solution.

Recent landfill studies have found that the students' degradability solution does not work. To decompose, degradable materials must be exposed to water, light, and oxygen. In modern landfills, buried waste is sealed from the environment. Archeologist William Rathje has excavated landfills from New York to California and found that virtually no degradation takes place. Newspapers are still readable more than 20 years after being thrown away. Food, such as steaks and carrots, remain unchanged for more than a decade. As Rathje said on "Saturday Night with Connie Chung," "I don't think there is a myth in the United States that is more popular than biodegradation, other than Santa Claus."

Courtesy Dow Chemical Company

The EPA's preferred alternative to degradability is recycling. Dow and others in the plastics industry were already investing in a growing plastics recycling industry. The plastics recycling industry is the fastest growing materials-recycling industry in the United States and currently recycles 28 percent of plastic soft drink bottles, as well as substantial quantities of other disposable plastics. Demand for recycled plastic is strong. According to Rubbermaid, its use of recycled plastic is limited only by the availability of materials.

To change students' focus from degradability to recycling, Dow undertook to educate and inform U.S. high school students, as one element in a national plastics recycling research and awareness effort.

Research

Six focus groups — two each in Los Angeles, Chicago, and Boston — were conducted with more than 50 high school students. We found that the students got most of their environmental information from MTV; were concerned about trash, but did not know where it goes when it leaves the curb; had a disproportionately negative opinion of plastics; felt that people need an incentive, perhaps financial, to recycle.

To paraphrase the words of the students, being the "Nightmare-on-Elm-Street" generation, they felt fear works well as an incentive; being the "Just-Say-No" generation, they said positive messages get more attention; as the MTV generation, they wanted music, excitement, and fast action — translated, they get bored quickly; being teenagers, they resented being "talked down to" — they wanted interaction, not a lecture; they had low expectations of assembly programs, in general.

Planning

Research, development, and planning activities began in November 1989. *Recycle This!* debuted its nationwide high school tour on March 22, 1990.

Objectives

- To provide high school audiences with accurate information about solid waste, degradability, and the recyclability of plastic, aluminum, paper, and glass
- To raise awareness of and involvement in recycling, in general, and specifically with regard to plastics

Audience

- High school students, and through them, their parents
- Educators
- Community officials
- Local recyclers
- The media, and through them, the community at large

Strategy

We planned the show to visit large high schools in major metropolitan areas to reach the maximum number of students possible per performance. Local public officials, recyclers, and media were invited to the performances. We provided information on local recycling activities to the students and media to encourage their participation. The budget was $600,000 for all facets of program development and implementation, as well as on-the-road management of the program.

Execution

Ketchum and Dow developed the concept, determined the relevant environmental teaching points, and outlined the elements of the program, including skits, songs, and the game show involving audience participants. Ketchum then hired a professional producer to script and stage the show. *Recycle This!*, a 45-minute long, live performance, involves a cast of five and crew of five, and uses music, humor, dance, skits, and video to convey a total of 88 separate environmental teaching points. Before the final production, members of the environmental sciences committee of the National Science Teachers Association (NSTA) reviewed the script with Ketchum, suggesting minor revisions.

In 1990, Ketchum booked *Recycle This!* visits to high schools in 53 cities in the United States and Canada. The summer program included a one-week visit to the Virginia Museum of Science in Richmond, and extended appearances at Six Flags Over Georgia, Great America (Chicago), and Great Adventure (New Jersey) amusement parks.

A highlight of the 1990 schedule was performing by invitation of NSTA for 400 science teachers at their annual meeting. The performance garnered a standing ovation and a steady stream of requests for the program. Ketchum has scheduled *Recycle This!* visits with high schools in 47 cities in 1991, ending its tour with a "command performance" to the plastics industry at the National Plastics Exposition, the world's largest plastics expo, in June 1991.

Recycle This! audiences receive a flyer detailing where to recycle locally and a recycled plastic cassette tape of the show's theme music. Dow's 800 information number is on the tape for callers to request a community action kit on how to start local recycling programs.

Evaluation

Recycle This! will directly reach more than 250,000 students, teachers, and parents by June 1991. To date, the impact has been remarkable.

Written praise from administrators and teachers commends *Recycle This!* as environmental education at its best, providing accurate, unbiased information to students in a memorable, motivational format. *Recycle This!* has spurred the initiation or expansion of recycling programs in schools visited from New York to Illinois to California. A follow-up survey that Ketchum conducted with schools visited in 1990 revealed a dramatic difference in awareness of recycling issues before and after, and an equally dramatic improvement in awareness that plastics are recyclable. The program also precipitated behavioral changes: Conard High School in West Hartford, Connecticut, revised its 1990–1991 calendar of special programs to focus exclusively on the environment. Northport High School on Long Island initiated a program to recycle paper, plastics, and aluminum as a result of *Recycle This!*

Currently, Dow fields approximately 175 calls each month on their 800 number. These are requests for the show to visit a particular high school, information on community recycling, information on plastics recyclers, and educational materials.

Recognition has come from industry, as well. Impressed with the response from academic and environmental audiences, Wal-Mart, Phillips Petroleum, Rubbermaid, Kodak, General Motors, Exxon, BFGoodrich, and others have invited *Recycle This!* to visit cities where they will sponsor the program in local high schools.

Furthermore, the media has extended the message that plastics are recyclable, as are aluminum, paper, and glass, to more than 106.7 million Americans. CNN, *Time* magazine and *Newsday* have reported on *Recycle This!* nationally; local media have reported on *Recycle This!* in every city visited.

To meet the demands of schools to whom Dow cannot bring the program, a 30-minute network-quality video of *Recycle This!* is now available at no cost to schools requesting it. A classroom version of Environmental Jeopardy, the game-show centerpiece of *Recycle This!* that quizzes students on their environmental knowledge, will soon be available for use with the video.

Exhibit 9–1a   *Recycle This!* Brochure

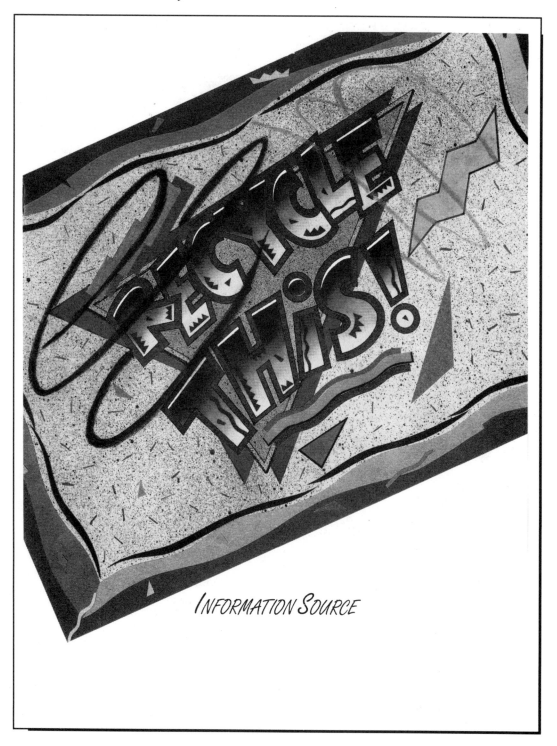

INFORMATION SOURCE

Courtesy Dow Chemical Company

RECYCLE THIS!

Recycling of all materials is no longer just for the eco-crowd. It's not a fad. It's becoming a new way of life.

Television stories of the Long Island garbage barge searching for an open dump raised public awareness that the United States is running out of landfill space in many places. Recycling more of our renewable resources — traditionally considered trash — has been suggested as a way to help solve this problem. In addition, recycling has many other benefits, including energy and resource conservation.

DO WE HAVE A LANDFILL SHORTAGE?

The cast of *RECYCLE THIS!* introduces the problem of overcrowded landfills.

In the RECYCLE THIS! video, the cast sings, "We didn't start the landfills." This is true since landfills and dumps have been the final resting place for most of the nation's solid waste for years. However, it would be inaccurate to sing that "we aren't filling them up." Almost two thirds of the nation's landfills closed over the last 10 years and 40 percent of those still open could be shut down today because they are operating without government approval.

Because 74 percent of the waste currently generated in the United States each year goes into landfills, a shortage of landfill space means solutions need to be found. The Environmental Protection Agency suggests placing a greater emphasis on source reduction, recycling and waste-to-energy incineration to extend the life of the nation's landfills.

Number of Available U.S. Landfills

18,500 — 1979

6,500 — 1988

3,250 — 2000

WHAT IS IN OUR TRASH CANS?

The solid waste stream is that never-ending flow of garbage we all create — newspapers, steel and aluminum cans, glass bottles and jars, plastic containers and more.

Paper and plastic represent the largest potential supply of recyclables based on volume according to a study conducted by the Franklin Associates and supported by the EPA. The "other" category in this chart includes wood, clothing, shoes, old tires and miscellaneous throw-aways.

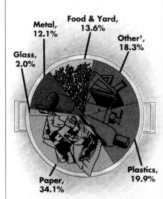

Metal, 12.1%

Food & Yard, 13.6%

Glass, 2.0%

Other†, 18.3%

Plastics, 19.9%

Paper, 34.1%

Municipal Solid Waste by Material Type and Volume

†*Other* includes wood, clothing and miscellaneous throw-aways.

WHAT ABOUT DEGRADABILITY?

A member of a University of Arizona archaeological team holds a newspaper that had been buried in a landfill for 12 years.

Many people think landfills are the easiest and best way to get rid of waste because they believe that biodegradable materials decompose quickly in landfills. Recent research, however, presents a much different picture.

Archaeologists from the University of Arizona, examining excavated landfill debris buried 20 years earlier, discovered "green grass clippings, a T-bone steak . . . and five hot dogs," all in excellent condition. Also, long-buried newspapers could be accurately dated from their perfectly preserved pages. After cataloging large quantities of like-new trash, the researchers concluded that biodegradability in landfills is a "myth."

These studies indicate that even highly degradable natural materials undergo little or no decomposition in landfills because the waste isn't exposed to air, water or sunlight. This lack of degradability is preferred because the by-products of degradation pose a threat to the environment. To keep liquid produced by decomposing materials from leaving landfills and going into groundwater, modern landfills are often lined with clay or heavy-duty plastic and covered at night with a thin layer of soil or compost.

A more realistic plan for solid waste management than waiting for things to degrade is to use source reduction, recycling and waste-to-energy incineration to reduce waste. Materials that can't be handled by these other waste management methods are landfilled.

Artie and Doc examine waste stored in a landfill for 30 years.

WHAT IS SOURCE REDUCTION?

Jimmy Jam sings "reduce, reuse and recycle." He says "source reduction" means using less.

Plastic soft drink bottles are now 20 percent lighter than in 1977.

Manufacturers use source reduction to minimize production and disposal costs. For example, products may be supplied in concentrated form, requiring smaller containers. Thinner packaging also may be used. In recent years, makers of plastic soft drink bottles have trimmed the container's weight by 20 percent. This conserves about 175 million pounds of plastic each year.

Companies have found a variety of ways to reduce waste at the source. By making its drinking straws 20 percent lighter, McDonald's has eliminated one million pounds of waste per year. Employees of The Dow Chemical Company at a plant in Allyn's Point, Connecticut, eliminated 90,000 pounds of waste per year by removing an intermediate step in the production of polystyrene resins.

Individuals can apply source reduction techniques as well. These include buying refills and selecting concentrates so that less packaging is used. Other ways are using reuseables when appropriate and considering whether a product is truly needed.

WHY RECYCLE?

Recycling is another key waste reduction method. Up to 50 percent of the four pounds of solid waste that every person produces per day on average could be recycled, but only 13 percent is currently recycled.

By using materials more than once, we conserve natural resources and the energy required to produce and process new materials. Recycled newspaper, for example, uses only 20 to 30 percent of the energy required to manufacture newsprint from new pulp. Each recycled aluminum can saves the energy equivalent of six ounces of gasoline. In fact, it takes 95 percent less energy to make a new can from recycled aluminum.

Recycling is also a way to divert waste from landfills and conserve landfill capacity for nonrecyclables. In addition to its environmental and conservation benefits, recycling creates jobs and business opportunities.

WHAT IS BEING RECYCLED?

$1,175/ton

Soft Drink Container Recycling Rates

Glass, 15%

Plastic, 28%

Aluminum, 61%

Aluminum cans are often the most commonly recycled material in the waste stream partly because they are the recyclable with the highest value per ton. In 1989, 61 percent of aluminum cans used in the United States were recycled. The economics of recycling are seen as you look at the next most recycled product — the plastic soft drink bottle — which has the second highest value as a recyclable and next to aluminum cans is the second most recycled soft drink container.

Here are a few other recycling success stories. In 1989, Americans recycled:

- 15 million tons of paper and paperboard boxes
- 145 million pounds of high density polyethylene plastic bottles (milk jugs, shampoo and detergent bottles)
- 42 percent of all soft drink containers

Even aerosol cans are being collected for recycling in some places.

And, we can expect recycling to continue growing. For example:

- The steel industry, which has always recycled scrap metal, formed the Steel Can Recycling Institute in 1988 to increase recycling and has six mills participating in the effort.

- The goal of the Glass Packaging Institute is to have used glass constitute 50 percent of the glass industry's raw material.
- The goal of the National Polystyrene Recycling Company is to recycle 25 percent of all disposable polystyrene (plastic used to make plastic foam plates, cups, bowls, etc.) products by 1995.

These national trends may not always reflect local conditions. The best way to find out what is being recycled locally is to contact city or county waste management officials. There is also a list of organizations at the end of this brochure that can supply information about recycling.

CAN PLASTICS BE RECYCLED?

Most people are aware that paper, glass, aluminum and steel discards are recyclable and being recycled. However, plastic is a relatively new material and hasn't been widely recycled at the consumer level until recently.

Already 500 cities in the United States include plastics in their recycling programs. In addition, the amount of plastics being recycled is expected to grow by about 30 percent per year. Finding new uses for recycled plastics is the mission of many scientists and engineers. Plastics industry members are committed to increasing recycling and are investing several hundred million dollars yearly in plastics recycling research and businesses.

The RECYCLE THIS! rapper challenges a group of scientists to find uses for recycled plastics.

Value of Recyclables Per Ton

$54/ton — Glass

$58/ton — Steel

$162/ton — Plastic

$1,175/ton — Aluminum

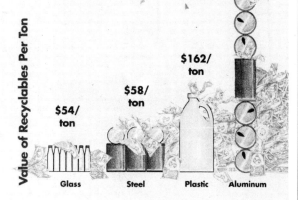

HOW CAN YOU IDENTIFY DIFFERENT TYPES OF PLASTIC?

To help consumers identify plastics when sorting them for recycling, the plastics industry has started a voluntary program of coding plastic packaging with a recycling symbol and number on the bottom of the package. The code indicates which type of plastic was used to make that particular product.

1
PETE
Polyethylene Terephthalate (PET)

2
HDPE
High-Density Polyethylene

3
V
Vinyl/Polyvinyl Chloride (PVC)

4
LDPE
Low-Density Polyethylene

5
PP
Polypropylene

6
PS
Polystyrene

7
Other
All Other Resins and Layered Multi-Material

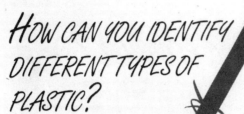

HOW IS RECYCLED MATERIAL USED?

The following are common uses for recycled materials:

Paper: Some newsprint, stationery, paperboard packaging, corrugated boxes, tissues and paper towels.

Recycled paper and plastic find a second life as packaging for many of the products found on store shelves.

Plastic: Base cup for soft drink bottles; fiberfill for jackets and sleeping bags; detergent bottles; plastic lumber for benches, picnic tables and boating docks; audio and videotape cassettes; carpeting fiber; and many other applications for plastics where food contact is unlikely.

Glass: Glass bottles and jars. Some scrap glass is pulverized and used as a filler for road surfacing.

Aluminum: Cans or other aluminum products.

Steel: Virtually all steel products.

Yard Waste: Compost for use as a soil additive.

HOW TO START A RECYCLING PROGRAM

Keys to starting a successful recycling program include:

- Investigate which recyclables local recyclers and brokers will accept and, of course, only collect what you can market.
- Increase volume by including neighboring organizations and communities in your program.
- Inform program participants about what is being accepted. Repeat messages frequently to raise participation levels and to cut down on contamination of desired recyclables by having them mixed with unwanted items.
- Include experienced professionals in your planning. At the end of this brochure is a listing of some of the organizations that have information on how to manage recycling programs. These groups also may be able to help identify outlets for the recyclables you collect.

WHO'S RESPONSIBLE?

All of us have responsibility for safely handling municipal solid waste because we all help create it. The first step is to try to minimize at the source through responsible purchasing and reuse of products. When disposal time comes, everyone can help reduce the amount of material going into landfills by composting yard waste, recycling and working with local waste management officials to understand what disposal approach works best for our own communities.

Moving away from an overdependence on landfills for disposal will require public support of more aggressive recycling programs and other waste management methods. Since solid waste is managed at the local level, change will be most likely when prompted and supported by concerned citizens who help form effective partnerships in their communities between government, industry and the public.

Here are some suggestions that anyone can do to further the recycling effort:

- Find out what is being recycled in your area.
- Save your recyclables and participate.
- Volunteer to help at a recycling collection center.
- Campaign for recycling by becoming more informed about recycling trends and options. Then, write federal, state and local government officials, telling them you support recycling and why.
- Start a recycling program in your school. Call Dow at 1-800-441-4369 and request a copy of "How to Set-Up a School Recycling Program," published by The Council for Solid Waste Solutions.

An Akron, Ohio, resident carries her recyclables to the curb as part of the city's recycling program. Her commitment to recycle represents the active role all citizens must play to solve our solid waste problem.

RECYCLE THIS! raises awareness that all of us should be part of making needed changes and supporting community recycling programs. You can make a difference. Volunteers have successfully launched recycling programs by creating and publicizing drop-off locations for recyclables or by helping establish recycling programs that involve curbside pick-up.

However, we don't need to wait until everything is in place to start recycling. Already, more than 1,200 communities have some type of recycling program and, with a little effort, most of us can **RECYCLE NOW!**

FOR ADDITIONAL INFORMATION

The following organizations may be contacted for more information on the solid waste challenge:

Center for Plastics Recycling Research
Rutgers, The State University
of New Jersey
Busch Campus, Bldg. 3529
P.O. Box 1179
Piscataway, NJ 08855-1179
908/932-4402

Council for Solid Waste Solutions
1275 K Street, NW Suite 400
Washington, DC 20005
202/371-5319

Council on Plastics and Packaging
in the Environment
1275 K Street, NW Suite 900
Washington, DC 20005
202/789-1310

Flexible Packaging Association
1090 Vermont Ave., NW Suite 500
Washington, DC 20005
202/842-3880

Foodservice & Packaging Institute
1025 Connecticut Ave., NW
Suite 513
Washington, DC 20036
202/822-6420

Keep America Beautiful, Inc.
Mill River Plaza
9 West Broad Street
Stamford, CT 06902
203/323-8987

National Association for Plastic
Container Recovery
4828 Parkway Plaza Blvd., Suite 260
Charlotte, NC 28217
704/357-3250

National Polystyrene Recycling
Corporation
25 Tri-State International
Lincolnshire, IL 60069
708/945-1991

National Recycling Coalition
1101 30th Street, NW Suite 305
Washington, DC 20007
202/625-6406

National Soft Drink Association
1101 16th Street, NW
Washington, DC 20036
202/463-6732

National Solid Waste
Management Association
1730 Rhode Island Ave., NW
Suite 1000
Washington, DC 20036
202/659-4613

Polystyrene Packaging Council
1025 Connecticut Ave., NW
Suite 508
Washington, DC 20036
202/822-6424

The Society of the Plastics Industry, Inc.
1275 K Street, NW Suite 400
Washington, DC 20005
202/371-5200

Southern Aerosol Technical
Association
1091 Lake Drive
Marietta, GA 30066

RECYCLE THIS!
The Dow Chemical Company
2040 Dow Center
Midland, MI 48674

DowBrands, Inc.
9550 Zionsville Road
P.O. Box 68511
Indianapolis, IN 46268

Printed in U.S.A.

Funding for RECYCLE THIS!
was provided by Dow Plastics
and DowBrands. For further
information call Dow at
1-800-441-4369.

Printed on recycled paper.

*Trademark of The Dow Chemical Company
Form No. 304-00293-291-P&M

McKAY99043/REQ200530

The Upjohn Company targeted Hispanic Americans in two large population centers: Los Angeles and San Antonio. The market leader in oral antidiabetes therapy in the United States, Upjohn selected a highly vulnerable public. Hispanic Americans are three times more likely to develop diabetes than the general public. Working with local chapters of the American Diabetes Association in both cities, Upjohn staged a health fair in Belvedere Park in East Los Angeles and a diabetes screening at a special game of the San Antonio Missions baseball team. Exhibit 9–2a is a diabetes awareness news release used in San Antonio. Exhibit 9–2b is a news release announcing the participation of campaign spokesman, "Catfish" Hunter, at the "Strike Out Diabetes Night" in San Antonio, and Exhibit 9–2c is a media alert for "Strike Out Diabetes Night." Exhibit 9–2d is a set of two public service announcements by singer Vicki Carr, announcing the "United Against Diabetes" fiesta at Belvedere Park in East Los Angeles.

| Case 9–2 | ## "Unidos Contra la Diabetes" (United Against Diabetes) |

The Upjohn Company, Kalamazoo, MI, with Manning, Selvage & Lee Public Relations, New York, NY

The Background

Diabetes with its complications is the third leading cause of death by disease in the United States. Yet, while an estimated 12 million Americans have diabetes, only half of them know it. Because of lifestyles and genetic heritage, Hispanics are three times more likely to develop diabetes than is the general public. Hispanics are also the fastest growing minority in the country. Health care authorities report that, because of economic and educational disadvantages, many Hispanics do not take advantage of the health care system. For these reasons, The Upjohn Company, the market leader in oral antidiabetes therapy in the United States, recognized both an educational and social need and a business opportunity for its prescription products. A pilot public relations program was begun in 1988 to address this situation.

Courtesy The Upjohn Company and Manning, Selvage & Lee, Inc.

Despite the challenges of language barriers and ethnic differences, including a frequently fatalistic attitude about disease, the program has begun to evince a measurable impact among the target audiences in the two cities where it was introduced.

Research

To better understand the problems at hand, we undertook the following research:

1. We reviewed published findings on the obstacles faced by both physicians and Hispanic patients in the diagnosis, treatment and long-term care of diabetes.
2. We talked with 10 geographically diverse American Diabetes Association (ADA) educators to learn about previous successful and unsuccessful efforts in reaching out to the Hispanic community.
3. We analyzed major Spanish-speaking markets with significant Spanish-language news media available for publicity efforts.
4. We analyzed proprietary Upjohn marketing research identifying target diabetes patients.

The above research determined that:

1. The Roman Catholic Church could be a key ally in these efforts.
2. The oldest woman in the family frequently makes most family health care decisions in the Hispanic community.
3. Respect for language and cultural differences is essential for credibility with the Hispanic community and media.
4. Finding strong Hispanic partners at the community level is equally essential for detailed special event planning and execution.
5. East Los Angeles and San Antonio, Texas, had news media offering great potential to support our efforts.

To better evaluate the success of our completed work, we adopted the following measures:

1. We set a publicity goal of generating repeated, positive, event-related educational information about diabetes in at least 75 percent of the Hispanic media available in the geographical areas we planned to work in.

2. We set a target audience goal of stimulating use of ADA bilingual screening questionnaires to assess diabetes risk among participants in planned educational activities.

Planning

Two separate but similar programs were developed to reach target audiences in East Los Angeles and San Antonio.

Responsibilities were shared by The Upjohn Company; Manning, Selvage & Lee; and local community organizations recruited for these efforts.

Program objectives were to:

1. Motivate 1,000 Hispanic Americans at risk for diabetes to see a health professional for a diabetes evaluation.
2. Generate major Hispanic and English news media coverage discussing the symptoms, risk factors, and treatments for diabetes.
3. Create events that function as positive, goodwill-building vehicles for Upjohn to point to as illustrations of the company's continuing commitment to diabetes education and patient service.

Audiences

The primary target audience was composed of Hispanics at risk for diabetes. The secondary target audience included doctors and other members of the health professional community in East Los Angeles and San Antonio.

Channels used to communicate to our target audiences included news media publicity, radio promotion, direct mail, free-standing newspaper inserts, church newsletters, and special community events.

The 1988 budget for both programs was $100,000 split between Los Angeles ($55,000) and San Antonio ($45,000), including all agency service and out-of-pocket production expenses.

Execution

Los Angeles

1. "Unidos Contra la Diabetes" health fair: Working with the Los Angeles affiliate of the American Diabetes Association, we organized a six-hour magnet event in Belvedere Park in predominantly Hispanic East Los Angeles. The event served

as a community focus for diabetes-related publicity, promotion, and advertising and became the setting for hundreds of diabetes risk-assessment screenings and clinic referrals by diabetes educators at the scene. In addition to patient screening in Spanish, there were informal talks and question-and-answer sessions in Spanish by a local physician, a nutritionist, an exercise expert, and several other health professionals. The Saturday morning and afternoon event also included entertainment, free eye examinations, and distribution of diabetes education materials in Spanish and English. News media and Upjohn corporate representatives also attended the event and spoke with physicians highly regarded in the Hispanic community.

2. Preevent publicity: For 10 days prior to the event, the local community witnessed repeated agency-arranged publicity and television and radio interviews with Spanish-speaking physicians and others discussing "Unidos Contra la Diabetes" and the warning signs of diabetes. In addition, singer Vicki Carr, a popular local celebrity, recorded radio public service announcements in English and Spanish used throughout the Los Angeles market. Finally, a Spanish, two-color insert promoting "Unidos Contra la Diabetes" and the warning signs of diabetes was published in eight separate Spanish-language daily and weekly newspapers.

San Antonio

1. "Strike Out Diabetes Night": We worked with the San Antonio affiliate of the ADA and a local health advocacy organization, the Center for Health Policy Development. Together, we forged a series of local events that created opportunities for major news media publicity and for diabetes risk assessment among Hispanics. These events included a kickoff luncheon with Archbishop Patricio Flores as the key speaker to honor program volunteers and The Upjohn Company and subsequent church-centered diabetes risk screenings. A special "Strike Out Diabetes Night" was arranged with the local San Antonio Missions baseball team, complete with "Strike Out Diabetes" giveaway towels, an Upjohn-ADA diabetes educational display, diabetes risk screening, live remote broadcasts in Spanish and English from the ballpark on KBUC-AM/FM stations, and a special appearance and ceremonial first pitch by Mayor Henry Cisneros.

2. Preevent publicity: A successful preevent media tour by The Upjohn Company's national diabetes spokesman Jim "Catfish" Hunter, the Baseball Hall of Fame pitcher who never let diabetes stop him, yielded several informational diabetes interviews on TV and radio and in print media. Topping off the event, the *San Antonio Express* became a media sponsor and printed more than six stories over the course of the week.

Evaluation

Los Angeles

Nearly 1,000 Hispanics attended the "Unidos Contra la Diabetes" event, 563 people were evaluated for diabetes, and 85 percent were found by ADA staff to be at risk for diabetes and referred to Spanish-speaking physicians for further testing and evaluation at no charge. In addition, there were four separate Spanish television news reports, six Spanish newspaper articles, and ten radio broadcasts in Spanish and English conveying all copy points. All totaled, 4.4 million impressions on diabetes education reached Hispanics in East Los Angeles.

San Antonio

Close to 3,000 spectators attended "Strike Out Diabetes Night" at the San Antonio Missions ballpark, where they heard and saw diabetes educational messages. More than 1,500 people were evaluated for diabetes by ADA staff; 12 percent tested positive for diabetes and were referred to Spanish-speaking physicians for further testing and treatment. Eight newspaper articles, six television broadcasts, and six radio interviews created 3.2 million impressions for diabetes education messages carried to the Hispanic/ Anglo community. The events also generated diabetes discussion nationwide on the Univision Hispanic network and in *Hispanic* magazine. Publicity more than exceeded goals.

On the strength of (1) overwhelmingly positive evaluations by local ADA chapter leaders and Mayor Cisneros, (2) excellent media coverage generated in 95 percent of available Hispanic media, and (3) significant, measurable success surpassing goals set for diabetes screening, the program is being continued in 1989 and expanded to include Miami.

Exhibit 9–2a   Diabetes Awareness Campaign News Release

Upjohn NEWS RELEASE

THE UPJOHN COMPANY
KALAMAZOO, MICHIGAN 49001
(616) 323-4000

from   MANNING, SELVAGE & LEE, INC.
79 MADISON AVENUE NEW YORK N.Y. 10016
(212) 213-0909

CONTACT: Jan AufderHeide
          (616) 323-6546

RELEASE: IMMEDIATE

CONTACT: John Creamer
          (212) 213-7127

CONTACT: Molly Morgan
          (212) 213-7132

DIABETES AWARENESS CAMPAIGN
TARGETS HISPANIC COMMUNITY

SAN ANTONIO, Aug. 15 -- Prevention and control are the bywords of the San Antonio Campaign for Diabetes Education, a series of activities beginning this week, directed toward the Hispanic community and designed to increase awareness of diabetes and its considerable toll.

Diabetes among the local Hispanic community is a cause of major concern, medical and public health authorities report.

According to the American Diabetes Association, more than 40 percent of the estimated 700,000 people with diabetes in Texas are Mexican-American. In fact, Mexican-Americans have a diabetes incidence rate that is 300 percent higher than the general population's. With its complications, diabetes is the third leading cause of death by illness in the United States.

"The Campaign for Diabetes Education is a local response to mounting evidence about the prevalence of diabetes among Hispanics in south Texas," says Juan Flores, executive director of the San Antonio Center for Health Policy Development. "The Mexican-American community is growing rapidly and a large

- more -

Courtesy The Upjohn Company and Manning, Selvage & Lee, Inc.

portion of this population is poor and at a heightened risk for diabetes. The personal and economic costs to the community will be tremendous if we don't do something about it."

Better understanding among Hispanic people of just what a diagnosis of diabetes means is an important aim of the campaign, says Robert P. Treviño, M.D., a local internist active in the Campaign for Diabetes Education.

"Too many people take a fatalistic attitude about diabetes," says Dr. Treviño. " They think, 'Oh, I've got diabetes. There's no solution. I'll probably lose my leg or my eyesight.' And they give up.

"We've got to make people understand that, though there isn't a cure, diabetes and its complications can usually be controlled through certain changes in lifestyle. And these problems can be prevented in the first place by adopting healthful habits early."

Obesity is one of the major risk factors for diabetes. More than three-fourths of all those with the disease are overweight. Treatment for the most common form of diabetes, the non-insulin-dependent variety, usually requires weight loss through a regimen of diet and exercise. Sometimes, patients are prescribed oral anti-diabetes agents, which improve the body's utilization of the hormone insulin, a substance responsible for converting food into energy.

"Diabetes is usually preventable or controllable, but it requires a personal adjustment in diet, and that's a big adjustment," says Dr. Treviño. "People have to learn to eat smaller amounts of food and to prepare food in a healthier way, using vegetable oil instead of lard, for example, or eating one tortilla instead of three or four.

"And poverty aggravates the situation. Many who are poor base their diets on processed foods, foods high in simple carbohydrates and high in fats, which are generally cheaper."

- more -

Screening and Follow-up

According to Juan Flores, the Campaign for Diabetes Education month is meant to stimulate diabetes prevention in the Hispanic community by getting as many people as possible screened for diabetes in order to catch it early before complications set in. "And for those we identify as requiring medical attention, " Flores says, "we mean not only to provide them with medical attention but also to follow up on them later on to be sure the attention is consistently delivered."

Variety of Activities Planned

Several individuals and public and private institutions are lending assistance to the Campaign for Diabetes Education in the form of organization help, financial backing, manpower, publicity, supplies and medical follow-up. For example, the San Antonio chapter of National Association of Hispanic Nurses, guided by Evelyn Garcia, is providing volunteers to administer diabetes risk analysis questionnaires at various church-group meetings around the city.

Other groups supporting the education effort include: the Center for Health Policy Development; the American Diabetes Association (ADA) and its Minority Initiative Task Force, chaired by Helen Ayala; The Upjohn Company; the Hispanic Chamber of Commerce; the Mexican-American Physicians Association; the Archdiocese of San Antonio, the Barrio Family Health Care Center, and the University of Texas Health Science Center.

Here is a run-down of upcoming campaign activities:

- The Campaign for Diabetes Education gets underway on August 17 with a luncheon that will gather the project organizers and volunteers to galvanize their support.

- On Sunday, August 21, The Upjohn Company is sponsoring Strike Out Diabetes Night at V.J. Keefe Stadium. Before and during the game

- more -

between the Missions and the Midland Angels (game time 7 pm), fans can visit the American Diabetes Association (ADA) table beneath the grandstand and receive a free diabetes risk analysis, a short questionnaire (available in both English and Spanish) designed to determine a person's risk for developing the disease. ADA volunteers will be on hand to provide information on where to go for further diabetes screening. The first 1,000 people in the ballpark will receive a free Strike Out Diabetes beach towel.

- On September 12-13, the University of Texas Health Science Center at San Antonio will sponsor a symposium on the health status of the Hispanic elderly. The conference will examine health problems and issues affecting the elderly populations along the Texas/Mexico border.

- On September 17, the Campaign for Diabetes Education will come to La Plaza de las Islas (Main Plaza) in front of San Fernando Cathedral. Beginning at noon, free diabetes blood-screening, a simple blood test to determine blood-sugar level, will be available. The ADA will be on hand to provide valuable health information and to answer questions. A mobile van parked nearby will provide free screening for retinopathy, a diabetes complication that, left untreated, can result in blindness. Volunteers will be able to refer participants to local public and private health centers and clinics, where further testing and treatment will be available at little or no cost. Musical entertainment, nutrition presentations and other helpful diabetes information will be available throughout the afternoon.

- Also in September, Spanish-language station KWEX channel 41 will present a half hour program devoted to the nutritional needs of diabetic patients. A nutrition expert will demonstrate healthful ways of preparing meals. Throughout the month as well, channel 41 will be airing two-minute public service announcements devoted to diabetes prevention and control. Community leaders and individuals with success stories to tell about controlling their own diabetes will be featured.

# # #

Exhibit 9-2b   Diabetes Awareness Campaign News Release

Upjohn NEWS RELEASE

THE UPJOHN COMPANY
KALAMAZOO, MICHIGAN 49001
(616) 323-4000

from: MANNING, SELVAGE & LEE, INC.
79 MADISON AVENUE, NEW YORK, N.Y. 10016
(212) 213-0909

CONTACT: Jan AufderHeide
(616) 323-6546

RELEASE: IMMEDIATE

CONTACT: John Creamer
(212) 213-7127

CONTACT: Molly Morgan
(212) 213-7132

HALL OF FAMER "CATFISH" HUNTER
IN SAN ANTONIO TO HELP STRIKE OUT DIABETES

SAN ANTONIO, Aug. 15 -- Hall of Fame pitcher Jim "Catfish" Hunter is back in the minor leagues.

No, the former American League ace isn't suiting up with the Missions to start a new career, but he is in town today nonetheless to pitch his message about diabetes to San Antonians and to urge them to attend Strike Out Diabetes Night at V.J. Keefe Stadium on Sunday, August 21.

Diabetes is a special concern to Hunter. Ten years ago he found out he had the disease, and since then he's spent several weeks every year as a spokesman for The Upjohn Company, giving interviews and appearing at health fairs, alerting people to the symptoms and risk factors of diabetes. His main message is that, while there is no cure for diabetes, it can be controlled.

Diabetes and its complications is the third-leading cause of death by illness in the United States. It's a particularly severe problem in South Texas with its large Mexican-American population. According to the American Diabetes Association (ADA), some 700,000 Texans have the disease. Of these, 300,000 are

Mexican-Americans, who have a 300 percent greater likelihood of developing diabetes than the general population.

Diabetes strikes other minorities in similar disproportion. Blacks have a 33 percent greater chance of developing diabetes than whites, and over 20 percent of the adults in some Native American tribes also suffer from the disease.

Strike Out Diabetes Night

Hunter is urging San Antonians to do themselves a favor and go out to V.J. Keefe Stadium on Sunday night, August 21, for Strike Out Diabetes Night, during the game between the San Antonio Missions and the Midland Angels, which begins at 7 pm. Fans can stop by the American Diabetes Association (ADA) table under the grandstand and receive a free diabetes risk analysis, a short quiz that helps determine whether or not a person may be at risk for diabetes. Also, the first 1,000 fans into the ballpark will receive a free Strike Out Diabetes Night beach towel, compliments of The Upjohn Company. Country and western radio station KBUC will be broadcasting live from the Stadium beginning two hours before game time.

Strike Out Diabetes Night marks the first of several diabetes awareness events slated for the month of September in San Antonio under the banner, "A Su Salud" (To Your Health), an effort targeted for the Hispanic community. The activities will include diabetes public service announcements and a half-hour program on diabetes nutrition on a local cable channel, symposia on health problems faced by elderly Hispanics and diabetes blood-screening at San Fernando Cathedral on September 17.

Diabetes is estimated to affect some 12 million people nationwide, but only half are said to know they have the disease. It is a major cause of cardiovascular disease, blindness, kidney disease, amputations, strokes and birth defects. Each year, 150,000 people die from diabetes and probably another 150,000 more succumb to its complications.

Symptoms of non-insulin-dependent diabetes, by far the most common form of the disease, include: frequent urination and unquenchable thirst; weakness and fatigue; extreme hunger; blurred vision; tingling or numbness in the feet or hands; itchy skin; slow healing cuts or frequent skin infections

The Upjohn Company is a worldwide, research-based manufacturer and marketer of human health care products and services, agronomic and vegetable seeds, animal health products and pharmaceutical and specialty chemicals. The company's headquarters are in Kalamazoo, Michigan.

# # #

Exhibit 9–2c   "Strike Out Diabetes Night" Media Alert

THE UPJOHN COMPANY
KALAMAZOO, MICHIGAN 49001
(616) 323-4000

from   MANNING, SELVAGE & LEE, INC.
79 MADISON AVENUE NEW YORK, N.Y. 10016
(212) 213-0909

MEDIA ALERT:

TO: Health, science, sports, news reporters and assignment desks.

WHAT: Strike Out Diabetes Night

First event of the San Antonio Campaign for Diabetes Education, a month-long series of activities designed to enhance diabetes awareness, prevention and control among the Hispanic community.

Before and during the Missions' game fans are invited to take a short diabetes risk-analysis quiz at the American Diabetes Association table beneath the grandstand. Also, the first 1,000 fans entering the ballpark will receive Strike Out Diabetes beach towels, compliments of The Upjohn Company and the American Diabetes Association.

WHEN: Sunday night, August 21 (Before, during Missions-Midland Angels baseball game, 7:00 PM.

WHERE: V.J. Keefe Stadium (St. Mary's University, 36th and Culebra)

WHY: Diabetes is the third leading cause of death by illness in this country. Yet it is estimated that half of those who have the disease don't know it. Mexican-Americans are 3 times as likely as the rest of America to develop diabetes. Approximately one out of seven Hispanics has diabetes.

CONTACT: *John Creamer*, (212) 213-7127, *Jeanne Longo* (212) 213-0909; MS&L Public Relations, New York; *Juan Flores*, Center for Health Policy Development (512) 226-9743; *Jim Wehmeier*, PR Director, San Antonio Missions, (512) 434-9311; Susanne Barham, American Diabetes Association (512) 697-0854.

Courtesy The Upjohn Company and Manning, Selvage & Lee, Inc.

Exhibit 9–2d Diabetes Awareness Campaign Public Service Announcements

COPY PSA's DIABETES EVENT

15"

Hi! I'm Vicki Carr... Please join the American Diabetes Association with The Upjohn Company at the "UNITED AGAINST DIABETES" fiesta this Saturday the 27th, from 11 a.m. to 3 p.m. at Belvedere Park, corner of First and Mednik, in East Los Angeles. Entrance is free and there'll be music, food and lots of activities for the family ... We'll see you there!

30"

Hi! I'm Vicki Carr... Did you know that one out of seven Hispanics has diabetes...Don't risk it...Inform yourself! Please join the American Diabetes Association and The Upjohn Company this Saturday the 27th at the "UNITED AGAINST DIABETES," Fiesta at Belvedere Park, corner of First and Mednik in East Los Angeles from 11 a.m. to 3 p.m...There will be music, food, exercise demonstrations and lots of activities...Entrance is free...Bring the family...WE'LL SEE YOU at "UNITED AGAINST DIABETES," THIS SATURDAY AT BELVEDERE PARK FROM 11 TO 3 P.M.!

Courtesy The Upjohn Company and Manning, Selvage & Lee, Inc.

*In June 1990, the "Nutrition During Pregnancy" report of the
National Academy of Sciences reversed earlier conventional
medical wisdom that the use of multivitamins containing folic
acid during early pregnancy reduced the risk of serious birth
defects called neural tube defects (NTDs). Publicity following
the report advised pregnant women to skip vitamin supplements. Hoffman-La Roche, a manufacturer of bulk vitamins,
decided to counteract the academy's report with a program
that included publicizing new research studies with findings
contrary to those of the academy. The outcome of this effort
was that in 1992, the U.S. Public Health Service issued a recommendation that all women of childbearing age should consume 0.4 milligram of folic acid daily for the prevention of
neural tube birth defects. Exhibit 9–3a is a news release announcing the nutrition and pregnancy conference that ultimately led to present U.S. Public Health Service guidelines.*

Case 9–3   **Vitamin Nutrition in Pregnancy and Prepregnancy**

Hoffman-La Roche, Inc., Nutley, NJ, with Ketchum Public
Relations, New York, NY

The Background

As early as the 1960s, there were reports in the medical literature
linking use of multivitamins (MV) containing folic acid (a B vitamin) during early pregnancy to a reduced risk of serious birth
defects called neural tube defects (NTDs), the *leading cause of
infantile paralysis* in the United States. By the mid-1980s, two
large population studies made a very strong case for the protective
power of MV supplements taken periconceptionally (about 3
months before and after conception). However, in June 1990, the
"Nutrition During Pregnancy" report of the National Academy of
Sciences stated that supplementation during pregnancy is unnecessary except during the second and third trimesters, and even
then, only after individual dietary and nutritional assessment of
the patient. Although there were many other facets of the report,
media coverage headlined the antisupplement message. Clinical

Courtesy Hoffman-La Roche Inc.

trials that would provide definitive scientific proof that MV and/ or folic acid could help prevent NTDs had not yet been completed; still, some scientists believed the evidence strong enough for pro-supplement recommendations to women and their doctors, and even a public health policy. Indeed, some felt that further clinical trials would be unethical in light of what was already known. Ketchum urged its client, Hoffmann-La Roche Inc., a manufacturer of bulk vitamins, to take a leadership role on the issue, despite the fact that Roche does not market consumer products. Roche, deeply concerned over the potentially devastating consequences to thousands of children of the future, agreed to support a program of both scientific activities and public relations.

Research

An avalanche of publicity following the publication of the academy's report advised pregnant women to "forget vitamins," "skip supplements," and "try none a day." The report had cautioned doctors to assess the nutrient intakes of their patients before prescribing supplements. Recognizing that most doctors have little time to spend on nutrition assessment, Ketchum recommended that Roche sponsor research to determine:

1. The extent to which doctors were currently assessing their patients' diets
2. Their knowledge of the NTD/MV link
3. Whether they currently prescribed prenatal vitamins
4. Whether the report had affected their practices

A survey of ob/gyns was developed and executed by the Nutrition Information Center at Cornell Medical Center, in collaboration with the Research Department of Ketchum Public Relations, as well as a focus group of New York area ob/gyns. This research was intended to provide both a baseline of knowledge/opinions and substance for later tactical publicity elements. As expected, it was found that doctors rarely assessed their pregnant patients' nutritional status apart from a simple measure of weight gain; that they almost always prescribed prenatal vitamins, and almost never counseled patients about their nutritional habits before pregnancy. Shockingly, only one in ten of the ob/gyns in the focus group was aware of the NTD/MV reports, and those who were unaware were quite skeptical of their veracity.

Planning

Ketchum proposed a multiyear plan of action to raise awareness of the folic acid/NTD link among opinion-leading target audiences. It was recommended that Roche use its existing vehicle, the Vitamin Nutrition Information Service (VNIS), to disseminate scientific information, build a prosupplementation consensus among health professionals, and publicize the information.

Objectives

- To raise awareness of the importance of MVs containing folic acid during preconception and pregnancy
- To develop a consensus of professional opinion supporting MV use among all women of childbearing age

Strategy

- To use results of ob/gyn research as a platform for discussion of periconceptual supplementation
- To collaborate with credible third-party organizations to reach professional organizations and opinion leaders
- To create "pull-through" by communicating the importance of preconception nutrition to consumer audiences

Audience

- Health/nutrition professionals: Ob/gyns, family physicians, dietitians, nutrition counselors, public health nutritionists, and nutrition educators
- Health/nutrition communicators: Health/nutrition editors, writers, and producers
- Influentials: Opinion leaders and policy-makers
- Consumers: Women in their childbearing years (18 to 49) and significant others

Execution

Without positive results from the clinical trials on vitamins and NTDs (which were ongoing at the time the program was started), this program could not have achieved what it did. But such results were obtained, and Ketchum's role in the long process of obtaining a public health recommendation in favor of vitamins was to raise and keep the issue alive before the target audiences. Basic tactical elements included the following:

- Scientific research and background information: Landmark research articles and other background materials were distributed to opinion-leading health and nutrition professionals and communicators

- Professional knowledge/opinion research: Results of the ob/gyn survey and focus group were used in several ways. Preliminary results were presented to editors of national women's magazines by Dr. Barbara Levine of the Nutrition Information Center, Cornell Medical Center, at an editor roundtable, which also featured NTD researcher Dr. Aubrey Milunsky, director of the Center for Human Genetics in Boston. Then the results were developed into a professional abstract and presented as a poster session at a professional conference. Finally, they were written as a professional research article and submitted to a peer-review journal.

- Professional conference: A conference on "Maternal Nutrition and Pregnancy Outcome," organized by the New York Academy of Sciences and Roche nutrition scientists, served as a forum for gathering all the relevant research and researchers together and focusing scientific attention on the topic. Ketchum publicized the conference as well as Dr. Levine's poster session to both short- and long-lead media.

- Professional newsletter: An overview of research, based on the conference, was developed for ob/gyns and distributed by the Nutrition Information Center, Cornell Medical Center.

- Research and symposia publicity: Ketchum publicized new research as studies were completed and results became available (for example, a United Kingdom trial by Nicholas Wald, M.D., published in *The Lancet*, July 1991, and a Hungarian trial by Andrew Czeizel, M.D., published in the *New England Journal of Medicine*, December, 1992).

Budget and Staffing

The pregnancy program was able to run economically because it was a subcomponent of the larger, existing Roche program and was staffed by the same account team at Ketchum. About $80 million per year of the VNIS budget was earmarked for the preconception/pregnancy program. The staff included a senior counsel, an account manager, a registered dietitian, an account coordinator, technical writers, and an account assistant.

Evaluation

A consensus conference of health professionals was convened by the Centers for Disease Control (CDC) in July 1992 to review NTD/MV/folic acid research and to discuss public health and policy issues. This meeting was largely an outgrowth of the New York Academy of Sciences conference, which had been attended by CDC representatives working in the area of NTDs. As a result of the consensus of professional opinion achieved at this conference, in September 1992, the U.S. Public Health Service issued a recommendation that *all women of childbearing age should consume 0.4 milligram of folic acid daily for the prevention of neural tube birth defects.*

The collaborative effort between Roche scientists—who supported the clinical trials, tirelessly networked with their colleagues, and created platforms for discussion—and the Ketchum communications team—who effectively used public relations to build a professional consensus of opinion and to raise public consciousness of the issue—was a major factor in changing the official public health policy in the United States. Ketchum's activities with health professional audiences and the health and nutrition media not only helped focus scientific attention on the topic, but also helped build both public and professional interest to the "critical mass" needed to effect change.

On the consumer communications side, Ketchum raised awareness by generating positive coverage of the issue via national media, including *U.S. News and World Report, USA Today, Time,* "CBS This Morning," "Good Morning America," *Good Housekeeping, Parents,* CBS news radio, *Glamour, Medical World News,* and *Self.* In place of the negative headlines that dominated the press when the program was begun, there are now provitamin statements such as "U.S. Backs a Vitamin to Foil Birth Defects" (*The New York Times*), "New Study Finds Vitamin Supplement Can Sharply Lower Severe Birth Defects" (*The Wall Street Journal*), and "Folic Acid Could Cut 75% of All Neural Tube Defects" (*Medical Tribune*). In 1992 alone, Ketchum placed NTD/multivitamin/folic acid stories reaching 18.5 million people in the top regional markets and 31.4 million via national media, for a total audience reach of *50 million.* Through this public service effort, Ketchum and Roche succeeded in placing the issue of vitamin nutrition during prepregnancy and pregnancy on the national agenda, with the result that thousands of babies may be spared the crippling consequences of inadequate maternal vitamin status. According to the CDC, the public health impact of preventing the occurrence of NTDs is comparable to that of the polio vaccine.

Exhibit 9–3a **News Release Announcing Maternal Nutrition Conference**

VNIS News Release

S News Release **VNIS News Release** VNIS

May, 1992
FOR IMMEDIATE RELEASE

From: Ketchum Public Relations
       1133 Avenue of the Americas
       New York, NY 10036
       Contact: Maureen Ternus, M.S., R.D.
       212-536-8837

MATERNAL NUTRITION KEY TO POSITIVE PREGNANCY OUTCOMES

SAN DIEGO, CA -- Mounting research underscores the importance of adequate vitamin and mineral status among women, not only during pregnancy, but in the months before conception. More than 50 scientists convened at the "Maternal Nutrition and Pregnancy Outcome" conference sponsored by the New York Academy of Sciences, to share their research and discuss its implications.

One of the most exciting reports was that supplementation with multivitamins including folic acid, a B vitamin, during the preconception period and early pregnancy can protect against first-time occurrence of neural tube birth defects (NTDs). This was presented by Andrew Czeizel, M.D., lead investigator of the neural tube defects arm of the Hungarian Family Planning Program.

This large-scale, ongoing trial allows evaluation of pregnancy outcomes in general and has included a randomized blind

-more-

The Vitamin Nutrition Information Service • Hoffmann-La Roche, Inc. • Nutley, NJ 07110 • (201) 365-0167

HHN-0497/0592

Courtesy Hoffmann-La Roche Inc.

study to test whether periconceptional multivitamin supplementation effectively reduces the rate of first occurrence of neural tube defects. Previous clinical data have shown that multivitamin supplements lowered the risk of recurrence, and a recent trial found that folic acid alone significantly reduced recurrences.

"Our findings are important from a public health standpoint, because 95 percent of NTDs occur among women who have not had a previously affected pregnancy. Only five percent of cases are recurrences," explained Dr. Czeizel, who is a medical geneticist in the Department of Human Genetics and Teratology of Hungary's National Institute of Hygiene.

NTDs occur when the neural tube -- which becomes the future spine and brain of the developing embryo -- fails to close properly, resulting in anencephaly (a partially or completely missing brain) or spina bifida (a gap in the protective sheath covering the spinal cord). These defects typically occur between the third and fourth week of pregnancy.

The new data from the Hungarian trial will be taken into consideration by the Centers for Disease Control (CDC), Atlanta, GA, as they review their nutrition policy for American women of childbearing age.

-more-

The CDC currently recommends folic acid supplements only for women who have already had an infant with an NTD. "An important public health question is whether all women of reproductive age in the United States should take folic acid-containing supplements," said Godfrey Oakley, M.D., Director of the Division of Birth Defects and Developmental Disabilities at CDC.

Providing nutrition counseling to women before they become pregnant is an area that needs professional education and attention, according to Barbara Levine, Ph.D., R.D., Assistant Professor of Nutrition in Medicine at Cornell University Medical Center/New York Hospital. Dr. Levine conducted a survey to determine the extent to which ob/gyns currently evaluate the diets of either their pregnant patients or their patients who are planning pregnancy to determine their need for dietary changes and/or supplements.

In a sample of 566 ob/gyns, only 10.1 percent reported that they saw their patients prior to the fourth week of pregnancy, and only 5.5 percent reported that they saw their patients before conception to prepare the woman for pregnancy.

"Fifty-eight percent of the doctors did not ask their pregnant patients such basic questions as whether they have made any changes in their diets, how may calories they are taking in and the types of food they are eating," said Dr. Levine.

-more-

4

Nine out of ten doctors in the survey (94 percent) claimed to provide nutrition counseling to their patients, but, "all too often their 'advice' consisted of vague admonishments to 'eat right' or to 'avoid alcohol,'" explained Dr. Levine.

Although official recommendations on nutrition during pregnancy assume that most women eat a balanced diet and therefore meet their nutritional needs, "many women, particularly those who are economically deprived, are not meeting the Recommended Daily Allowances (RDAs) for a variety of micronutrients," said Gladys Block, Ph.D., Professor of Public Health Nutrition at the University of California, Berkeley.

Women below or near the poverty line typically eat diets that are insufficient in iron, zinc, folic acid, vitamin A, vitamin C and B6, according to data from two national nutrition surveys -- the Second National Health and Nutrition Examination Survey (NHANES II) and the Continuing Survey of Food Intakes of Individuals (CSFII). Dr. Block analyzed these surveys to determine the nutritional status of women during their childbearing years.

"Even middle class women aren't eating as well as they should," Dr. Block said. "For example, average intakes at the 25th percentile were only about half the RDA for vitamin E, zinc and calcium. The RDA for folic acid is 180 micrograms (mcg) for

-more-

adult women and increases to 400 mcg during pregnancy, but poor
women had median daily intakes of only 150 mcg. Furthermore, 25
percent of women above the poverty level averaged folic acid
intakes of only 142 mcg."

Several researchers discussed how nutritional status may
interact with other lifestyle factors to produce birth defects
and other adverse pregnancy outcomes.

Lifestyle factors such as drug abuse, alcoholism and
cigarette smoking can compromise the nutritional status of
pregnant women, according to Adrianne Bendich, Ph.D., Senior
Clinical Research Coordinator at Hoffmann-La Roche Inc. "These
lifestyle factors adversely affect a woman's nutritional status
during pregnancy by depressing the appetite, decreasing
absorption of nutrients and altering metabolism," she said.

Conversely, nutritional deficits appear to exacerbate the
negative effects of cigarette smoking, drug abuse and alcohol use
during pregnancy, which are known to increase the risk of
miscarriage, stillbirth and delivering a baby with developmental
or physical handicaps.

"According to current estimates, ten percent of newborns in
the U.S. are exposed to one or more illicit drugs in the womb,"
said Dr. Bendich. "Factors such as AIDS, teenage pregnancy and
poverty also compromise a woman's nutritional status during
pregnancy."

-more-

"To lower the risk of adverse pregnancy outcomes, dietary recommendations during pregnancy should take into account the effects of these various lifestyle and environmental factors on maternal nutrition," she said.

In the case of maternal alcoholism, "there is increasing evidence that micronutrient deficiencies may be associated with Fetal Alcohol Syndrome (FAS)," pointed out Ivor Dreosti, Ph.D., D.Sc., leader of the Nutrition and Cancer Group of Australia's Commonwealth Scientific and Industrial Research Organization.

"Alcohol abuse depletes certain antioxidant vitamins and trace elements such as zinc, which may increase free radical damage to fetal cells. The degree of severity of FAS is dependent upon how much damage occurs to fetal cells. This, in turn, is mediated in part by the mother's nutritional status during pregnancy," Dr. Dreosti said.

More than 50 doctors and scientists from the United States, England, Canada, Hungary and Australia presented their research to their colleagues at this conference held by the New York Academy of Sciences. It was the first time that the lead investigators of all the major NTD trials in the world, both observational and clinical studies, have convened in an open forum.

###

*In response to its extensive, nationwide research indicating a
lack of knowledge about child care among working parents,
the Dayton Hudson Corporation developed a program called
"Child Care Aware" to help parents identify, access, and demand quality care in their communities. Exhibit 9–4a is a
"Child Care Aware" news release. Exhibit 9–4b is a tip sheet
that includes a checklist for evaluating child care and five
steps to finding quality child care.*

Case 9–4	**Child Care Aware**

Dayton Hudson Corporation, Minneapolis, MN, with Burson-
Marsteller, New York, NY

The Background

Dayton Hudson Corporation, a Minneapolis-based retailer, developed "Child Care Aware" to help educate parents about quality
child care and how to find it. Many Dayton Hudson employees and
customers are working parents — with a substantial number having children of day care age. Dayton Hudson research showed that
these parents were concerned that affordable, quality care was
not readily available.

Research

Because of the appropriateness of the issue to its customer base,
the company used primary and secondary research to further
define key child care issues.

Dayton Hudson partnered with 32 nonprofit child care organizations to access their expertise on child care issues. Additionally,
it commissioned a third-party research firm to conduct 23 focus
groups with working parents nationwide.

The conclusions were that parents, especially first-time parents, were: (1) dissatisfied with the quality of their child care
arrangements, (2) unable to identify key characteristics of quality
care, and (3) unaware of and unable to adequately use local child
care resources.

Academic studies and the results of Dayton Hudson customer
interviews further confirmed the need for child care education.
Moreover, information from the Bureau of Labor Statistics showed

Courtesy Dayton Hudson Corporation

the breadth of the market: six out of every 10 families in the United States have the sole or both parents working.

Objectives

The objectives of "Child Care Aware" were:

- To raise awareness of the importance of quality child care among Dayton Hudson employees, parents, employers, and public policy-makers nationwide
- To help parents identify the components of quality child care
- To enable parents to access quality care in their communities
- To encourage parents to demand quality care

Strategy

The strategy was to partner with local child care organizations as credible spokespersons/resources and to use the Dayton Hudson network of Target and Mervyn's stores to distribute educational materials. A checklist consisting of 20 questions to consider when evaluating child care and a five-step plan to finding quality care were also created as key educational tools. The checklist was designed to help parents monitor components of quality care, including interaction between the children and caregivers, discipline practices, and whether activities are right for certain age groups. The five-step plan was also created as an evaluation tool. The plan advises parents, for instance, to make unannounced visits to potential caregivers and to count the number of children for each caregiver.

"Child Care Aware" was also developed with a consumer response system—a toll-free hot line. This enabled Dayton Hudson to not only provide a real link to the community, but also to measure the success of the campaign. Results of a grassroots and national media initiative and public service announcements also helped evaluate the program.

The budget totaled approximately $2.7 million, with 22 percent devoted to advertising.

Execution

The campaign activities were:

- A media initiative was designed to extend from the national to the grassroots level, reaching a range of audiences through diverse media

- A media kickoff was timed to coincide with the July National Democratic Convention and took advantage of the attention child care would receive during the convention period. An "exclusive" placed in the *Wall Street Journal's* "Work and Family" column quoted the "Child Care Aware" key spokesperson, featured the quality care checklist, and described the campaign and Dayton Hudson's efforts to improve child care quality and increase assistance for parents

- Public service announcements were distributed to broadcast outlets nationwide. These introduced a national toll-free hot line that linked parents to local child care resources and provided brochures with the quality child care checklist

- A grassroots media effort was initiated with more than 100 one-on-one interviews scheduled with local child care experts in approximately 32 markets

- In-store information booths were set up in 11 cities, and the Dayton Hudson network of 771 stores displayed 30,000 posters and distributed 1.7 million brochures, 125,000 buttons, and more than 20 million shopping bags bearing the "Child Care Aware" checklist.

- More than 50 community events, such as parades and zoo days were coordinated to attract working parents and their children and to distribute campaign information

- Dayton Hudson's president delivered speeches on the need for corporate involvement in child care education. The speeches were directed toward key target audiences (CEOs and human resource managers)

- Existing promotional vehicles — Target and Mervyn's Sunday circulars that reach more than 50 million people — were used to showcase the quality care checklist and feature the hot line number in target markets

- Billboards and transit ads reminded parents of what to look for in day care

Evaluation

The success of "Child Care Aware" was evident by the number of responses to the toll-free hot lines, the hot line survey, media impressions, PSA pick-ups, and recognition the company received.

Toll-free Hot Line and Survey

Calls into the toll-free nationwide hot line totaled approximately 19,000 in six months. In addition, an estimated 9,600 calls were received by local child care agencies, while 14,400 calls were tracked via local toll-free numbers in six states. An informal survey of national toll-free number respondents showed that 41 percent used the "Child Care Aware" checklist in evaluating options and 77 percent of respondents were first-time parents—a key target audience. Callers also confirmed that messages on how to properly assess quality care in their communities were communicated.

Media

The "Child Care Aware" media initiative generated more than 46.5 million impressions. A dozen major national placements—including the *Wall Street Journal, Fortune, Working Mother, Parents, Donahue*, ABC-TV's "Prime Time Live" and CBS-TV's "This Morning"—featured the "Child Care Aware" quality care checklist and/or the toll-free hot line number.

National media impressions totaled more than 34.3 million. Regional print and broadcast coverage yielded more than 12.3 million impressions. Local publicity included *The Dallas Morning News, Houston Chronicle, Los Angeles Times*, and *San Francisco Peninsula Parent*. Stories also ran in child care organization newsletters and aired on local television network and independent affiliates.

Public Service Announcements

Broadcast PSA's aired an estimated 17,000 times, including approximately 11,800 radio broadcasts and more than 5,100 television broadcasts.

Awards/Program Recognition

As a result of its "Child Care Aware" initiative, Dayton Hudson and its Target and Mervyn's stores received widespread recognition for leadership in child care education. Awards and recognitions, for example, were given by the Michigan House Republic Task Force on Child Care, the California Child Development Administrators Association, the International Women's Forum, Minnesota Governor Arnie H. Carlson, and Wisconsin Lieutenant Governor Scott McCallum.

Child Care Aware.

A PARTNERSHIP FOR QUALITY CHILD CARE

CONTACTS:

Barbara Reisman
Child Care Action Campaign
(212) 239-0138
Denise Nelson
National Assn. of Child Care Resource & Referral Agencies
(507) 287-2220

Laura Anders
Child Care Aware/Dayton Hudson
(612) 370-6622

FOR IMMEDIATE RELEASE

CHILD CARE AWARE OFFERS TIPS TO STRESSED-OUT PARENTS ON HOW TO FIND SUMMER CHILD CARE

MINNEAPOLIS, June 7 -- Stress is up for working parents these days as they scramble to make summer child care arrangements, according to a recent survey conducted by the National Association of Child Care Resource and Referral Agencies (NACCRRA). The survey asked counselors at child care resource and referral agencies across America about the types of questions they are getting from parents during this annual shift in child care arrangements.

The agencies are all participants in the Child Care Aware national public education program on quality child care. The $2.8 million campaign, sponsored by Dayton Hudson Corporation, its foundation and its Target, Mervyn's, Dayton's, Hudson's and Marshall Field's stores, is a cooperative effort with prominent child care organizations:

MORE

Courtesy Dayton Hudson Corporation

Child Care Action Campaign, NACCRRA, the National Association for the Education of Young Children (NAEYC) and the National Association for Family Day Care.

"Resource and referral agency counselors are reporting that parents are under stress in trying to arrange high-quality, affordable child care this summer," said Denise Nelson, NACCRRA's Community Coordinator.

Parents' Concerns

The most common concerns parents are presenting to counselors this summer are:

1) finding programs that offer high-quality, age-appropriate activities;

2) the additional cost of care for school-age children who must now be supervised during workday hours;

3) transportation safety and convenience of location;

4) ability of the child care provider to accommodate parents' working hours;

5) finding programs for kids over age 10 (too young to be unsupervised, not happy in traditional child care);

6) licensing and monitoring of programs and providers;

7) the child's interest in the activities offered;

8) easing the child's transition into the program.

"School's out soon for an estimated 18 million children whose parents work during the day," said Barbara Reisman,

MORE

executive director of Child Care Action Campaign.

"Securing adequate summer child care is a major national headache each year because there is no unified system of care in this country. Parents with fewer resources often face very troubling choices -- including leaving children unsupervised or settling for low-quality child care. In fact, in a recent NAEYC study, nearly one-third of parents reported leaving their children unattended during summer workdays," she said.

Help for Parents

To help parents seek out quality summer child care, Child Care Aware provides parents with a toll-free national information line at 1-800-424-2246 to put them in touch with the child care resource and referral counselors in their own communities. The campaign also has developed a five-step plan and some tips for working parents (see attached pages).

Dayton Hudson Corporation, based in Minneapolis, Minn., is one of America's largest retailers and corporate philanthropists with 1992 revenues of $17.9 billion and a corporate giving program totaling more than $20.7 million. The Corporation has committed $10 million over seven years to improve the quality of child care in America. Dayton Hudson operates 848 stores in 33 states.

93ccasm   #   #   #

Exhibit 9–4b   Child Care Tip Sheet

CHILD CARE AWARE℠
A PARTNERSHIP FOR QUALITY CHILD CARE

PARENTS QUALITY CHECKLIST

YES NO

BASICS
☐ ☐ Is the program licensed or registered?
☐ ☐ Is the group's size okay for my child's age?
☐ ☐ Is the caregiver trained and experienced?

THE PLACE
☐ ☐ Is there enough space?
☐ ☐ Are there different places for different activities?
☐ ☐ Is the outdoor play area fenced, hazard-free and completely visible to the caregiver?
☐ ☐ Is the space bright and pleasant?
☐ ☐ Is there an acceptable child-to-staff ratio?

DO THE CAREGIVERS
☐ ☐ Genuinely like children?
☐ ☐ Talk to children at their eye level?
☐ ☐ Share your beliefs about discipline?
☐ ☐ Greet your child when you arrive?
☐ ☐ Comfort children when needed?
☐ ☐ Keep you up-to-date on your child's activities?
☐ ☐ Make themselves available to answer your questions?

ACTIVITIES
☐ ☐ Are active and quiet experiences balanced?
☐ ☐ Are activities correct for the child's age?
☐ ☐ Are toys safe for each age, clean and available?

PARENTS' ROLE
☐ ☐ Are unannounced visits okay?
☐ ☐ Are there ways for you to get involved?

CHILD CARE AWARE
A PARTNERSHIP FOR QUALITY CHILD CARE

Source: Child Care Aware, a national community service campaign sponsored by the Dayton Hudson Corporation, its foundation and Target and Mervyn's store divisions in cooperation with: Child Care Action Campaign, the National Association of Child Care Resource and Referral Agencies, the National Association for the Education of Young Children, the National Association for Family Day Care.

5 STEPS TO FINDING QUALITY CHILD CARE

1. LOOK
Do the caregivers enjoy talking and playing with children at the children's eye level? A good relationship is essential to quality care.

2. LISTEN
Is the environment calm, dull, happy or loud? The sound can tell you a lot about activities, relationships and discipline.

3. COUNT
How many children are in the caregivers' care? The fewer children, the more attention your child will receive.

4. ASK
What experience or training do the caregivers have? Studies show that trained caregivers are more likely to provide quality care.

5. BE INFORMED
For further information, contact your local Child Care Resource and Referral agency. Or call the Child Care Aware Hotline at (800) 424-2246 or the National Association of Child Care Resource and Referral Agencies at (507) 287-2220.

CHILD CARE AWARE
A PARTNERSHIP FOR QUALITY CHILD CARE

Source: Child Care Aware, a national community service campaign sponsored by the Dayton Hudson Corporation, its foundation and Target and Mervyn's store divisions in cooperation with: Child Care Action Campaign, the National Association of Child Care Resource and Referral Agencies, the National Association for the Education of Young Children, the National Association for Family Day Care.

PART THREE

Emergency Public Relations

Chapter 10 Emergency Public Relations

In preparation for emergencies, the practitioner should be generally aware of the four aspects of the process model, although its use in this form of public relations will be limited.

Research

Some research will be helpful in reaching a state of readiness for an emergency. The three types of research used for other forms of public relations are appropriate.

Client Research

Client research should focus on preparing as many "worst-case" scenarios as possible. What can go wrong? Is the organization's physical plant vulnerable to fire, explosion, or other crises? Is dangerous equipment located on the premises? All division heads in the organization should be asked by the director of public relations to prepare a list of potential trouble spots that could erupt in their respective areas. Whenever possible, corrective action should be taken to neutralize these problems before an emergency can occur. Research may also examine the client's handling of past crises.

Opportunity or Problem Research

Emergency public relations is generically reactive in nature. Some practitioners argue that it is impossible to really get ready for a sweeping disaster. Emergency planning, however, must be pro-active in order to be prepared for a proper reactive response to an emergency.

Audience Research

The practitioner should make a list of internal and external publics to be immediately notified in case of an emergency. Internal publics would include the chief executive officer and other top organizational officials on a "need-to-know" basis at first. As the emergency progresses, the entire work force can be notified through existing internal channels of communication. External audiences in an emergency should include, in priority order, law enforcement officials; the next of kin of the injured or dead, notified before the public release of their names; the mass media; governmental agencies, if appropriate; and trade publications. These internal and external audiences are a suggested starting point. The practitioner needs to be much more specific in creating an emergency contacts list designed to notify all concerned parties in a timely fashion.

Objectives

Because of the exceptional nature of emergencies, objectives for this form of public relations cannot be carefully planned. Nonetheless, some general guidelines are applicable:

1. to provide accurate, timely information to all targeted internal and external audiences
2. to demonstrate concern for the safety of lives
3. to safeguard organizational facilities and assets
4. to maintain a positive image of the organization as a good corporate or community citizen

These guidelines will serve the practitioner well in preparing for the two areas of responsibility involved in programming.

Programming

Programming for emergency public relations should focus on two major actions or areas of responsibility: establishing a public relations emergency headquarters and a media information center.

The Public Relations Headquarters

The public relations emergency headquarters (PR HQ) will probably be the regular public relations office itself. If more space is needed, other offices may also be designated as part of the PR HQ. This office will be responsible for notification of all internal and external emergency audiences, for preparation of material for the media, and for the establishment of a public information center to answer inquiries and to control rumors. The director of public relations should remain in the PR HQ to supervise these three functions.

Notification, the first function of PR HQ, will be the top priority of this office as soon as a crisis occurs. The internal and external audiences were discussed above and will be reviewed in Exhibit 10–a, the "Emergency Public Relations Checklist."

Names of the injured or dead should be withheld from public release until the next of kin are notified or for 24 hours, whichever comes first.

The second function of the PR HQ will be preparation of materials for the media. A company or organizational backgrounder, fact sheet, biographies of major officers, and their captioned photographs should already be prepared and waiting in the files. Along with assembling these background materials, the public relations staff should immediately begin the task of preparing its first basic news release on the crisis. A good rule of thumb is that this should be ready for release *no more than one hour* after the occurrence of the emergency. The release should include all known facts, such as what happened, how, when, where, who, and how many were involved. The question of why may be omitted since the organization may run the risk of involving itself in litigation through an admission of fault. This matter should be handled by the legal department. The release should be cleared as quickly as possible with senior management, the legal department, and possibly the personnel department. Then the news release should be issued immediately to local and national mass media, specialized publications, employees, community leaders, and pertinent government agencies. In addition to the first basic release, PR HQ should issue frequent statements to the media in ongoing crises and should coordinate media interviews with the CEO as warranted.

Through all of these emergency public relations procedures, two principles are recommended: a *one-voice* principle and a *full-disclosure* principle. Above all other considerations, the organization should *speak with one voice*. All employees should be briefed to give information to the media or other concerned parties only from official organizational statements, issued by PR HQ. The full-disclosure principle refers to giving all known information, with the exception of why the emergency occurred if this might involve admission of fault.

The third function of the PR HQ is to establish a *public information center (PIC)*. The responsibilities of the PIC include responding to telephone inquiries with accurate information, providing information to groups to combat rumors, and holding meetings with groups as needed to clarify misinformation. The organization's switchboard should be briefed in advance to refer all calls in an emergency to the PIC, and the one-voice and full-disclosure principles should be observed at all times in its operation.

The Media Information Center

If media people will be gathering at the site of an emergency or disaster, the director of public relations should set up a *media information center (MIC)* at some location near the crisis area but away from the PR HQ. Public relations staff members at the PR HQ must be allowed to perform their required tasks without the interruption of news people wanting information. The MIC should, if possible, designate some staff people to escort media representatives if there is a hazardous disaster area. Reporters should not be permitted to wander freely through a dangerous zone, although they usually want unrestricted access to everything. The MIC should be a suitable room, preferably an auditorium if available, where journalists can remain to receive news releases about the emergency. A high-credibility spokesperson and several alternates should be designated in advance and, once chosen, a single spokesperson should be on duty as long as necessary at the MIC to read news releases. Directors of public relations should never be designated MIC spokespersons. They should remain at the PR HQ to supervise all operations. The spokesperson, however, should be a high-ranking officer in the organization; otherwise, the organization's credibility could suffer. Needless to say, the one-voice and full-disclosure principles should be stringently applied in the operation of the MIC.

Uncontrolled and Controlled Media

In an emergency situation, most of the communication will be uncontrolled in the form of news releases, interviews with organizational officials, and perhaps photographs, although the media representatives will usually take their own photos. Controlled media will be used sparingly, usually as prepared background material or as in-house bulletins posted for employees.

Effective Communication

Two-way communication and audience participation may assume greater than usual importance in a crisis. The targeted audiences, especially the media, will want to be involved and interact with the spokesperson as much as possible. But in general, all the previously discussed principles of communication should be observed.

Programming for emergency public relations, then, concentrates on the two major responsibilities of creating a public relations emergency headquarters and a media information center (see Exhibit 10–a). Beyond that, customary use of uncontrolled and controlled media and principles of effective communication are appropriate.

Exhibit 10–a	**Emergency Public Relations Checklist**

I. Public relations emergency headquarters (PR HQ). The PR director stays in PR department or designated PR HQ and supervises:
   A. Notification and liaison
      1. Internal: Notify the CEO and other top officials on immediate "need-to-know" basis
      2. External: Notify the media; law enforcement officials; governmental agencies; next of kin of injured or dead, before public release of names (24-hour rule suggested)
   B. Preparation of materials for media
      1. Have company backgrounder, fact sheet, and bios of officers already prepared
      2. Prepare basic news release on crisis as soon as possible (one-hour rule suggested)
         a. Include all known facts — what happened, how, when, where, who, and how many involved — not why (fault)
         b. Be certain all information is accurate; never release unconfirmed information

       c. Withhold names of victims until next of kin are notified (or 24 hours, whichever comes first)

       d. Clear release with senior management, legal department, personnel department

       e. Issue release immediately to local and national mass media, specialized publications, employees by bulletin boards and phone, community leaders, insurance company, pertinent governmental agencies.

    3. Issue timely statements to media in ongoing crises

    4. Use *one-voice principle* — information only from official organizational statements

    5. Use *full-disclosure principle* (except admission of fault)

  C. Public information center (PIC)

    1. Establish and announce a public information center in PR HQ

    2. Respond to telephone inquiries with accurate information

    3. Provide accurate information to groups where rumors are circulating

    4. Hold meetings with groups as needed to clarify misinformation

    5. Have switchboard refer all pertinent calls to PIC

    6. Direct company employees to make no unauthorized statements to media people

    7. Use *one-voice principle* — information only from official organizational statements

    8. Use *full-disclosure principle* (except admission of fault)

II. Media information center (MIC)

  A. Designate a place for media people to gather, if necessary

  B. Locate MIC at site near crisis area, but away from PR HQ. (Media people admitted to disaster site must be *escorted* by PR personnel)

  C. Have sole spokesperson on duty day or night at MIC

    1. Use *one-voice principle* — information only from official organizational statements

    2. Use *full-disclosure principle* (except admission of fault)

Evaluation

The evaluation of emergency public relations will be less precise than for other forms of the discipline. Since emergencies are unplanned, the PR objectives must be, at best, general and nonquantitative guidelines. In a quiet period well after the organization's recovery from the emergency, it will be appropriate to review the general guidelines previously mentioned and informally assess the PR department's degree of success in meeting them. Such a review should also include analyzing media coverage; tracking complaints from consumers, community, employees, and other relevant publics; holding internal meetings on the crisis plan and its implementation, and assessing damage to the organization's image. Of course, a formal survey of all participants can also be taken. The results may be used for a variety of purposes, possibly including improvement of emergency public relations procedures.

Summary

Although the ROPE process has limited applicability in emergency public relations, it should not be forgotten or discarded.

Research is useful in preparing for emergencies. Worst-case scenarios should be prepared to determine what problems could possibly develop. Although emergency public relations is inherently reactive, planning for such crises should be proactive. Emergency contacts lists should be made, including all internal and external individuals, groups, and agencies that are to be notified in a crisis.

Objectives for emergency PR tend to be of an impact nature. They usually concentrate on providing information to important audiences as needed; safeguarding lives, facilities, and assets; and protecting the credibility of the organization.

Programming should include establishing a public relations emergency headquarters and, if necessary, a media information center. The functions of the emergency headquarters include notification and liaison and preparation of materials for the media. If reporters will be gathering at the site of a disaster or crisis, a media information center should be established near (but usually not on) the site, and an organizational spokesperson should be designated to be on duty to read statements to the journalists as long as the crisis lasts.

Evaluation for emergency PR is usually less formal than for other types. If objectives have been set before a crisis occurs, each should be appropriately evaluated. If not, the organization should, after the emergency, want to review its notification functions, its general accessibility and service to the media, and, of course, its media coverage during the event.

Readings on Emergency Public Relations

Barton, Laurence. *Crisis in Organizations: Managing and Communicating in the Heat of Chaos.* Cincinnati, OH: South-Western Publishing Co., 1993.

Bernstein, Alan B. *The Emergency Public Relations Manual,* 3rd ed. Highland Park, NJ: PASE, 1990.

Dougherty, Devon. *Crisis Communications: What Every Executive Needs to Know.* New York: Walker, 1992.

Fink, Stephen. *Crisis Management: Planning for the Inevitable.* New York: AMACOM, 1986.

Horne, G. N. "Mediating Conflict in a Crisis." *Public Relations Journal* 39, January 1983, pp. 22ff.

Katz, Anthony R. "Checklist: 10 Steps to Complete Crisis Planning." *Public Relations Journal* 43 (November 1987): 46–47.

Lerbinger, Otto. *Managing Corporate Crises: Strategies for Executives.* Boston: Barrington Press, 1985.

Levy, Robert. "Crisis Public Relations." *Dun's Business Review,* August 1983, pp. 50ff.

Lukaszewski, James E. "Checklist: Anatomy of a Crisis Response." *Public Relations Journal* 43 (November 1987): 45–46.

Newton, C. *Coming to Grips with Crisis.* New York: AMACOM, 1981.

Pines, W. L. "How to Handle PR Crises: Five Dos and Don'ts." *Public Relations Quarterly,* Summer 1985, pp. 16ff.

Pinsdorf, Marion K. *Communicating When Your Company Is Under Siege: Surviving Public Crisis.* Lexington, MA: Lexington Books, 1987.

Reinhardt, Claudia. "How to Handle a Crisis." *Public Relations Journal* 43 (November 1987): 43–44.

Ressler, Judith A. "Crisis Communications." *Public Relations Quarterly,* Fall 1982, pp. 8ff.

Walters, Lynne Masel, and Lee Wilkins, eds. *Bad Tidings: Communication and Catastrophe.* New York: Erlbaum, 1988.

Werner, Lawrence R. "When Crisis Strikes Use a Message Action Plan." *Public Relations Journal* 46 (August 1990): 30–31.

Wilson, James. "Managing Communication in Crises: An Expert's View." *Communication World,* December 1985, pp. 13ff.

Emergency Public Relations Cases

*An apparent hydrocarbon vapor release in polyethylene plant
number 5 at the Phillips Petroleum Company's Houston
Chemical Complex triggered the largest fire and explosion in
the company's history and one of the worst accidents in the
petrochemical industry in recent years. Here Phillips has provided us with two separate public relations work plans, one
for media and community relations and the other for employee relations. The exhibits include only a sampling of the
company's many news releases about this accident. Exhibit
10–1a is the first "bare-bones" news release issued after
the accident took place. Exhibit 10–1b is a later, and more
detailed, news release that was issued the same day. Exhibit 10–1c is a news release issued the following day, and
Exhibit 10–1d is a news release prepared 10 days after the
event. Exhibit 10–1e is a company photograph of the fire itself.*

Case 10–1   ## The Houston Chemical Complex

Phillips Petroleum Company, Bartlesville, OK

Media and Community Relations Work Plan

Need

On October 23, 1989, the Corporate and Media Communications
staff of Phillips Petroleum Company responded to a major fire and
explosion at the company's Houston Chemical Complex (HCC) in
Pasadena, Texas. As a result of the accident, 23 workers were
killed and another 35 were hospitalized. It was the worst accident
in Phillips' history and the worst accident in the petrochemical
industry since the Texas City explosion in the 1940s, which killed
more than 550 people. The blast was felt as far as 25 miles away.
At Rice University, scientists gauged the explosion as the equivalent of 3.5 on a Richter scale. Windows were shattered as far as
three miles away, and several hundred vehicles were damaged.
The explosion destroyed Phillips' polyethylene facilities, the largest of their kind in the world. Within an hour of the explosion,
some 150 representatives of the media, representing 40 news organizations, were at the site.

Courtesy Phillips Petroleum Company

There was an immediate need to respond to the news media and reassure the local community and employees through them. In addition, Phillips' crisis response needed to:

- Preserve and restore Phillips' reputation as a safe, concerned employer
- Reassure the local community of Phillips' commitment to the area
- Provide full details of the accident to the media and chemical trade press
- Maintain media goodwill by being as responsive as possible to special requests and by providing photo opportunities as soon as possible
- Confirm the company's basic health to the financial media

Communications were aimed at the following audiences:

- The media: Covering the HCC accident were more than 40 news organizations, representing local, state, national, and international media, and the chemical trade press
- Residents of the Pasadena area, where most HCC employees reside: Pasadena is a community of some 116,000 residents; it is also an important suburb of Houston, a city of some 3.6 million people

Objectives

In keeping with Phillips' policy of open, honest, and timely communications, the goals and objectives of the crisis communications effort were the following:

- Be open and responsive to the media
- Demonstrate top management's concern for employees and the community
- Reassure the local community
- Reassure the financial community

These goals were adopted because of the seriousness of the accident to employees and company property, the effect of the accident on the community, and the intense media interest the accident generated.

Corporate and Media Communications has a standing crisis communications plan for all field locations. Specific details for implementing the plan vary by event and are always governed by local conditions. In an emergency, Corporate and Media Communications works with local management and with a pre-designated local official who has received training in media response. (A main objective of Corporate and Media Communications is to have trained spokesmen at all field locations.) Because of the seriousness of this event, Corporate and Media Communications recommended that top management be part of the communications effort and that corporate communications specialists go to the site to assist local management. In addition, the plan called for the following:

Media Relations

- An announcement would be made to the press as soon as possible.
- Press briefings would be held routinely and with regard to media deadlines.
- Media rooms would be established at HCC and the Bartlesville, Oklahoma, headquarters complex.
- The press would be taken to the site of the accident as soon as possible in order to help them understand — and relay to the public — the difficulty of the search and rescue effort under way.

Community Relations

- The company would use the media, paid advertising, and personal letters to show appreciation for the aid and assistance received in responding to the crisis.

Funding for the HCC emergency response was paid for from a special account established for insurance purposes. Expenditures were approved as the need arose, following expedited approval processes. The time schedule was dictated by events and by the company's commitment to respond quickly and accurately.

Execution

The accident occurred at 1:05 P.M. on October 23. Within 15 minutes of the accident, Corporate and Media Communications professionals in Bartlesville met with the president and chief operating officer of the company, as well as with the executive vice president in charge of Petroleum Products and Chemicals.

The following actions were taken:

Media Relations

- The local spokesman responded immediately to press inquiries and worked with emergency crews to assess damage and determine any casualties.

- Glenn Cox, Phillips president and chief operating officer, accompanied by two Corporate and Media Communications professionals, arrived at the site at about 4 P.M. By this time, the press was out in full force. Some 150 media representatives and six satellite trucks were across the road from the plant, where a temporary command center had been established. Cox met with the press at 5 P.M. and 9:30 P.M., in time for the media to meet their deadlines.

- By the second day, media interest was focusing more on personnel and technical questions. As a result, the role of spokesman was shifted to the vice president of plastics resins, the highest executive at HCC. Meanwhile, upon returning to Oklahoma, Cox held another press conference with the media there.

- For the next two weeks, Corporate and Media Communications professionals acted as spokesmen.
  - There were two key spokesmen and eight professional communicators assigned to the HCC emergency. They answered close to 1,000 press inquiries, wrote a dozen background papers and prepared 29 news releases in the two-week period between October 23 and November 13.
  - In addition, a five-man video/photography crew was sent to the site the day of the accident and remained there through November 13; two video professionals remained at the site through mid-January.
  - Media rooms were established at HCC and Bartlesville, with five professionals manning each. Fourteen telephone lines were dedicated at HCC for media calls, and 10 lines at the Bartlesville media facility. For the first two days of the crisis, the media rooms were staffed around the clock. Through November 13, they were staffed from 6 A.M. to 11 P.M.
  - Press briefings were held three times a day during the initial phase of the crisis, then on an as-needed basis as the situation became more stable.
  - On October 25, the media were taken to the accident site and allowed to photograph it.
  - On October 27, a hot line was established at HCC to keep employees and the media updated on the status of the facility, memorial services, and so forth.

— A Bartlesville-based Corporate and Media Communications professional was assigned to HCC through mid-January to assist with media, employee, and community relations.

Community Relations

- Interviews were arranged with Phillips' environmental experts to allay the public's concern about the environmental impact of the explosion and fire.
- Phillips executives took every opportunity in interviews to praise those who offered aid and assistance.
- Phillips purchased two full-page ads in Houston-area newspapers to thank appropriate parties for their help.
- Names were taken of all who lent assistance, and personal letters were mailed to each. This represented some 200 individuals and organizations.
- Corporate and Media Communications assisted Pasadena officials with a memorial service; it was attended by top management and by local plant management.

A major problem to overcome was the difficulty of communicating with HCC in the early hours of the accident. The explosion severely damaged HCC's administration building, the predetermined site for an emergency command center and media room. As a result, it wasn't until about 2:30 P.M. that a temporary command center could be established and phone lines dedicated to answering media calls. To alleviate the problem, the company had AT&T transfer HCC's incoming calls to the Bartlesville command center. This assured that all media inquiries were answered and enabled family and friends to inquire about HCC employees. By 6 P.M., HCC was in a position to begin receiving calls.

Results

Because of the nature of the crisis, formal evaluation was not programmed into the original plan. However, there are strong reasons to believe that Phillips' media relations efforts were successful.

- Coverage in both the print and broadcast media was fair and accurate; in addition, Phillips received far less criticism from this accident than other companies have received for less severe events.

- The local community knows that Phillips' commitment to HCC is permanent.

- The fact that Phillips' stock did not decline precipitously following a major loss of capacity shows that the financial community was reassured of the company's basic health.

- Laudatory articles appeared in the *Houston Chronicle, Houston Business Journal,* and *Adweek* about the Phillips' media team. In addition, the local IABC chapter praised Phillips' communications efforts. Several invitations have been received from communications groups asking Phillips professionals to share their experiences in dealing with the HCC emergency.

- The manager of Corporate and Media Communications has been asked to chair a companywide task force dealing with all aspects of emergency response.

Although Corporate and Media Communications believes its crisis response was effective, the staff convened in late November to review its performance and suggest ways to improve its response should another emergency situation occur. Among their recommendations:

- Devise a better method of sharing information among the staff

- Create a more functional media room for Bartlesville staff

- Ensure that established methods of recording media inquiries are followed in crisis situations

Employee Relations: Work Plan

Need

On October 23, 1989, the Corporate and Media Communications staff of Phillips Petroleum Company responded to a major fire and explosion at the company's Houston Chemical Complex (HCC) in Pasadena, Texas. As a result of the accident, 23 workers were killed and another 35 were hospitalized. It was the worst accident in Phillips' history.

There was an immediate need to communicate the following:

- Phillips' concern for employees and their families, including the employees and families of subcontractors working at the site

- Phillips' future plans at HCC

Because Phillips is a highly integrated company, the loss of capacity at HCC could impact employment across the company. As a result, communications were aimed at two audiences:

- Employees of HCC and their families: Approximately 900 people are employed at HCC
- All other Phillips employees: Phillips employs 21,000 people worldwide

Objectives

In keeping with Phillips' policy of open, honest, and timely communications, the goals and objectives of the crisis communications effort were the following:

- Demonstrate top management's concern for employees and their families, including the employees and families of subcontractors working at the site
- Keep employees informed of events on a timely and ongoing basis

These goals were adopted because of the seriousness of the accident to employees and company property.

Corporate and Media Communications has a standing crisis communications plan for all field locations. Specific details for implementing the plan vary by event and are always governed by local conditions. In an emergency, Corporate and Media Communications works with local management and with the local Human Resources professional to communicate with affected employees. Because of the seriousness of this event, Corporate and Media Communications recommended that top management be part of the communications effort and that corporate communications specialists go to the site to assist local management. In addition, the plan called for the following:

HCC Employees

- Glenn Cox, Phillips' president and chief operating officer, would go to Houston immediately to meet with affected employees and their families and to answer questions from the media. He would be accompanied by the executive vice president of Petroleum Products and Chemicals.

- A group of Corporate and Media Communications professionals would accompany Cox to Houston to assist with local employee, media, and community relations. Five other professionals would remain in Bartlesville to provide communications for the rest of the company.

- Employee meetings, long a mainstay of plant communications, were impossible. Therefore, personal letters and the Houston-area media would be used to provide key information to affected employees until direct communications could be established.

- A hot line would be established at HCC as soon as possible to keep employees (and the media) informed of important events.

- Employees would be notified as quickly as possible about employment and wages, as well as about Phillips' plans for restoring its polyethylene facilities.

Other Employees

- The accident would be announced to all employees as soon as possible.

- Employees would be kept informed daily of events at HCC.

- Employees would be notified as soon as possible of the business impact of the explosion on Phillips.

- A memorial would be conducted for those killed.

Funding for the HCC emergency response was paid for from a special account established for insurance purposes. Expenditures were approved as the need arose, following expedited approval processes. The time schedule was dictated by events and by the company's commitment to respond quickly and accurately.

Execution

The accident occurred at 1:05 P.M. on October 23. Within 15 minutes of the accident, Corporate and Media Communications professionals in Bartlesville met with the president and chief operating officer of the company, as well as with the executive vice president in charge of Petroleum Products and Chemicals. Corporate and Media Communications recommended, and the following actions were taken:

- The president and executive vice president, along with Corporate and Media communications professionals, left immediately for Houston. That evening the president met with employees and their families in the command center and held two news conferences.

- The accident was announced to all employees (approximately 5,000) at the Bartlesville, Oklahoma, headquarters within one and a half hours after notification. Simultaneously, the announcement was wired to all Phillips' in-plant communicators (approximately 60) and sent by electronic mail to another 8,000 employees worldwide.

- The severity of the damage to HCC meant that most employees could not enter the premises for more than a week. As a result, it was virtually impossible to have direct communications with them. To compensate, the company sent personal letters to their homes and relied on the Houston media to provide critical information. This included telephone numbers to call to obtain information about counseling services, the status of the plant, wage and employment news and news of the injured and missing.

- A hot line was established on October 27. It contained information on the status of HCC, as well as information about counseling services, memorial services, and those hospitalized.

- Bulletins (a total of nine) were wired daily to field editors for posting and also sent by electronic mail to another 8,000 employees worldwide. In Bartlesville, PA announcements were made daily for the first week to keep employees updated.

- A five person video/photography crew was sent to the scene immediately. On October 26, a special HCC show aired throughout Phillips' worldwide operations. Two follow-up news shows, also distributed worldwide, appeared on November 16 and December 6.

- *Philnews*, Phillips' corporate magazine, covered the accident in the November issue.

- On October 25, the company reassured employees of the company's financial health with a bulletin stating that its insurance coverage was sufficient to replace damaged facilities and cover earnings losses from the HCC accident.

- On October 26, Phillips announced that wages and benefits would continue for all HCC employees through the end of the year. (As of January 17, there had been no layoffs at HCC.)

- Corporate and Media Communications worked with Pasadena officials on a memorial service for those killed in the explosion. Top management and their spouses attended the event. Approximately 2,500 were present for the service, most of them HCC employees and their families.

- Corporate and Media Communications coordinated the establishment of a memorial fund for the families of those killed in the accident.

- Corporate and Media Communications recommended and coordinated a companywide tribute to the victims of the accident. At 1:05 P.M., November 6, two weeks after the accident, a moment of silence was held at Phillips' facilities worldwide in memory of the victims.

- On November 8, the company announced that rebuilding would begin soon at HCC to replace the polyethylene facilities.

- On December 11, Corporate and Media Communications made a presentation to the board of directors on the HCC emergency response; in addition, a video prepared by the staff was shown to the Management Committee and board.

A major problem to overcome was the damage to HCC's administration building, the predetermined site for an emergency command center. As a result, it wasn't until about 2:30 P.M. that a temporary command center could be established and phone lines linked between Corporate and Media Communications professionals at HCC and Bartlesville. To alleviate the problem, the company had AT&T transfer incoming calls to HCC to the Bartlesville command center. This assured that all inquiries were answered and enabled family and friends to inquire about HCC employees. By 6 P.M., HCC was in a position to begin receiving calls.

Results

Because of the nature of the crisis, formal evaluation was not programmed into the original employee communication crisis plan. There were informal indications that communications were well received. Among them:

- Media interviews with HCC employees indicated continued company support.

- The board was complimentary of Corporate and Media Communications during the emergency.

- More than a dozen employees contacted the vice president of Corporate Affairs to express their appreciation for sending bulletins through electronic mail. (The HCC emergency was the first occasion that electronic mail was used to disseminate employee news.)
- Related to the above, several employees have suggested that Corporate and Media Communications transmit all future employee bulletins by electronic mail, as well as by other methods.
- HCC requested that a Corporate and Media Communications professional remain at the facility through mid-January to assist with employee communications.

Although Corporate and Media Communications believed its crisis response was effective, the staff convened in late November to review its performance and suggest ways to improve its response should another emergency situation occur. Among the recommendations, devise a better method of sharing information among the staff and make better use of electronic mail in disseminating employee information.

Exhibit 10–1a   **First News Release Issued After the Accident**

news release

PHILLIPS PETROLEUM COMPANY

BARTLESVILLE, OKLAHOMA 74004
CORPORATE AFFAIRS

Explosion and Fire at
Houston Chemical Complex

October 23, 1989

FOR IMMEDIATE RELEASE:

BARTLESVILLE, Okla. -- An explosion and fire have occurred at the Phillips 66 Company Houston Chemical Complex. The accident occurred at about 1 p.m. CDT. The plant produces polyethylene, polypropylene and butadiene-styrene polymers. There are reports of injuries, but the extent is not known at this time. Communications into the plant are poor.

A team headed by Glenn Cox, Phillips president and chief operating officer, have left for the scene and are expected to arrive at the plant late this afternoon.

# # #

CONTACT: 918/661-4982
             661-5204
             661-4987
             661-6422

Courtesy Phillips Petroleum Company

Exhibit 10–1b   Later News Release

news release

PHILLIPS PETROLEUM COMPANY
BARTLESVILLE, OKLAHOMA 74004
CORPORATE AFFAIRS

One Fatality Confirmed
At Phillips Houston Facility;
109 Treated for Injuries

October 23, 1989
10:15 p.m. CDT

FOR IMMEDIATE RELEASE:

BARTLESVILLE, Okla. -- One fatality has been confirmed as a result of a fire and explosion at Phillips Petroleum Company's Houston Chemical Complex.

The incident occurred at 1:05 p.m. CDT, when there was an apparent hydrocarbon vapor release in polyethylene plant No. 5 at the complex.

Glenn A. Cox, Phillips president and chief operating officer, told reporters late Monday night that 20 Phillips people and three contract employees were still unaccounted for. "We have begun to send Phillips representatives to visit with the families of employees who are unaccounted for," Cox said.

According to Dr. Paul Pepe, director of emergency medical services for the city of Houston, 109 people have been sent to area hospitals from the Houston Chemical Complex. Of that number, 33 were admitted to the hospital and five or six were listed in serious to critical condition.

-more-

Courtesy Phillips Petroleum Company

One Fatality Confirmed
At Phillips Houston Facility;
109 Treated for Injuries

Add One

At this time, Phillips officials are not able to get back in the facility to thoroughly check the area where the explosion took place. All operations have been shut down and efforts continue to put out the fire.

Said Cox, "We deeply appreciate the efforts of local authorities and industries along the Houston Ship Channel in helping us bring the fire under control."

# # #

CONTACT: (918) 661-5204
                661-4987
                661-4982
                661-6422

Exhibit 10–1c   News Release, Day Two

news release

PHILLIPS PETROLEUM COMPANY
BARTLESVILLE, OKLAHOMA 74004
CORPORATE AFFAIRS

Search, Rescue Teams
Continue Efforts to Locate
Workers at Houston Complex

October 24, 1989   5:00 p.m.

FOR IMMEDIATE RELEASE:

BARTLESVILLE, Okla. -- Search teams continue to comb the damaged Houston Chemical Complex in an effort to locate 22 workers who are unaccounted for after Monday's fire and explosion at the complex. Their efforts have been slowed by the massive extent of damage that occurred in the polyethylene area of the plant.

So far, two fatalities have been confirmed.

Glenn A. Cox, president and chief operating officer of Phillips Petroleum Company, told reporters in Houston today, "If an employee was in the heavily damaged portion of the plant when the accident took place, then that person would probably not have survived."

Cox added that counseling for employees and their families is being offered by Phillips, and company representatives have attempted to visit all hospitalized employees, when the injured person's condition permits.

Thirty-three persons remain hospitalized.

The company will continue to pay employees while damage is being assessed. In addition, the company will explore possible employment opportunities for some employees at other Phillips facilities. Because of the extent of the damage at the polyethylene facilities, it is unlikely that full employment will continue at the facility.

CONTACT: 918/661-6172; 4987; 4982; 6422; 5204

Courtesy Phillips Petroleum Company

Exhibit 10–1d   News Release 10 Days After the Accident

news release

PHILLIPS PETROLEUM COMPANY
BARTLESVILLE, OKLAHOMA 74004
CORPORATE AFFAIRS

Plastics Production To Resume
At Houston Chemical Complex

November 3, 1989

FOR IMMEDIATE RELEASE:

BARTLESVILLE, Oklahoma -- Phillips 66 Company today announced plans to resume production of plastic resins from operations not seriously damaged in the October 23 explosion and fire at the Houston Chemical Complex in Pasadena, Texas.

Startup production procedures have begun at the complex's K-resin plant and similar measures at the polypropylene plant are scheduled to begin the middle of next week.

Phillips also has announced its intention to continue polyethylene resin production at the Pasadena complex and will provide a more specific rebuilding schedule in a few days.

Nineteen fatalities have been confirmed as a result of the accident, including a hospitalized contract worker who died earlier this week. Search teams are continuing to comb accessible areas for four Phillips employees who remain missing. In addition, a rappelling search team has covered the upper levels of the 200-foot high plant 5 reactors.

As announced earlier, Harris County Fire Marshal investigators and Phillips structural experts have concluded that demolition of some structures is necessary in order to permit safe completion of the search for missing employees. Unstable damaged steel and concrete structures made the decision necessary. Demolition in some areas is expected to begin Monday.

-more-

Courtesy Phillips Petroleum Company

Plastics Production To Resume
At Houston Chemical Complex

Add One

Four Phillips employees and one contract worker remain
hospitalized primarily from burns and all are listed in good to
guarded condition. Counseling services for all employees of the
complex and their families is continuing at a company-sponsored
counseling centers located at Humana Hospital Southmore and at the
Houston Chemical Complex.

Phillips has been working with area residents and businesses
since the day of the explosion to settle claims stemming from the
accident. Some 1707 claims have been filed. As of Friday
morning, the company had paid claimants $445,000, representing
full or partial payment of 862 claims.

# # #

CONTACT: 918/661-4982; -5204; -4987; -6422; -6172

Exhibit 10–1e   **Photograph of the Fire at HCC**

Firemen battle the blaze at Phillips Petroleum Company's Houston Chemical Complex.

Courtesy Phillips Petroleum Company

Caught off guard without an adequate crisis plan during Florida's freak Christmas freeze of 1989, Florida Power & Light (FPL) entered 1992 with a revised crisis program that would soon be tested by the most devastating natural disaster in the nation's history, Hurricane Andrew. The company's extensive training programs for personnel at all levels paid handsome dividends as FPL competently managed its comprehensive recovery program in the wake of the hurricane. Exhibit 10–2a is a print advertisement used during the aftermath of the storm. Exhibit 10–2b is an FPL news media summary.

Case 10–2 **Florida Power & Light: Out of Andrew's Shadow**

Florida Power & Light Company, Miami, FL

The Background

On December 25, 1989, the state of Florida experienced a freak winter freeze that left millions of homes and businesses without electricity. Christmas turkey dinners went uncooked. Homes were dark — and cold. Holiday lighting didn't twinkle. Utility customers' tempers flared and the news media — citing lack of planning and communication by the utilities — took the state's electric companies to task. The Christmas blackouts were to remain a sore point and a communications challenge for months and years to follow. New Year 1990 brought legislative hearings and finger wagging by state agencies. Florida Power & Light Company's consumer research showed that customer confidence in the company, which serves 3.2 million customers in 35 Florida counties, plunged 12 percent and remained depressed for a year. With the support of FPL's senior management, the Corporate Communications department revamped its crisis communication plans, devoting special attention to major emergencies: capacity, nuclear, fuel shortage, and hurricane.

On August 24, 1992, Hurricane Andrew tested FPL's new crisis communication plans at a level no one anticipated. Our plan and its implementation received worldwide scrutiny.

Courtesy Florida Power & Light Company

Objectives

Customer satisfaction, system electrical reliability, and safety of the general public and our employees rank high among FPL's corporate goals. Specific departmental goals under our crisis plan are to ensure that timely, consistent, factual information is provided to our customers, our employees, and the financial community. Through such a communications effort, we hope to not only help protect the health and safety of our employees and the general public, but foster a high level of confidence in the company's ability to handle and recover from a crisis, avoiding a repeat of the Christmas blackout scenario that severely damaged FPL's image among its various constituents. We seek to take the initiative with the news media and to make senior FPL management available and accessible to ensure that our messages will be listened to and acted upon by the public. Success of our efforts will be measured by customer attitudes during and after a recovery effort, by media coverage, and by the tone with which our efforts are treated in the press and broadcast media, by the reaction of the financial community in the days and months following recovery from the crisis, and by the demonstrable performance and safety-related efforts of our employees.

Execution

Florida Power & Light entered 1992 with a new, revamped crisis communication plan that, although having received nationwide recognition (including a 1991 IABC Gold Quill Award of Merit and a PRSA Silver Anvil) as a model crisis plan, was still untested under actual storm conditions. In early 1992, in the aftermath of a company-wide reorganization months earlier that eliminated 1,900 jobs and nearly a third of the Corporate Communications staff, we conducted a "dry run" of the hurricane crisis plan and found that work was still needed. We had a corporate staff primarily "green" to the sensitivities of crisis response and a field organization—plus 3.2 million customers—that had not experienced a full-scale hurricane in decades. We needed to educate and media-train new executives on the breadth and immediacy of information needs and to prepare key field personnel to know how and when to respond, and we needed to give both groups the content to do the job well.

The five-person media staff has overall responsibility for the crisis communications plan. To remedy the plan's shortcomings as a result of the reorganization, we found employees who had experienced hurricanes and asked their help to develop written responses to the forty-five "most asked" questions. These became the cornerstone of our communications. Field media liaisons — company managers who help the media staff in emergencies — were given special training. Key executives who would lead the storm recovery effort for the first time received news conference training. Letters were sent to line crews and field personnel encouraging them to talk to customers and the media if a disaster occurred, with guidelines provided. A full package of materials was issued to customer phone representatives so the "single voice" of the company could be maintained. Finally, every corporate communications employee received role training with specific instructions on what he or she would be required to do and an overview of what others would be doing. In an informal survey conducted with the news media, we asked how and when they would most like to receive information during a crisis, and we incorporated that into our new plan. We were wrapping up our efforts as "hurricane season" officially got under way June 1.

On Saturday, August 22, indications were that Hurricane Andrew would hit Florida. The Media Relations section convened at our offices early Sunday and began issuing detailed information to the media on electrical safety and FPL's recovery plan. Material was also provided to media liaisons and phone centers around the state, since we had no idea where the hurricane would strike. Prepositioned broadcast media ads were activated. We staffed the headquarters storm center and prepared to ride out the storm.

Hurricane Andrew — the most devastating natural disaster in the nation's history — struck south Florida in the predawn hours of Monday, August 24, with sustained winds clocked at 145 miles per hour (mph) and gusts recorded in the 175–200 mph range. The storm's center came ashore south of downtown Miami, cut a path across the Everglades, and exited into the Gulf of Mexico. In its aftermath, 1.4 million homes and businesses lost electricity. Much of FPL's transmission system lay toppled. Devastation was awesome. The company's Turkey Point Nuclear Plant was in the eye of the storm; 25,000 homes were destroyed and 80,000 severely damaged; 600 FPL employees — including some of the Corporate Communications staff — became part of the "new homeless"; public use of portable generators threatened the safety of FPL restoration crews; crews were impeded in their efforts by impassable, traffic-clogged roads; scavengers stole materials before FPL crews could turn on the lights; and, to add further insult, afternoon rainstorms dumped more water into already damaged buildings and handicapped FPL crews in their restoration efforts. All of this combined to challenge FPL's communications efforts.

Media Relations

During the 18 days immediately following the storm, the Media Relations staff scripted and conducted news conferences daily. The daily briefings enabled FPL to set the scope, tone, and direction of information being provided and quell rumors quickly. Company executives — the CEO, president, and vice presidents for customer service and distribution — were available and participated in every news briefing and were available around the clock for special interviews, to answer operational questions, and to provide fast approval of media releases and statements. We distributed videos of the morning briefings to media outside the storm area unable to attend the live briefings. Over the 34-day restoration period, we handled 1,600 media calls (in English and Spanish), issued 66 written media releases and backgrounders, coordinated special morning and evening photo opportunities and arranged for media tours and crew interviews, including helicopter fly-overs. We provided round-the-clock communications coverage for the first week and 18-hour-a-day coverage for the duration of the restoration period. Hispanic media also received direct attention from Spanish-speaking media liaisons.

Internal Communications

The Internal Communications section logged long hours communicating with FPL's 14,500 employees, including simulcasts of the morning press briefings over FPL's inhouse television network, followed by taped replays every hour to FPL locations around the state. This gave birth to a daily live news program that had been planned for development in 1993 but was created literally overnight to meet employee needs. Written communications were prepared to explain numerous programs developed to assist employees, particularly those whose homes had been damaged and yet were called upon to work grueling hours restoring service to customers. Working with the Human Resources department, Internal Communications developed and distributed lists of contractors and other special services that would enable employees to get new housing or repair work done more easily. The staff prepared materials offering employees tips on how to cope with the crisis and supported special family training classes on adjusting after the crisis. They issued multiple daily status reports via fax to field personnel and also provided copies to federal, state, and local officials and the military present in south Florida throughout the recovery. After restoration, a 45-minute documentary was produced for each of FPL's 14,500 employees and CEO's of utilities that helped us, along with a letter of "thank you for a job well done" from the chairman.

Financial Communications

The department's Investor Relations group responded to fifty analyst calls in the first three days after the storm and by the fourth day had organized a teleconference with our CEO and 75 analysts and portfolio managers. Storm restoration updates were faxed periodically to utility analysts, and a special hurricane package was prepared specifically for them. Shareholder relations, through the aid of a toll-free 800 line, responded to approximately 750 phone calls and letters from shareholders, using much of the information developed for the media to ensure a consistent message. A storm update letter was included with dividend checks to approximately 80,000 shareholders in early September. Investor Relations and Executive Communications (speechwriters) staff also spelled the Media Relations staff during those early days when coverage was being provided 24 hours a day.

Advertising

Advertising department staff members worked closely with the media staff to ensure the consistency of our public messages. Under their direction, FPL's external advertising agency not only initiated prepositioned media advertising at appropriate times, but developed new communications to disseminate important safety and service restoration advertising during the days and weeks immediately following the storm. Ads were also created to communicate information to, and provide recognition for, FPL employees.

Results

By September 27 — 34 days after Hurricane Andrew struck — ALL customers whose homes and businesses were capable of accepting electricity had service restored — a feat that has earned the highest praise from industry peers and customers who, seeing a landscape resembling a war zone, expected to be without electricity for months. It was a herculean effort on the part of our personnel and those from other utilities who helped.

Communications played a major part in that success. Keeping our key audiences abreast of all aspects of the recovery effort through continuous updates helped us establish the credibility and understanding our customers needed to be patient. It helped our employees stay focused and committed. Repeated safety messages resulted in NO customer electrical injuries or deaths and less than a half-dozen injuries among the more than 4,000 field crew members working around the clock in Florida's hot, humid climate. Our stock price remained stable. The Nuclear Regulatory Commission, in part because of special communications initiated by FPL, authorized the restart of the nuclear reactors that had received a direct hit from the hurricane (something never before experienced by an operating nuclear plant). More importantly to those of us in Corporate Communications, posthurricane surveys of customers show that satisfaction with the company has actually increased by 20 percent. Surprisingly, survey data showed that high levels of satisfaction came from customers in areas most severely damaged and without electricity longest. Media coverage was balanced, supportive, and occasionally laudatory. We continue to receive letters of praise from customers, even children who remember our communications messages following the storm.

The company is continuing the extra effort to bring the community and our employees out of the shadow of this devastating storm. We have launched tree give-away programs to help "re-green" Dade County; we have sought and received Public Service Commission permission to extend special energy conservation services, programs, and incentives to those customers faced with rebuilding their homes and businesses; we have initiated special rebuild news stories and printed rebuild guidelines; and we continue to provide crisis counseling and other services to storm-stressed employees.

Budget

Corporate Communications maintains a $15,000 budget for annual media training for crisis communications. Additional storm communications costs were covered under FPL's Public Service Commission–mandated $70 million storm restoration fund. No budgetary limitations were set.

Evaluation

Hurricane Andrew was the first major test of FPL's revamped crisis communication plan. The corporate reorganization proved very beneficial during hurricane recovery efforts as the reduced layers of management and increased employee empowerment allowed for quicker response and approvals on critical communications and storm recovery issues.

However, like all plans, ours must be continually reviewed based on experience. Under lessons learned, while we have backup emergency electrical supplies, we were fortunate to have been able to retain critical telephone and fax services, as well as our own fiberoptic television lines, throughout the storm. We will be looking for backup alternatives to these systems. The storm made it extremely difficult for some staffers to get to the office quickly to relieve those who rode out the storm. We will be reevaluating staff deployment. And because of our multilingual community, we will be adding additional Hispanic and Creole translation capabilities.

Corporate Communications is proud of its role in helping to bring our community out of the shadow of Hurricane Andrew. And we're confident that as a result of our communications efforts preceding, during, and after Hurricane Andrew, the stigma of the Christmas blackout of 1989 is behind us.

Exhibit 10–2a   **Florida Power & Light Print Advertisement**

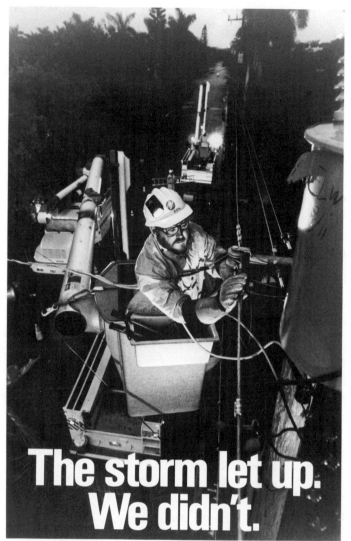

The storm let up.
We didn't.

This has been one of the worst storms to hit Florida in years.

But even before it left the area, FPL crews had begun working to fix the damage it caused.

And now that the storm has passed, every available FPL employee continues to work long hours to restore power quickly.

But until we can restore it, we ask for your patience. And ask that you do a few things that can help...and keep you safe, too.

Please stay away from downed or low-hanging wires, or nearby standing water. Water touching a live wire is as dangerous as the wire itself.

If you do see a downed line, call FPL immediately. Otherwise, try to keep the phone lines free for emergency calls.

Please don't trim trees until FPL crews are finished working in the area.

And don't block access to poles or transformers with debris. The faster we can get to a problem, the faster we can fix it.

If you watch or listen to the news for regular updates, we'll let you know how repairs are going.

We can't guarantee that things will be fixed overnight.

But we can guarantee that we won't rest until they are.

FPL
an FPL Group company

Courtesy Florida Power & Light Company

Exhibit 10–2b   Florida Power & Light News Media Summary

FPL NEWS MEDIA SUMMARY

August 30, 1992

HURRICANE ANDREW RESTORATION OVERVIEW

Comments from FPL President Steve Frank:

- This is day 6 of the company's hurricane plan implementation, and this morning we have fewer than 300,000 customers out of service in Dade and Broward counties.

- The number of customers without service in Broward is approximately 12,000. FPL hopes to remain on schedule for completing Broward tonight. In Dade County, the count is approximately 275,000.

- Our damage survey work in Dade is about 85 percent complete. The assessments will help us efficiently deploy crew members still moving into the county. As we previously announced, more than 3,300 FPL employees and other workers will be on the job in Dade by Monday afternoon. We also are evaluating the need for even more people available to us from other sources.

- Our focus on hurricane restoration is being hindered by thunderstorms that caused quite a few power outages yesterday. The storms flooded some areas and lightning created additional safety problems for customers and our field crews. Some outages affected customers who had just been restored after losing service to the hurricane. The forecast today calls for afternoon thunderstorms.

- The thunderstorms raise an important issue that we would like our customers to be aware of -- and that is the still-fragile nature of our repaired system. Lightning struck a major transmission line Saturday, and because of the hurricane we were not able to recover as quickly as would have been possible in normal circumstances. In many hurricane-affected areas we do not have the backup and redundant transmission systems that would normally be available to us. Redundant systems allow us to recover from thunderstorm outages relatively quickly, but it will be some time before FPL can rebuild backup transmission lines and other facilities.

- Customers can help in this matter by moderating their use of electricity to the extent possible. For example, when businesses open on Monday and more people return to workplaces, it would be helpful if everyone keeps their air-conditioning thermostats on comfortable -- but NOT extra-cool -- settings. Let me emphasize that this is a matter of coping with a fragile network, not a matter of having insufficient generating capability.

- MORE -

Courtesy Florida Power & Light Company

Before Bob Marshall and Bill Hamilton provide some additional information, we offer two important reminders:

-- FPL is bringing in 20-25 tractor trailer-loads of materials every day, and new crews are headed south into Dade today and Monday -- but it is taking too long because of traffic. Dade residents can help FPL's restoration efforts by staying off the roads whenever possible.

-- They can also help by staying off the telephone unless absolutely necessary. Keeping the road and telephone networks clear will help not only FPL, but also many of the government and private agencies participating in the restoration effort.

FPL NEWS MEDIA SUMMARY

AUGUST 30,1992; 10 A.M.

HURRICANE ANDREW RESTORATION REPORT

Comments by Bob Marshall, vice president - power distribution

BROWARD--Approximately 12,000 customers remain out of service (2 percent)

ATLANTIC BOULEVARD NORTH--Essentially 100 percent of service restored.

595 NORTH TO ATLANTIC--99 percent restored from I-95 west; 98 percent restored from I-95 east to the beach.

COUNTY LINE NORTH TO 595-- 99 percent restored from Florida Turnpike west; 95 percent from the turnpike east.

DADE--Approximately 275,000 customers remain out of service (33 percent)

MBO--Miami Beach area approximately 85 percent restored.

NWO--North Dade area approximately 84 percent restored.

SWO--Coral Gables area approximately 42 percent restored.

WEO--West Dade/Hialeah areas approximately 78 percent restored

CEO--Miami Central/Liberty city areas approximately 82 percent restored.

PNO--Southern Dade County approximately 36 percent restored.

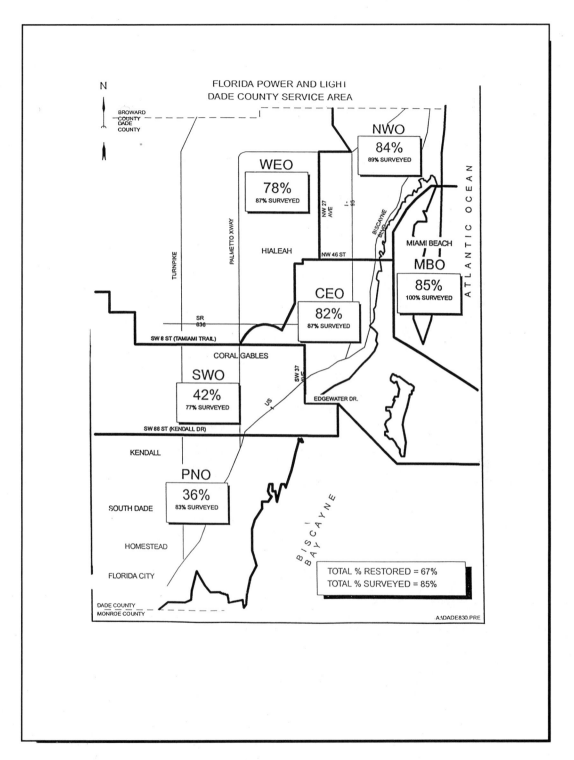

FLORIDA POWER AND LIGHT
DADE COUNTY SERVICE AREA

TOTAL % RESTORED = 67%
TOTAL % SURVEYED = 85%

A:\DADE830.PRE

439

FPL NEWS MEDIA SUMMARY
AUGUST 30, 1992

HURRICANE ANDREW RESTORATION OVERVIEW

Comments from Bill Hamilton, vice president of customer service:

· CUSTOMER SAFETY AND THE SAFETY OF OUR EMPLOYEES
who are working to restore service continues to be our utmost concern,
especially in the highly damaged areas we are now working in Dade
County

· If you're using PORTABLE GENERATORS, again we recommend
that you locate the generator in a well-ventilated area, preferably
outside your home. Plug appliances directly into the generator. Do not
exceed the recommended wattage noted on the generator. Use
extension cords if necessary. Avoid connecting the generator to the
home's main wiring at the circuit breaker. Improper use of generators
can cause electricity to flow backwards into the power lines,
endangering our workers or possibly even neighbors served by the same
power line.

· If you're without electricity and you haven't already done so, turn off all
of your CIRCUIT BREAKERS in the circuit breaker box, except for
one or two that would operate a light. If you do not know how to do
this, then turn off appliances, leaving only a lamp or light switch on.

· IF YOU HAVE ANY CONCERNS THAT THE ELECTRICAL
SYSTEM IN YOUR HOUSE MAY BE IN AN UNSAFE
CONDITION, CALL A LICENSED ELECTRICIAN. REMEMBER
STANDING WATER ANYWHERE NEAR ELECTRICAL
OUTLETS OR ENTERING THROUGH DAMAGED WALLS OR
ROOFS MAY CREATE AN UNSAFE CONDITION.

· Customers should know that DADE COUNTY BUILDING &
ZONING department personnel are attempting to survey the same hard
hit areas where we are working. If they determine a home is damaged
to the extent if may be unsafe -- structurally or for any other reason --
they will post a notice to this affect. FPL will not be permitted to
connect electric service to these homes for the safety of the occupants.

· ACTION CUSTOMERS CAN TAKE THAT WILL FACILITATE
SERVICE RESTORATION -- In some cases there are situations in
hurricane damaged neighborhoods where customers can take action to
speed the process of electric service restoration.

For example, if you have damage to the area and equipment above and
around your electric meter, you may need to call a licensed electrician
to make repairs before FPL crews can re-energize the power line to
your house.

- **To evaluate the need to call a licensed electrician,** look at the area near your electric meter where the power line is or would connect to your house. If you see damage to the house connection, to the pipe that carries wires down the wall to the meter or damage to the metal box that surrounds the meter, you may want to call an electrician. Once a professional makes repairs to the house wiring connection -- called a weatherhead -- and to the piping and meter box, if necessary, your house should be ready to receive electric service when crews arrive. If the meter itself is damaged, FPL will repair or replace it.

- **VISUAL INSPECTION SHOULD BE DONE FROM THE GROUND. DO NOT GET ON A LADDER FOR A CLOSER LOOK. DO NOT TOUCH ANY ELECTRICAL EQUIPMENT OR LINES THAT MAY BE AROUND THE ELECTRICAL EQUIPMENT. YOUR ELECTRICIAN SHOULD BE THE ONLY ONE TO MAKE A CLOSE INSPECTION.**

- If your neighbor has a similar problem, consider making your request together to allow your electrician to make the most of the visit. If you're not sure about what is needed, FPL crews will be able to advise you when they come to make repairs to power poles and power lines at your house.

- FPL crews are reporting that piles of YARD DEBRIS and other trash stacked near power line poles or where power line poles used to be is slowing their ability to get electric service restored.

  Please keep all utility easements -- areas under power lines either in the front or rear of your home or business -- clear of all debris.

  FPL is NOT recommending that customers attempt to remove debris that the storm may have deposited in and around electrical equipment -- especially downed power lines. FPL ONLY asks that you not add to any debris in these areas as it will slow the task of getting to downed power poles, lines and transformers that need to be replaced or repaired.

  PLEASE SHARE THIS INFORMATION WITH YOUR NEIGHBORS SO THAT WE CAN MAXIMIZE OUR EFFORT WHEN WE REACH YOUR NEIGHBORHOOD.

- FPL has had a few reports that certain individuals are posing as FPL contractors willing to cut and remove fallen or storm-damaged trees for money. **FPL does not charge customers whe it is necessary to cut trees in order to access power lines and equipment for service repairs,** nor does FPL authorize anyone to charge to cut or remove trees for power

441

line access. **Those who are authorized to clear access to our equipment --** including special tree clearing crews and FPL contractors -- are paid by FPL. At the same time, we know many customers are having yard work done, and to the extent that it will make it easier for our crews to get to electrical service equipment in their yard, we're most appreciative.

· We also have a special announcement for our EMPLOYEES who may be listening. Many of you are among the homeless or those who have suffered serve damage. Many too, have been working in locations with limited communications or little time to address personnel problems. Please know that FPL has set up a special EMPLOYEE ASSISTANCE HOTLINE to help you with housing and other needs. That number -- for FPL EMPLOYEES ONLY -- is 1-800-222-4FPL.

· Since that line is for employees only, let me mention that the CUSTOMER LINES -- **for emergencies and downed sparking wires only at this time** -- are 797-5000 in BROWARD and 442-8770 in DADE.

· FPL is also aware that many DADE FAMILIES ARE RELOCATING TO BROWARD COUNTY. Please be patient with us regarding requests for establishing service at your new location. Restoration of electric service to the severly damaged areas of Dade County is still our number one priority, but we are attempting to address your new needs in Broward, so that those of you who have already suffered so much can begin to get on with ~~your~~ the rest of the issues of putting your life back together again.

· And finally a reminder to help us devote our attention to emergency situations -- please do not call FPL to report that you are out of service or ask when service will be restored. We are fully aware of areas that need electrical service restoration and we are doing our best -- with the assistance of the news and broadcast media -- to provide electrical service restoration progress reports. DO CALL if you see a downed power line that is sparking. For the many without phones, the same is true. You do not need to come into an FPL office to report your service is out. We know you are out and we are work as hard as possible to get to you.

Appendixes

Questions for Class Discussion and Case Analysis

The following questions can be used in class discussions of each of the cases in this textbook. Students can gain valuable experience by leading class discussions.

Research

Does the case give adequate background information about the organization itself? What was the major reason for conducting this program? Was the program proactive or reactive? Which audiences were targeted for communication? Should other audiences have also been targeted? How were research data about each audience obtained? Were the data as complete as necessary? Is there anything unusual about the research phase of this case? What are the research strengths and weaknesses of this case?

Objectives

Categorize this case's objectives. Which are impact objectives? Specify informational, attitudinal, or behavioral. Which are output objectives? Should they have been more quantitative? Should they have used time frames? Were output objectives used when the ultimate goal was really impact? What is your overall assessment of the objectives used in this case?

Programming

Evaluate the theme (if any) used in this case. Is it short, catchy, memorable, to the point? What major message or messages are communicated in this case? Evaluate the central actions or special events in this case. Are they truly worthwhile and newsworthy? Are they "pseudoevents"? Evaluate the types of uncontrolled and controlled media that were used. Were any forms of communication omitted that should have been used? Was adequate use made of interpersonal communication? Did the communication achieve a sense of "grassroots involvement" through interpersonal communication, or was there overreliance on mass media publicity placement or impersonal forms of controlled media? Discuss the use of such communication principles as source credibility, salient information, effective nonverbal and verbal cues, two-way communication, opinion leaders, group influence, selective exposure, and audience participation. How effectively were these principles used? Explain.

Evaluation

Was each of the case's objectives separately evaluated? Describe the evaluative methods used. How appropriate and effective were these methods? Did the program achieve its stated objectives? Was there a real *link* between the case's objectives and its evaluation?

Overall Judgments

As a whole, how effective was this public relations program? What are its major strengths? major weaknesses? Explain. What are the major PR lessons or principles to be learned from this case? What, if anything, would you do differently if you were assigned a public relations problem like this one?

Appendix II Case Problems and Exercises

1. Oral Report

Prepare a 10- to 15-minute oral report on the operations of the Public Relations department of a local organization. The report should include background information on the organization, the definition of its target publics, research methods used, objectives, communication methods, and evaluation procedures. The report will be evaluated using the criteria listed below. Since all PR practitioners should be accomplished public speakers, the report will be graded on both content and delivery.

Oral Report Evaluation

1. *Organization:* Name of organization, background data, characteristics
2. *Definition of target public(s):* How the organization's PR department segments publics
3. *Research methods:* Discussion of quantitative and non-quantitative methods used by the organization in gathering data
4. *Objectives:* Statement of PR objectives used by the organization

446

5. *Communication methods:* Explanation of communication activities used to reach public(s) and subsets: (1) action or special event(s); (2) uncontrolled media; (3) controlled media — print, audiovisual, interpersonal; illustration of report with some of the organization's communication materials

6. *Evaluation:* Explanation of evaluation procedures used by the organization to measure PR effectiveness

7. *Presentation of report:*
   a. Organization
      (1) Clear delineation of sections of the report
      (2) Appropriate explanation and details for each section
      (3) Attention-getting introduction
      (4) Appropriate conclusion and summary
   b. Delivery
      (1) Eye contact with class during report
      (2) Conversational quality, avoidance of excessive reading
      (3) Effective use of visual aids — charts, slides, transparencies, chalkboard, and/or other media

2. Media Relations

Aunt Tillie's Fruit Tarts

For 100 years Aunt Tillie's Fruit Tarts Incorporated of Minneapolis, Minnesota, have been filling cookie jars across the United States. This soft, fruit-filled cookie is an American classic that has been carried in lunch boxes and eaten as a snack by several generations. The cookie company prides itself on its small town, homemade image. Each package of fruit tarts prominently displays a drawing of the grandmotherly Aunt Tillie with hair in bun, glasses on nose, and apron. Although Aunt Tillie's Fruit Tarts have a strong core of repeat customers, the company feels that its visibility should be higher to successfully compete with some of the newer cookie brands on the market. Using the ROPE method as a guideline, prepare a media relations campaign, in keeping with the company's image, designed to celebrate the 100th anniversary of Aunt Tillie's Fruit Tarts and the general visibility of the product.

New Orleans River Boat Museum

New Orleans is rich in a history relating to the Mississippi River. The river boat was an integral part of river life and river culture, bringing visitors, goods, and news to the city in the 1800s. To both celebrate and educate about this rich period of New Orleans' history, the New Orleans River Boat Museum has been established by noted philanthropist, Andre Pierce Beauregard Delacroix. Built with both the New Orleans community and tourists to the city in mind, the museum will feature several boats to be toured with costumed interpreters, educational exhibits about river life in the nineteenth century, a movie designed to capture the essence of the river boat culture, and a restaurant for visitors that could have been on board a boat of the time. This new and unique museum has been in the planning and construction stages for several years, and now it is ready to open its doors to both the city of New Orleans and all visitors to the city as well. Use the ROPE format to prepare a "grand opening" campaign for the New Orleans River Boat Museum that will reach both the local and tourist communities.

The Modern Bookbinders Group

Bookbinding, until the advent of the mass-produced clothbound and paperback book, was considered a high art form. Binders took great care in choosing the correct leathers, marbled papers, and stitching materials so that a book would look beautiful on its shelf and last for years. Bookbinding, the art form, is making a comeback because of both its practical and esthetic values. The Modern Bookbinders Group (MBG), in reaction to the yellowed paperbacks and broken spines of mass-produced books, has decided to revive the lost art of bookbinding. Members of MBG use the methods of the past, as well as some of today's technology, in creating beautiful bindings for individual books that will last for years. Bookbinders in the group now work mostly on limited editions created by artists and in rebinding people's favorite books that have been damaged. The organization wants the general public to know more about it and to appreciate both the artistic and archival qualities of bookbinding methods. Using the ROPE process, how do you, as a PR practitioner, assist them?

3. Employee Relations

Rangerwell College

Rangerwell College is a small liberal arts college located in a midsized town in Texas. The college, founded in 1932, is relatively young. Its history has seen both spurts of growth and times of cutbacks. Due to several years of mismanagement, a too small endowment, and a dwindling number of students, the Rangerwell administration is now faced with difficult financial choices if Rangerwell is to survive. After much deliberation by the college administration, the choices that have been made include the elimination of both the continuing education and summer school divisions. These decisions, although necessary for the future of the college, will eliminate numerous faculty and staff and will shake the entire Rangerwell community. As director of employee relations for the college, use the ROPE method to devise a strategy for the college administration to make the announcement of these cutbacks in the most positive manner possible. Also discuss preparing the administrators to deal with potential employee reactions and to offer relocation assistance.

Consolidated Stationery Corporation

The Consolidated Stationery Corporation (CSC) has for many years had its large corporate headquarters offices on the upper peninsula of Michigan, in a town called Escanaba. Management has now decided to move the headquarters, employing some 300 people, to Maine. In Maine, the general health of the logging and paper economy, along with the economy in general, is better than it is in Michigan. The transition from Michigan will take place in phases over the course of a year. All employees from the Michigan office will be asked to go to Maine to continue working with CSC. However, it is feared by CSC executives that many employees will not move to Maine because of the great distance and leaving friends and family. Management knows that this is the right move for the corporation as a whole, but they are greatly concerned about making the announcement about the office relocation. Using the ROPE model, outline your strategy and the advice you would give the CSC president in making the actual relocation announcement and any follow-up provisions that may be of assistance to CSC employees.

Diversified Motor Company

Diversified Motor Company (DMC) began as a small, family-run company that made small motors for a variety of products, including electric mixers, shavers, and so on. The company, located in the heart of Omaha, Nebraska, prides itself on the family atmosphere of the factory. The owners demonstrate a great deal of concern for the general well-being of their employees above and beyond the turkey each receives on Thanksgiving and hefty holiday bonuses. This concern for the employees, plus a well-run company, has led to both continued success and growth for DMC. Now in its third generation, the family of owners have maintained this familylike atmosphere even with the rapid success and growth. However, the company has recently been purchased by a large Japanese conglomerate. Promises were made that things after the sale would remain pretty much as they have always been at the company. Employees, though, are still very concerned about keeping their jobs and keeping alive the family atmosphere that has made their jobs enjoyable. Using the ROPE method, as Diversified Motor Company's PR officer, devise a program to handle employees' fears about the buyout and its potential impact on company morale.

4. Member Relations

Happy Traveler Auto Club

With offices located around the United States, Canada, and Mexico, the Happy Traveler Auto Club has been in existence for several years. Club membership provides trip planning and special member discounts on hotels and tourist attractions. Its most popular benefit, though, is that of emergency roadside service. As of late, numerous complaints have been flooding the Happy Traveler Auto Club Member Relations office about the excessive waiting time required for this service. Membership literature promises service within one and one half hours, but reports of three to four hour waits are not uncommon. One-third of Happy Traveler's members have left because of their dissatisfaction with Happy Traveler services. As the PR director of the Happy Traveler Auto Club, what can you do to improve member relations and restore confidence and trust in your services. Using the ROPE model, design an effective member relations campaign for the Happy Traveler Auto Club.

Rideshare

Rideshare is a local commuter information organization serving the Chicago metropolitan area. Their several hundred members are people who must travel into and out of the city each day for work. Over the past several years, the volume of Chicago's commuter traffic has steadily increased. Highways surrounding the city are continuously backed up. They were not designed with such high volume in mind. Rideshare was founded as a grassroots response to this increase in commuter traffic. The group's mission is to have commuters teach other commuters about the need for carpooling and alternate methods of getting to and from work. In its educational campaign, Rideshare emphasizes the current problems of gridlock, poor air quality, and lack of parking that face the city. It also keeps the bigger picture in mind when educating commuters. Rideshare voices concerns about the global environmental issues arising from the use of fossil fuels, global warming due to depletion of the ozone layer, and so forth. Members feel that something must be done immediately about the commuter problem facing Chicagoans. For the future, Rideshare plans to begin a major campaign directed at city officials requesting specialized high occupancy (carpool) lanes and toll booths on the major commuter routes as incentives to promote carpooling. During this campaign, Rideshare will continue its work in educating the general public on the need for fuel and auto awareness. In order for Rideshare to meet all of its educational goals for the coming year, the group is going to need more members. Rideshare needs commuters who are motivated to help work on the educational campaigns. Using the ROPE method, devise a plan for Rideshare to make its cause known and in the process recruit new members.

Association of Tax Form Preparers

The Association of Tax Form Preparers (ATFP) is a 5,500 member organization representing income tax preparation centers and private accountants throughout the country. The association acts as a clearinghouse of information for its members with regard to tax laws, issues, and actual forms. The association was established some 15 years ago in order to help tax professionals deal with the numerous annual changes in tax law, tax forms, and general tax preparation methods. A monthly member newsletter is published with in-depth articles on current concerns. A toll-free expert information line is also made available to members that they can call for specific tax information and filing advice.

The association has a strong history of providing good information to its members. Despite this, things have not been going well over the past couple of years. Members have grown frustrated since the newsletter is often not published and incorrect information is often given by the so-called experts operating the toll-free help line. The membership renewal rate is starting to reflect these problems.

As the group's membership coordinator, you need to devise a strategy to regain the trust, support, and renewals of your disgruntled members. Use the ROPE process in planning your program.

5. Community Relations

Safeplace

Safeplace, a shelter for battered women and their children, is located in a quiet residential neighborhood in Sandy Beach, Florida. The shelter has been open for five years with several quiet success stories to its credit. These have involved helping women and their children in getting on their own feet, both emotionally and physically, after the horrible experiences of domestic violence.

The neighborhood surrounding Safeplace has been very supportive of the shelter from its start. Many volunteers from the area donate their time for baby-sitting, cleaning, cooking, and so on. Many others support the shelter through donations of food, clothing, and money.

Recently there have been several unpleasant incidents at Safeplace and in its neighborhood. In a few isolated, but disturbing instances, upset husbands of women staying at Safeplace have come, individually, to the shelter in the middle of the night shouting from the street for their wives and children to come home and driving recklessly around the area. When these incidents have occurred, the police have been called. It has been a scary situation for all involved. The residents of the neighborhood are starting to become afraid for their general well-being. They wholeheartedly support the work of Safeplace, but these incidents have caused a definite strain in the Safeplace/neighborhood relationship.

As the public relations advisor for Safeplace, develop a strategy to calm the neighborhood residents and strengthen the shelter/neighborhood relationship once again. Use the ROPE method.

Big City Police Department

The police department of Big City is facing a crisis in its relationship with the various inner-city communities it serves. The past year has seen a high rate of murder, assault, and theft in these communities. There have also been allegations of police brutality, harassment, and unnecessary search and seizure. This less than positive relationship is felt every time police officers respond to a call in the inner-city communities. The police/community relationship is currently at its worst in the Hispanic neighborhoods. Police officials fear that a riot may occur in one of the Hispanic neighborhoods the next time the police are called. The police department has been undergoing an intense process of self-evaluation, and several officers have been fired for their inappropriate behaviors and attitudes.

Using the ROPE method, devise a strategy for the police department to use in improving its image as well as to make people aware of the changes that have been made within the department.

Rodalia

The southern city of Rodalia is proud of its unique downtown historic district. This four-block historic area is filled with houses once owned by officers in the Civil War. The architecture in the area has been kept as historically uncompromised as possible. The carefully kept clapboard, the shuttered windows, the brick sidewalks, and the carriage houses all work together to make a quaint and charming spot in Rodalia's landscape. The historic district is the site of numerous community events, including Christmas caroling, a fall festival, Independence Day festivities, and so on.

Recently, it has been announced by city officials that Rodalia's historic district will now be managed by the state parks and recreation department. The department plans to build a visitor center, provide costumed interpreters as tour guides, and establish three new parking lots. This takeover will be good for the town in that tourists from outside the area will visit, bringing increased business to local hotels, motels, restaurants, and retail outlets.

Unfortunately, the people of Rodalia are in an uproar. They are glad for the good economic news, but they fear for the loss of their own historic district. They do not want to lose this community center. They have logistical concerns as well. How heavy will traffic be? Where will these new parking lots be built? There is much anxiety about what the future will hold.

As a PR practitioner for the state parks department, you must work to calm the community so that the new center and ownership may get off to a good start. Use the ROPE method to devise your strategy.

6. Public Affairs

Small Farmers in Indiana

These days it is tough going to be a small farmer. Equipment, labor, and supplies are all very expensive. Making a substantial profit is feasible only if you own one of the huge incorporated farms. The days of the small, family-owned farm seem to be numbered. A group of farmers in southern Indiana have banded together to try to keep the smaller farms alive for as long as possible. They feel that special state property and sales tax exemptions would be the key to help these farms survive. Some Indiana lawmakers have said they will consider the farmers' proposal.

For purposes of this exercise, assume that you represent the farmers. Outline your lobbying plans for them in the following three areas:

1. Coalition building
2. Direct lobbying
3. Indirect (grassroots) lobbying

Be specific. Use names of real organizations, members of the Indiana legislature, local media outlets, community leaders, and so on. Use the ROPE format for your overall proposal.

Braille Books for Blind Children

In the early 1920s, the national agency Braille Books for Blind Children (BBBC) was started in an effort to open the world of learning and reading for blind children. Braille books are quite expensive, and often schools cannot afford them for their blind students. The BBBC raises funds specifically for book purchases and awards the books to schools around the country. Their record is impressive. They have helped numerous students and have made a lasting impact on many school systems across the country. However, the BBBC is feeling slighted in receiving government support. The group has applied for funding from the Department of Health and Human Services grant agency on several occasions but has not had any success.

You are hired to gain support for BBBC's position. They want you to line up other agencies that serve the sight-impaired to help BBBC have some influence in Washington. You must come up with a way to gain support and develop a strategy for lobbying the Department of Health and Human Services. Using the ROPE model, how would you do this?

The National Association of Word Processors

The National Association of Word Processors (NAWP) is a national organization with more than 15,000 members. It prides itself on looking out for typists, stenographers, and secretaries across the country. Through its newsletters, annual conventions, and local chapter meetings, the group has developed a loyal membership. Recently, however, many members have been seriously afflicted by carpal tunnel syndrome. This affliction, affecting the fingers, wrists, and lower arms of those who type a great deal, can be quite painful and immobilizing. It can cause people to miss several days and sometimes months of work. The syndrome can be avoided if typists have chairs and desks that keep their hands in the proper position. The association wants to lobby Congress to pass an act requiring employers to provide the proper furniture from which typists can work safely.

You are hired to gain support for this position. The association wants you to line up organizations that will also support its position and that may help it to gain influence in Washington. You must come up with a way to gain support and develop a strategy for lobbying Congress. Using the ROPE model, how would you do this?

7. Investor Relations

Bixby Town Traveler

The Bixby Town Traveler has been the most successful midsize luxury car on the market for the past 10 years. The public seems to love the combination of its sporty exterior and its lush interior. It has been the mainstay for the Bixby Motor Company. The company's other models have never caught on as well as the Town Traveler.

However, bad news is on the horizon for Bixby Motor Company shareholders. Recent findings about a series of automobile accidents have brought to light a serious design flaw in the Town Traveler that causes severe autobody stress when the cars turn corners at high rates of speed. This flaw cannot be remedied without totally redesigning the look of the Town Traveler. There is hope that the new Town Traveler will do as well as the original, but it will be difficult for Bixby Motor Company to recover from both the bad news and the new design.

You have been hired as a PR consultant by the company. Using the ROPE model, devise a strategy to inform stockholders of the termination of the Town Traveler line, the only significant profit-making model the company has, and of the new design yet to come. Bixby Motor Company needs the support of its shareholders now more than ever. How will you effectively communicate the long-term goals of the company's management while retaining its present base of shareholders?

Darling Donuts

Robert Raskins is founder, president, and CEO of Darling Donuts. Darling Donuts began in 1956 with a few coffee shops in Philadelphia. It has since become known throughout the United States through the numerous Darling Donut franchise operations that serve people every day on their way to work. The franchises do well individually, and the Darling Donut Corporation does well for its stockholders.

Recently, Darling Donuts was audited by the Internal Revenue Service. In the audit process, the IRS discovered that a great deal of revenue seemed to be disappearing from the books. After an extensive search at the Darling Donuts Corporate offices, the audit discovered that Raskins was embezzling the profits that should have been going to the shareholders. The corporation has been shaken badly by Raskin's arrest.

You have been hired as a PR consultant by the Darling Donut Corporation. Using the ROPE model, devise a strategy to reassure its stockholders.

Southwestern Inns

Bob and Ruth Smith moved to Taos, New Mexico, more than 25 years ago. They so loved the natural beauty of the mountains, desert, and people of the area that they decided to open an inn for vacationers so that others could share in the beauty. The first inn was an immediate success with its southwestern charm of adobe walls, cacti, local food, and the natural beauty of the inn's surroundings.

With their initial success, the Smiths decided to open a few more inns in the southwest region of the United States. To do so they borrowed from banks and their friends. The Smiths are now operating 36 inns. Their loans have been long repaid, and their friends are now stockholders receiving hefty premiums.

The vast Withson Hotel group has made the Smiths an offer for all of their inns that is too good for them to pass up. The inns will continue to be run in the manner begun by the Smiths, but under the management of the Withson Hotel group.

You are hired by the Withson Hotel group to inform the current investors of the takeover. Using the ROPE model, devise a strategy for informing them. You must assure the investors that the inns will not lose their identity and their simple charm. Remember, too, that although there will be the bonus of the large group's profits, under the new management, the shareholders will have a smaller interest in the inns than they once did.

8. Consumer Relations

Growing Healthy

Growing Healthy baby food products were on the market for several years. With the food's strong nutritional base and the exceptional safety of the company's other infant products, the baby food was trusted by parents around the nation. Five years ago this trust in Growing Healthy was destroyed when eight cases of botulism were linked to Growing Healthy food. The company was devastated. In response to the crisis, it recalled its products from all its vendors. The company has remained in business for the past five years by selling only nonfood items. This has meant a considerable drop in market share and thus profits.

Growing Healthy has decided that it is time to get back into the baby food market. They know that this will be difficult, but they feel their product is worth the struggle. You have been hired as a PR consultant for Growing Healthy. Using the ROPE model, devise a plan to restore consumer confidence in Growing Healthy. The company's executives want to assure parents that it is once again safe to feed Growing Healthy products to their children.

Petal Dew Facial Mud Masque

Petal Dew Facial Mud Masque, manufactured by the Petal Dew Company, has been on the market for three years. If used correctly, the product promises to firm the skin, rid it of impurities, and reduce signs of aging. It has done quite well for the Petal Dew line. The company's marketing strategy of department store demonstrations and dramatic before-and-after photographs in print advertisements has been very successful.

Recently, though, several stories have reached the newspapers of women using the product developing a painful and long-lasting rash. On interviewing these women, Petal Dew discovered that they were using the product more frequently and for longer periods of time than recommended on its packaging. But although the rash was the consumer's mistake, it has scarred the sales of Petal Dew Facial Mud Masque.

As the PR director of Petal Dew cosmetics, you need to promote the concern your company feels for its consumers. What will you do to regain consumer trust and confidence both in the product and for the Petal Dew line in general? Use the ROPE model as a guideline.

Cradleform Shoe Company

Cradleform Shoe Company has built a strong reputation based on its traditional, comfortable, quality line of footwear for both men and women. Its products are worn by waitresses, doctors, security guards, and other people who are on their feet for long periods of time around the world.

Cradleform is facing a crisis now in consumer trust. This crisis developed a few months after the much celebrated debut of the company's new "Good for Your Legs" line. The shoes in this line featured a uniquely shaped sole and arch support designed to provide extra comfort. After great initial success, complaints about Achilles tendon discomfort from Good for Your Legs wearers began to flood into the Cradleform offices. The shoes were placing too much stress on the tendon. Cradleform's new product, marketed as good for the body, was in fact harmful.

You have been hired as their PR counsel. Using the ROPE model, how would you deal with the problems Cradleform faces? Company executives are worried that product sales will decline and that consumer trust in Cradleform footwear may be at risk.

9. Special Publics

Senior Share Center

The rate of clinical depression among the elderly is very high. The depression often stems from lack of contact with others. Elderly persons may never leave their homes because of a physical condition, lack of money, or fear of a fast-moving world.

As a new community agency, Senior Share Center (SSC) has as its mission to get elderly people involved with life and with each other. Located in Framingham, Massachusetts, the center offers a free hot lunch program each day, health screenings, and social programs, but its officers are interested in expanding the center's services.

You have been hired by SSC to assist in its further development of services and to disseminate information about the center to the elderly. Using the ROPE process, how will you get the information to people who do not have, in general, a great deal of contact with the world beyond their homes.

New Directions

Once they leave prison, ex-offenders often find that life is not as good for them as they had hoped. The public holds negative stereotypes of the ex-offender group as being untrustworthy, violent, and unemployable in general. New Directions is an agency designed to help ex-offenders to face this distrust and more general issues. Based in Seattle, New Directions provides employment assistance coupled with a supportive network of services to program participants upon their return to the community. New Directions has had several success stories in helping ex-offenders. However, the agency feels that progress on improving the negative stereotypes could still be made. Using the ROPE method as a guideline, plan a campaign that targets potential employers and the business community's awareness of both what the New Directions agency accomplishes and what ex-offenders in general are like and can accomplish to diminish the constraints of the stereotypes.

Boston's "Chinatown"

A high concentration of Boston's Asian citizens live in an area of the city known as Chinatown. Chinatown's atmosphere is charged with the foreign smells, sights, and sounds of the Far East. But Chinatown is also known for numerous crimes suspected to be linked to Asian organized crime and gangs. Murders and robberies are numerous. Often there are several witnesses to a crime. The Boston Police Department, however, has had little success in ending the crimes because Chinatown residents are afraid, both of the criminals and of the police because of negative experiences with authorities in their native countries. Organized crime's grip on the area grows stronger every day.

As the community relations officer for the Boston Police Department, what can you do to encourage Chinatown's residents to speak to police investigators? Use the ROPE model in your strategy.

10. Emergency Public Relations

Rosewood Castle

Rosewood Castle is an imposing mansion nestled in the hills of southern California. Built by railroad tycoon Walter Rose in the 1920s, the mansion is filled with priceless antiques and art objects. When Mr. Rose died in 1961, the house and its surrounding gardens were opened to the public as a museum. Hundreds of visitors come each day.

Late last night, five men disguised as police officers forced their way into the museum. They tied up the night watchmen, jammed the castle's sophisticated alarm system, and stole eight paintings. The thieves knew exactly what they wanted. They took the best of Rosewood's collection. The night watchmen and the crime were discovered the following morning when the next shift of guards arrived.

You are in charge of public relations for Rosewood Castle. Your job is to control the flow of press information as much as possible. Keep in mind that you are working with numerous authorities including the FBI in trying to recover the stolen works. Information regarding the building's security system and the actual paintings taken is very sensitive. Using the ROPE model, how will you respond to the numerous media, both national and international, standing on the front lawn of the mansion?

Reaching Out Ministries

Reaching Out Ministries is a multidenominational social service agency located in Butte, Montana. Funded by several local churches, the agency, headed by Reverend Bill Wenham, serves members of the community. Reaching Out provides whatever type of assistance the citizens of Butte may need. Food when they are hungry, clothing and shelter when their houses burn down, counseling when their lives are falling apart, canned foods at Thanksgiving, and gifts for the children at holiday time are but a few examples. Reverend Wenham is a familiar and welcome sight around Butte. He personifies Reaching Out Ministries.

Unfortunately, scandal has touched Reaching Out Ministries. The local police have formally charged Reverend Wenham with sexually abusing three young boys who were receiving help from the Ministries.

You are in charge of public relations for Reaching Out Ministries. Using the ROPE model, how will you present the information to the press about the incident? You want to portray the continuing works of the Ministries in a positive light, without minimizing the seriousness of the charges brought against Reverend Wenham. You should keep in mind the effects this will have on the community as a whole.

Fordham Festival Hotel

The Fordham Festival Hotel opened in San Francisco in 1989. It is the flagship of the Fordham Fine Hotel chain, which operates 455 hotels across the country. The Festival, with 600 rooms, 6 restaurants, fine shopping opportunities, large conference facilities, and golf and tennis courts, offers visitors a complete package of the "finer things" in life. Guests may stroll in the large atriumlike lobby, ride in the glass elevators, and enjoy the view of the wharves through the numerous windows of the hotel's contemporary architecture.

Tragedy struck early on a Sunday morning when a fire broke out in one of the guest rooms. The fire spread quickly, trapping several people on the upper floors. Firefighters did the best they could to put out the fire, but it was tough going. When the fire was finally extinguished, three guests were dead and several more were seriously injured.

As the public relations coordinator for the Fordham Fine Hotel chain, how do you respond to the media about the fire? Using the ROPE method, describe how you will represent the hotel chain's position to the public over the next few weeks.

PRSA Code of Professional Standards for the Practice of Public Relations

This Code was adopted by the PRSA Assembly in 1988. It replaces a Code of Ethics in force since 1950 and revised in 1954, 1959, 1963, 1977, and 1983. For information on the Code and enforcement procedures, please call the chair of the Board of Ethics through PRSA Headquarters.

Declaration of Principles

Members of the Public Relations Society of America base their professional principles on the fundamental value and dignity of the individual, holding that the free exercise of human rights, especially freedom of speech, freedom of assembly, and freedom of the press, is essential to the practice of public relations.

In serving the interests of clients and employers, we dedicate ourselves to the goals of better communication, understanding, and cooperation among the diverse individuals, groups, and institutions of society, and of equal opportunity of employment in the public relations profession.

Courtesy Public Relations Society of America

We Pledge:

To conduct ourselves professionally, with truth, accuracy, fairness, and responsibility to the public;

To improve our individual competence and advance the knowledge and proficiency of the profession through continuing research and education;

And to adhere to the articles of the Code of Professional Standards for the Practice of Public Relations as adopted by the governing Assembly of the Society.

Code of Professional Standards for the Practice of Public Relations

These articles have been adopted by the Public Relations Society of America to promote and maintain high standards of public service and ethical conduct among its members.

1. A member shall conduct his or her professional life in accord with the public interest.

2. A member shall exemplify high standards of honesty and integrity while carrying out dual obligations to a client or employer and to the democratic process.

3. A member shall deal fairly with the public, with past or present clients or employers, and with fellow practitioners, giving due respect to the ideal of free inquiry and to the opinions of others.

4. A member shall adhere to the highest standards of accuracy and truth, avoiding extravagant claims or unfair comparisons and giving credit for ideas and words borrowed from others.

5. A member shall not knowingly disseminate false or misleading information and shall act promptly to correct erroneous communications for which he or she is responsible.

6. A member shall not engage in any practice which has the purpose of corrupting the integrity of channels of communications or the processes of government.

7. A member shall be prepared to identify publicly the name of the client or employer on whose behalf any public communication is made.

8. A member shall not use any individual or organization professing to serve or represent an announced cause, or professing to be independent or unbiased, but actually serving another or undisclosed interest.

9. A member shall not guarantee the achievement of specified results beyond the member's direct control.

10. A member shall not represent conflicting or competing interests without the express consent of those concerned, given after a full disclosure of the facts.

11. A member shall not place himself or herself in a position where the member's personal interest is or may be in conflict with an obligation to an employer or client, or others, without full disclosure of such interests to all involved.

12. A member shall not accept fees, commissions, gifts or any other consideration from anyone except clients or employers for whom services are performed without their express consent, given after full disclosure of the facts.

13. A member shall scrupulously safeguard the confidences and privacy rights of present, former, and prospective clients or employers.

14. A member shall not intentionally damage the professional reputation or practice of another practitioner.

15. If a member has evidence that another member has been guilty of unethical, illegal, or unfair practices, including those in violation of this Code, the member is obligated to present the information promptly to the proper authorities of the Society for action in accordance with the procedure set forth in Article XII of the Bylaws.

16. A member called as a witness in a proceeding for enforcement of this Code is obligated to appear, unless excused for sufficient reason by the judicial panel.

17. A member shall, as soon as possible, sever relations with any organization or individual if such relationship requires conduct contrary to the articles of this Code.

Official Interpretations of the Code

Interpretation of Code Paragraph 1, which reads, "A member shall conduct his or her professional life in accord with the public interest."

The public interest is here defined primarily as comprising respect for and enforcement of the rights guaranteed by the Constitution of the United States of America.

Interpretation of Code Paragraph 6, which reads, "A member shall not engage in any practice which has the purpose of corrupting the integrity of channels or communication or the processes of government."

1. Among the practices prohibited by this paragraph are those that tend to place representatives of media or government under any obligation to the member, or the member's employer or client, which is in conflict with their obligations to media or government, such as:

   a. the giving of gifts of more than nominal value;
   b. any form of payment or compensation to a member of the media in order to obtain preferential or guaranteed news or editorial coverage in the medium;
   c. any retainer or fee to a media employee or use of such employee if retained by a client or employer, where the circumstances are not fully disclosed to and accepted by the media employer;
   d. providing trips, for media representatives, that are unrelated to legitimate news interest;
   e. the use by a member of an investment or loan or advertising commitment made by the member, or the member's client or employer, to obtain preferential or guaranteed coverage in the medium.

2. This Code paragraph does not prohibit hosting media or government representatives at meals, cocktails, or news functions and special events that are occasions for the exchange of news information or views, or the furtherance of understanding, which is part of the public relations function. Nor does it prohibit the bona fide press event or tour when media or government representatives are given the opportunity for an on-the-spot viewing of a newsworthy product, process, or event in which the media or government representatives have a legitimate interest. What is customary or reasonable hospitality has to be a matter of particular judgment in specific situations. In all of these cases, however, it is, or should be, understood that no preferential treatment or guarantees are expected or implied and that complete independence always is left to the media or government representative.

3. This paragraph does not prohibit the reasonable giving or lending of sample products or services to media representatives who have a legitimate interest in the products or services.

4. It is permissible, under Article 6 of the Code, to offer complimentary or discount rates to the media (travel writers, for example) if the rate is for business use and is made available to all writers. Considerable question exists as to the propriety of extending such rates for personal use.

Interpretation of Code Paragraph 9, which reads, "A member shall not guarantee the achievement of specified results beyond the member's direct control."

This Code paragraph, in effect, prohibits misleading a client or employer as to what professional public relations can accomplish. It does not prohibit guarantees of quality or service. But it does prohibit guaranteeing specific results which, by their very nature, cannot be guaranteed because they are not subject to the member's control. As an example, a guarantee that a news release will appear specifically in a particular publication would be prohibited. This paragraph should not be interpreted as prohibiting contingent fees.

Interpretation of Code Paragraph 13, which reads, "A member shall scrupulously safeguard the confidences and privacy rights of present, former, and prospective clients or employers."

1. This article does not prohibit a member who has knowledge of client or employer activities that are illegal from making such disclosures to the proper authorities as he or she believes are legally required.

2. Communications between a practitioner and client/employer are deemed to be confidential under Article 13 of the Code of Professional Standards. However, although practitioner/client/employer communications are considered confidential between the parties, such communications are not privileged against disclosure in a court of law.

3. Under the copyright laws of the United States, the copyright in a work is generally owned initially by the author or authors. In the case of a "work made for hire" by an employee acting within the scope of his or her employment, the employer is considered to be the author and owns the copyright in the absence of an express, signed written agreement to the contrary. A freelancer who is the author of the work and is not an employee may be the owner of the copyright. A member should consult legal counsel for detailed advice concerning the scope and application of the copyright laws.

Interpretation of Code Paragraph 14, which reads, "A member shall not intentionally damage the professional reputation or practice of another practitioner."

1. Blind solicitation, on its face, is not prohibited by the Code. However, if the customer list were improperly obtained, or if the solicitation contained references reflecting adversely on the quality of current services, a complaint might be justified.

2. This article applies to statements, true or false, or acts, made or undertaken with malice and with the specific purpose of harming the reputation or practice of another member. This article does not prohibit honest employee evaluations or similar reviews, made without malice and as part of ordinary business practice, even though this activity may have a harmful effect.

An Official Interpretation of the Code As It Applies to Political Public Relations

Preamble

In the practice of political public relations, a PRSA member must have professional capabilities to offer an employer or client quite apart from any political relationships of value, and members may serve their employer or client without necessarily having attributed to them the character, reputation, or beliefs of those they serve. It is understood that members may choose to serve only those interests with whose political philosophy they are personally comfortable.

Definition

"Political Public Relations" is defined as those areas of public relations that relate to:

a. the counseling of political organizations, committees, candidates, or potential candidates for public office; and groups constituted for the purpose of influencing the vote on any ballot issue;
b. the counseling of holders of public office;
c. the management, or direction, of a political campaign for or against a candidate for political office; or for or against a ballot issue to be determined by voter approval or rejection;

    d. the practice of public relations on behalf of a client or an employer in connection with that client's or employer's relationships with any candidates or holders of public office, with the purpose of influencing legislation or government regulation or treatment of a client or employer, regardless of whether the PRSA member is a recognized lobbyist;

    e. the counseling of government bodies, or segments thereof, either domestic or foreign.

Precepts

1. It is the responsibility of PRSA members practicing political public relations, as defined above, to be conversant with the various statutes, local, state, and federal, governing such activities and to adhere to them strictly. This includes, but is not limited to, the various local, state, and federal laws, court decisions, and official interpretations governing lobbying, political contributions, disclosure, elections, libel, slander, and the like. In carrying out this responsibility, members shall seek appropriate counseling whenever necessary.

2. It is also the responsibility of the members to abide by PRSA's Code of Professional Standards.

3. Members shall represent clients or employers in good faith, and while partisan advocacy on behalf of a candidate or public issue may be expected, members shall act in accord with the public interest and adhere to truth and accuracy and to generally accepted standards of good taste.

4. Members shall not issue descriptive material or any advertising or publicity information or participate in the preparation or use thereof that is not signed by responsible persons or is false, misleading, or unlabeled as to its source, and are obligated to use care to avoid dissemination of any such material.

5. Members have an obligation to clients to disclose what remuneration beyond their fees they expect to receive as a result of their relationship, such as commissions for media advertising, printing, and the like, and should not accept such extra payment without their client's consent.

6. Members shall not improperly use their positions to encourage additional future employment or compensation. It is understood that successful campaign directors or managers, because of the performance of their duties and the

working relationship that develops, may well continue to assist and counsel, for pay, the successful candidate.

7. Members shall voluntarily disclose to employers or clients the identity of other employers or clients with whom they are currently associated, and whose interests might be affected favorably or unfavorably by their political representation.

8. Members shall respect the confidentiality of information pertaining to employers or clients past, present, and potential, even after the relationships cease, avoiding future associations wherein insider information is sought that would give a desired advantage over a member's previous clients.

9. In avoiding practices that might tend to corrupt the processes of government, members shall not make undisclosed gifts of cash or other valuable considerations that are designed to influence specific decisions of voters, legislators, or public officials on public matters. A business lunch or dinner, or other comparable expenditure made in the course of communicating a point of view or public position, would not constitute such a violation. Nor, for example, would a plant visit designed and financed to provide useful background information to an interested legislator or candidate.

10. Nothing herein should be construed as prohibiting members from making legal, properly disclosed contributions to the candidates, party, or referenda issues of their choice.

11. Members shall not, through use of information known to be false or misleading, conveyed directly or through a third party, intentionally injure the public reputation of an opposing interest.

An Official Interpretation of the Code As It Applies to Financial Public Relations

This interpretation of the Society Code as it applies to financial public relations was originally adopted in 1963 and amended in 1972, 1977, 1983 and 1988 by action of the PRSA Board of Directors. "Financial public relations" is defined as "that area of public relations which relates to the dissemination of information that affects the understanding of stockholders and investors generally concerning the financial position and prospects of a company, and includes among its objectives the improvement of relations between corporations and their stockholders." The interpretation was prepared in 1963 by the Society's Financial Relations Committee, working with the Securities and Exchange Commission and with the advice of the Society's legal counsel. It is rooted directly in the Code with the full force of the Code behind it, and a violation of any of the following paragraphs is subject to the same procedures and penalties as violation of the Code.

1. It is the responsibility of PRSA members who practice financial public relations to be thoroughly familiar with and understand the rules and regulations of the SEC and the laws it administers, as well as other laws, rules, and regulations affecting financial public relations, and to act in accordance with their letter and spirit. In carrying out this responsibility, members shall also seek legal counsel, when appropriate, on matters concerning financial public relations.

2. Members shall adhere to the general policy of making full and timely disclosure of corporate information on behalf of clients or employers. The information disclosed shall be accurate, clear, and understandable. The purpose of such disclosure is to provide the investing public with all material information affecting security values or influencing investment decisions. In complying with the duty of full and timely disclosure, members shall present all material facts, including those adverse to the company. They shall exercise care to ascertain the facts and to disseminate only information they believe to be accurate. They shall not knowingly omit information, the omission of which might make a release false or misleading. Under no circumstances shall members participate in any activity designed to mislead or manipulate the price of a company's securities.

3. Members shall publicly disclose or release information promptly so as to avoid the possibility of any use of the information by any insider or third party. To that end, members shall make every effort to comply with the spirit and intent of the timely-disclosure policies of the stock exchanges, NASD, and the SEC. Material information shall be made available on an equal basis.

4. Members shall not disclose confidential information the disclosure of which might be adverse to a valid corporate purpose or interest and whose disclosure is not required by the timely-disclosure provisions of the law. During any such period of nondisclosure members shall not directly

or indirectly (a) communicate the confidential information to any other person or (b) buy or sell or in any other way deal in the company's securities where the confidential information may materially affect the market for the security when disclosed. Material information shall be disclosed publicly as soon as its confidential status has terminated or the requirement of timely disclosure takes effect.

5. During the registration period, members shall not engage in practices designed to precondition the market for such securities. During registration, the issuance of forecasts, projections, predictions about sales and earnings, or opinions concerning security values or other aspects of the future performance of the company, shall be in accordance with current SEC regulations and statements of policy. In the case of companies whose securities are publicly held, the normal flow of factual information to shareholders and the investing public shall continue during the registration period.

6. Where members have any reason to doubt that projections have an adequate basis in fact, they shall satisfy themselves as to the adequacy of the projections prior to disseminating them.

7. Acting in concert with clients or employers, members shall act promptly to correct false or misleading information or rumors concerning clients' or employers' securities or business whenever they have reason to believe such information or rumors are materially affecting investor attitudes.

8. Members shall not issue descriptive materials designed or written in such a fashion as to appear to be, contrary to fact, an independent third-party endorsement or recommendation of a company or a security. Whenever members issue material for clients or employers, either in their own names or in the names of someone other than the clients or employers, they shall disclose in large type and in a prominent position on the face of the material the source of such material and the existence of the issuer's client or employer relationship.

9. Members shall not use inside information for personal gain. However, this is not intended to prohibit members from making bona fide investments in their company's or client's securities insofar as they can make such investments without the benefit of material inside information.

10. Members shall not accept compensation that would place them in a position of conflict with their duty to a client, employer, or the investing public. Members shall not accept stock options from clients or employers nor accept securities as compensation at a price below market price except as part of an overall plan for corporate employees.

11. Members shall act so as to maintain the integrity of channels of public communication. They shall not pay or permit to be paid to any publication or other communications medium any consideration in exchange for publicizing a company, except through clearly recognizable paid advertising.

12. Members shall in general be guided by the PRSA Declaration of Principles and the Code of Professional Standards for the Practice of Public Relations of which this is an official interpretation.

Index